THE GOLDEN

HOME AND

THE GOLDEN HOME AND HIGH SCHOOL ENCYCLOPEDIA, while sufficiently comprehensive and detailed for family use, has been created principally for students at the high school level.

The aim of this reference work is twofold: first, to serve the student's immediate need for authoritative information on a wide range of subjects, and, second, to set forth and explain the many areas of knowledge, so that a student may explore them and thus more competently plan his educational future.

Arranged alphabetically in twenty volumes, here are thousands of full, accurate entries, written and reviewed by experts. The text is abundantly illustrated with full-color photographs and paintings.

Designed to complement the high school curriculum, this encyclopedia offers help with assignments and valuable guidance in the use of other reference tools —dictionaries, atlases, and various library materials. Extensive cross-references and a complete index direct the reader quickly to the information he seeks. A special feature of this work is the sound career information it offers in scores of job and professional fields.

Among the many subjects encompassed in these volumes are the newest developments in science, from microbiology to radioastronomy; fine arts and literature; history and government; religion and philosophy; the physical world, its plants and animals; the social sciences; invention and industry. Four-color maps and latest census figures contribute to an up-to-date view of the world, its continents, nations, and peoples.

Every care has been taken to make *The Golden Home and High School Encyclopedia* lively and stimulating, without sacrifice of accuracy. It is the hope of the editors that these volumes will be used with both advantage and pleasure.

VOLUME V

HIGH SCHOOL ENCYCLOPEDIA

in 20 Volumes

Civilization • Defoe, Daniel

GOLDEN PRESS • NEW YORK

FIRST PRINTING, 1961
Library of Congress Catalog Card Number: 61-13292
© Copyright 1961 by Golden Press, Inc. Designed and produced by Artists and Writers Press, Inc. Printed in the U.S.A. by Western Printing and Lithographing Company. Published by Golden Press, Inc., New York.

Illustrations from GOLDEN BOOKS, © 1949, 1950, 1951, 1952, 1953, 1954, 1955, 1956, 1957, 1958, 1959, 1960, 1961 by Golden Press, Inc.; and from the Basic Science Education Series (Unitext), published by Row, Peterson and Company, Evanston, Illinois © 1944 by Row, Peterson and Company.

CIVILIZATION refers to social and technical development usually related to the growth of cities. (See CITY.) The word also means a society that has reached this stage of development.

Some people use the word *civilization* to mean the culture of a certain group. In this case the word *culture* or *society* could be substituted. For example, people say "British civilization" for "British society" or "British culture."

The word *civilization* was used by Dante to mean "a large social entity extending beyond the individual and family." The French Encyclopedists, such as Voltaire, used *civilization* to mean "mental enlightenment." In this sense, Europe of the Renaissance was a higher civilization than Europe of the feudal period during the Middle Ages.

We can contrast civilized people with people of earlier times who collected their food. They did not think about much except where their next mouthful was coming from or what magic to use for good hunting. With the development of agriculture, people no longer had to spend all their waking hours gathering food, and the foundations for civilization began. Specialization and division of labor brought about leisure time for thinking of, and producing, new things.

In the material sense, civilization entails fully efficient food production, cities and urbanization, formal laws, a formal political state, social classes, writing, and monumental works of art.

Along with the material developments, there are social ones. A civilized person participates in the formal laws of his society. His interest extends to people in general. Usually he abhors the sacrifice of human life.

Not everybody agrees about what civilization is. Many persons believe that the Aztecs reached civilization. Some people would argue that the Aztecs were not civilized because they practiced human sacrifice.

CIVIL RIGHTS, the liberties granted an individual by a state. Civil rights include substantive rights, such as freedom of speech, freedom of the press, and freedom of worship. Procedural civil rights include habeas corpus, the right to a trial by jury, and protection from unreasonable seizures or searches. The civil rights granted by dictatorships differ greatly from those given by democracies. Even in democracies a continuous effort must be made to protect civil rights and to extend them to all citizens.

The civil rights enjoyed by U.S. citizens have their basis in English practice. The English received their traditional rights from the Magna Charta (1215), the Petition of Right (1728), and the English Bill of Rights (1689). This tradition of civil rights was transplanted to this country by the colonists. The Declaration of Independence accused the king of denying the colonies their civil rights. (See DECLARATION OF INDEPENDENCE.) When the Constitution was drawn up, it nowhere mentioned civil rights, and critics objected that individuals did not receive sufficient safeguards against the power of the government. Therefore the Bill of Rights, the first ten amendments, was added. The Bill of Rights, supplemented by the "reconstruction amendments" (13, 14, and 15), guarantees civil rights to an individual in relation to the federal government.

In 1875 a civil rights act was passed that would have protected individuals against discrimination in public places (restaurants and the like). The act was adjudged to be unconstitutional where it placed the protection of individuals from other

The map below shows the locations of early civilizations. The earliest civilizations arose in Egypt, Mesopotamia, and northwestern India. Somewhat later civilization arose in China, and much later it arose in Mexico and Peru. Some civilizations developed forms of writing, as shown below. The quipu writing of the Incas of Peru was not writing in the strict sense but a means of keeping accounts.

individuals in the hands of the federal government rather than with the state governments. In 1911 citizens were given the right to protect their civil rights in the district courts. In 1954 the Supreme Court ruled against segregated schools. The Civil Rights Act of 1957 set up a six-member Commission on Civil Rights to look into cases of denial of voting rights and to collect information on any denial of equal protection under the laws. And the 1960 Civil Rights Act further extended the power of the federal government to protect the voting rights of American citizens. In addition to government measures, civil rights are also protected by the work of private organizations, such as the American Civil Liberties Union.

The United Nations seeks to protect civil (or human) rights on an international scale. Its Commission on Human Rights began work in 1947 under the direction of Eleanor Roosevelt. The Universal Declaration of Human Rights was prepared by the commission and adopted by the General Assembly in 1948. See BILL OF RIGHTS; DEMOCRACY.

CIVIL SERVICE IN THE UNITED STATES, all services other than military, naval, legislative, and judicial that are rendered to and paid for by the federal government. The government is the nation's largest employer. Its employees, the civil servants, work in every state. Many have acquired a high level of technical specialization as lawyers, doctors, engineers, and scientists. The skilled artisans and mechanics in their ranks staff the shipyards, arsenals, and industrial plants. During the 1950's almost half of all civilian employees of the government worked for the Department of Defense.

The civil service included only a few hundred people when George Washington became president in 1789. Politics was then a profession practiced by the well to do, and it seemed natural that politicians should take civil service jobs. The first transformation of the civil service came during the presidency of Andrew Jackson from 1829 to 1838. The civil service became a tool of political patronage, in which well-paying government jobs were given to loyal party members. This practice, known as the spoils system, dominated the civil service until 1883. By then the dishonesty, incompetence, and inefficiency of the system threatened the administration of the country. Unqualified persons were chosen for important positions, while other persons were tempted to use their offices for personal gain.

Agitation for a reformed civil service began in the 1850's. But success did not come until Jan. 16, 1883, when the Civil Service Act was passed. This law, the basic provisions of which are still in effect, based the civil service on a merit system and declared it to be a nonpolitical organization. Henceforth, appointments to government jobs were made on the basis of fitness for office, determined by competitive examinations. Later, employees were forbidden to hold public office.

A person is prepared for a civil service examination by schooling, vocational training, and employment experience. Those who achieve the highest grades are placed at the head of the civil service list. When a federal agency has a job to fill, it usually asks the Civil Service Commission for this list of eligibles.

CIVIL WAR, AMERICAN. On Apr. 12, 1861, the Confederate batteries fired on Fort Sumter in South Carolina. Thus, the four-year war between the Union and the Confederacy began.

The question of slavery was the predominant cause of the Civil War. Slavery was an important part of Southern plantation life. This form of life, so different from that of the North, produced a sharp separation between the two sections of the country. (See PLANTATION LIFE IN THE SOUTH.) By the time the Civil War broke out, each side was afraid that the other was trying to impose its own way of life upon the whole country. The conflict became apparent in the 1820's, when many Southerners began to think that slavery was a good thing and necessary for the development of the best type of civilization. At the same time, abolitionists began preaching against slavery and thus intensified Southern resentment toward the North. (See ABOLITIONIST MOVEMENT.) The Southerners soon became fearful that Congress would prohibit slavery in the new territories of the United States. The establishment of free territories meant that eventually free states would outnumber slave states and would be able to dictate to them. The Missouri Compromise in 1820 and the Compromise of 1850 calmed these fears temporarily. See COMPROMISE OF 1850; MISSOURI COMPROMISE.

During the 1850's incidents such as the bloody civil war between proslavery and antislavery settlers in Kansas, the Dred Scott case, and John Brown's raid on Harpers Ferry, Va. (now W. Va.), brought tempers on both sides to the point of explosion. (See BROWN, JOHN; DRED SCOTT DECISION.) The election victory in 1860 of Abraham Lincoln and the Republicans, who stood for prohibition of slavery in the territories, was the signal for secession to begin. (See CONFEDERATE STATES OF AMERICA; FORT SUMTER.) Despite the excitement over the slavery issue, the main purpose of Lincoln and the North was to preserve the Union, not to free the slaves. President Lincoln did not issue the Emancipation Proclamation until nearly two years after the Civil War had begun. See EMANCIPATION PROCLAMATION.

The first battle of the war was fought at Bull Run in Virginia. The Union armies attacked, hoping to drive on to capture Richmond, Va., the capital of the Confederacy. Both sides were so untrained that when the Union soldiers fled, the Southerners were too surprised to follow them. (See BULL RUN, BATTLES OF.) Robert E. Lee, who commanded the Southern forces and led the Army of Northern Virginia, was more than a match for George McClellan and the other leaders of the Army of the Potomac. Again and again General Lee defeated that army but was unable to capture Washington, D. C. Whenever he came near, as he did in 1862 at Antietam, Md., he was turned back. See ANTIETAM, BATTLE OF.

Meanwhile the Union armies in the West, under Ulysses S. Grant and William Tecumseh Sherman, gained control of the Mississippi River, thus splitting the Confederate States from north to south. The chief events of the campaign to control the Mississippi were Grant's capture of Fort Henry and Fort Donelson in Tennessee early in 1862; the Battle of Shiloh in Tennessee in April, 1862; the capture of New Orleans by the Northern navy under David G. Farragut later the same month; and finally, Grant's capture of Vicksburg, Miss., over a year later.

Lee tried to counteract Union successes in the West by invading Pennsylvania. However, General George Gordon Meade defeated Lee at Gettysburg, Pa., at the same time that Grant was capturing Vicksburg, Miss. See GETTYSBURG, BATTLE OF; GETTYSBURG ADDRESS.

Courtesy of the Seventh Regiment

Courtesy of the Seventh Regiment

NORTHERN SUPERIORITY IN MANPOWER AND MATERIAL RESOURCES

61% Population

66% Railroad Mileage

74% Bank Deposits

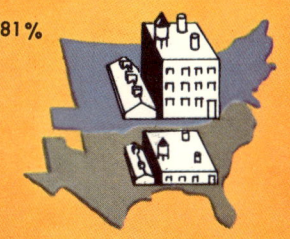
81% Factories

67% Farms

This print from an oil painting, "The March Down Broadway" by Thomas Nast, shows New York's 7th Regiment as it departed fully equipped in April, 1861, for Washington, D.C.

The Confederate uniform was gray; the Union one was blue.

From HARPER'S WEEKLY
Above is a bivouac of New York's 7th Regiment on its memorable march to the relief of Washington, D.C., in April, 1861.

Union states in the Civil War were New Hampshire, Vermont, Maine, Massachusetts, Rhode Island, Connecticut, New York, New Jersey, Pennsylvania, Delaware, Maryland, Ohio, West Virginia, Kentucky, Indiana, Michigan, Wisconsin, Illinois, Minnesota, Iowa, Missouri, Kansas, Oregon, and California. Confederate states were Virginia, North Carolina, South Carolina, Georgia, Florida, Tennessee, Alabama, Mississippi, Arkansas, Louisiana, and Texas.

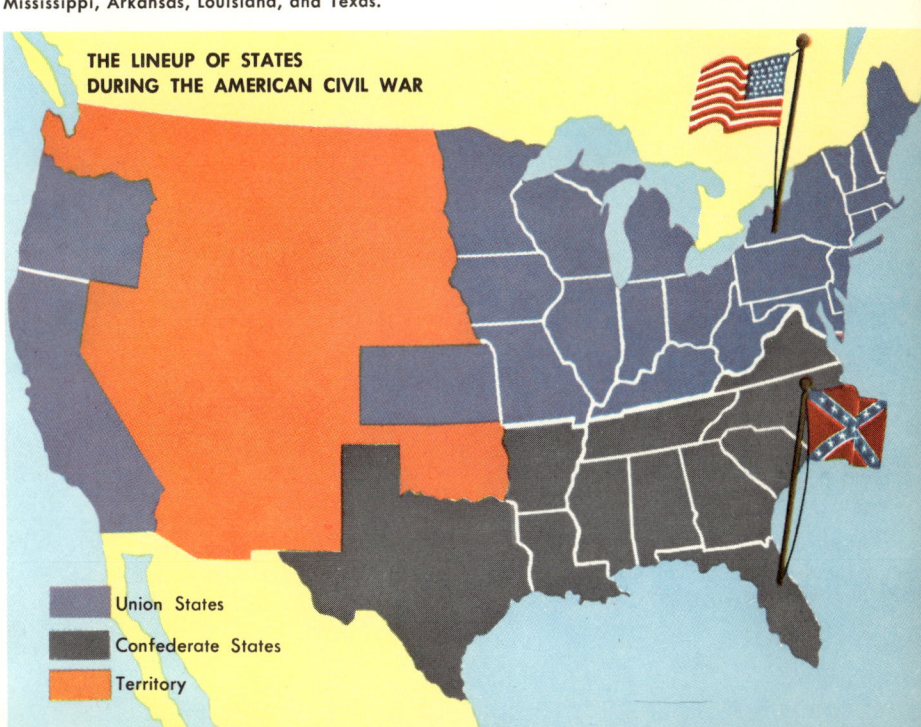
THE LINEUP OF STATES DURING THE AMERICAN CIVIL WAR

Union States
Confederate States
Territory

Collection of Oliver Jensen

History's first battle between ironclads occurred on Mar. 9, 1862, between the South's armored *Merrimac* and the North's *Monitor*.

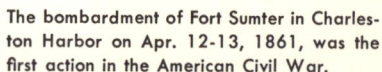

Above is a Currier & Ives lithograph of the Battle of The Wilderness, in Virginia, on May 5 and 6, 1864. After the battle, which was indecisive, both armies withdrew.

This huge gun (right), mounted on a fort on Morris Island, was used in the shelling of Charleston, S.C. Its projectile weighed 200 pounds. Such cannon were generally used only for sieges; they were too large to accompany field armies.

Natl. Archives

Zouave,
5th New York

The bombardment of Fort Sumter in Charleston Harbor on Apr. 12-13, 1861, was the first action in the American Civil War.

Library of Congress

Above is a lithograph of notorious Andersonville Prison, where some 13,000 Union soldiers died. The rations were those of the Confederate soldiers, but crowding and exposure caused a high death rate.

CIVIL WAR, AMERICAN 601

Below is General Grant (seated, second from left) and his staff. The photograph was taken at City Point, Va., in June, 1864, shortly after the bloody repulse of Union forces by General Lee at Cold Harbor, Va.

Chicago Hist. Soc.
Jefferson Davis became president of the permanent government of the Confederacy on Feb. 22, 1862.

This picture of President Lincoln (center), Allan Pinkerton (left), and Major General John A. McClernand (right) was taken at Sharpsburg, Md., by Mathew Brady after the main battle of the Antietam campaign.
Chicago Hist. Soc.

Chicago Hist. Soc.
This is Libby Prison, which was in Richmond, Va. The former tobacco warehouse became a prison for Union officers. The horrors of this notorious prison were, in large part, the result of the South's own privation.

CIVIL WAR, AMERICAN

Chicago Hist. Soc.

The painting above of "Sheridan's Ride" depicts the arrival of Philip Sheridan from Winchester to inspire Union soldiers to victory at Cedar Creek, in Virginia, in 1864.

Library of Congress

Many Southern cities were heavily bombarded before surrender.

Library of Congress

In April, 1861, President Lincoln proclaimed a blockade of Confederate ports. Here the Union fleet is anchored at Hampton Roads, off Old Point Comfort, in Virginia.

Virginia Department of Conservation and Development

The sessions of the Congress of the Confederate States of America met in the state Capital of Virginia, at Richmond, from 1861 to 1865.

CIVIL WAR, AMERICAN

U.S. Army Photograph

Both armies in the Civil War relied mainly on volunteers, who were enticed by bounties. At this Union recruiting station a new recruit was offered a total of $677.

George W. Kurten

Above is a view of Gettysburg National Military Park, which commemorates the Battle of Gettysburg. The defense of Gettysburg halted Lee's invasion of Pennsylvania.

This is a Civil War Union staff officer in field uniform. He was a member of New York's famous 7th Regiment.

Courtesy of the Seventh Regiment

The historic print above shows Sherman's March to the Sea, which occurred in late 1864. Sherman's destructive march destroyed the war potential of Georgia.

Chicago Hist. Soc.

Shown at the left is General Lee (seated, foreground) surrendering to General Grant (seated, center) at Appomattox Court House, Va. The surrender was signed Apr. 9, 1865, at the home of Wilmer McLean.

After capturing Vicksburg, Union armies in the West concentrated on Chattanooga, in southeast Tennessee. That city connected railroads through the Confederate states and also provided a good point from which the Southerners could attack Ohio. The Confederate soldiers very nearly defeated Union forces at Chickamauga near Chattanooga. Defeat was prevented by Union General George Henry Thomas, who became known as the Rock of Chickamauga. Grant was then summoned to Chattanooga, and Sherman marched his army up from Vicksburg. Grant and Sherman won at Chattanooga, Lookout Mountain, and Missionary Ridge. Sherman moved on to Georgia and the sea. Grant was then made commander in chief. With overwhelming numbers and great skill and determination, Grant pushed the Union frontal attack against Lee, while Sherman rounded up the remaining forces of the Confederacy and moved north, through the Carolinas and into Virginia. Grant beat Lee at the Wilderness and Spottsylvania Courthouse, besieged and took Petersburg, captured Richmond, and received the surrender of Lee at Appomattox Courthouse on Apr. 9, 1865. (See APPOMATTOX COURTHOUSE, SURRENDER AT.) The only remaining large Confederate army, which, under General Johnston, was being driven north through the Carolinas by General Sherman, surrendered some days later.

During the war the Navy made a great record. David Dixon Porter was of great service to Grant, operating gunboats on the western rivers, at Fort Henry, and at Vicksburg. A strict blockade of the whole southern coast prevented the Confederates from selling their cotton crop in England and from getting aid from abroad. When the South put the ironclad *Merrimac* in action, it seemed as though that ship could break up the blockade of wooden ships, but this hope was destroyed by the appearance of the Union's ironclad ship, *Monitor*. (See MONITOR AND MERRIMAC.) The Union ships also destroyed Confederate commerce raiders. However, even at the outset of the Civil War, a Northern victory was probable because of Northern superiority in manpower and material resources. The Union contained 61 percent of the population, 66 percent of the railroad mileage, 74 percent of the bank deposits, 81 percent of the factories, and 67 percent of the farms.

The United States had its diplomatic troubles during the war. At first, public sentiment in England and France favored the South. The Confederate government tried to get help from England, and once when some of its envoys were taken off an English ship by an American man-of-war, there was nearly a war between the United States and England. After the Emancipation Proclamation, however, public opinion both in England and France turned in favor of the Union.

The costs to the United States of the Civil War cannot be accurately measured. The deaths from all causes in the Union army totaled 360,000 and in the Confederate army 260,000. The total cost in money to the North and the South has been estimated at well over $20,000,000,000. No one can estimate the social and moral costs of the war. These effects continued to be felt by later generations of Americans.

CIVIL WAR, ENGLISH, was the climax of the long struggle between the supporters of Puritanism and of the rights of Parliament on one side and the supporters of the Established Church and of the divine-right absolutism of Charles I on the other. (See PURITANS.) The war really consisted of two wars, the first lasting from 1642 to 1646 and the second fought during 1648.

Parliamentary discontent, already present during the reign of Elizabeth I, came to a head after James I succeeded her in 1603. James asserted that, as king, he drew his powers from God and was therefore free from control by Parliament or by law. He followed up this claim by imposing taxes without the customary consent of Parliament.

By attempting to impose a strict Anglican form of worship on all British inhabitants and to make the Anglican bishops as absolute in church matters as the king claimed to be in political matters, both James I and his son Charles I further angered Parliament, many of whose members were Puritans, and the Scots, most of whom were Presbyterians. Especially hated for his campaign for religious uniformity and absolutism was Charles I's aide William Laud, archbishop of Canterbury, who censored the press and suppressed all but Anglican religious meetings. Also resented were courts, such as the Star Chamber, through which the kings handed down harsh judgments and imposed their royal wills on their subjects.

Parliament opposed James I and Charles I at various times by refusing to grant them money unless they would observe the rights of Parliament and accept other limitations of their powers. Several acts expressing Parliament's demands, including the Petition of Right of 1628 and a group of acts passed in 1640 and 1641, eventually became fundamental parts of the English constitution. See PETITION OF RIGHT.

James and Charles retaliated against Parliament by dissolving it several times and by arresting some of its leaders. Charles's attempted arrest of Parliamentary leaders in 1642 touched off the English Civil War.

The part of Parliament that opposed the king quickly raised its own army, called the Roundheads, which was victorious over the king's forces, which were known as the Cavaliers. The decisive forces in the war were the New Model army, that part of the Parliamentary army raised and organized by Oliver Cromwell, and the New Model army's cavalry, called the Ironsides. These troops were recruited from the most extreme Protestants. Part of their strength was their conviction of the righteousness of their cause. The two great Parliamentary victories of the war were at Marston Moor in 1644 and at Naseby in 1645. Charles surrendered in 1646, and Parliament and the king began to confer on reforms.

However, a split developed in Parliament. The majority members wished to establish Presbyterianism, the religion of the Scots, as the official state religion. Cromwell's New Model army, whose members were known as Independents, wanted no state religion. Charles tried to use the split to refuse the reforms and to gain the support of the Scots and Presbyterian members of Parliament against the army. Thus began the second part of the English Civil War, with Royalists, Scots, and other Presbyterians pitted against the army, under Cromwell, and a minority of Parliament. This war was quickly ended; the army purged Parliament of those members who did not support the Independents. The remainder of Parliament, which was known as the Rump Parliament, tried Charles for treason and condemned him to death in 1649.

Though monarchy was restored in 1660, no king after the war ever attempted to rule England without the consent of Parliament.

CLAM

CLAM, a salt-water or fresh-water mollusk related to the oyster. There are two kinds of clams that are much used for food on the Atlantic coast of the United States—the soft clam and the hard clam.

The soft clam burrows in the sand and mud along the beach. It is most abundant along the New England coast, and at low tide clam diggers go out in great numbers with baskets and shovels. The soft clam has a thin, oval shell, which consists of two hinged valves. When closed the valves have two openings through which water and food enter. Within the shell is the body of the clam, wrapped in a fold of leathery skin— the mantle, which lines the shell. The mantle also secretes the shell. Pearls are formed within the shells of some clams. At one end the mantle is prolonged into a long, elastic neck containing a double tube or siphon, which projects out of the shell and can be thrust up to the surface and opened when the

Razor Clam

Soft Clam

Natt Dodge
Gweducs

Channeled Duck Clam

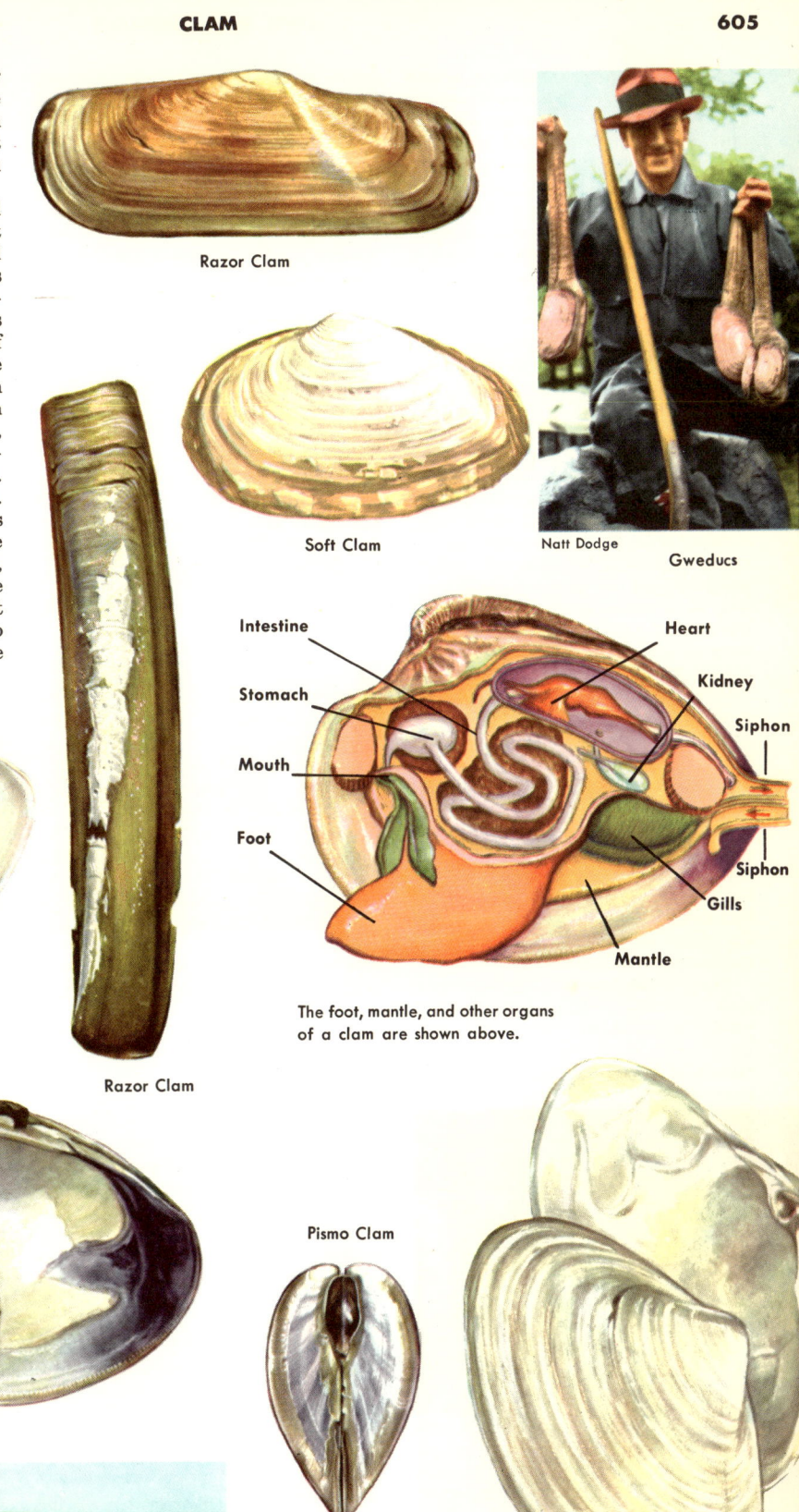

Razor Clam

The foot, mantle, and other organs of a clam are shown above.

Northern Quahog

Pismo Clam

Atlantic Surf Clam

tide is in. Water bearing oxygen and bits of food flows through the tube, and waste-laden water spurts out. Gills are the organs of breathing. A stomach, intestine, and pumping heart lie within the mantle.

The hard clam has a thick, hard, round shell and does not burrow deep in the sand. It lives under 1 to 6 fathoms of water and is taken out by raking the bottom. It is found chiefly from Cape Cod to Florida. It is able to close its shell very tightly; this fact explains the old name of clamp that was used in colonial days.

CLARINET, a wind musical instrument consisting of a tube with a bell mouth. It is made of either granadilla wood or plastic and usually has 6 finger holes, a thumb hole, and 17 keys. The tone is made by a thin piece of reed set in the mouthpiece. The reed vibrates when the player blows into the mouthpiece. In fullness of tone, the clarinet is sometimes said to be the most perfect of wind instruments, and it has a compass of over $3\frac{1}{2}$ octaves. Several differently pitched clarinets are used, of which the commonest is the B-flat soprano clarinet. Others include the E-flat clarinet, the orchestra A clarinet, the bass clarinet, and the contrabass clarinet. Usually three different clarinets are used in an orchestra. Two or more are used in a band, in which it takes the leading part, as the violin does in an orchestra.

Many composers, including Mozart and Beethoven, have written music for the clarinet. It is a German improvement of the instrument known as a shawm in the Middle Ages and has been used in orchestras since the latter part of the 18th century.

Clarinets are important band instruments.
Washington Park High School, Racine, Wis.

Ind. Hist. Bur.

"The Fall of Fort Sackville," above, is an oil painting depicting the capture by George Rogers Clark in 1779 of that fort in Vincennes, Ind., from the British.

CLARK, GEORGE ROGERS (1752-1818), American soldier and frontiersman, was born near Charlottesville, in Virginia. He served the British against the Indians in one campaign and in 1776 moved to Kentucky, then a district of Virginia, where he served as a surveyor for the Ohio Company. Gaining the settlers' confidence, he represented Kentucky in the Virginia legislature. He was a leader in organizing Kentucky as a separate county and was successful in procuring a large amount of gunpowder that was much needed for protection. In the Revolutionary War Governor Patrick Henry of Virginia made him a lieutenant colonel and gave him charge of raising troops to conquer the so-called Illinois country. Clark quickly captured Kaskaskia, and the American flag soon flew over Cahokia and Vincennes. General Hamilton, the British commander of Detroit, recaptured Vincennes. When Clark, who was at Kaskaskia, heard this, he gathered together 170 men and, marched through swamps and thick forest in midwinter, attacked Vincennes and forced the British commander to surrender on Feb. 25, 1779. He was fighting the British and the Shawnee Indians at the close of the war. In 1786 he led an unsuccessful expedition against the Wabash Indians. After he retired, he lived in poverty until within a few years of his death, when he was voted a tract of land and a small pension by the Virginia legislature.

He was of great service to his country. His conquest of the Northwest Territory gave the United States a claim to the lands between the Mississippi and Allegheny rivers and formed the basis of the peace in 1782-1783.

CLARK, WILLIAM (1770-1838), was a leader of the Lewis and Clark Expedition and was also the brother of George Rogers Clark. He was born in Virginia. He fought the Indians from about 1786 to 1796, holding the rank of lieutenant of infantry in the United States Army (1792-1796). At Merriwether Lewis' invitation in 1803, he joined Lewis in plans for their notable expedition across the continent from St. Louis to the mouth of the Columbia River (1804-1806).

In 1807 Clark was appointed brigadier general of militia for the Missouri Territory, and from 1807 until 1838 he was superintendent of Indian affairs at St. Louis. He was governor of the Missouri Territory (1813-1821) and was surveyor general of Illinois, Missouri, and Arkansas (1824-1825).

CLASSICAL MUSIC may be thought of as the best musical works that survive in any period of musical history. Popular pieces are usually shorter and have an immediate, but only temporary, appeal. This may also imply that classical music is composed for a select audience, while popular music is written for the masses. However, the differences between the two kinds are not well defined. Some music now considered classical was once popular. The chorales from Bach's *St. Matthew's Passion*, for example, were sung by Lutheran congregations in his own time. Similarly, in the United States the best popular songs of a generation are often referred to as classics.

Historically, the period of classical music extended from the end of the 17th century to the beginning of the 19th century and centered around Vienna. It included such composers as Scarlatti, Haydn, Mozart, and the early Beethoven. The classical school began as a movement away from the musical dramas—operas and oratorios mostly—of the 16th and 17th centuries.

Classical music is often contrasted with romantic music, which emphasizes intense personal emotions, freely expressed, and virtuoso performance. Thus, the performer becomes almost as important as the composer himself. The composers Beethoven and Schubert are difficult to classify as either romantic or classical, since their music contains important elements of both types. The classical style is characterized by a greater concern for technical and formal perfection in composition and performance.

CLASSICISM, an attitude or spirit associated with ancient Greek and Roman culture, particularly in literature and philosophy. More specifically, by "ancient Greek and Roman culture" is meant Greece of the 5th and 4th centuries B.C. and Rome under Julius Caesar and Augustus (from about 60 B.C. to A.D. 17). In a larger sense works that are called classical are the very best of an age or within a literary form. Thus, Cervantes' *Don Quixote* is referred to as a classic in Spanish literature or as a classic among novels. In many cases the main inspiration of such classical works cannot be traced to Greek or Roman culture at all. The term *classicism*, however, always implies Greek or Roman values.

Classicism is often opposed to romanticism as a spirit that arises from a sense of proportion rather than from a preoccupation with the extremes of emotion. Certainly the architecture and sculpture of ancient Greece exhibit a fundamental unity and balance of parts. The simplest geometrical figures are used in architectural designs—circles, equilateral triangles, squares, and rectangles. Strong vertical thrusts are met by equally strong horizontal thrusts. In the symmetrical figures of Greek sculpture one sees a perfection of the human form. The blank, serene faces of both athlete and god reflect self-mastery. The figures are typical and ideal representations of human character. See GREEK ARCHITECTURE; GREEK SCULPTURE.

The revival of classical ideals was most spectacular in the art of the Renaissance. Florentine architects, sculptors, and painters did not merely copy from ancient models. They absorbed the very spirit of classical art and made it live again in new forms. (See RENAISSANCE ART.) Neoclassical art of the 18th and 19th centuries was not nearly so successful in making this transformation. Yet several artists of considerable stature emerged from the mass of imitators and second-rate talents. The Scottish architect Robert Adam, the Italian sculptor Canova, and the French painters David and Ingres all incorporated classical elements in their work without sacrificing force of expression. See NEOCLASSICAL ART.

Classicism in music is usually associated with the 18th-century school of composers that centered around Haydn and Mozart. Although the Greek musical modes are the direct ancestor of our diatonic scale, very few actual compositions were left to us by the ancients. Thus, European music of the 18th century cannot be said to have revived Greek or Roman qualities except in a very general sense. In their emphasis on form, balance, and symmetry Bach, Handel, and Mozart were bringing classical principles to bear on their musical compositions, but they were certainly not inspired by musical works of the Greeks in the way that Donatello and Brunelleschi, for example, were inspired by fragments of classical sculpture and architecture. See CLASSICAL MUSIC; MUSIC.

In classical literature there is much more that we can study at first hand. Philosophy, poetry, and drama all bespeak a love of proportion and of the virtues of temperance and justice. Yet neither Plato nor Aeschylus nor Aristophanes denies appetite and feeling. On the contrary their works show an acquaintance with the most violent human passions. At the same time they insist on the rule of reason over the more unruly parts of the soul and stress the importance of good actions. To the Greek dramatists a well-ordered tragedy made lesser dramatic elements subordinate to the form, or plot. Most of their plays are also marked by a unity of design, in which a single theme dominates the entire work.

The actions of Greek tragedy take place within the family, where emotional ties are strongest and consequently most explosive. Incest, murder of parent by child or child by parent, madness, self-mutilation, exile are among the most familiar tragic themes. Usually the characters represented are noble, of a royal house, such as that of Atreus in the *Oresteia* of Aeschylus. Furthermore, they are typical of the human character rather than being specific and personal. The disasters they bring upon themselves are consequently understood to have general, human significance.

The feeling of repose and justness at the close of a Greek tragedy— that restoration of harmony and balance so dear to the classical mind —thus comes after one has witnessed dreadful suffering. But suffering must have meaning, or life would be outrageous. One of the Greek dramatists spoke of suffering as a strange gift of the gods, for it is by knowing pain that man becomes wise.

Of the various neoclassical literary movements that sprang up in Europe after the Renaissance, that of France is most highly esteemed.

Indeed, Molière, Corneille, and Racine are still considered the chief French dramatists. Certain features of classical tragedy are evident in the plays of Corneille that were written after his most famous work, *Le Cid*. Like the Greek tragedians, he concentrated on a single theme, most frequently the conflict between passion and duty in human beings. Racine, too, made conflicting forces in character bold and clear cut. The noble human being under stress, torn by a possessive and maddening kind of love, is often the subject of his plays. Both playwrights were also influenced by the current school of French criticism that prescribed strict rules in the writing of poetry and drama. As a result, a great many of their plays observe the unities of action, time, and place.

Dryden and Pope, the great neoclassical writers of England, made their finest contributions in verse forms rather than in the drama. Their gifts were particularly well suited to odes in the style of Pindar and Horace, to satire, and to pastoral verse. English poets and dramatists who came closer to the full-bodied emotion and moral sinew of Greek tragedy and comedy were those of the late 16th and early 17th centuries—Webster, Shakespeare, Marlowe, and Ben Jonson. See ENGLISH LITERATURE; FRENCH LITERATURE; GREEK LITERATURE; LATIN LITERATURE; ROMANTICISM.

CLAY, HENRY (1777-1852), known as The Great Compromiser, was born in the part of Hanover Co., Virginia, known as The Slashes. Clay's formal education was slight. In 1797, after studying under the noted jurist George Wythe, Clay was licensed to practice law. Finding conditions in Richmond too crowded, he moved to Lexington, Kentucky, where he became noted as a criminal lawyer.

In 1803 Clay was elected to the state legislature. In 1806 and 1807 he filled an unexpired term in the U.S. Senate. He was then reelected to the legislature and chosen speaker. In 1809 he was again picked to fill an unexpired term in the U.S. Senate.

In 1810 Clay was elected to the national House of Representatives and immediately named its speaker. He became the advocate of western interests and was the leader of the War Hawks, who pushed the United States into the War of 1812. In 1814-1815 he was a member of the U.S. delegation to the peace conference at Ghent, Belgium.

Under President James Monroe Clay declined various posts, preferring the role of administration critic in Congress. In this capacity he authored the American System. This was a program of internal improvements, a national bank, protective tariffs, and adequate national defense. During this period Clay also did much to secure the passage of the Missouri Compromise.

After two years' absence he returned to Congress in 1823, secured a high tariff in 1824, and in the same year was defeated for the presidency. In the runoff election in the House, he supported John Quincy Adams against Andrew Jackson. When Adams was elected and Clay was named secretary of state, enemies charged a "corrupt bargain." There is evidence of none, but the cry affected Clay's later career.

Clay retired after Jackson became president in 1829. But Clay returned to Congress in 1831 as head of the opposition and became the leader of the new Whig movement. Defeated for the presidency in 1832, he forgot his disappointment in the nullification crisis of 1833, which he settled by his compromise tariff. Clay remained in the Senate until 1842, opposing both Jackson and his successor, Martin Van Buren.

Clay's hedging of his former stand against annexation of Texas cost him the presidency in 1844. Four years later he failed to get the Whig nomination and, because of his opposition to military men in the presidency, refused to support the campaign of Zachary Taylor. Clay returned to the Senate the following year and served there until his death. See COMPROMISE OF 1850.

CLAY is a general term for naturally occurring, earthy, very fine-grained material composed mainly of hydrous aluminum silicate minerals. Nearly all clays are plastic (easily molded and shaped) when mixed with a limited amount of water. Many types of clays are known, and there are several groups of clay minerals.

Nearly all clays consist of minute, flake-shaped crystalline particles. The particles are less than 0.005 millimeters in their greatest dimension. Many clay particles are of colloidal size—of less than 0.001-millimeter dimension. Many of the properties of clay are the result of small particle size.

Clays have many different chemical compositions. Some of the aluminum in the hydrous aluminum silicate minerals is often replaced by iron or magnesium. Other elements or compounds are present as impurities. Finely divided organic material may be included in a clay. Two clays of similar chemical composition may have very different properties.

Clay minerals carry cations (positive ions) on their surfaces. The cations are not a part of the clay minerals. Some clay minerals are capable of exchanging the cations they carry for other cations that are present in water solutions. This process is called ion exchange or base exchange. The structure of a clay mineral is not affected by ion exchange, but the properties of a clay may be greatly affected.

Henry Clay (below) often propounded before the U.S. Congress his American system: high tariffs and internal improvements.

Library of Congress

At the upper left is a map showing the distribution of clay deposits in the United States. Clay has a variety of uses, as indicated above. Heavy clay products include building brick, structural tile, and sewer pipe. Clay is used in portland and other hydraulic cements. As firebrick it is used to line furnaces.

As shown above, clays are found in various colors, depending on the impurities they contain. Basically clay is a hydrous aluminum silicate, but no two clays are exactly alike. For most uses chemical composition is unimportant. The important properties of clay include plasticity, dry and fired color, and resistance to heat.

The plasticity of a clay depends on the chemical composition of the clay minerals, the cations attached to the surfaces of the clay minerals, the clay particle sizes and orientations, and the impurities present in the clay. When clay particles are mixed with water, each clay flake is surrounded by a film of water a few molecules thick. The clay particles slide past each other on their water films as the clay is molded into different shapes.

Clays have important uses in many industries. The ceramic industry is the principal user of clays. Most ceramic products are made mainly of clay. (See CERAMICS.) Some important ceramic products made mostly of clay are bricks, tiles, sewer pipe, terra cotta, firebrick, refractories (materials to withstand high temperatures), pottery, stoneware, and porcelains for electrical and chemical uses. The petroleum industry and the manufacturers of vegetable oils use adsorbent clays. The clays are used to remove impurities and decolorize the petroleum and vegetable-oil products. Clays are used as lubricants and particle carriers in drilling muds. Drilling muds are used during the drilling of oil wells. The paper industry uses large quantities of a type of clay called kaolin. The clay is used as filling in the body of a sheet of paper and as a coating on the surface of paper. Clays are used as a filler in calcimine and in casein paints. Clays are incorporated in rubber products. Clay makes the rubber stiffer, tougher, and more resistant to wear. Rubber containing clay is used in such products as shoe soles and heels, floor tile, matting, bicycle tires, and hose.

CLAYTON ANTITRUST ACT, a law passed by the U. S. Congress on Oct. 15, 1914, as a supplement to the Sherman Antitrust Act of 1890. The author of the act was Henry De Lamar Clayton, a Democratic congressman from Alabama.

The Clayton Antitrust Act declared that federal antitrust laws could not be applied to labor and agricultural organizations pursuing legitimate activities. The act also prohibited interlocking directorates of industrial combinations and certain banks, that is, a person could not be a director of two or more companies in the same industry or corporation. Furthermore, officials of companies were held personally responsible for violation of antitrust laws.

CLAYTON-BULWER TREATY, a convention between the United States and Great Britain, named for John M. Clayton, U. S. secretary of state, and Sir Henry Bulwer, British minister at Washington, D. C. It proposed to govern the actions of the two nations in the construction of a canal in Central America. It was ratified in 1850. It provided that neither party should "obtain or maintain for itself any exclusive control over the said ship canal" or "erect or maintain any fortifications commanding the same" or "occupy, or fortify, or colonize, or assume or exercise a dominion" in the territory surrounding any such canal. As the reality of the building of such a canal by the United States began to materialize and the possibility of such action by Great Britain began to diminish, the pact was supplanted in 1901 by the Hay-Pauncefote Treaty.

CLEMENCEAU, GEORGES (1841-1929), a French statesman, was born the son of a doctor in the Vendée and spent his early childhood in the family's castle, Château de l'Aubraie. He took a degree in medicine at the University of Paris. In 1865 he visited the United States and contributed articles to *Le Temps*.

After the Franco-Prussian War Clemenceau played a part in Paris politics. He became a member of the House of Deputies in 1876 and was soon the leader of the Radicals. He made many political enemies and was not reelected in 1893. In 1903 Clemenceau was back in politics as a member of the Senate, and from 1906 until 1909 he was prime minister. As such he strengthened the alliance with England, created the ministry of labor, and nationalized the Western Railroad.

Clemenceau was again called upon to form a ministry during the bleak war year of 1917. Following World War I he set about to make Germany incapable of another war. In his role in preparing the Treaty of Versailles he was attacked by Britain and the United States for harshness and by the French for leniency. His interests were anti-German and exclusively European. Above all, Clemenceau wanted a free, civilized, and peaceful Europe. He was cautious about the League of Nations, but he was nevertheless willing to give it a chance to work. In 1920 Clemenceau lost the election to the French presidency and retired from public life to one of contemplation and writing. Of his numerous written works his most famous is *In the Evening of My Thought*. See VERSAILLES TREATY.

CLEMENS

MARK TWAIN

To the left is Mark Twain as remembered by lecture audiences of the 1870's and 1880's. Shown below is the author's boyhood home in Hannibal, Mo. Two modern Tom Sawyers lean against the fence immortalized by the whitewashing episode recounted in *Tom Sawyer*.

Mo. News Magazine

A number of Mark Twain's best known works are identified by the drawings below. The Mississippi River steamboat, left, quite similar to the ones that were once piloted by the author himself, symbolizes the life and times so faithfully recollected in Mark Twain's masterpieces.

Life on the Mississippi

The Adventures of Huckleberry Finn

A Connecticut Yankee in King Arthur's Court

The Prince and the Pauper

The Celebrated Jumping Frog of Calaveras County

CLEMENS, SAMUEL (1835-1910), an American author better known as Mark Twain, was born in Florida, Mo. In 1839 the Clemens family settled in Hannibal, Mo., and here he passed the boyhood so vividly recalled in his writings. Clemens left school after his father's death in 1847 and was apprenticed to a printer. Later, he worked on his brother's newspaper and as a journeyman printer. Clemens became a Mississippi steamboat pilot but gave this up when the Civil War halted the operations of the boats.

In 1862 Clemens began writing for a Virginia City, Nev., paper. At this time he adopted the name Mark Twain, which means "two fathoms deep," a phrase used in making soundings on the Mississippi. It was originally a pseudonym of Isaiah Sellers, a pilot who wrote for the New Orleans *Picayune*. Clemens, in the New Orleans *True Delta*, used the name in parodies he did of Sellers' articles.

In 1865 Clemens wrote his famous story "The Celebrated Jumping Frog of Calaveras County," which was collected with other stories and published in 1867. In *The Innocents Abroad*, published in 1869, Clemens describes a tour he made of the Mediterranean and the Holy Land. *Roughing It* was published in 1872, and in 1873, *The Gilded Age*, a novel written in collaboration with C. D. Warner.

In 1876 Clemens wrote that perennial favorite among boy's books *The Adventures of Tom Sawyer*. In 1880 came *A Tramp Abroad* and in 1882 *The Prince and the Pauper*. In the following two years Clemens published the American classics *Life on the Mississippi* and *The Adventures of Huckleberry Finn*. His fantasy of medieval England, *A Connecticut Yankee in King Arthur's Court*, was published in 1889.

Clemens had become a partner in a publishing house, and in 1894 the firm went bankrupt. To pay his debts, Clemens made a worldwide lecture tour, which he recorded in *Following the Equator*, published in 1897. During this decade, the last of the 19th century, Clemens published many works, but these were inferior to his early productions. These works include *The Tragedy of Pudd'nhead Wilson*, *Personal Recollections of Joan of Arc*, *The American Claimant*, *Tom Sawyer Abroad*, and *Tom Sawyer, Detective*. In 1898 he succeeded in discharging his debts.

Clemens' last works are known for their pessimism. They include "The Man that Corrupted Hadleyburg," "What is Man?," and "The Mysterious Stranger." After Clemens' death his letters were collected, and his authorized life was written by his secretary, Albert Bigelow Paine.

Intrigues of the beautiful Cleopatra are the subject of several great works of literature, among them Shakespeare's *Antony and Cleopatra* and Shaw's *Caesar and Cleopatra*.

CLEOPATRA (about 69-30 B.C.), queen of Egypt. Her father, Ptolemy XI Auletes, died when she was 17 years old and left his throne to her and her brother Ptolemy XII.

When Ptolemy tried to take the power from her, she made up her mind to ask Julius Caesar, then in Alexandria, to help her. She could not go to him openly because she was watched by her brother's friends. She got a servant to carry her on his back in a roll of carpeting into the room of Caesar, and when the carpet was unrolled, the beautiful girl sprang out, threw herself at the feet of the Roman general, and begged him for help. Caesar promised it, and he did not leave Egypt until Ptolemy had been killed and Cleopatra had regained her throne.

Some years later Caesar was murdered, and Mark Antony became the most influential man in Rome. Cleopatra was summoned by Antony to answer charges of treachery. Antony was then at Tarsus, a city of Asia, on the Cydnus River. Cleopatra had a splendid ship built. It was ornamented with gold and silver. The sails were of purple silk, and the silver oars kept time to soft, sweet music. She lay on a couch under a canopy of gold cloth.

Antony was so charmed that he accompanied her back to Egypt. On her account he divorced his wife, Octavia, the sister of Octavian, who later became Augustus Caesar and who soon declared war against Cleopatra. She was with Antony at the Battle of Actium in 31 B.C. and was the first to flee. Antony followed her to Egypt. After he had killed himself, she was taken prisoner by Octavian. He ordered her to be watched carefully, intending to take her to Rome to grace his triumph. But she had a poisonous serpent called an asp brought to her in a basket of figs. She dressed herself in her royal robes and, with her crown on her head, put the asp on her breast. She died in a few moments from its bite. See MARK ANTONY.

CLEPSYDRA. See WATER CLOCK.

CLEVELAND, STEPHEN GROVER (1837-1908), 22d and 24th president of the United States, born in Caldwell, N.J., Mar. 18, 1837. In 1841 his parents moved to Fayetteville, N.Y., where he received a common-school education. In 1855 he entered a law office in Buffalo, N.Y., and in 1859 he was admitted to the bar.

From 1871 to 1874 he was sheriff of Erie Co., New York, and in 1882, mayor of Buffalo. In the same year he was elected governor of New York by an immense majority and served until 1884.

He was then elected, on the Democratic ticket, president of the

Grover Cleveland

United States. In 1888 he was nominated for reelection but was defeated by Benjamin Harrison. Cleveland was nominated a third time and reelected in 1892.

During his presidential career he advanced the cause of civil service reform. In addition, he forced Congress to repeal the clause of the Sherman Silver Bill that required the treasury to buy a certain quantity of silver every month. By encouraging the overproduction of silver, this act had resulted in the silver dollar's being worth only 56 cents in gold. This drop in the value of the silver dollar was one of the causes of the panic in 1893.

During Cleveland's administration the Department of Agriculture and the Interstate Commerce Commission were created, and the Chinese Exclusion Act and a law barring laborers brought into the United States under contract were passed. Cleveland vigorously asserted American rights in the Canadian fisheries dispute with Great Britain. He also gave the protection of the Monroe Doctrine to Venezuela concerning boundary claims that it considered unjust. Cleveland advocated a tariff large enough for revenue only and opposed the McKinley Tariff Bill, which the Republican administration had passed, because he said the great surplus of revenue in the treasury led to reckless public expenditure.

CLEVELAND is a major inland port and a great iron and steel center. The largest city in Ohio, it is located in the northern part of the state, on Lake Erie, at the mouth of the Cuyahoga River. Its population in 1960 was 876,050.

Besides iron and steel the principal products manufactured in the city are electrical equipment, aircraft engines, automobiles and parts, machine tools, and food products.

In 1796 Moses Cleaveland surveyed land for the Connecticut Land Company and founded the town of Cleveland. Even though the town was named after Cleaveland, people got in the habit of spelling the name without the *a*. After the construction of the Ohio and Erie Canal in 1832 the growth of Cleveland was rapid, and it was incorporated as a city in 1836. John D. Rockefeller organized the Standard Oil Company here in 1870.

Western Reserve University is located in Cleveland, as are Case Institute of Technology, Fenn College, John Carroll University, and Ursuline College for Women. Cultural institutions include the Cleveland Museum of Art, the Cleveland Museum of Natural History, and the Cleveland Symphony Orchestra. A most unusual institution located here is the Cleveland Health Museum, the first in America.

CLIFFDWELLER, one of a group of Indians who lived in the cliffs bordering on the valleys of the Rio Grande and Colorado. No one knows when the first dwellings were cut into the cliffs. The Indians who used them may have lived there in order to hide from the more warlike tribes who wandered into the region. By the time of Coronado's famous visit to these areas in the 16th century, most of the cliff dwellings were no longer occupied. The Pueblo Indians, who still occupy these regions, are the descendants of the cliffdwellers.

Some of the cliff dwellings are almost inaccessible. They were reached by a series of ladders made of wood or carved into the rock. These ladders led up almost perpendicular precipices. Nearly all the original ladders have been destroyed by the crumbling of the rocks.

The door to a cliff dwelling was a small hewn opening. Inside, there was one or more chambers, which were often below the level of the entrance. Sometimes there were two or more stories of rooms. The walls and floor were plastered with clay. Sometimes the walls had simple painted designs. Near the entrance was a fireplace, with a smoke vent that led outside. Numerous alcoves and storage spaces were carved into the walls. Porches were occasionally built in front of the entrance. They were supported by timbers inserted into holes in the face of the cliff. Inside the dwellings explorers have found the remains of baskets, cloth, pottery, implements and utensils of stone, ornaments, and weapons. The cliffdwellers had agricultural implements, and they probably lived by growing corn. See PUEBLO INDIANS.

CLIMATE, the effect of weather over a long time. Four things make up weather: temperature, precipitation and humidity, wind, and air pressure. These are the elements we check before leaving the house in the morning, so that we may know whether to wear a raincoat, an overcoat, or no coat at all.

Climate is the general picture of day-by-day weather conditions over a long time. It is not necessarily an average picture, because variations from the average are important in the overall climatic picture. For example, the average temperature over the period of a year may be 50° F. in a certain location. But this average annual temperature could be the average monthly temperature every month. Or the average monthly temperature could vary greatly because some months are very cold and other months are hot. The weatherman must collect weather information daily for a period of years and fit it together before he has a picture of the climate of a locality.

The four elements that make up weather and climate do not produce the same conditions throughout the world. The Arab, riding through the hot, dry desert, is subjected to climatic conditions very different from those experienced by the South Sea Islander in his balmy, humid, forested home. The conditions that cause the four elements of weather to differ are called climatic controls.

One of the most important climatic controls is latitude, which determines the intensity and duration of the sun's rays. The distribution of water and land also has an important effect on climate. By way of example are Portland, Ore., and Minneapolis, Minn., both of which lie at about the same latitude, or distance from the Equator. The mean temperature in Portland's coldest month is about 40° F., but in Minneapolis it is 12° F. This difference is due to Portland's being near the moderating influence of the Pacific Ocean, while Minneapolis is in the middle of a huge body of land. Winds are important climatic controls. It makes a great difference whether winds consistently blow from the ocean and carry great quantities of moisture or whether they sweep from the land, in which case they may be very dry. High-pressure and low-pressure belts, as at the Equator and at approximately 30 degrees north and south latitudes, cause calm belts of little wind movement. Altitude also affects climate. A climber on Mt. Whitney in southern California may be shivering with cold, while Death Valley, less than 80 miles away, may have a temperature of over 100° F.

Life among the cliffdwellers is shown in the artist's drawing at the left. The time is between 1050 and 1300. Their position made these dwellings easy to defend but very inconvenient. Hundreds of such cliff dwellings may still be seen today at Mesa Verde National Park, which is in Colorado.

Climate varies in general with latitude, but it also depends upon local conditions. Climatic belts around the earth are charted on the globe at left as follows: 1, polar; 2, tropical; and 3, temperate. Local variation is illustrated by conditions in the western United States. Winds from the Pacific Ocean, indicated by arrows, are laden with moisture, but most of the moisture is intercepted by high mountain systems—the Cascades and the Sierra Nevada. The result is a desert area beyond the coastal mountains.

Mountain barriers have a profound effect on climate.

The climate of northwestern Europe is tempered by the warm ocean current that drifts northward across the Atlantic from the vicinity of the Gulf of Mexico. The northeast coast of Asia has no such warm current and is therefore much colder —and much less inhabited.

These major climatic controls operate on the four elements of climate to produce the characteristic climate of your city or state.

Vegetation is a good gauge of climate. Plants cannot move around like people, and they are dependent on weather conditions. So the type of vegetation that grows in a locality can tell us a great deal about the climate there. See HUMIDITY; PLANT GEOGRAPHY; PRECIPITATION; SEASON; STORM; WEATHER; WIND CIRCULATION.

CLINOMETER, a portable instrument used with a ceiling light to measure cloud heights at night. The ceiling light casts a beam of light directly overhead to the base of the cloud layer. The weatherman stands at a known distance from the ceiling light (about 800 to 1,000 feet) and adjusts his clinometer so that the spot of light on the cloud layer is reflected in it. This adjustment gives him a reading on the clinometer that tells him the elevation angle from the ground to the base of the cloud layer. By trigonometry the weatherman can find out the height of the cloud base and can report the ceiling. See CEILING.

CLIPPER SHIP. The clipper ship was the fastest cargo-carrying sailing vessel ever built. Its speed and grace were due to its narrowness in proportion to its length, its tall masts, its enormous sail area, and the sharpness of its bow.

Clipper design was evolved by American shipbuilders to meet the commercial challenge of early steam-propelled vessels. In competition

The clipper ship *Lightning* set two records on her maiden voyage in 1854. She covered 436 miles in one day and made the Boston-to-Liverpool run in 13 days 19½ hours.

with each other and with steam vessels, clippers established speed records during the California and Australian gold rushes and in the fruit, opium, tea, and slave trades—especially during the height of the clipper-ship era, from 1840 to 1855.

The first true clipper was the *Ann McKim*, built in 1832. Most notable were the *Thermopylae*, the *Flying Cloud*, the *Comet*, and the *Cutty Sark*. The *Cutty Sark* established a brief sailing record of 363 miles in one day. Clippers were faster than nearly all steamships built before 1865. Several of them made the voyage from New York or Boston to San Francisco in less than 100 days. Clipper ships were generally of 1,500 to 2,000 registered tons. With the decline of the American carrying trade after the Civil War and the rise of British steamers, the clipper-ship era came to a close.

CLIVE, ROBERT (1725-1774), an English adventurer who was largely responsible for Great Britain's acquisition of India. At 18 years of age Clive went to India as a clerk for the British East India Company. However, he hated office routine, and the situation in India provided great opportunity for his talents. After war broke out in 1746 between the French East India Company and the British East India Company, which were competing fiercely for trade and power in a highly disunited India, Clive joined an English garrison. In 1751 he and a handful of men ousted the French from the Carnatic.

Clive then returned to England but came back to India three years later and shortly thereafter established the East India Company's power over Bengal. Soon after taking Calcutta, Clive conspired with Indian merchants to replace the native ruler. In 1757 he defeated him and his French backers at the Battle of Plassey. The prince was replaced, and Bengal was thereafter controlled by the British East India Company. Although Clive had taken bribes and used illegal means to gain his ends, he stopped the corrupt practices of the company and reorganized the army after he became governor in 1765. When he returned to England two years later, a parliamentary committee found him guilty of fraud in the Bengali conspiracy. However, the committee also agreed that he had done great service to his country. His death was by suicide.

CLOCK

Elgin Natl. Watch Co.

Courtesy of Sessions Discount Center

Courtesy of Sessions Discount Center

The 18th-century outdoor clock at the lower left is set in a wall of Sainte-Chapelle, Paris. The device at the left, designed by Galileo, is an early attempt to use the pendulum in clockwork. The modern clock at the right is powered by a tiny transistor unit. Early pocket watches of the type at the lower right were called Nuremberg eggs because they were first made in that German town and their elaborately decorated cases were egg shaped. At the far right is shown a richly ornamented wooden cuckoo clock.

Robert J. Bezucha

Elgin Natl. Watch Co.

CLOCK, an instrument used for measuring and indicating the passage of time. The first instrument of this sort was the sundial. However, this was of no service at night or on cloudy days, so the hourglass soon made its appearance. Next came the clepsydra, a type of water clock, which was subsequently improved by the addition of a toothed wheel and an index, or sort of dial. The most famous clock of this type was the one built at Athens by the great astronomer Andronicus of Cyrrhus as part of the noted structure known as the Tower of the Winds. The next improvement in clockmaking was the substitution of a weight for water to turn the wheel. This invention was attributed to Archimedes. Some other mechanism was necessary to regulate this weight in order to make the index pass over equal spaces in equal time. This mechanism's work had to be accomplished by a pendulum or escapement of some kind. A rude form of an escapement was invented about A.D. 1000, and in 1360 an improved model appeared.

Accuracy in marking time on a clock was not attained until the idea of attaching the pallets of the escapement to the pendulum rod and making the escapement horizontal occurred to Christian Huygens, a Dutch mathematician, about 1658. The anchor escapement, developed in the latter half of the 17th century, and the deadbeat escapement, in the early 18th century, gave a new impetus to clockmaking.

There has been no material change since 1700 in the principles on which clocks are made, except the substitution of steel springs for weights, the use of finer movements, and the addition of the hairspring to regulate still further the action of the escapement or pendulum. Electricity and compressed air have been used since about 1875 for the motion and control of clocks.

The electrical clocks of today are of two kinds: the synchronous type, which is operated from a central control, and the independent type, which has small electrical motors to measure time in accord with the flow of electrical current.

CLOTH, any fabric woven, knitted, or pressed from animal, vegetable, mineral, or manmade fibers or from a combination of these types of fibers. Except for the felts, which are formed by heat, moisture, and pressure, cloth is the final product of four basic processes: the production of a fiber such as cotton, wool, or rayon; the preparation and spinning of the fibers into yarn; the arranging of the yarn, according to certain patterns, into cloth as in weaving and knitting; and, finally, the finishing of the cloth for the tailor, the dressmaker, the sailmaker, or other craftsmen.

Illustrated below are the three basic weaves of rayon fabric, as follows: **1**, plain, which produces even-surfaced goods; **2**, twill, which produces diagonal ribs; and **3**, satin, which produces goods with a glossy surface.

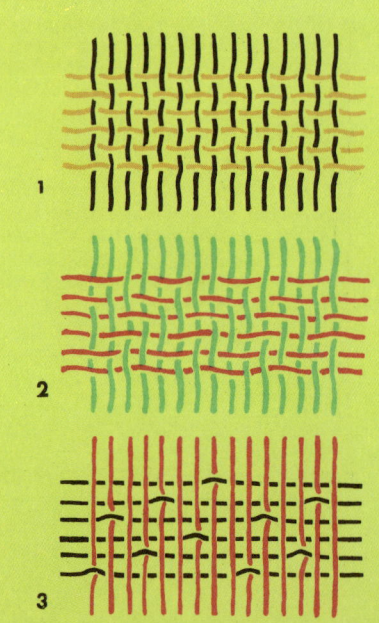

The weaving of cloth probably followed the weaving of baskets. Bits of cloth have been found among the remains of the ancient lake dwellers of Switzerland, in Egyptian tombs, and in tombs in Denmark, England, and Ireland. The origin of cloth is lost in the fog of antiquity because cloth, made from animal and vegetable fibers, decays rapidly in damp, warm soil.

In terms of raw materials, cloth-making has developed in three stages. The first stage was cloth from vegetable fibers, such as flax, nettles, and the inner bark of trees. The extensive use of cotton is relatively new, dating from the end of the 18th century. The second stage began with the use of animal fibers, especially wool and silk. Very ancient remains of woolen cloth have been found in Mesopotamia. Silk came to Western Europe and to America from China. The third stage in the history of clothmaking began in the late 19th century with the development of manmade fibers like rayon and with the introduction of nylon. The manmade materials are not only used to make totally new kinds of cloth but are also combined with the old vegetable and animal fibers for improved strength, wearing ability, and other qualities.

CLOTHING, HISTORY OF. Clothing is influenced by climate, occupation, and daily needs. Other influences on clothing are religious beliefs and ideas of modesty and beauty.

The Ona people in the cold country of Tierra del Fuego often wear no clothing, and the Arabs in hot countries are often fully clothed. Usually, where people wear less clothing, there is more body decoration. The Ona, for example, often paint their bodies. The Amish, members of a religious sect, do not use buttons because they believe them to represent luxurious or militairstic standards.

The earliest known clothing was worn by men in the last part of the Old Stone Age. They wore beads or body ornaments of bone, animal teeth, and shell. Probably they wore cut-and-sewed skins. During the New Stone Age spinning was invented, and clothing was made of woven cloth dyed in various colors. Clothing was simple at first—a kilt for women and a loincloth for men. A large piece of cloth, worn over the shoulders, was used as a blanket at night. In cold weather people wore cloaks of sheepskin or goatskin.

Clothing reflects the entire life of a people, just as does art, architecture, and literature. In the Middle East women of the Mohammedan religion were heavily veiled and covered. They were usually secluded. In Turkey and in Egypt, with political and social changes in the 20th century, changes in dress became evident. The veil went out of fashion, and European styles were adopted.

In Europe during the Middle Ages the lines of the towering cathedrals were reflected in the tall headdresses and sharply pointed

Illustrated above are some dress styles worn before 1700. **1.** This Greek is wearing the chiton, basic garb for both sexes in ancient Greece. **2.** The uniform of the Roman soldier weighed as much as 50 pounds. **3.** The barbarian's battle garb included chain mail. **4.** Costumes like these were worn at Charlemagne's court. **5.** This was a bishop's garb during the early 13th century. **6.** Dresses with long trains became popular during the Renaissance. **7.** With the conquistador are three Aztec Indians. **8.** The Puritans' dress was severely plain. **9.** This was the costume worn by an English gentleman during the 1670's.

CLOTHING

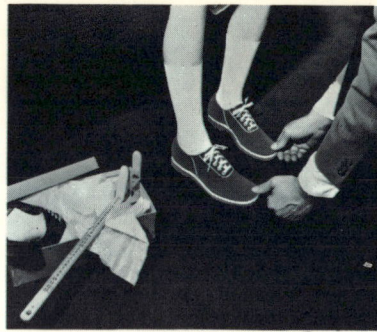

Natl. Shoe Inst.

The salesman is checking the distance from the end of the foot to the shoe tip. Shoes should fit snugly yet comfortably.

CLOTHING, SELECTION AND CARE OF. The places you go and the things you do regularly should be kept in mind when you are planning to buy clothing. Such factors as the quality of clothing, the type of fabric, the workmanship, the fit, and the care required must be considered. Different fabrics have different wearing qualities, and these must be known. (See CLOTH.) Signs of good workmanship are correct cut, lengthwise or crosswise of the threads; close, even stitches; proper matching of patterns at seams; and buttonholes made with close, even stitching.

Clothes should be placed on hangers immediately after they have

Features to look for when selecting a new coat include a strong and durable lining, A; well-made buttonholes, B; quality fabric of the desired color, weight, and weave, C; and a well-finished set of buttons, D.

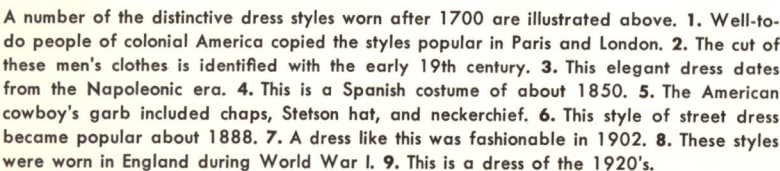

A number of the distinctive dress styles worn after 1700 are illustrated above. 1. Well-to-do people of colonial America copied the styles popular in Paris and London. 2. The cut of these men's clothes is identified with the early 19th century. 3. This elegant dress dates from the Napoleonic era. 4. This is a Spanish costume of about 1850. 5. The American cowboy's garb included chaps, Stetson hat, and neckerchief. 6. This style of street dress became popular about 1888. 7. A dress like this was fashionable in 1902. 8. These styles were worn in England during World War I. 9. This is a dress of the 1920's.

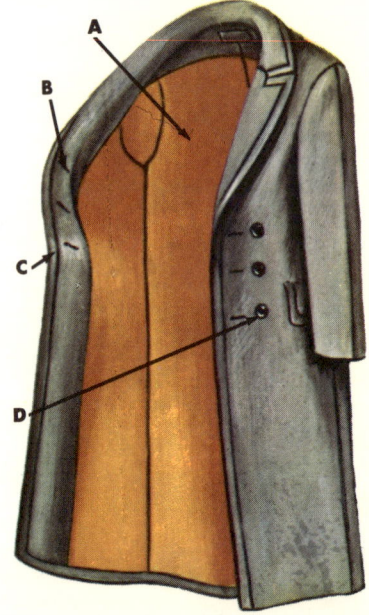

shoes of the people. In the late 18th century after Pompeii was discovered, interest was revived in classical antiquity. Costumes of Greek or Roman type, with flat slippers and flowing, draped garments, were in fashion. In France, after the revolution that began in 1789, plainer clothing was substituted for the more elaborate garments of the Old Regime.

Variability or stability in fashions usually reflects social and political situations. During the calm Victorian times costume variations were small compared with the changes in the more turbulent years shortly before and after World War II.

CLOUD

been worn, and they should be brushed between cleanings. Spots and stains should be removed. Suitable work clothes should be worn for all work activities. Stained clothes should not be pressed before they are cleaned. It is well to follow the laundering directions that come with your clothes. Temperature of the water is important to many fabrics. All clothing should be clean, but no starch should be used, before storing. One may use moth repellent preparations at home to prepare woolens for storage, or they may be sent to dry-cleaning plants.

CLOUD, a formation in the atmosphere originating from water vapor. The atmosphere contains a great deal of water vapor that is drawn from water surfaces, such as the sea, by the heat of the sun. So dependent on the sun are clouds, in fact, that when the sun cannot replenish their water supply, as at night, they sometimes die of thirst. Once water vapor is a part of the atmosphere, it is carried hither and yon by the winds.

You may have watched a cloud being formed and may not have realized it. When hot bath water is run into the tub in a slightly chilly bathroom, the steam that you see is actually a cloud. The warm, moist air over the hot water loses some of its water as steam when the warm air mixes with the colder air around it.

This is one way that clouds are formed outdoors. The cold air of a cold front mixes with warm, moist

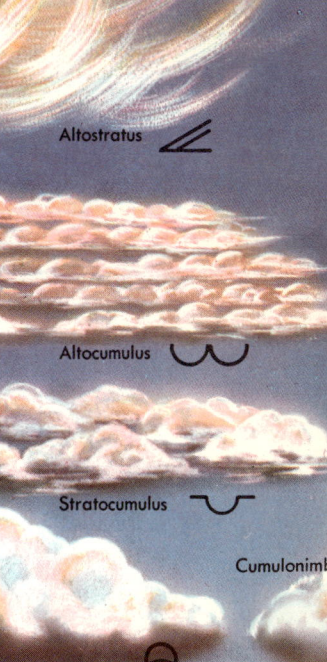

The diagram above illustrates a basic pattern of cloud formation. The red arrow indicates the course of a warm airmass pushing over a cold airmass. As the warm air rises it cools below its saturation point. The water vapor it bears condenses to form clouds and rain.

The clouds in the foreground (below) are of the cumulus type; the layered ones in the distance are stratus clouds. This cloud bank was photographed over Sierra Leone.

Artha Hornbostel

At the right are cloud types and symbols. Altostratus and altocumulus clouds, middle clouds, form between 6,500 and 20,000 feet. Clouds above and below, except for vertically developed cumulus and cumulonimbus clouds, are called high and low clouds, respectively.

Low clouds or fog (a cloud on the ground) may form when the earth cools quickly, as on a clear night. Air in contact with the earth is cooled below its saturation point.

Clouds may also form as warm ocean or lake air moves in over a cool land surface. The moisture-laden airmass is cooled below its saturation point, and the moisture condenses to form clouds.

Cloud formation may occur when warm air is lifted by a mass of heavier cold air acting as a wedge. Again, clouds form as the warm air is cooled below its saturation point.

Clouds may be formed through adiabatic cooling, or the cooling of a rising airmass, whenever winds move up a mountain slope.

Most clouds are formed by the cooling, called adiabatic cooling, that occurs whenever air rises. Heated by contact with a warm land surface, air expands and begins to rise. As it rises, it cools at the rate of about $5\frac{1}{2}°$ F. for each 1,000 feet of rise.

air, and the warm air loses some of its water to form clouds. Clouds are also formed when air moves northward across the colder surface of the earth. And when warm air rises, it cools. The cooler air, since it can carry much less water with it, leaves its burden of water behind as clouds. That is why mountains are often hidden in mantles of cloud: Air is cooled as it rises over a mountain barrier. Air is also forced to rise as an air current when it is heated by the sun. And, once again, the rising air reaches colder and higher regions of the atmosphere, cools, and casts off its burden of water as clouds.

In a "cloudy" bathroom, the mirror over the sink will often gather moisture. This shows that moisture needs something to condense on. And, in fact, before clouds can form, something also must be present in the air for water to gather, or condense, on. These tiny "mirrors" are furnished by the countless particles of smoke, sea salt, and dust that are always present in the air.

Clouds are useful signposts for the weatherman. He can sometimes predict what the next day's weather may bring if he observes the clouds. See ATMOSPHERIC CONDENSATION; CLOUD SEEDING; FOG.

CLOUD SEEDING is a means of scientific rainmaking. Like many other scientific discoveries, cloud seeding was discovered almost by accident. Scientists working on the problem of preventing ice formation on airplanes seeded clouds with bits of dry ice. They discovered that snow was sometimes formed. Many people were excited about the news that rain and snow could be artificially created. Some went so far as to predict that drought and deserts were things of the past. But the job of the scientist was a difficult one. He studied the formation of rain, and he tried numerous cloud-seeding experiments, but the results were not spectacular. But perhaps cloud seeding is the first step to the control of weather and climate. For example, the law establishing the National Science Foundation states that one of the purposes of this agency is to "initiate and support a program of study, research, and evaluation in the field of weather modification, giving particular attention to areas that have experienced floods, drought, hail, lightning, tornadoes, and hurricanes."

Cloud seeding is done by sowing particles of dry ice, salt, water, or silver iodide in large cumulus clouds. The dry ice causes the tiny drops of water in clouds to form rapidly growing crystals. The crystals finally become so heavy that they fall. Silver iodide or salt works simi-

Cloud seeding with Dry Ice (below) causes a partly cleared strip to form in stratus clouds below the airplane. A plane seeds a cumulus cloud (right) with about a pound of Dry Ice. The seeding produces a shower over a small area.

CLOWN

Red clover is native to Europe and Asia but is also widely cultivated in North America.

larly. The silver iodide becomes a core (or nucleus) that gathers cloud droplets as ice. Finally the ice particles become heavy, fall, and melt into rain as they descend. This is also how natural rain or snow is formed.

So far, cloud seeding is unable to do more than give nature a boost. The conditions for seeding must be such that natural precipitation is about to occur. In fact, scientists who study cloud seeding have had to be careful in recording their results. They must make certain that they allow in their statistics for those situations in which rain would have fallen without cloud seeding. See PRECIPITATION; RAIN; RAINMAKING.

CLOVE, the dried flowerbud of a kind of myrtle tree, native to the Molucca Islands in the East Indies but now grown chiefly on the islands of Pemba and Zanzibar, off the east coast of Africa. The clove is a beautiful tree, 25 to 30 feet tall, shaped like a pyramid and covered with shiny evergreen leaves. The flowerbuds are picked before they begin to open and are dried in the shade. The little ball at the end of the clove is the flower folded up. Cloves are used as a spice in cooking. The oil of cloves is used in perfumery, in medicine, and for the relief of toothache and other pains. The word *clove* comes from the Latin *clavus* (nail). The spice is so called because it looks like a little nail.

CLOVER, a plant much used for pasture and hay and often used in lawns. It is a legume, belonging to the same family as the pea and bean. Like them it benefits the soil in which it grows because, through the bacteria that grow in little nodules on its roots, it is able to make use of the nitrogen in the air. Most plants cannot do this. The leaves of the clover plant are each made of three leaflets. The flowers are tiny and are borne in close heads, or clusters. There are many different kinds of clover. Most of the cultivated kinds are natives of Europe.

Red clover has fragrant flowers of a dull rose and pink. Bees visit the red clovers and fertilize them. Red clover is one of the principal legumes grown and dried for hay. Because of its high protein content it is particularly valuable as a winter feed for livestock. White clover is a low plant with a creeping stem, which roots at the joints and forms in this way a very dense sod. It is well suited for use in pastures because it withstands the tramping of animals and grows quickly after having been eaten closely.

CLOWN, a term loosely applied to any funny fellow, whether he is so by intention or by mistake. In traditional drama, however, a clown differs from the utter fool of real life and the straight vaudeville comedian in that he tends to act his part both as a player and as a real person. For this reason he is more complex than the other characters on the stage.

The evolution of such legendary stage types as Harlequin, Pierrot, Joey, and Auguste reveals the chief types of clown: the simpleton; the knave; the jester, or professional fool; and the universal spirit of mirth. As adapted by English drama especially, the dramatic function

Photos, Robert H. Bradley

The famous clown Emmett Kelly (above) appears as Weary Willy, a sad hobo. Traditionally the clown is a carefree fellow, such as the great English clown "Joey" Grimaldi (below) or the modern whiteface clown (right).

The Bettman Archive

of the clown was often comparable with that of the Greek chorus or the *raisonneur* (a serious personage who discussed the action or moral of the play) of early French drama.

In the popular mind, however, the clown is a circus figure, a buffoon with a red-and-white painted face. He wears the traditional clown suit, with ruffs at the neck, wrists, and ankles. His tricks are based on exaggerations of human weaknesses—greed, conceit, mental simplicity, and physical awkwardness. Some of the most popular modern clowns are wistful and pathetic figures. Humor is provoked by the clash of their tattered dignity with the facts of a harsh world.

Famous clowns have included Joseph Grimaldi (originator of Joey), Joe Jackson, Toto, Grock, the Arnauts, the Fratellinis, and Emmett Kelly.

CLUB MOSS, a plant that grows along the ground in the manner of a creeping shrub. Club mosses are not true mosses, even though some of them resemble mosses, but are closely related to the ferns. Some club mosses resemble miniature spruce or pine trees. Club mosses are so named because of club-shaped reproductive structures that grow upward from the tops of some of their branches.

Millions of years ago the ancestors of the club mosses, which were as big as our biggest trees, grew together in extensive forests that covered large areas of the earth. Much of our coal was formed millions of years ago from the ancestors of the club mosses and of the ferns.

Present-day club mosses are native to tropical and subtropical forests and to the dense, damp woodlands and mountain slopes of the temperate region of eastern North America.

Giant club moss, **1**, is shown $\frac{1}{300}$ actual size. Present-day club mosses—horsetail, **2**, and common club moss, **3**—are $\frac{1}{6}$ actual size.

COAL, a solid mineral of vegetable origin used for fuel and various by-products. Coal is one of the chief minerals of the earth and is composed mostly of carbon with some hydrogen, oxygen, and nitrogen. It is found in beds laid down in various geologic ages and generally ranges from brown to black in color. In a general way, coal may be defined as a fossil fuel of black color and stony consistency.

There are a number of varieties of coal, the four major divisions being anthracite (hard coal), bituminous (soft coal), subbituminous, and lignite. The term *anthracite* is applied to all coals that contain more than 86 percent of fixed carbon, the highest carbon content being about 98 percent. The other divisions are graded according to their fixed carbon content, volatile matter, and lack of ash and, in some cases, by the size of the lumps in which they are marketed.

The generally accepted theory of the origin of coal is that the rank and luxuriant vegetation that prevailed during the Carboniferous period grew and decayed upon land raised but slightly above the sea. By subsidence this thick layer of vegetable matter sank below the water and became gradually covered with sand, mud, and other mineral sediment. Then, by some light upheaval of the sea bottom or other process, a land surface was once more formed and was covered with a dense mass of plants. These plants in course of time decayed, sank, and became overlaid with silt and sand as before. At length thick masses of stratified matter accumulated and produced great pressure. This pressure, acting with chemical changes, gradually mineralized the vegetable layers into coal.

Reference to the use of coal by ancient civilizations is rather vague. Some reference was made to it during the time of the Greeks, but it is generally understood that the use of coal to any great extent began around the 13th century in London. In 1316 the English Parliament petitioned the king, Edward II, to prohibit the use of coal. A proclamation was issued, but owing to the high price of wood, its use soon became general in London. It was for a time known in England as sea coal because it was imported over the sea.

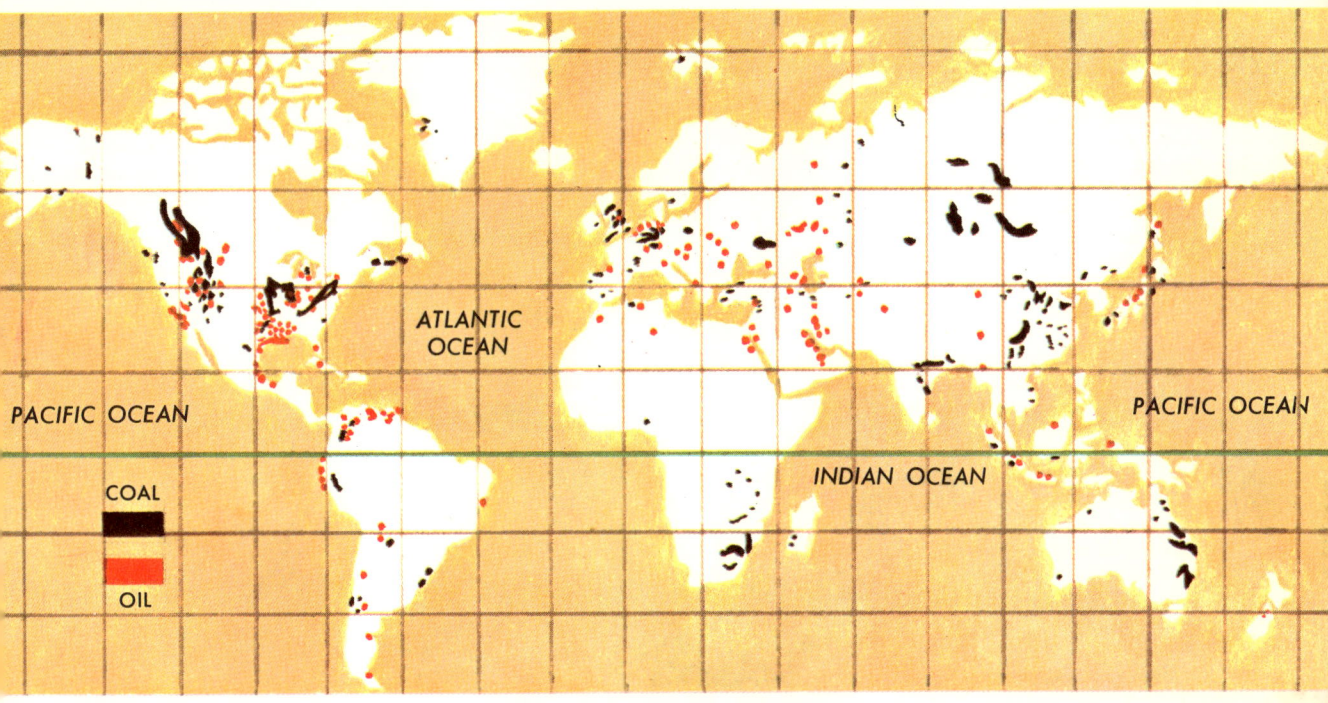

Major areas in production of coal and oil are charted above. Both of these important minerals come from remains of living things.

A gradual increase in its use occurred later, and many countries have found ample sources of coal through the centuries.

On the continent of Europe productive coalfields are found in Belgium, France, Poland, Czechoslovakia, and Germany. The British Isles have a great supply, the largest in Europe. The U.S.S.R. also has several fine coalfields. Other countries that have good fields are Colombia, Chile, Argentina, and Brazil in South America; China, India, and Indochina in Asia; parts of Africa; and Australia and New Zealand in the South Pacific. In North America lie the greatest coal reserves of the world, nearly 40 percent of the known reserves. In the United States the largest known reserves are found in the northern Great Plains area; however, these reserves have not been developed. The Appalachian region, extending from western Pennsylvania to northern Alabama, is the major producing area. Other producing areas include the midwestern states, the Gulf states, the Rocky Mountain area, and the Pacific coast. In Canada the coalfields extend across the provinces of Alberta, British Columbia, and New Brunswick and are also found in Nova Scotia. The estimated coal reserves of the world are about 2½ to 3 trillion tons, spread over all the continents. See COAL MINE.

COAL MINE, an open pit or a system of underground tunnels from which coal is dug. Coal is found beneath the earth's surface in beds, averaging about 5½ feet thick and often extending for hundreds of square miles. About three-fourths of American coal comes from underground mines. The rest comes from strip mines.

In underground mines coal is broken and removed from the face of the mine in several ways. Some mines undercut the coal with a chain-saw machine that cuts a narrow slot as deep as 9 feet. Above this slot horizontal holes are bored in the coal with auger drills; the holes are then charged with explosives, which are detonated. The broken coal is loaded into mine cars on rails or into rubber-tired shuttle cars by mechanical loading machine that handle about 6 tons a minute. Other mines use continuous mining machines that need no crew ahead of them to undercut, drill, and blast. They rip the coal out of the seam and load it into shuttle cars or onto extensible belt conveyors that advance with the continuous mining machine.

Some drift and slope mines use only conveyor belts, made of canvas and rubber, for transporting the coal to the preparation plant on the surface. Other mines use electric locomotives and mine cars on rails, and still others use both systems. In shaft mines the coal is hoisted to the surface by large buckets, called skips. Two skips operate simultaneously; one is being lowered while the other is being hoisted. Modern skip hoists are completely automatic. No operators are needed to load or unload the skips or to control the hoist motor.

As coal is removed and the mining area expands, pillars of coal are left to support the overburden. Sometimes the roof between the pillars also has to be supported by wooden posts or by long roof bolts that reinforce the thin beds of shale above the coal by tying them together. In areas where subsidence of the surface is permissible, the pillars of coal can also be mined, and the roof is allowed to cave.

The U.S. Bureau of Mines is experimenting with a process called underground gasification, which would do away with all machines by burning the coal at the face of the seam to produce commercially usable gas and immense quantities of heat.

In strip mines the coal is first laid bare by removing the overburden with gigantic electric power shovels, draglines, or wheel type excavators. The coal is then loaded into large trucks with smaller shovels. When the overburden becomes too high and it is no longer economical to remove it, many strip mines use great boring machines with augers up to 4 feet or more in diameter to recover additional coal under the high wall. Others use remote-control continuous mining machines that cut oval openings or tunnels 10 feet wide and 1,000 feet long. The coal is carried out by conveyor belts that follow the mining machine, which is operated by one man outside the tunnel.

Safety in a mine is a never-ending struggle. Safety inspectors with gas-detection lamps are constantly checking for accumulations of gas, which may be ignited by a spark into a killing explosion. Rock-dusting machines blow fine, noncombustible limestone onto the mine walls and roofs to inactivate the coal dust. In many mines underground springs can erupt into floods; and in some anthracite mines many tons of water have to be pumped to the surface for every ton of coal mined. Aboveground ventilating fans force 6 tons of air through the mines for every ton of coal removed. Despite all these precautions and the use of dust masks, silicosis and pneumonia kill some miners. However, during the past 40 years fatal accidents have been reduced by about 70 percent, and 90 percent of the bituminous coal mines in the United States do not have a single fatal accident in the course of a year.

COAL OIL. See KEROSENE.

COAL PRODUCTS, numbered in the tens of thousands, are chiefly derived from the carbonization of soft coal in coke ovens. (See COKE.) The other four primary coal products are coal tar, coal gas, ammonia liquor, and light oil. From 1 ton of coal processed in a byproduct coke oven are recovered about 1,410 pounds of coke, 19 pounds of coal tar, 280 pounds of coal gas, 20 pounds of ammonia liquor, and 17 pounds of light oil. The further refinement of each of these products constitutes a huge industry in itself.

In 1709, at Coalbrookdale, England, the coal-products industry began with the discovery of the advantages of using coke to make iron. During the American Revolutionary War, when the supply of pitch from the colonies fell off, British shipbuilders found an alternative supply in coal tar, a byproduct of the coke oven. A little later, the Scottish roadbuilder J. L. McAdam found an unlimited use for coal tar. And about the same time, the third main product, coal gas, began to be used in England for street and home lighting.

Americans, richly endowed with wood, petroleum, and natural gas, disregarded England's technological superiority in the utilization of coal and its byproducts. However, after the Civil War coke replaced charcoal in the smelting of iron and steel. As late as 1910 Pennsylvania and Ohio were dotted with wasteful beehive coke ovens, which polluted the air with their valuable volatile tars and gases. In 1907 a German scientist, Heinrich Koppers, persuaded American steel companies to build closed coke ovens to produce not only coke but thousands of other valuable products as well.

Among these products are coal tar for highways; creosote for preserving railroad ties and fenceposts; ammonia for refrigeration and fertilizers; nitric acid for explosives, plastics, lacquers, and camera films; pyridine for sulfa drugs, vitamins, and water repellents; and benzine for perfume and saccharin.

COAL-TAR PRODUCTS. Coal tar is the thick, black liquid exuded when coal is subjected to destructive distillation in coke ovens at temperatures between 700° F. and 1,900° F. and then condensed. The quality of the tar and the kinds of products obtained from it depend upon the nature of the coal and the intensity of the heat used in the airtight coke ovens. Coal tar is the principal byproduct of the coke, coal gas, and ammonia industries. Although pure coal tar is composed of only carbon, hydrogen, nitrogen, and oxygen, thousands of products for the construction industries, iron and steel mills, farms, hospitals, and homes are refined and synthesized from coal tar.

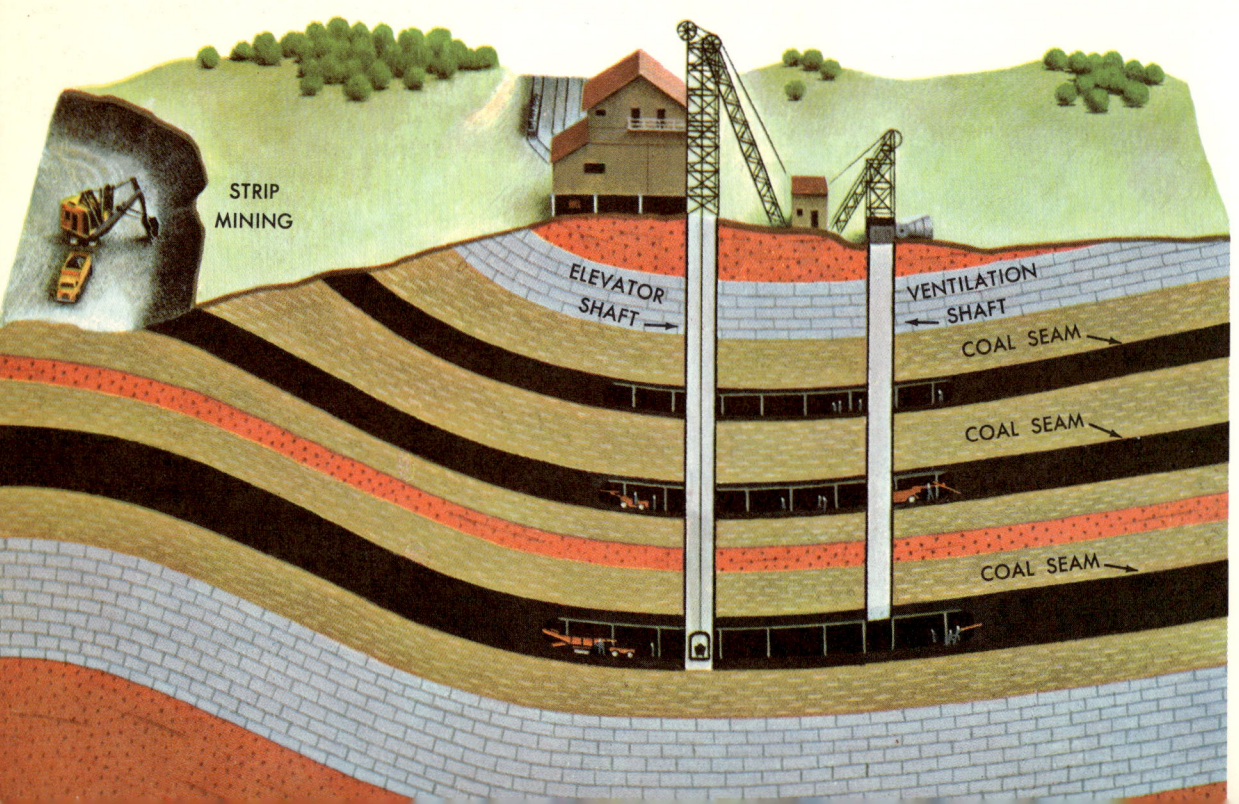

A longitudinal diagram of a coal mine shows how vertical shafts are driven down to coal seams, which are then mined by tunneling. Coal is removed through the elevator shaft; the other shaft is for ventilation only. Note the strip mining of a seam at the surface.

Coal tar was first produced in England during the middle of the 18th century when the shortage of charcoal forced iron manufacturers to use coke. The coal tar produced by the beehive ovens was a waste product until the shortage of pine pitch during the American Revolution forced English shipbuilders to use coal tar for caulking and preserving seams and timbers. Creosote made from coal tar is still used for preserving fenceposts and railroad ties.

The second great use of coal-tar products was for the binding of crushed-stone roads made by the Scotch engineer John Loudon McAdam in the early 19th century. In the United States, as the iron and steel industry converted from charcoal to coke, coal tar was utilized as a cheap fuel. As it rose from the top of the coke ovens, it was condensed and piped back to the furnaces and the coke ovens.

The great development of coal-tar products did not get under way until about 1880, when German chemists, building on British discoveries, developed the first stable coal-tar dyes. Twenty years later the coal-tar dye industry began in the United States but as late as 1916 was so small that the United States had to undertake a crash program when World War I cut off dye imports from Germany.

Of minor importance in terms of tonnage of coal tar consumed but of enormous importance to individuals are the coal-tar perfumes and the coal-tar drugs. From 25 tons of violets only one ounce of natural oil can be extracted, and 3,200 ounces of roses must be pressed to make an ounce of the pure rose oil used in perfume. Natural-lilac and lily-of-the-valley fragrances are unobtainable from the flowers because the oils break down in processing. All of these are now made from coal tar, and in addition we enjoy other perfumes not even found in nature.

In medicine, the coal-tar products include aspirin, saccharin, and sulfa drugs, many of which have been rendered obsolete by even more powerful coal-tar derivatives. Germs that have been difficult to identify under a microscope are now easily detected by the use of coal-tar medical dyes.

On the farm, DDT for fly control, 2,4-D for weed control, creosote for termite control, and tar paper are now everyday coal-tar products.

For the automobile, coal tar can be a great source of gasoline, and has already added tens of thousands of miles to the life of tires.

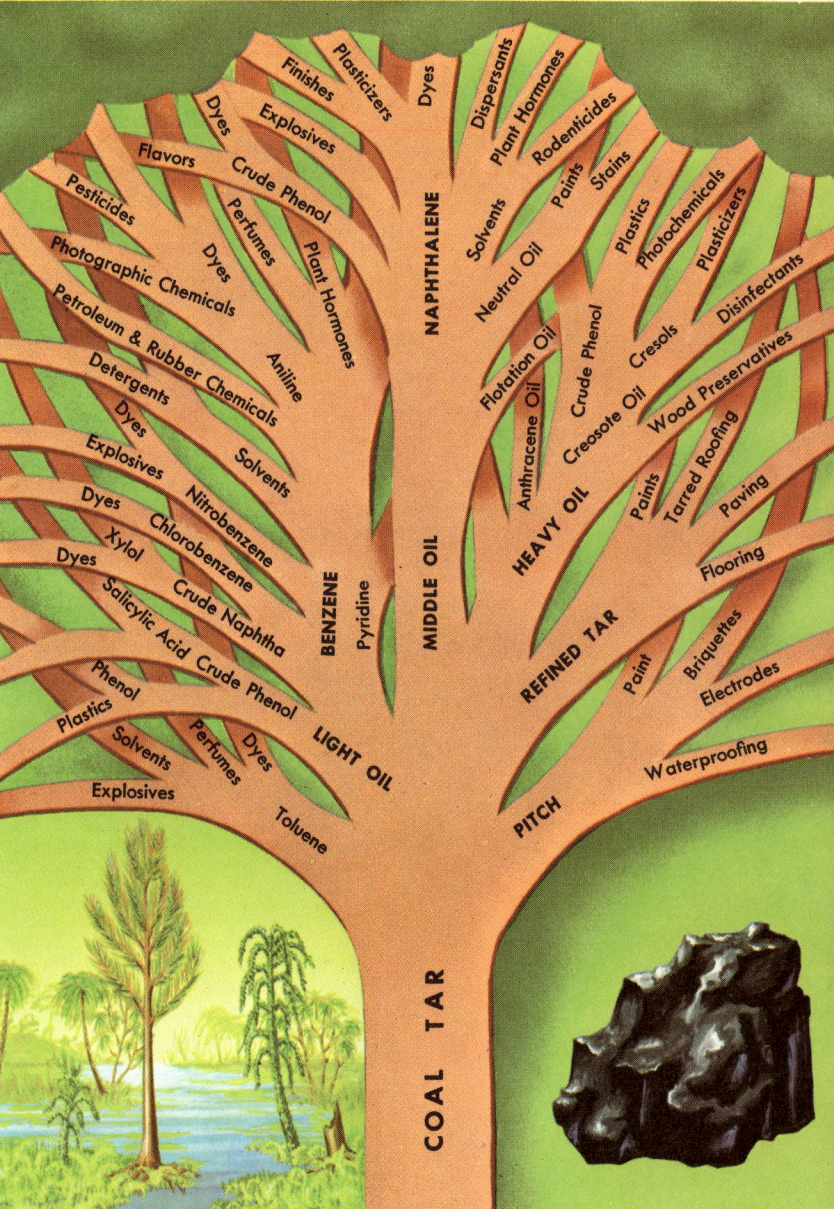

Adapted from Du Pont

Coal tar—a thick, black, and evil-smelling liquid—yields more than 200 different substances through distillation. The "tree" above shows how some of the substances are used.

COAST RANGES, in western North America, a mountain belt stretching south along the Pacific coast from Alaska, through British Columbia, Washington, Oregon, and California and into Lower California in Mexico. The ranges do not always lie in a continuous ridge.

In the United States the Coast Ranges include the Diablo Range, the Santa Lucia Range, the San Rafael Mountains, and Mt. Pinos, all in California; the Klamath Mountains, situated on the Oregon-California border; and the Olympic Mountains in northwestern Washington. The highest peak in the Olympics is Mt. Olympus, which rises to 7,954 feet and has seven glaciers. It is the center of Olympic National Park, where a famous rain forest is located.

There is abundant rainfall in the Coast Range area beginning north of San Francisco and extending to the southern part of Alaska. Within this region there are valuable coniferous forests. The Coast Range lands south of San Francisco are notably dry except for the higher

COAT OF ARMS

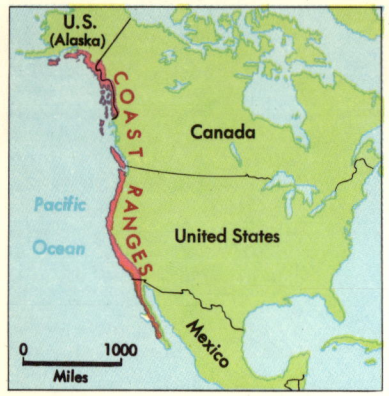

altitudes, where forests are supported. Many valleys of the ranges, however, include valuable farmland. Waterpower has been developed in the streams between southern British Columbia and northern California.

The southern portions of the Coast Ranges consist largely of recently folded, sedimentary rocks, which are still subject to extensive faulting. Most California earthquakes are caused by such faulting.

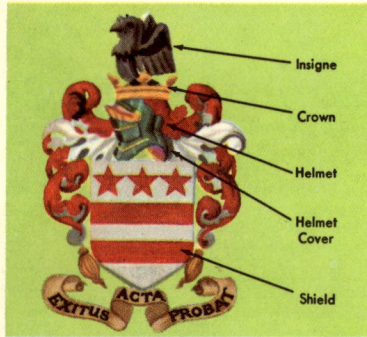

George Washington's coat of arms is shown above, with the basic parts identified.

COAT OF ARMS was a practical device by which the wearer of armor in the Middle Ages was recognized as being of the noble class. Knights or warriors of that time were often covered from head to toe in metal suits when they went to war or jousted in tournaments.

The colorful pattern on his shield, overcoat, or crest of his helmet (mantling) identified the hidden knight. Each knight chose a pattern unlike that worn by any other knight. This pattern remained unchanged and was transmitted in a family from father to sons. Later, students of history used these coats of arms to trace the fortunes of important families. This study was called heraldry, or the science of describing coats of arms.

As time went on, knights engraved their coats of arms on all kinds of objects belonging to them, even on furniture. They displayed coats of arms over the gates of castles and on their seals, which were attached to letters, messages, and documents.

Methods of warfare changed after the 15th century, and metal suits and shields were discarded. But seals bearing coats of arms continued to appear in correspondence, and shields were kept for ornamental purposes.

Newly created nobles received coats of arms from princes and kings as a reward for their services to the royal family or to the country. These new coats of arms, unlike those in the Middle Ages, were embellished by crowns, animals, and plants. In modern times, states have used coats of arms on their seals, and these have become a mark of high office. The president of the United States uses a seal with coat of arms.

COBALT, a silvery-white metallic element used in alloys, as a radioisotope, and as a pigment. Its chemical symbol is Co. The principal sources of cobalt are the Congo Republic and Ontario in Canada.

Cobalt alloys include stellite, carboloy, and alnico. Stellite, a cobalt-chromium alloy, is used for metal-cutting tools. Carboloy, a hard, tough alloy of cobalt and carbide of tungsten, is used for cutting steel, glass, and porcelain. Alnico, composed of aluminum, cobalt, iron, and nickel, is a strong magnet and constitutes the permanent magnet in such devices as loudspeakers and telephones.

The radiation from radioactive cobalt is used for medical treatment of deep-seated tumors. It is used by industry for the detection of internal flaws in metal parts. Cobalt compounds are used as pigments for paint, ceramics, and glass.

COBB, TY (1886–1961), in full, Tyrus Raymond Cobb, known as the "Georgia Peach," American baseball player, was born in Narrows, Ga. At the age of 17 Cobb decided to become a baseball player. Rejecting his father's suggestions that he become a doctor or lawyer, Cobb wrote to every baseball club in the South Atlantic League. He got a reply from the Augusta, Ga., club and was hired as a center fielder. When he missed a flyball and lost the game for his team, the manager sold him to another club for $2.00. But that club's owner canceled the sale, and Cobb rejoined the Augusta club. From 1905 to 1926 he played with the Detroit Tigers and served as manager from 1921 to 1926. For several years, he played with the Philadelphia team in the American League.

Before his retirement at the age of 42, he held the league records in batting and base stealing. He stole 892 bases, made 4,191 hits, scored 2,244 runs, and amassed a batting average of .367. For 12 seasons he paced the league in batting, 9 of them in a row. He batted .400 or over three times. He is in the Baseball Hall of Fame.

Cobalt may be obtained from a variety of ores. Among the major ores are the two above—cobaltite (left) and skutterudite.

This diagram of a cobalt atom shows how the 27 electrons (−) are arranged around a nucleus of 27 protons (+) and 32 neutrons. Cobalt has atomic number 27; the atomic weight of the most abundant isotope is 59.

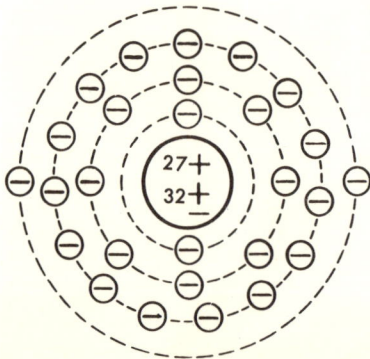

COBRA, an extremely poisonous snake of which there are several species. Cobras are found in Africa and southern Asia. All of these snakes are able to distend the neck to form a hood when aroused. The best known species of cobra is the common cobra of India.

The Indian cobra is 4 to 6 feet long. It is nocturnal in its habits and often enters houses in search of prey. It eats toads, frogs, birds, small animals, and other snakes. When attacked, it boldly raises the

COCKROACH

Cockfighting is a popular sport in the Philippine Islands. In every village there is a building where the fights are held. Betting among the spectators is very keen. *Standard Oil Co. (N.J.)*

front part of its body from the ground. With bent body, dilated neck, and threatening head, it presents a formidable appearance. Its bite is generally fatal to man, often within a few moments. It rarely bites unless it is stepped on, but cobras are so abundant in India that every year thousands of people are killed by them.

The Indian jugglers apparently handle cobras without harm to themselves and make frequent use of cobras in their performances. They pretend to employ powerful medicines that make them safe from the serpent's bite, but the truth is that the cobra's poison fangs are extracted. These cobras execute certain movements resembling a rude dance while keeping time to the movements of the musician.

A cobra spreads its hood (left) for a Pakistani snake charmer. The cobra below was photographed in Bangkok, the capital of Thailand.

COCKFIGHTING, a sport in which two or more cocks (roosters) fight each other in a cockpit or ring. It is a very old sport, but it is now illegal everywhere except in Spain, the Far East, and some Latin American countries.

Cockfighting probably began in India, Persia, or China and spread from there to ancient Greece and Rome. It is said that the Romans took the sport to England. Several English kings were very fond of it, especially Henry II, Henry VIII, and the Stuart kings. It was also popular in some of the American colonies. The breeding and training of gamecocks was an important industry in the 17th and the 18th century.

The commonest kind of cockfighting is the single battle, with two cocks who fight until one is killed or stops fighting. Sometimes the natural spurs of the animals are cut off, and steel or silver ones are fastened on. Cockfighting in the United States has been illegal for many years.

Cockroaches belong to the most ancient group of insects now in existence. The American species (above) is about 1 3/8 inches long.

COCKROACH, an insect that has successfully adapted itself to human habitations, where it eats available human food. The cockroach belongs to the order of straight-winged insects, or Orthoptera. Other members of this order are the grasshoppers and the crickets. Although the male cockroach has wings, it can fly only for short distances. The female is almost wingless. The cockroach has long, slender legs and a flat body, which enable it to squirm through the tiniest cracks and hide in the smallest crevices.

Cockroaches infest houses, stores, warehouses, wharves, and ships. Although they originated in the Orient, they are now found in almost every region of the world, especially in seaports. Cockroaches issue from their crevices at night in search of food. They will eat small amounts of bread, cake, meat, vegetables, and almost any other types of accessible food. They are not primarily objectionable because of the small amount of food that they eat but because of the disagreeable odor they impart to the food they touch and because of their carrying of diseases. When a light is turned on at night and cockroaches are caught in their stealthy scavenging, they will immediately scurry for safety to their crevices. The cockroach most likely to infest houses in North America is the yellowish-brown German species, which came originally from Europe. Other species that may be encountered in North America and elsewhere in the world are the Oriental, the American, and the Australian.

COCOA. See CHOCOLATE AND COCOA.

A workman is cutting pods from a cocoa tree on a plantation in New Guinea. The cocoa beans are the seeds lying within the pods.

These three cocoa pods were grown on different species of the cocoa tree.

COCOA TREE, the tree from whose seeds cocoa and chocolate are made. The tree is 20 to 25 feet high, is a native of tropical America, and is much cultivated in the tropics of both hemispheres, especially in the West Indies and Central and South America. It is also called the cacao.

The seeds, or cacao beans, are contained in pointed, oval pods, which are from 6 to 10 inches long. Each pod contains about 50 beans embedded in a white, sweet-tasting, jelly-like pulp. A typical cocoa tree bears between 20 and 40 pods each year. The pods are attached directly to the trunk and branches of the tree. The cacao beans, which are nutritious and contain much fat, have an agreeable flavor and can be eaten raw. They must be fermented, roasted, and pulverized before they can be made into cocoa or chocolate.

COCONUT, the fruit of the coco palm, found chiefly on the islands of the Pacific and Indian oceans. The coco palm grows 60 to 100 feet high. It has no branches, but at the top is a crown of 15 to 20 huge, feather-like leaves, each 12 to 20 feet in length, under which the big, round nuts hang in bunches. The shell of the nut is very hard when ripe and is lined on the inside with a layer an inch or so thick of white coconut meat—the kernel. In the cavity is a cupful or so of a sweet liquid called coconut milk. The nuts are gathered or, far more often, are allowed to fall to the ground as they ripen.

The meat of the coconut is a very important article of commerce. From most of the coconuts the meat is removed from the shell on the plantations and is dried in the sun or in kilns. In this form it is exported under the name of copra. Copra is the source of coconut oil and is shredded to make the form of coconut used in cakes, cookies, pies, and candies. The coco palm is one of the most valuable trees in the world, nearly every part of it being useful to man. Natives make cups and bowls from coconut shell. They make house rafters, canoes, and fenceposts from the trunk of the tree. Young leaves are cooked and eaten as a vegetable; old leaves are made into cloth, hats, and baskets. The leaf ribs are used for boat paddles, spears, and torches.

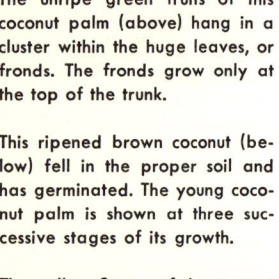

The unripe green fruits of this coconut palm (above) hang in a cluster within the huge leaves, or fronds. The fronds grow only at the top of the trunk.

This ripened brown coconut (below) fell in the proper soil and has germinated. The young coconut palm is shown at three successive stages of its growth.

The yellow flower of the coconut palm, a green coconut at three stages of growth, and a longitudinal section of a ripened brown coconut are shown at the right.

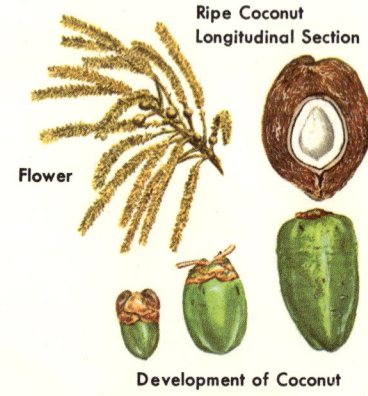

COCOON. A fuzzy caterpillar, upon being hatched from its egg, is called a larva. After some weeks or months of life, a larva will partially or completely enclose itself in a small sac, called a cocoon. The larva spins this cocoon of fine, silken threads from within its body. The larva usually fastens its cocoon to a tree limb or other object.

While appearing to lie dormant within its cocoon, the insect is busily changing itself into a moth. While in the cocoon it is called a pupa. The cocoon keeps the helpless pupa warm and dry and protects it from harm. Butterflies, bees, and other insects also begin life as wormlike larvae but do not spin cocoons for themselves before passing into the pupal stage.

Some cocoons, like that of the silkworm moth, are beautiful to behold and are spun from fine, delicate, strong threads. Silk is made from the cocoon of the silkworm moth. Man has never been able to produce artificially any fabric of as fine a quality as that produced from the silkworm's cocoon.

Robert H. Bradley

Polyphemus Moth

Cecropia Moth

Isabella Moth

Promethea Moth

Luna Moth

The worker is examining the silkworm cocoons that are being cultivated for their silk in straw mats called nests. The cocoons of various moths are also shown above.

COD, one of the most important food fishes. It is found in the North Atlantic, the North Pacific, and the Baltic Sea. The chief American cod fisheries are on the Grand Bank and other banks off the coast of Newfoundland, where for hundreds of years English, French, and American vessels have gone to engage in the fishing.

The cod is a deepwater fish, living at depths of 10 to 70 and more fathoms. It moves in small schools, going into deeper water in hot weather and coming nearer the coast in the winter to spawn.

A single mother cod produces 5,000 to 2,000,000 tiny eggs, which float upon the surface of the sea. Only part of these develop into sizable fish, for great numbers of them do not hatch or are destroyed, and many of the young are eaten by larger fish.

From the days of earliest settlement, the cod fisheries have been of great importance to New England. Cod was its first colonial export, and the drying and salting of the fish has always been a valuable industry. Cod can be eaten fresh, salted and preserved, canned, or frozen. Cod-liver oil is an important product of codfish.

CODE, a means of communicating (often secretly) with someone through the use of symbols rather than language.

In 1942 a powerful Japanese fleet headed toward Midway in the Pacific Ocean to take it by surprise. Little did the Japanese realize that the United States Navy had concentrated near Midway ships from as far away as 3,000 miles. The Japanese fell into the ambush and suffered the worst naval defeat in their history. The tide of World War II had turned. The valor of the men in the ships and planes had won the battle. But there was one other hero, who remained unknown until well after the war. His name was Magic. The Japanese knew nothing at all about Magic. Magic was a small machine, constructed by the United States long before the fatal attack on Pearl Harbor, Hawaii. It was built by cryptographers (experts in codes) to duplicate the decoding device hidden by the Japanese in Tokyo. Experts had been studying Japanese codes and had decoded, or "broken," an important one. After once learning the code, the experts could build their own machine and decode those messages as easily as the Japanese could.

Codes have been used in warfare and diplomacy since the beginning of written history. The Spartans used a very clever code to carry orders to their army commanders. Julius Caesar used a code. But Caesar was no cryptographer, and

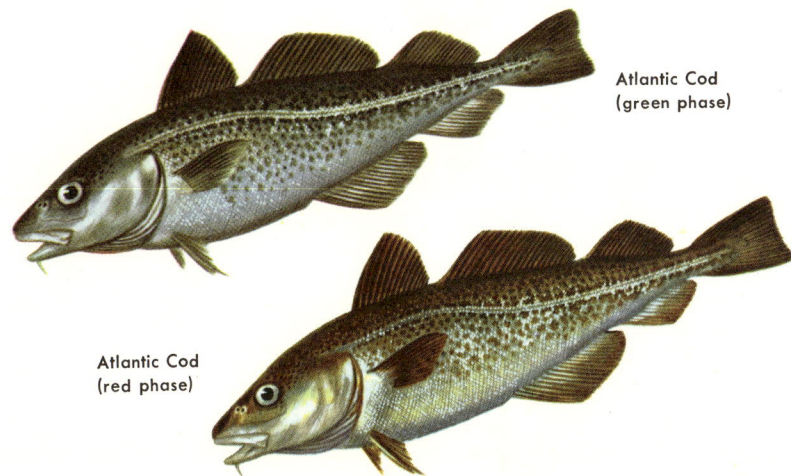

The color of the Atlantic cod varies from gray green to red brown. Its maximum length is 6 feet. About 75 million pounds of this cod are caught annually.

Atlantic Cod (green phase)

Atlantic Cod (red phase)

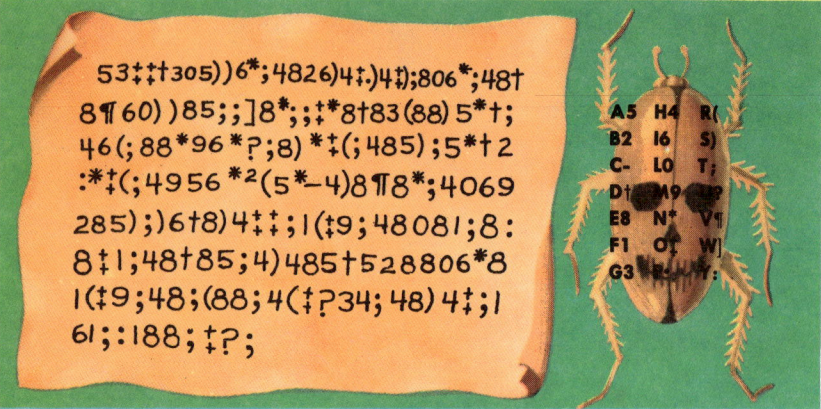

In Edgar Allan Poe's mystery story "The Gold Bug" these strange numbers and symbols were used to record in a secret code the mysterious and perplexing directions for finding the buried treasure. The code can be deciphered by studying the key.

his code could have been broken with ease by a decipherer. Charlemagne used a much cleverer code. During the Renaissance codes were very popular. Many people had complicated private codes. In fact, a letter written by Charles I of England consisted entirely of numbers. No one (except the recipient, of course) was able to decipher the letter until 1858.

Codes are so varied and intricate that it would take many books to describe all of them. But almost every code can be broken by a clever cryptoanalyst. When the great mathematician François Viete broke the Spanish code in the 16th century, it appeared so uncanny to some people that they accused him of being in league with the devil. The Pope, amused at the dilemma of the Spaniards, did not press charges against Viete, however. He know that cryptography, despite its dramatic results was not magic.

Francis Bacon was a good cryptographer. He said that a good code must be easy to read and to write but very difficult to decipher. Also it must not attract suspicion.

The idea of codes has been adapted to a great many useful purposes. See BRAILLE; DEAF SPEECH; HAND SIGNAL; LANGUAGE; MORSE CODE; SEMAPHORE; SHORTHAND; SIGN LANGUAGE.

COD-LIVER OIL. When a baby is about two weeks old, the doctor will probably want to give him an important protective food. It is often spoken of as cod-liver oil, though other fish-liver oils are often used. Pure cod-liver oil is given babies less now than formerly, as concentrated preparations of vitamin D are simpler to give and usually cost less.

Liver oils of certain fish supply vitamin D. Summer sunlight makes vitamin D in a person's skin. Since it is not possible in most places for babies to get enough sunlight, they must be given a substitute for it.

When a baby takes vitamin D, it helps his body to make use of the calcium he is getting in his milk. Without the vitamin D this calcium, necessary to build strong bones and teeth, might not be absorbed. Without enough calcium the bones fail to grow normally, and the disease called rickets results. A person keeps right on needing this special protection as long as he is growing. The doctor will tell which form of vitamin D to use and when to start giving it. It is important to give no more of a concentrated form of vitamin D than the doctor advises.

CODONAS. See FLYING CODONAS.

CODY, WILLIAM FREDERICK (1846-1917), nicknamed "Buffalo Bill," a famous American scout and showman, was born in Scott Co., Iowa. At 15 he became one of the first riders of the pony express. When the Civil War broke out, he was a government scout and guide. In 1863 he joined the 7th Kansas Cavalry.

After the war he supplied buffalo meat to the builders of the Kansas Pacific Railway, thus getting the name of Buffalo Bill. From 1868 to 1872 he was again a government scout and in the latter year entered the Nebraska legislature. In the Sioux War of 1876 he served with the 5th Cavalry and killed Chief Yellow Hand.

In 1883 he organized Buffalo Bill's Wild West Show and toured the United States with it, going to Europe in 1887 and creating a sensation there. He kept on touring the world with his show for many years. Everywhere he was a great favorite with the public, particularly with children.

COELACANTH, a present-day primitive fish that is anatomically similar to the fossil fish from which the amphibians are thought to have evolved more than 250 million years ago.

Prior to 1938 no living coelacanth had been discovered, and paleontologists had concluded that the coelacanths had become extinct long ago. However, in 1938 a living coelacanth was found in the Indian Ocean, near the southern extremity of Africa. The coelacanth was different from most present-day fish but was anatomically similar to coelacanths that had lived between 100 million and 300 million years ago. Both the fossil and present-day coelacanth have fringed fins, cartilaginous skeletons, and other anatomical characteristics not possessed by most other present-day fish. The coelacanths have undergone little evolutionary change during the 300 million years in which they have inhabited the oceans. Both fossil and present-day coelacanthine species belong to the large primitive group of fish called Crossopterygii, most other species of which also lived hundreds of millions of years ago and are now extinct.

Since certain fossil crossopterygians are anatomically similar to the oldest fossil amphibians, zoologists think that the amphibians evolved from these crossopterygians between 250 million and 300 million years ago.

The coelacanth, which is much older than any other known living fish, has taught biologists much about the anatomy of the primitive fish that lived millions of years ago.

FEEDING POLYP OF OBELIA
(Internal Structure)

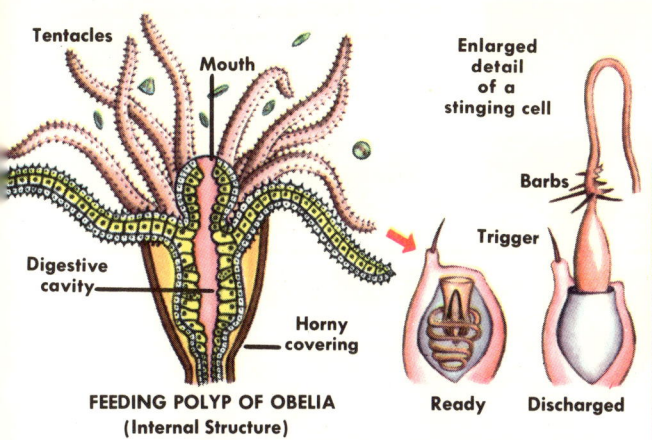

A diagrammatic longitudinal section of a food-ingesting polyp of Obelia, a colonial coelenterate, is shown above. Obelia consists of food-ingesting polyps and reproductive polyps.

Representatives of the three coelenterate classes—Anthozoa, Hydrozoa, and Scyphozoa—are shown below. The Anthozoa, which include sea anemones and many types of corals, are sessile and have flowerlike forms. The Hydrozoa include the solitary sessile hydra, the colonial sessile Obelia, and the colonial motile Portugese man-of-war. The Scyphozoa include many jellyfishes, most of which are motile.

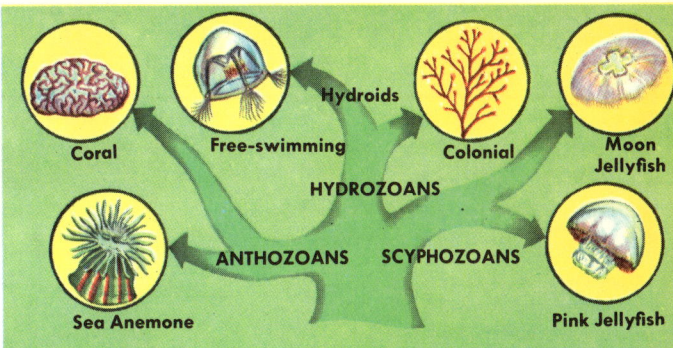

COELENTERATE, a primitive, multicellular, aquatic invertebrate that is considered to represent an early stage in the evolution of the more complex multicellular animals. The coelenterates constitute the phylum Coelenterata, which occupies a low position in the evolutionary scale.

The coelenterates, all of which appear more like plants than animals, include corals, polyps, hydras, jellyfish, sea anemones, and the Portuguese-man-of-war. Corals and sea anemones are sessile, that is, they remain permanently attached to a submerged rock or to the ocean bottom. Jellyfish swim freely under water. Hydras are both sessile and motile. The Portuguese man-of-war is actually a motile colony of four specialized types of individual polyps. One type is specialized to form the float that buoys up the colony. The second type is specialized for ingesting food. The third type is specialized for fighting by means of stingers called nematocysts. The fourth type is specialized for reproduction. Corals, which live together in vast sessile colonies, have hard, brittle, limy skeletons that collectively constitute coral reefs.

Biologists rank the phylum Coelenterata just above the phylum Porifera, or the sponges, in the evolutionary scale. The coelenterates are the lowest animals to manifest extensive cell specialization and the differentiation of cells into distinct tissues. A typical coelenterate, such as a hydra, has two layers of tissue: an external epidermis and an internal gastrodermis. Ectodermal cells are variously specialized for bodily movement, for touch, and for the lethal stinging of tiny prey. The stinging cells, or nematocysts, enable coelenterates to obtain food and to defend themselves against enemies. The nematocysts of a Portuguese man-of-war can pierce a man's skin and paralyze him. The endoderm encloses the gastrovascular cavity, into which food and water enter through a terminal mouth. The functions of the gastrovascular cavity are to digest food and to distribute it to all of the endodermal cells. Endodermal cells are variously specialized for digestion, for secretion of digestive enzymes, and for touch.

Coelenterates exist in two distinct body forms. The polyp form has a body stalk; the jellyfish, or medusa, form does not have a body stalk. The ectodermal sensory cells are connected with a complex network of specialized cells that transmit sensations to all bodily parts and that coordinate bodily responses. This cellular network is the forerunner of the nervous system possessed by higher phyla.

The coelenterates are ranked lower in the evolutionary scale than most other multicellular phyla because their tissues are not organized into organs and organ systems. For example, coelenterates do not have special digestive organs; digestion is accomplished by specialized endodermal cells that surround the gastrovascular cavity.

However, coelenterates are thought to represent an early stage in the evolution of the higher multicellular phyla because of their extensive cell specialization; their differentiation of cells into distinct tissues; their central, enclosed digestive cavity; and their coordinating nerve cells.

COEUR, JACQUES (about 1395-1456), a French merchant-banker who was one of the richest men of his age. He was born of a modest merchant family in Bourges. Around 1427 he began his rise to wealth and power with a voyage to the Mediterranean and the Near East, where he established trade relations with Christians, Jews, and Moslems. His financial ability soon earned him great profits. He dealt in every kind of merchandise, supplied customers of many lands, and through his agents in them kept well informed about business conditions. He operated from strategically placed warehouses and built a private fleet, the galleys of which plied the waters of the Mediterranean and the English Channel.

In 1440 Coeur became paymaster, or financial minister, to Charles VII of France. Later Coeur served as a member of the royal council and master of the royal mint. In return for lending increasingly large sums to the King and the nobility he received mines and a title of nobility and was given important diplomatic missions. During the last years of the Hundred Years' War his contributions greatly helped the French expel the armies of England from France.

Coeur's wealth, however, earned him many enemies, and many of his debtors, including the king, defaulted in their payments. He was eventually accused of poisoning the king's favorite, Agnès Sorel. He was tortured and banished from France, and his property was confiscated. He sought refuge at the papal court and died shortly after on the island of Chios while on an expedition against the Turks.

Courtesy of the Pan American Coffee Bureau

About its fifth year the coffee shrub produces what the farmer considers his first crop. The field at left is located in Brazil.

The coffee berries are picked when they turn cherry red (below). The berry consists of two coffee beans surrounded by a pulp.

Courtesy of the Pan American Coffee Bureau

Colombian workers (below) spread coffee beans in the sun to dry. In the wet method of processing, berries are fermented and then depulped by machine. They are dried about two weeks.

Annan Photo Features

Most of the world's coffee is obtained from the Arabian coffee shrub, an evergreen plant with shiny, oblong leaves. The fragrant, pure-white flowers last for only a short time; they are followed by the berries, which turn dark red as they ripen. Each berry contains two seeds, or beans.

Standard Oil Co. (N.J.)

The roasting process (above) develops the flavor-producing agents in the coffee bean.

COFFEE is prepared from roasted seeds of a small tree native to eastern Africa. It is cultivated on large plantations in Brazil and other parts of South America, in Central America, in Africa, and on the Arabian Peninsula. The tree is usually kept trimmed so that it is not over 5 to 10 feet high. The dark-red fruit looks something like short-stemmed cherries. As a rule, each fruit contains two hard, bluish-green seeds—the coffee beans, or berries. In preparing the coffee for market, it is necessary to pick the fruit when fully ripe, remove the pulp, dry the beans, remove the parchment, and clean away the chaff. The coffee is then ready for export. However, before it is used, it has to be roasted and ground. Roasting changes it to a dark-brown color.

Coffee is said to have been used in Persia over 500 years ago, but it was not known in Europe until about 300 years ago. The first coffeehouse in London was opened in 1652. It was about 75 years later that coffee plants were first brought to the Western Hemisphere. Brazil is now the world's leading coffee producer, while the United States leads the world in coffee consumption.

COHAN, GEORGE M. (1878-1942), American actor and dramatist, was born in Providence, R. I. He first appeared on the stage when he was nine years old. He was in vaudeville with his family for many years in a song-and-dance act billed as "The Four Cohans."

He wrote many plays, most of which he also acted in and produced. Among them were *Get-Rich-Quick Wallingford* and *The Song-and-Dance Man*. He also starred in Eugene O'Neill's *Ah, Wilderness*. He was especially noted for his patriotic and sentimental songs, such as "Over There," "You're a Grand Old Flag," "I'm a Yankee Doodle Dandy," "Give My Regards to Broadway," and "Mary Is a Grand Old Name." In 1941 he was awarded a Congressional medal for his patriotic songs. His autobiography is entitled *Twenty Years on Broadway and the Years It Took To Get There*.

COHESION AND ADHESION are forces of attraction between molecules or neutral atoms. Cohesion is the ability of molecules or atoms to attract and cling to like molecules or atoms. Adhesion is the ability of molecules or atoms to cling to unlike molecules or atoms.

COIN COLLECTING

When a small quantity of water is spilled on a level, nonabsorbent surface, the water does not spread evenly over the surface—rather, it gathers in drops or small puddles. The water gathers in drops and puddles because of cohesion between water molecules. If a piece of glass is dipped in water, certain of the molecules cling to the surface of the glass after it is removed from the water. The water molecules cling to the glass because of adhesion between glass and water molecules. Gums, glue, and cement also cling to surfaces because of adhesion.

Cohesion causes waterdrop, **1A**, to form on paraffin; detergent makes drop wet paraffin, **1B**. Weight opposes cohesion, so larger mercury drops are less nearly spherical, **2**.

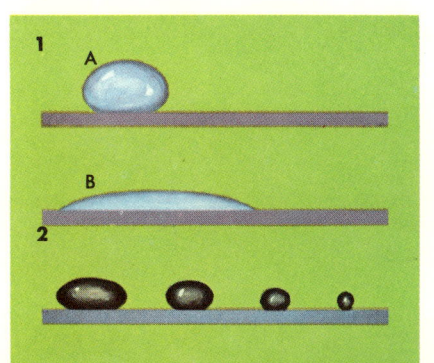

Adhesion is attraction between unlike molecules. Whether a liquid will adhere to, or wet, a solid is indicated by whether its surface curves upward or downward where it touches the solid. Thus mercury does not wet glass. Water wets glass but not paraffin.

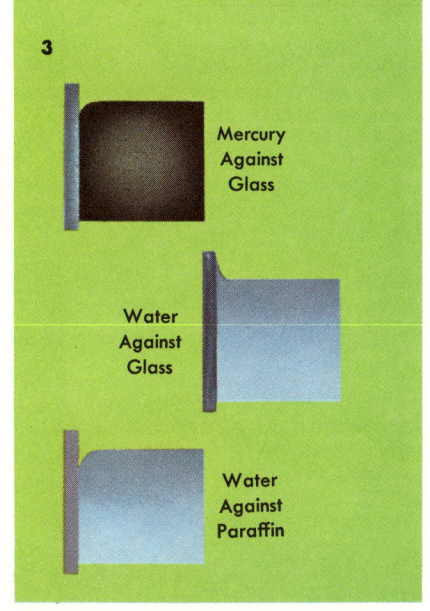

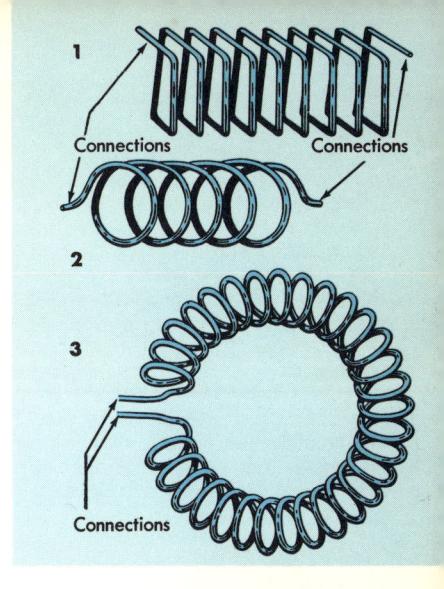

Electrical coils are wound in several different forms, including **1**, square coil; **2**, helical coil; and **3**, toroid coil.

COIL, in electricity, is made up of successive turns of insulated wire. There are usually a large number of turns, and they are wound closely together. The coil may or may not be wound around an iron core. A coil creates a magnetic field when an electrical current passes through it. When the coil is wound around an iron core, the iron becomes an electromagnet. (See ELECTROMAGNET.) Coils are widely used in electrical devices. The shape of the coil is less important than the number of turns and the amount of iron in the core; the inductance increases when either of these is increased. Coils may be used in several different ways. They may be electromagnets, or in relays, or in solenoids. They may be made parts of oscillating circuits, or they may be transformer windings. Two coils wound on the same iron core can be used to step up or step down the voltage of an alternating electric current; this is a transformer. See INDUCTANCE; TRANSFORMER.

COIN COLLECTING, a hobby that is popular all over the world. Coins from even the earliest times are so numerous that a beginner can easily form a good collection without great expense. Coin collecting creates an interest in history. Collectors usually find that they are more attracted to one period than to another and begin to specialize in the coins and history of their favorite period or sometimes of their favorite country. The best way to start a collection is to get in touch with experienced collectors and learn from them which dealers they have found to be reliable. The dealers will be glad to help the beginner by encouraging him to select coins suitable to his amount of spending money. The young collector should get in touch with other collectors who have just begun the hobby. Often they are able to trade duplicates. When a coin is bought, the collector should try to learn all he can about it. He should make use of the help of an older collector, a library, or a museum. Each coin may be kept in a small envelope with a description of the coin on the outside. The envelopes may be arranged in boxes or drawers. A catalogue of the collection should be made.

These numismatists, or coin collectors, are filling in two kinds of coin boards, one filled in by dates on the coins and the other by type of coin. The coin catalogues tell the value of the coins. The envelope file (left) represents another way to store collections.

COINED WORD, a word that somebody invents for a special purpose. Usually a coined word means a word of this type that has become part of the general vocabulary. An example of a coined word is the word *chortle*, first used by Lewis Carroll in the poem "Jabberwocky" in *Through the Looking-Glass*. It means "a combination of a chuckle and a snort."

Another example is the word *radar*, coined during World War II. It comes from the U.S. Army and is derived from "*radio detecting and ranging*." See BLENDS.

COKE, the residue of coal that has been subjected to destructive distillation in a closed retort or oven. Coke is a dark-gray, lumpy material, quite light for its bulk. It has a peculiar clinging quality that makes it difficult to shovel except from a hard surface, such as a cement floor. Coke produces a quick, hot, smokeless fire that burns down to a clean ash.

Coke used to be made in beehive ovens, which are great brick domes set over furnaces. All of the valuable byproducts were wasted either by burning them at the top of the oven or by letting them off to pollute the air. Since about 1920 coke has been cooked in byproduct ovens. Among these byproducts are ammonia for cleaning, refrigeration, and fertilizer; coal gas for heating and cooking; tar products for drugs, dyes, and explosives; and asphalt for roadmaking.

About four-fifths of the coke produced in the United States is used in the reduction and processing of iron, tin, copper, and zinc ores. Less than one-tenth is used for domestic heating.

In round figures, 100 million tons of the 500 million tons of bituminous coal mined each year in the United States go into coke ovens to produce 60 million tons of coke. The byproducts of the coke industry are worth more than one-third of the value of the coke itself.

COLD, in physics, the absence of heat. At the time of Robert Boyle, a British chemist of the 17th century, it was debated whether cold was a real quality or merely the absence of heat. Later, when scientists had learned more about heat, it was decided definitely that cold was simply the absence of heat. See HEAT.

By touching an object an individual can tell whether that object is at a lower-than-normal temperature. See ABSOLUTE ZERO; REFRIGERATION.

COLD, COMMON. A cold is a virus infection of the nose and throat. Your nose gets stuffy and runs, you sneeze, your head aches, and you may have a sore throat, chills, and a slight fever. Unless there are complications, a cold lasts about a week.

Colds spread easily from person to person in a family and at school and at work. To keep a virus from traveling from one person to another, a person with a cold should not touch another person or breathe in his face. He should use disposable tissues and keep his hands clean.

Rest in bed helps to get rid of a cold and prevents the development of complications. Any medicines should be prescribed by a doctor.

COLDBLOODED ANIMAL. Animals whose body temperature varies with the temperature of the environment are called coldblooded. A coldblooded animal cannot keep its body at a constant temperature. When the air or water in which it lives is warm, its body is warm; when its environmental air or water becomes cold, its body becomes cold. It cannot regulate the amount of heat its body produces or prevent this heat from escaping. Cold-blooded animals include reptiles, amphibians, fish, and all invertebrates.

All coldblooded animals that inhabit the Temperate Zones hibernate during winter. The turtle, for example, becomes sluggish as cold weather approaches. It burrows into the soft earth. Once safely underground, it falls into a deep sleep. Its heart nearly stops beating, and its blood circulates very slowly. Its breathing stops entirely. If you should pick up the turtle at this time, its body would feel very cold. It remains completely inactive. However, when the spring sun warms the earth again, the turtle's body becomes warm. It regains consciousness, crawls from its burrow, and resumes its normal activities. See WARMBLOODED ANIMAL.

COLD CREAM is a facial cream that is made with a solid water-in-oil emulsion. Beeswax and alkali are used as the emulsifying agent. There are many formulas for cold cream. It has been used as a cosmetic since the 2d century B.C. Cold cream has been popular because of its possibilities as a base for many kinds of creams. For example, there are cleansing creams, astringent creams, and emollient creams, all using a cold-cream base. Cold creams are mildly akaline but usually are not harmful.

The three illustrations below show a rapidly moving cold front, 1, and slow-moving fronts lifting stable air, 2, and unstable air, 3.

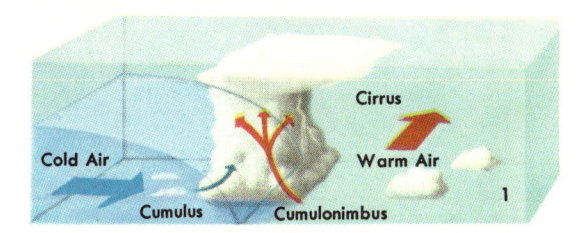

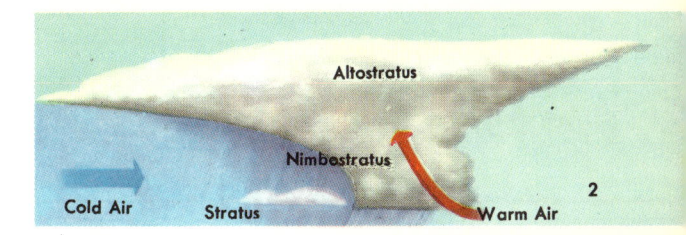

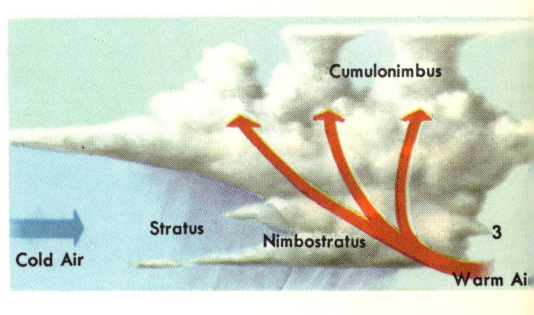

COLD FRONT, the surface of contact formed when cold airmasses push into warmer air. The cold airmasses that push down into the United States are formed in northern Canada and the polar regions. They tend to form cold fronts that move southward and eastward across the United States at a speed of about 25 miles per hour. The face of the cold front is very steep, so that the frontal weather usually extends along a narrow ribbon some 5 to 50 miles wide.

The frontal weather is formed as the cold front undermines the warm air ahead of it. The warm air rising over the cold airmass forms nimbostratus clouds and may produce rain. Sometimes the cold mountain of air moves very fast. The warm air may then rise more violently and form cumulonimbus clouds. Then, there may be thundershowers as the cold front passes.

The cold front is closely connected to other phenomena of weather. It is the result of the collision of two airmasses with different types of air. Cold fronts often push out from anticyclones. Or they are formed as cyclones draw in masses of air at different temperatures. The squall is another special phenomenon sometimes associated with a cold front. See AIRMASS; ANTICYCLONE; CYCLONE; SQUALL; WARM FRONT.

COLD SORE is a group of blisters on reddened skin. It is caused by a virus. Cold sores appear on the lips, as during a cold. They may also appear on the face and at other places, such as the nose, where the skin and mucous membranes come together. The infection can be serious if the virus gets into the central nervous system. Most people have the virus causing cold sores without having attacks of cold sores. Other people get cold sores whenever they have fever, the common cold, or have similar types of upsets. Medical science has not yet developed an effective treatment for this particular sore.

The actual slope of a cold front is shown (above, left) as cold air wedges under warm air.

Stable air may form nimbostratus clouds (above, right) from which falls a steady rain.

Unstable air (right) forms cumulonimbus clouds. Rain in sheets may fall through the cold air after the front has passed.

COLD STORAGE, refrigeration (by ice, carbon dioxide, or a gas circulated by machinery) that holds down the temperature of the air in a warehouse, railroad car, truck, or storeroom to about 30° F. Cold storage should not be confused with frozen storage, the upper limit of which is 0° F. The function of cold storage is to retard normal biological and chemical developments in foods, hides, furs, woolens, and metal parts, whereas the function of frozen storage is to stop these developments altogether. Many products that can be kept for months in cold storage would be completely altered or destroyed if they were to be placed in frozen storage.

Of the several methods of cold storage, each has its advantages and its limitations. Cold storage by ice in refrigerator cars was perfected for the meat industry about 1877. This type of cold storage is still widely used, despite annual losses paid by the carriers amounting to many millions of dollars. Moist cold storage tenderizes meat and keeps vegetables and fruits from drying out. Cold storage with ice has been greatly improved in warehouses and railroad cars by the forced circulation of air. Cold storage by carbon dioxide (Dry Ice), first used in 1924, is dripless, reliable, and in the case of fruits very valuable in preventing excessive evaporation. After the block of Dry Ice has lost its cooling power, the heavy, relatively harmless gas fills the container with an invisible protective blanket.

The greatest use of cold storage is by the food industries, especially for holding back seasonal excess supplies of meat, fruit and vegetables. Millions of cases of eggs are held in cold storage, but better methods of storage are coming to the fore. However, since 1947, many cold-storage plants have been converted to frozen-storage plants with the perfection of super-rapid freezing and vacuum dehydration at low temperatures. Many furs are held in frozen storage, but ordinary cold storage at close to 32° F. is sufficient for most woolens and other garments liable to moth damage. Cold storage generally does not kill the insects in the larval and pupal stages, but it renders them inactive. Hides can be held in cold storage as long as five years without deterioration. Scientists have found that airplane rivets held in Dry Ice are less liable to split when they are used to join sheets of aluminum.

COLD WAR, a struggle short of armed conflict between two nations or groups of nations. The weapons of such a war are chiefly a race for the latest and most terrifying instruments of destruction and attacks and counterattacks by means of diplomatic maneuvers, economic competition, espionage and fifth-column activities, and unceasing streams of propaganda. During a cold war armies of the great powers are trained and equipped for battle, but unlike during a hot war, they are never thrown against each other. Only rarely does a cold war become somewhat heated. That occurs when two minor nations or two factions within one such nation embark on

Huge British and United States supply planes airlifted a daily average of 8,000 tons of food and raw materials to the people of West Berlin when the Soviets blockaded all traffic from the West to that city from June, 1948, until May, 1949. The Soviet Union's aim was to control all Berlin, which, although located in East Germany (occupied by the Soviet Union), was divided into United States, British, French, and Soviet zones. The Berlin blockade was an early phase of the Cold War. Though the blockade failed, the Cold War spread from Germany throughout the world and became a serious danger to peace and survival.

hostilities, with each of the warring groups requesting and receiving limited assistance from the major power blocs.

The tension that existed after World War II between the United States and its allies on one side and the Soviet Union and the other nations of the Communist world on the other is the classic example of a cold war. In crushing Nazi Germany the Western world had recognized the Soviet Union as an ally, but as quickly as the Soviet armies wrested control of eastern Europe from German subjugation they began to impose upon it governments dominated by Communists and subservient to Moscow. While the West began the rapid demobilization of its armies, the U.S.S.R. kept its military strength at wartime peak. At the same time it sealed off from the rest of the world its own territory and that of its eastern European satellites by means of an iron curtain. (See IRON CURTAIN.) To the West these moves plus an increasingly hostile tone in international conferences gave the impression that the Soviet Union, no longer forgetful of belief in an irresolvable conflict between capitalism and communism, intended to expand in order to bring about the world triumph of communism.

Out of regard for its safety the West began to increase the size of its armies. On the other side the U.S.S.R. ended the U.S. monopoly of such superweapons as the atom and hydrogen bombs. To halt Communist expansion and subversion the West, particularly the United States, adopted programs of extensive economic and military assistance, which were designed to stabilize the economies and to improve the military positions of those nations friendly to the West. In order to woo many of these nations to its side the Soviet bloc later began a similar program of aid. By then the Communist onslaught in Europe had been halted; instead, the Communist world, which since 1949 had included the mainland of China, concentrated its efforts on the populous and more technologically backward areas of Asia, Africa, and Latin America. Hot but limited wars flared in Korea and Indochina, but they were settled by armistices in which neither side was permitted a complete victory.

Throughout this cold war both the Soviet bloc and the West continued to talk of peace and disarmament. Frequent negotiations were undertaken for their attainment, but mutual distrust always resulted in their failure.

COLERIDGE, SAMUEL TAYLOR

(1772-1834), English poet and philosopher, was born at Ottery St. Mary, Devonshire. He was educated at Christ's Hospital, London (one of England's best boys' schools), and at Cambridge University, which he left without taking a degree. In 1794 Coleridge met the poet Robert Southey, with whom he planned a utopian colony in the United States. The project collapsed because of lack of funds, but in the course of the planning Coleridge met and married Southey's sister-in-law, Sarah Fricker, by whom he had four children.

This portrait is of Coleridge as a young man.

Coleridge's first collection of poems was published in 1796. The following year he met the poet William Wordsworth, and thus began one of the most famous and productive friendships in literary history. Together they planned a volume of verse in which Wordsworth was to indicate the real poetry that is hidden in ordinary subjects, while Coleridge was to deal in supernatural subjects that illustrate the emotions common to all humanity. The result was *Lyrical Ballads*, published in 1798 and often considered to mark the beginning of the English romantic movement. Coleridge's principal contribution was "The Rime of the Ancient Mariner." During the same period Coleridge also wrote his two other poetic masterpieces, "Kubla Khan" and "Christabel."

After 1800 Coleridge's poetic inspiration seemed to fade rapidly. That year he completed his superb translation of Schiller's tragedy *Wallenstein* and in 1802 the "Ode to

Dejection," his last great poem. In his later years he turned increasingly to prose, producing some of England's best literary criticism as well as religious and philosophical works that profoundly influenced succeeding generations. The most famous of these later works is the *Biographia Literaria*, an autobiography with numerous digressions on literary subjects.

After 1799 Coleridge lived in London until in 1816 he moved to Highgate to take the cure for his opium addiction, which he had acquired at an early age. At both places he was visited by many literary figures and other important people, who reported that his conversation was even more brilliant and stimulating than his writing. His ideas brought him recognition as one of the most stimulating thinkers of his day; today, however, he is chiefly remembered for the imaginative poetry of his youth. See ENGLISH LITERATURE; WORDSWORTH, WILLIAM.

COLLAGE, a picture composed wholly or partly of materials other than paint. The variety of materials used is limited only by the artist himself and by the effect he seeks. Cloth, linoleum, wood, photographs, letters and numerals, and pieces of colored paper are the usual materials. Collage designers arrange fragments of such materials to stimulate fantasies in the mind of the observer. By presenting unusual combinations of ordinary articles, they try to invest the commonplace with new meaning.

The collage was first developed by the dadaists about the time of World War I and was later taken up by the surrealists. It had a considerable influence on commercial art.

Canvas-and-oil collage by C. di Marca-Relli
Courtesy of The Art Institute of Chicago, Mr. & Mrs. Frank G. Logan Purchase Prize

COLLECTIVE BARGAINING. The meeting of representatives of labor unions with representatives of industry to determine the wages and other conditions of employment of the union members is called collective bargaining.

A major union function is to represent employees in negotiating collective agreements with employers. This process is carried on by each union. Sometimes the local union represents the workers of an individual employer or group of employers. Sometimes a group of local unions bargain collectively with a group of employers in a city or area. Sometimes the parent national union bargains with a single large employer, a group of employers, or even with all or substantial portions of an entire industry. With the large number of unions and employers that exist in the United States, many thousands of labor-management agreements are constantly being negotiated by collective bargaining. In 1956, for example, there were over 125,000 collective-bargaining agreements in force between unions and employers.

The collective-bargaining agreement may deal with such subjects as wages; employee benefits such as holidays, vacations, pensions, and health and welfare provisions; working conditions, safety, and related subjects; work schedules, hours, and overtime arrangements; and layoff procedures, seniority, promotions, and transfers.

In the days before the Industrial Revolution, workers often labored side by side with the master of the shop. But with the growth of cities and factories, it became more usual for groups of workers to bargain with representatives of the employer. There was little collective bargaining before 1800. Although common in construction industries and some factories after 1870, it was not typical in mass production until the late 1930's.

COLLEGE. See UNIVERSITY AND COLLEGE.

COLLEGE CONFERENCES, regional organizations of college sports programs. Most colleges and universities in the United States belong to one of these organizations that govern the qualifications and competition of the teams of member schools. The teams of each college in the conference usually play all the other teams during a sport season. At the end of the schedule the team with the best won-and-lost record is declared the conference champion. Some of the best known college conferences are the Atlantic Coast Conference (Maryland, Virginia, North Carolina, and South Carolina); the Ivy League (New England States and New York); the Missouri Valley Intercollegiate Athletic Association (Iowa, Kansas, Missouri, Nebraska, and Oklahoma); the Southeastern Conference (Kentucky, Tennessee, Mississippi, Louisiana, Alabama, Florida, and Georgia); the Southern Conference (Virginia, District of Columbia, West Virginia, North Carolina, and South Carolina); the Southwest Conference (Texas and Arkansas); and the Western Intercollegiate Conference, or the Big Ten (Wisconsin, Iowa, Illinois, Indiana, Ohio, Minnesota, and Michigan).

The National Collegiate Athletic Association is the most powerful intercollegiate sports organization in the United States. It has a membership of 556 institutions, conferences, and athletic organizations. In addition to formulating and enforcing the rules governing many intercollegiate sports, the NCAA sponsors national and regional intercollegiate meets and tournaments.

The Eastern College Athletic Conference is similar in purpose and function to the NCAA. The ECAC has jurisdiction over 21 leagues and associations in which 121 eastern colleges and universities participate.

COLLOID, a term used to signify certain substances that have no regular internal structure, and which, therefore, do not crystallize.

Some substances, such as glue, starch, albumen, and gelatin are natural colloids, that is, they do not have to be reduced to the colloidal state. They have no crystalline structure, and if they are mixed with water and the water is evaporated, they do not form crystals.

When a colloid is mixed with water, we do not get a true solution, as in the case of the crystalloids, but a suspension, that is, the colloid divides into very minute particles, which remain suspended in the water. This suspension is called in chemical language a sol. Sometimes a sol, made with warm or hot water, sets as it cools and makes a jelly, as starch or gelatin will, for instance. This jelly is called a gel.

Colloids will not pass through a membrane by osmosis as solutes will. In this way, a mixture of a colloid and a crystalloid can be separated by being hung in a parchment

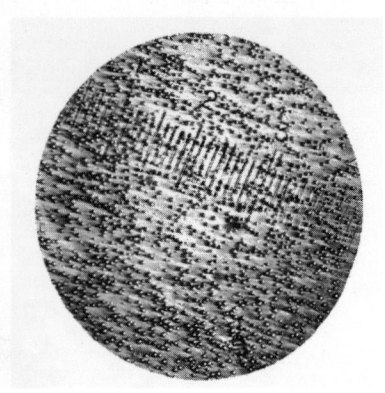

This is a photomicrograph of a colloid that has been magnified 500 times. One can see that the tiny particles are evenly distributed throughout the solution. — Premier Mill Corp.

envelope in water, for the crystalloid substance will penetrate its pores and escape, while the colloid remains behind. (See OSMOSIS.) Obviously the particles of the sol are bigger than the particles of the solute. They are not big enough to be seen by any microscope, however high powered, but they are large enough to diffuse light. If we send a ray of light through a tumbler of apparently clear starch and water in a dark room, the path of the ray through the sol will be seen as a milky blur.

By means of the ultramicroscope (an invention through which we see a beam of light reflected by the object rather than the object itself), we can observe the behavior of the particles in a sol, and it is seen that they are all in rapid and irregular motion. This is due to the fact that they are electrified.

There are all sorts of colloids. Smoke and dust in air act as colloidal mixtures, and that is why they are so difficult to eliminate. The most satisfactory device has been found to be an electrical separator, which, by using a high-voltage current, attracts the particles in the smoke or dust cloud, so that they separate and can be removed as solids.

The blood is a colloidal mixture, protoplasm is a colloid, and in fact most of the chemistry of living substances has to do with colloids.

COLLOQUIALISM, an expression in the accepted spoken idiom. Colloquialisms are used widely in everyday speech but are often considered unsuitable for formal writing.

Colloquialisms are often abbreviated expressions—*math, champ, gas*—or all-purpose words—*funny, fine, frightfully*. The all-purpose words are colloquial in some, though not necessarily in all, meanings. *Fine* in the sense of "excellent" is colloquial.

There are those who insist on the use of formal English, at least in books. However, many colloquialisms make their way into the dictionary and should not be rejected too hastily.

COLOMBIA is a republic of northwestern South America. The capital is Bogotá. The surface of the country is extremely varied. The lofty Andes occupy the western part, and vast lowland plains, covering more than half the country, lie in the almost uninhabited east. Colombia has an area of about 440,000 square miles. Its population is about 14,000,000.

The Andes spread out in three great ranges, forming valleys running north and south. Through one of these valleys the Magdalena River, Colombia's important transportation route, flows to the Caribbean Sea. The Cauca River is the Magdalena's chief tributary. The great eastern plain is covered with thick tropical rain forests in the south and grasslands in the north. Hot lowlands lie along the Pacific and Caribbean coasts.

The climate depends chiefly on altitude. It ranges from hot in the lowlands to cold in the highlands. The tops of the high Andean peaks are always snow covered. Temperatures remain practically the same throughout the year. Rainfall is seasonal, and the year is generally divided into wet and dry seasons, which vary in length in different parts of the country.

Although only a small part of the country is under cultivation, agriculture is the leading occupation. The wide range of climate allows many different kinds of crops to be grown. Livestock raising is of considerable importance.

In terms of value, coffee is by far the most important crop. Colombia is second only to Brazil in coffee production. Bananas again became important after the fungus disease that stopped production of this crop in the 1940's was controlled. Sugarcane, rice, wheat, corn, and tobacco are among other important crops. Most industrial activity centers around the production of consumer goods for the country's own use.

In 1961 the north coast was linked by rail with the interior. A railroad also extends to the west coast. Because of the high mountains, highway and railroad construction is difficult and costly. Air travel has partially solved the problem. The Magdalena River is still an important freight-shipping route. Coffee accounts for the bulk of Colombia's exports. Most of the foreign trade is with the United States.

Many Colombian people are of mixed Spanish and Indian ancestry (mestizo). In some communities are people of unmixed European origin. The people live mainly in the mountains and valleys of the Andes. Few live in the eastern lowlands.

The Spaniards explored the Caribbean coast of Colombia as early as 1500, but no successful settlement was made until 1525. In 1538 Jiménez de Quesada conquered the Chibcha Indians and founded Santa Fé de Bogotá, now called simply Bogotá. The entire area was ruled as a presidency of the Viceroyalty of Peru. Pirates repeatedly raided the towns along the Caribbean coast. Later the Viceroyalty of New Granada was formed from the territory that now is Colombia, Venezuela, Ecuador, and Panama.

A revolution against Spain broke out in 1810. After independence was won in 1819, Simón Bolívar was chosen president. In 1830 Venezuela and Ecuador withdrew from the new republic. Panama seceded from Colombia in 1903.

COLOMBIA

Area: 440,000 sq. mi.
Population: 14,000,000
Capital: Bogotá
Largest cities: Bogotá, Medellín, Cali, Barranquilla
Highest mountain peak: Cristóbal Colón (18,950 feet)
Chief river: Magdalena
Climate: Hot in lowlands, cold in highlands—seasonal rainfall
National flag: Top half yellow, bottom half two horizontal stripes of blue and red
National anthem: *Oh! Gloria inmarcesible* (Oh! Unfading Glory)
Form of government: Republic
Unit of currency: Peso
Language: Spanish
Chief religion: Roman Catholic
Chief economic activities: Agriculture (including livestock raising), mining, manufacturing
Chief crops: Coffee, sugarcane, corn, potatoes, rice, wheat
Chief minerals: Petroleum, gold, silver, platinum, emeralds
Chief manufactures: Food products, textiles
Chief exports: Coffee, petroleum, bananas
Chief imports: Machinery and vehicles, iron and steel, metal manufactures, chemicals

Over a million people live in Bogotá, Colombia's capital. Its modern buildings mingle with its colonial ones.

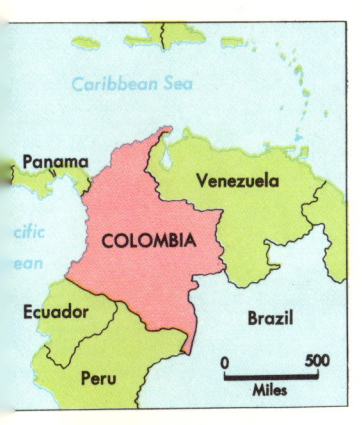

Bananas, grown on Colombia's northern coastal plain, are shipped green, mainly to Germany and The Netherlands. Banana blight once almost wiped out the industry, but the disease was later controlled.

The iron mines at Paz del Río (above) are 8,500 feet up in the Colombian Andes. The ore is taken by opencast mining and is moved by rail to the nearby steel mills. Coal and limestone, which are also necessary for the steel industry, are found in the vicinity.

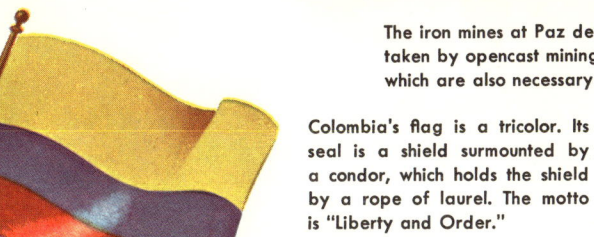

Colombia's flag is a tricolor. Its seal is a shield surmounted by a condor, which holds the shield by a rope of laurel. The motto is "Liberty and Order."

Colombia is well provided with iron ore. To the right is one of its new steel mills. Colombia's steel is consumed domestically and provides for about two-thirds of the nation's needs.

COLOMBO PLAN, a plan sponsored by the British Commonwealth for economic assistance and cooperation between nations of southern and southeastern Asia. The plan was published in 1950 after meetings of the Commonwealth Consultative Committee in Colombo, Ceylon; Sydney, Australia; and London, England. The members of the organization in 1951, the year the plan went into effect, were the United Kingdom, Canada, Australia, New Zealand, India, Ceylon, Malaya, Pakistan, North Borneo, and Singapore. Vietnam, Cambodia, Laos, Burma, Nepal, Indonesia, Japan, the Philippines, Sarawak, and Thailand joined later. The United States is admitted to the organization's meetings as a member and works with the committee.

The member nations are represented on a council that sponsors technical cooperation. The donor nations—Britain, Canada, Australia, New Zealand, Japan, and the United States—contribute much of the monetary aid. But other members have begun to exchange experts and to provide training institutes. The technical experts work in the fields of trade, industry, education, medicine, engineering, agriculture, and transportation. The Colombo Plan has been one of the most successful of the economic-assistance plans.

COLONIALISM. See COLONY; IMPERIALISM.

COLONIAL LIFE IN AMERICA. European customs and traditions, transplanted to the New World, formed the basis of colonial life during the 17th and 18th centuries. To a large extent it was the conditions encountered on the frontier that accounted for the difference between life in the Old World and life in the New World.

Although the frontier had a leveling effect, a social stratification, though certainly not strict, did develop. Most of the colonists belonged to the middle class. However, there there was a small upper class—rich merchants, plantation owners, and the New England clergy—and in addition a small working class. In the northern colonies the working class consisted primarily of indentured servants; in the southern colonies, Negro slaves.

The diversity of the industries and occupations carried on in the colonies was largely due to the varied nature of the environment. New England became a center for the

Colonial Williamsburg

Colonial Williamsburg

This children's room (above) contains furniture and toys of the type used during the colonial period. A huge open fireplace of brick dominated the kitchen portion of the early-American home shown below.

Shelbourne Museum, Inc.

Historic Raleigh Tavern (left), reconstructed on its original site in Williamsburg, Va., was a center of political as well as social activity. The apothecary shop (below) was a forerunner of the present-day drugstore.

Colonial Williamsburg

A colonial estate usually had a special laundry building (below).

Colonial Williamsburg

COLONIAL LIFE IN AMERICA

This hut (above), with its roughly hewn planks and thatched roof, is typical of the dwellings in which the Pilgrims lived during their first years in the New World.

From earliest colonial times merchants utilized waterways to ship goods to market. Below is a view of commercial traffic moving on the Delaware River about 1750.

The coach (below), halted at the Governor's Palace at Williamsburg, Va., is of 18th-century design. Time in the pillory (right) was a punishment for misdemeanors.

small farm and the industrial community. Farther south, in the middle colonies, both agriculture and industry flourished, while in the southern colonies agriculture predominated.

It is significant that while the French, Dutch, and Spanish were successful in transferring the tenant-lord relationship of land ownership to the New World, the English were unsuccessful in this respect. The English colonists demanded full ownership of their land. The manner in which the land was distributed was generally established in the original charter. The colony's promoter (proprietor or trading company) to whom the charter was granted was usually responsible for establishing a government. The degree of authority that the promoter maintained over the colony varied widely. However, in all cases English settlers were guaranteed their rights as royal subjects.

American representative government had its formal beginning with the founding of the Virginia House of Burgesses in 1619. The chief civil administrator in each of the English colonies immediately prior to the American Revolutionary War was the royal governor. This officer was selected by one of three methods. He was appointed by the king of England, nominated by the colonial proprietor and approved by the king, or elected.

The mainstream of religion in the English colonies was supplied by Protestantism from northern Europe. In several colonies the association between the church and the state was close, an extreme example being the administration of the early Puritan colonies. Although the church never controlled the government officially, a virtual theocracy existed for many years in Massachusetts. Similar association tended to exist in other areas where one religious denomination had a numerical advantage. The ties between church and state were gradually weakened and were officially severed by the state constitutions that replaced the colonial charters. An event important in the history of American religion was the Great Awakening, a revival that occurred during the mid-18th century. Its more significant results included a realignment within the Presbyterian and Congregationalist ranks and a gradual liberalization of the traditional Calvinist doctrine.

During the 17th and 18th centuries the educational systems were largely under religious control, a primary function of the schools being to prepare the young men of the community for service in the ministry. Tax-supported public schools were established in Massachusetts by an act of the General Assembly in 1647. In addition to their public schools many Massachusetts towns maintained Latin grammar schools (equivalent to the modern high school). In the middle colonies children were educated at parochial (church-sponsored) or private schools. Similarly, in the southern colonies, where the population was widely scattered, children were either sent to private schools or were educated by private tutors. As a general rule the youth acquired a higher education in England. After about 1750 the system of Latin grammar schools, which had spread to the middle and southern colonies, began to be supplanted by academies, which featured a broader and more practical curriculum. The academy system became especially popular in the southern colonies. American colleges were patterned after their European counterparts. Of the first nine, seven were founded under religious sponsorship.

Primarily because of lack of leisure, contribution to the arts and letters was limited until after the Revolutionary War. The conditions of pioneer life left little time for recreation or amusement. In early Puritan New England and early Virginia most forms of amusement were banned. This situation, which continued in the North, changed elsewhere. Throughout the colonies the rural population found relief from work at such social functions as house raisings and husking bees. By the end of the 18th century many of the Puritan restraints had been forgotten.

COLONY, a politically dependent territory, sometimes inhabited by persons who have emigrated from the mother country but more often populated by native peoples who have been brought under foreign domination. Examples of the first type were the 13 original American colonies: New York, New Hampshire, Massachusetts, Connecticut, Rhode Island, Pennsylvania, New Jersey, Delaware, Maryland, Virginia, North Carolina, South Carolina, and Georgia. The British crown colony of Hong Kong on the coast of China is an example of the second. Usually a colony is situated at some distance from the country to which it owes allegiance; distance alone (apart from such matters as differences of race and culture) makes it difficult to incorporate the territory completely as a part of the home state.

The Phoenician city-states along the eastern Mediterranean established colonies in many parts of the Mediterranean area to facilitate and expand the commercial activities of this great seafaring people. Utica and Carthage were the most important of the Phoenician colonies, the latter in time becoming the capital of a great empire with colonies of its own. The Greek city-states also sent out exploring parties to all parts of the Mediterranean area to found settlement colonies, even along the Black Sea, in Corsica and Sardinia, and on the coasts of France and Spain. These colonies followed the pattern of their homeland by setting up city-states almost completely independent of the mother states.

Modern colonialism was an outgrowth of the commercial revolution of the 15th and 16th centuries. Improved methods of navigation, new sea routes, and the desire for overseas trading posts gave a strong impetus to colonization. Portugal was the first great colonizer among modern countries. Before the discovery of America the Portuguese established trading posts and garrisons along the coast of northern and eastern Africa and a little later on the west coast of India and in many other areas in the Far East. About 1530 they began the colonization of Brazil, which became the greatest of all Portuguese colonies. Spanish colonization over large areas in both North and South America followed closely the discoveries by Columbus. The Dutch East India Company, formed in 1602, enjoyed phenomenal success in the East Indies, where it almost completely supplanted the Portuguese and thwarted most of the English efforts at penetration. The Dutch West India Company established a colony along the Hudson River; it was conquered by the British and became New York.

Of all the colonizing powers of Europe Great Britain has been by far the most successful. In 1600 the British East India Company began to penetrate India. The first successful English colony in America was established at Jamestown in Virginia in 1607. In Australia the British built their first penal settlement in 1788. The colonization of New Zealand began in 1840.

The claim of France to North America was established by Cartier in 1534, but not until 1608 did Champlain begin colonization with a settlement at Quebec. This was the beginning of New France in America, but it was later taken over by Great Britain. France was more successful in gaining and retaining large areas in other parts of the world, especially in Africa. Germany and Italy did not enter the race for colonies until late in the 19th century; the German colonies were lost as a result of World War I, and the Italian, as a consequence of defeat in World War II.

The modern trend has been toward independence for colonies. The 13 American colonies declared their independence in 1776. Most of the Spanish and Portuguese colonies in America became independent shortly after 1800. The most important British settlement colonies have become independent nations within the British Commonwealth of Nations. In the Netherlands East Indies, Indochina, and Africa independence movements became irresistible after World War II, with former colonies, one after another, becoming independent states.

COLOR. All colors are present in the colorless beam of sunlight which we call white light. By passing sunlight through a triangular glass prism, we can find out what the individual colors are. This spreading out of the colors of white light makes a color sequence that is called a spectrum. An example of a color spectrum is the rainbow. As in the rainbow, a color spectrum made by passing light through a prism consists of an endless number of colors. These colors we recognize as ranging from red through orange, yellow, green, and blue to violet.

It is not definitely known who discovered that sunlight can be analyzed, or separated, into the different colors that make it up, but Sir Isaac Newton was the first man to make important use of the fact. Newton put a prism to the hole of a shutter by which he was examining the action of a ray of light in a dark room, and to his astonishment he saw a band of colors, the color spectrum, on the opposite wall.

A color spectrum is caused by the refraction of light that takes place in a prism. Light passing through a prism is bent, or refracted, but the various colors that make up the light are not equally refracted. Thus the light is separated into its elementary colors.

Since white light can be split up into the elementary colors—red, orange, yellow, green, blue, and vio-

COLOR

let—combining lights of those colors in correct proportions should give us white light. This fact may be demonstrated by sending the spectrum we get from one prism through another prism reversed. The light, which had been split up by the one, is recombined by the other and comes out as a white ray again.

Three of these colors of the spectrum are called primary colors. These are red, green, and violet. (These primary colors are different from the primary colors, or, more correctly, primary pigments, of the painter.) The red, green, and violet of the spectrum, when mixed together, make white light. Also any recognizable color may be made by mixing different proportions of light of these colors. Red light mixed with green light, for example, will make yellow light. (We will get an entirely different result from mixing paints.)

Color, it should be noted, is what we see. Color does not belong to

The appearance of colors is affected by their backgrounds. **1.** Color surfaces of identical areas may appear different in size. The white square at bottom is exactly the same size as the black square at top. **2.** Identical colors may appear different in hue. The green squares are actually identical in hue.

Surfaces appear as a particular color because they reflect only that color and absorb the other colors of the spectrum. Thus red objects absorb all but the red portion of white light; green objects absorb all but the green.

Value scales representing the tints and shades of gray and orange are shown at left. Value refers to the relative lightness or darkness of the color. For example, apricot is one of the lighter values of orange. Light values are called tints, while dark values are known as shades.

The color wheel at right shows how color pigments may be mixed to produce intermediate colors. The three primary colors—red, yellow, and blue—are connected by the black broken lines, while the secondary colors—orange, green, and violet—are connected by the red broken lines. Blue lines connect the principal complementary colors.

Colors of the spectrum are produced by a prism because the prism bends shorter wavelengths of light more than longer wavelengths.

Actually the spectrum is a continuous range of colors that can only roughly be divided into bands, as in this stylized drawing.

things at all. Matter has no color in itself. A thing's color (as we call it) depends on the condition of its surface. This surface absorbs or reflects light. The light it reflects is what we see.

Suppose we see a leaf. We say, "The leaf is green." Actually, the light that causes the effect we call green is exactly what the surface of the leaf cannot take in and so rejects. This light comes to our eyes, and we call the leaf green in consequence.

Because the colors of objects depend on the nature of the light that falls on them as well as the nature of their own surfaces, things seem to be a different color by artificial light than they are by daylight. Few artificial lights have the same composition as sunlight. You might buy a suit that looks dark gray in a store lighted with electric light only to find, when you get home, it is purplish blue.

COLORADO, the Centennial State, is located in the western part of the United States. It has spectacular mountain scenery, a vast supply of natural resources, and a healthful climate. It is the highest state in the United States, with an average altitude of 6,800 feet. It is the eighth largest state in area. Its 104,247 square miles are greater than the combined area of New York, New Jersey, and Pennsylvania. Rectangular in shape, it measures 276 miles north-south and 387 miles east-west.

Denver is the capital and the largest city. Chief cities include Pueblo, Colorado Springs, Greeley, Boulder, Englewood, and Fort Collins. Colorado's population in 1960 was 1,753,947.

The Rocky Mountains run through the west-central portion of the state. They form the Continental Divide. Eastern Colorado consists of flat land rising slowly for 200 miles to the foothills of the Rockies. The western section is part of the Colorado Plateau, or the Western Slope. It is the plateau area west of the Rockies. The highest peaks in Colorado are Mt. Elbert (14,431 feet), Longs Peak (14,255 feet), and Pikes Peak (14,110 feet).

East of the Continental Divide rise the North Platte, the South Platte, and the Arkansas rivers. The Colorado River, the Rio Grande (which flows east), and tributaries rise on the western slopes. The streams are not navigable because of numerous waterfalls and diversions of water for irrigation. Dams on them provide much hydroelectric power.

Colorado's dry continental climate varies with the altitude. The winters are cold, but they are severe only in the mountains. The summers are hot. The humidity is relatively low, and there is considerable sunshine.

Minerals, forests, soil, climate, and potential waterpower are Colorado's natural wealth. Nearly one-half of the land is natural pasture. About one-third of the total area is forested. Cut timber is mostly Ponderosa pine, lodgepole pine, fir, and spruce. Wildlife is legally protected and includes antelope, bear, deer, lynx, red fox, marten, beaver, and wildfowl.

Mining is a leading industry in Colorado. Gold and silver were the most important minerals at first, but today molybdenum, zinc, and uranium are the major ores mined. Climax, Colo., produces over 70 percent of the nation's molybdenum. Other minerals include coal, copper, lead, vanadium, fluorite, feldspar, tungsten, and petroleum. Some 35 minerals are being extracted in the state.

Although mining is important, farming and livestock raising are the major occupations. Farming yields the largest agricultural income. Cattle and sheep raising predominate. Wheat is the main field crop. The irrigated valleys of the South Platte and Arkansas rivers produce enormous crops, especially sugar beets. Hay, broomcorn, sorghums, dry beans, potatoes, cantaloupes, and garden and flower seeds are important crops.

The refining of metals is a major industry. Iron and steel are produced in the Pueblo area, and there is general manufacturing in the Denver area. There are beet-sugar refineries, oil refineries, large meat-packing plants, flour and feed mills, and canning industries.

Colorado has magnificent scenery and derives a large income from tourists who visit the national parks (Rocky Mountain, Mesa Verde), national monuments, and forests. Unsurpassed engineering bridged and pierced the Rockies. The Royal Gorge suspension bridge is 1,053 feet above the river; tunnels eliminate the heavy grade across the Continental Divide.

The Spanish explored Colorado as early as 1541. Others followed. Zebulon Pike's explorations brought him to the area in 1806. Stephen Long's expedition in 1820 gave the eastern part of the state the reputation of being a desert. The American period of settlement in the region came with the great strikes of gold in 1859. Made a territory in 1861, Colorado was admitted to the Union in 1876. A railroad branch line to Denver (1870), mining booms at Leadville and Aspen, and the cattle industry built up the state. After 1900 Colorado turned more to agriculture, livestock, and manufacturing. In the 1950's western Colorado boomed with the development of uranium deposits in the area.

COLORADO

Nickname: Centennial State
Seal: Shield in the center, showing mountain peaks and miner's pick and shovel—the state motto below—the eye of God above, with golden rays around the triangle
Flag: Blue field with white strip across it—a red C on the white with a golden ball representing gold production and sunshine
Motto: *Nil Sine Numine* (Nothing Without the Deity)

The City and County Building, shown below, is one of a complex of public buildings and monuments that surround the Civic Center of Denver, Colo. The Colorado Capitol stands nearby.

Robert D. Bezucha

COLORADO

Flower: Rocky Mountain columbine
Bird: Lark bunting
Capital: Denver
Largest cities: Denver, Pueblo, Colorado Springs
Area: 104,247 sq. mi. (including 325 sq. mi. inland waters)
Rank in area: 8th
Population: 1,753,947
Chief universities: University of Colorado, United States Air Force Academy, Colorado State University, University of Denver
Highest mountain peak: Elbert (14,431 ft.)
Chief rivers: South Platte, Arkansas, Rio Grande, Colorado, Gunnison
Chief lake: Grand
Average temperature: Denver, 31° F. (Jan.), 74° F. (July)
Average annual rainfall: 17 inches
Chief economic activities: Mining, agriculture (including cattle and sheep raising)
Chief crop: Wheat, alfalfa, sugar beets
Chief minerals: Petroleum, coal, uranium, molybdenum, zinc
Notable attractions: Rocky Mountain and Mesa Verde national parks, Garden of the Gods, Pikes Peak, Royal Gorge
Important historical dates:
    1541 Part of territory explored by Coronado
    1803 Eastern Colorado acquired by United States through Louisiana Purchase
    1859 Pikes Peak gold rush
    1861 Colorado Territory created
    1876 Colorado admitted to Union as 38th state

Robert D. Bezucha
This abandoned mine (above) at Central City is a remnant of Colorado's colorful past.

This tent-amphitheater (left) near Aspen, the noted winter sports center, is annually the scene of a summer program of cultural events.

Carloads of sugar beets (below), part of the harvest from the fertile valleys of central and eastern Colorado, are ready for processing.
Courtesy State of Colorado

Artha Hornbostel

Two skiers (below) pause to admire the view near Berthoud Pass, a passageway across the Continental Divide about 40 miles northwest of Denver. In this vicinity is located some of the most spectacular scenery in North America.
Courtesy State of Colorado

COLORADO
State Capital
County Seat
Size of symbols and type indicates relative population
1 Inch = 34.5 Statute Miles
10 0 10 20 30
Lambert Conformal Conic Projection
RELIEF
Feet
5 000
2 000
1 000
500
100
Sea Level
500
5 000
109°
108°
107°
106°
41°
40°
39°
38°
37°
SWEETWATER
WYO.
Laramie
ALBANY
UINTAH
UTAH
GRAND
SAN JUAN
ARIZ.
APACHE
NEW MEXICO
SAN JUAN
RIO ARRIBA
TAOS
Longitude West of Greenwich
MOFFAT
ROUTT
JACKSON
LARIMER
RIO BLANCO
GARFIELD
EAGLE
SUMMIT
GRAND
BOULDER
GILPIN
CLEAR CREEK
MESA
DELTA
PITKIN
LAKE
PARK
CHAFFEE
GUNNISON
MONTROSE
OURAY
SAN MIGUEL
DOLORES
MONTEZUMA
LA PLATA
SAN JUAN
HINSDALE
MINERAL
ARCHULETA
RIO GRANDE
SAGUACHE
ALAMOSA
CONEJOS
COSTILLA
FREMONT
CUSTER
TELLER
Grand Junction
Ft. Collins
Boulder
Longmont
Leadville
Glenwood Springs
Montrose
Durango
Alamosa
Salida
Craig
Meeker
Delta
Gunnison
Steamboat Springs
Walden
Kremmling
Dinosaur Nat'l Mon.
Colorado Nat'l Mon.
Black Canyon of the Gunnison Nat'l Mon.
Mesa Verde Nat'l Park
Great Sand Dunes Nat'l Mon.
Hovenweep Nat'l Mon.
Rocky Mtn. Nat'l Park
Ute Mountain Indian Res.
Southern Ute Indian Res.
Colorado R.
Gunnison R.
White R.
Yampa R.
Rio Grande
Dolores R.
Uncompahgre R.
San Miguel R.
Animas R.
Highest Point in Colorado
Mt. Elbert 14,431 ft.
Mt. Massive 14,418 ft.
Mt. Harvard 14,414 ft.
Blanca Pk. 14,317 ft.
Uncompahgre Pk. 14,301 ft.
Longs Pk. 14,255 ft.
Pikes Pk. 14,110
San Juan Mountains
Sangre de Cristo Mts.
Elk Mountains
West Elk Mountains
Continental Divide
Middle Park
North Park
South Park
San Luis Valley
Grand Mesa
Uncompahgre Plateau
Flat Tops
White River Plateau
Wolf Creek Pass 10,850 ft.
Monarch Pass 11,302 ft.
Berthoud Pass 11,314 ft.
Loveland Pass 11,992 ft.
Moffat R.R. Tunnel
COSMO RELIEF COLORADO
Copyright by RAND McNALLY & COMPANY
Made in U. S. A.

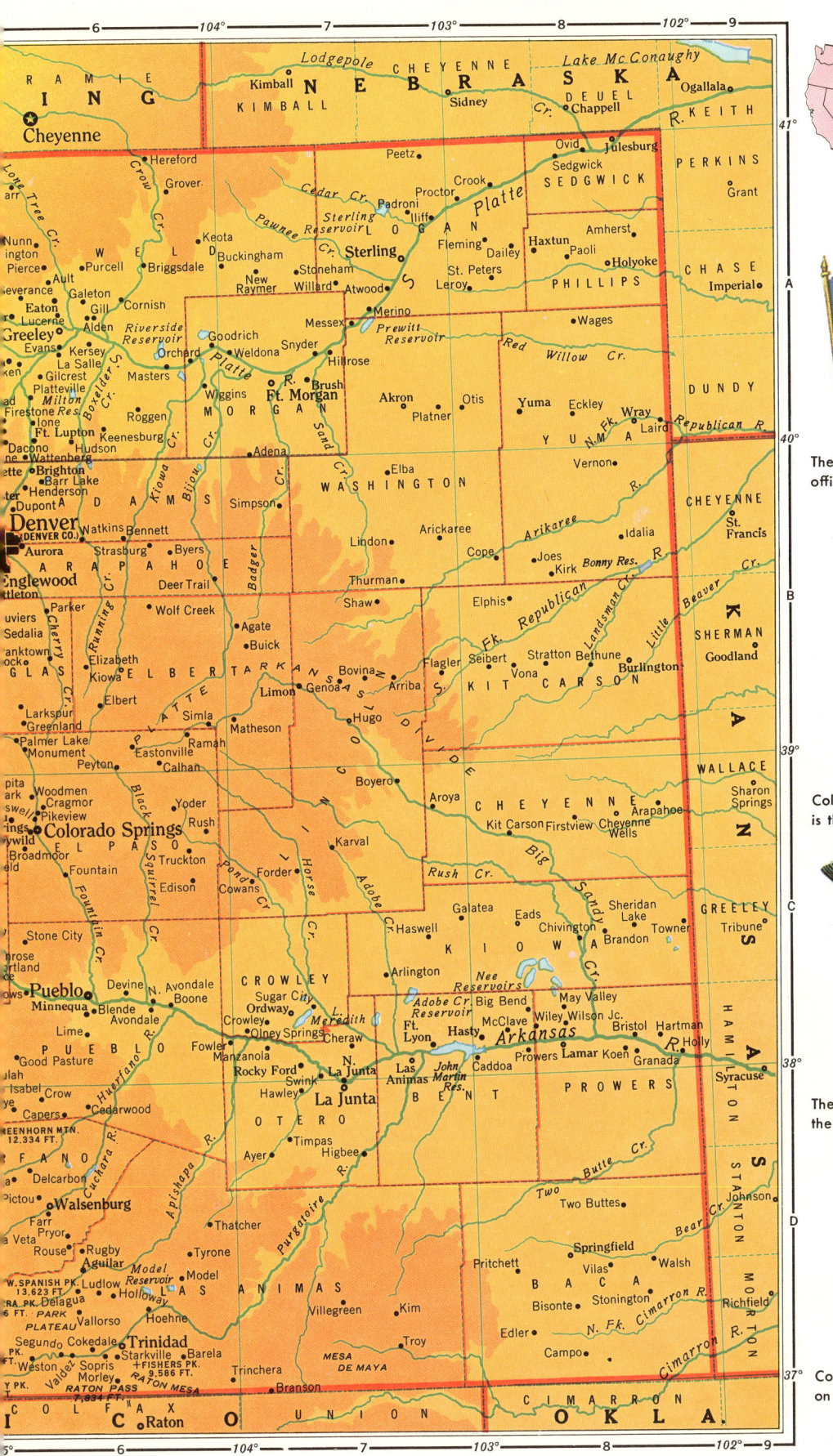

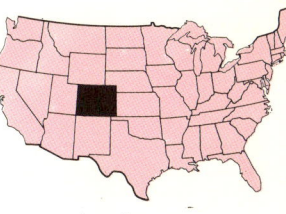

Location map

The state flag of Colorado was officially adopted in 1911.

Colorado's state flower (above) is the Rocky Mountain columbine.

The lark bunting, shown above, is the state bird of Colorado.

Colorado's date of admission is on the state shield (above).

For map index, see Volume 20.

COLORADO PLATEAU

COLORADO PLATEAU is a large, arid upland in southwestern United States. It includes much of Utah and Arizona and parts of New Mexico and Colorado. It is drained by the Colorado River system and covers an area of about 130,000 square miles. Deep canyons and high plateaus have made this region one of the most inaccessible in the United States. Scenic areas include the magnificent Grand Canyon in Arizona and Bryce Canyon and Zion national parks in Utah.

COLORADO RIVER, a river of southwestern United States. It rises in the Rocky Mountains in north-central Colorado and flows generally southwest, finally emptying into the Gulf of California in Mexico. Its length is about 1,400 miles. The Colorado forms part of the boundary between Nevada and Arizona. It also forms the boundary between Arizona and California and between Lower California and Sonora in Mexico. It drains some 242,000 square miles in the United States.

Some of the scenery along the Colorado is spectacular. The river cuts deep gorges and canyons throughout a mountainous region. Grand Canyon in Arizona was formed by this great river. The principal tributaries of the Colorado include the Dolores and Gunnison rivers in Colorado, the Green River in Utah, the San Juan River in Utah, and the Little Colorado and the Gila rivers in Arizona.

The river is used extensively for power and irrigation. Examples of such projects are the Colorado–Big Thompson project and the All-American Canal.

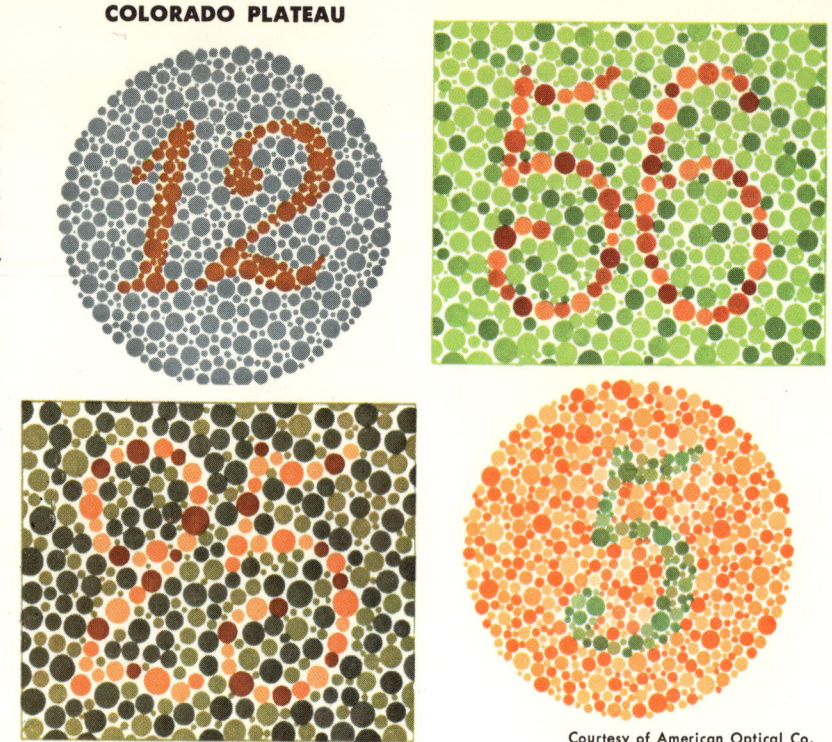

Courtesy of American Optical Co.

A person who has normal vision will see that some of the colored dots in the patterns shown above form the numbers 12, 56, 25, and 5. These illustrations, however, are not to be used for testing purposes; the reproductions simply show the type of patterns used.

COLOR BLINDNESS, an inability to distinguish between colors, particularly between red and green. However, some people cannot tell the difference between blue and yellow, and a very few people cannot tell the difference between any of the colors. A person is often tested for color blindness by being asked to sort yarns or look at colored charts of various shades of two colors, such as red and green. If he is color blind, he can distinguish the colors according to the brightness of the color but is unable to put them in a red series and a green series. Color blindness is usually inherited, and it usually occurs in boys. The cause of color blindness is a defect in the retina of the eye.

COLOSSUS OF RHODES. See SEVEN WONDERS OF THE ANCIENT WORLD.

COLT REVOLVER. The original Colt revolver was invented in the United States in 1836 by Samuel Colt. Since that time there have been many improvements, including metallic cartridges, double-action to make cocking after each shot unnecessary, and various safety devices. However, the basic principle of a revolving cylinder, containing several chambers for cartridges, remains unchanged. The most famous of Colt revolvers was known as the Peacemaker. The Peacemaker was first manufactured in 1873 as a .45 caliber six-shooter but was soon adapted for a .44 Winchester cartridge. In this form it became the revolver of the frontier. It was used by famous Westerners such as "Wild Bill" Hickok and Wyatt Earp. Issued to the Army and used in Indian campaigns and in the Spanish-American War, it had the longest popularity of any gun in the world and was produced until 1941.

Robert D. Bezucha

Robert D. Bezucha

Although there are several spectacular canyons (left) along the Colorado River's course through the American Southwest, all are dwarfed by the awe-inspiring Grand Canyon (above), situated in northwestern Arizona on the Colorado's middle course.

COLUMBIA is the capital and largest city of South Carolina. It is a manufacturing center that is supplied with abundant hydroelectric power from nearby projects. Columbia is situated at the head of navigation of the Congaree River in the central part of South Carolina. This city had a population of 97,433 according to the 1960 census.

The city has been a cultural center since the late 1700's. It is the seat of the University of South Carolina, Allen University, and Benedict College. Places of interest include the State House, the boyhood home of Woodrow Wilson, and some notable antebellum houses. A U.S. Army post, Fort Jackson, is nearby.

Columbia is an industrial, trade, and distribution center. The chief manufactured goods include textiles, fertilizer, and lumber and food products.

The city was settled in 1786, and the state legislature first met here in 1790. During the Civil War General Sherman burned much of the city.

COLUMBIA RIVER, of southwestern Canada and northwestern United States. It rises in the Rocky Mountains of British Columbia and follows an irregular course some 1,200 miles, to empty into the Pacific Ocean southwest of Tacoma, Wash. The Columbia forms part of the boundary between Washington and Oregon. It drains an area of about 259,000 square miles and is second to the Mississippi River in volume in the United States. The Columbia enters the United States in northeast Washington, and between this point and its confluence with the Snake River the Columbia is diverted into the Big Bend Region where the Grand Coulee Dam and reservoir are now located. The river is broken by many rapids and falls, and a deep gorge through the Cascade Range of mountains in Oregon is particularly beautiful. The mouth of the Columbia River forms a deepwater harbor.

The chief tributaries of the Columbia River system are the Clark Fork, the Kootenai, the Spokane, the Snake, the Deschutes, and the Willamette. Extensive salmon fisheries are located on the river. The Columbia basin project, sponsored by the federal government, includes Bonneville Dam, McNary Dam, the Grand Coulee Dam, and many smaller dams. In 1961 the United States and Canada signed a treaty for developing the river's resources.

COLUMBINE, the common name for a genus of plants of the crowfoot family. There are about 40 species, all from the North Temperate Zone. The columbine is a hardy perennial, with drooping, long-spurred flowers in a variety of colors. The wild columbine ranges widely over eastern North America. It has scarlet and yellow flowers and grows to a height of about 2 feet. The garden columbine has blue and white flowers and grows to a height of 3 feet.

Reddish spurs and yellow sepals mark the wild columbine of eastern North America.

COLUMBUS, CHRISTOPHER (about 1451-1506), discovered the New World when on Oct. 12, 1492, he landed on San Salvador (in the Bahama Islands) and claimed it in the names of Queen Isabella and King Ferdinand of Spain.

Columbus was born the son of a wool comber in the Mediterranean port of Genoa, Italy. As a young man he went to sea. During the next several years he made many voyages and studied the art and science of navigation. These studies led him to accept the idea that the earth was round and that he could reach China and Japan by sailing west. During these years he dreamed of the wealth and glory that would came to the man who could find a short sea route over which to bring the gold and spices of the East to Europe.

For a while Columbus lived in Portugal, where he married and had a son, Diego. He is said to have made some voyages along the northern coast of Africa in the service of the Portuguese crown. In any case, it was to King John II of Portugal that Columbus first presented his plan for finding a new sea route to the Indies. Failing here, he tried Isabella and Ferdinand of Spain. But they were uninterested, for their attention was occupied with a war to drive the Moors from their kingdom. Through his brother Bartholomew, Columbus tried unsuccessfully to get the patronage of the English and French courts.

When he finally gained a hearing with Isabella and Ferdinand, his proposal was rejected. To them his demands for a share in the venture were outrageous. Columbus wanted a principality of his own under Spain. In all the islands, seas, and continents he might discover, he asked to be known as Admiral of the Ocean. He also requested the viceroyalty of all these lands and a generous share of the revenue. At the last minute the Spanish monarchs changed their minds, and an agreement was signed. Columbus also received a royal letter of introduction to the ruler of Cathay (China).

On Aug. 3, 1492, Columbus and a crew of between 90 and 120 men sailed from Palos, Spain, for the Canary Islands and from there westward into the unknown. His ships were the *Santa María*, which he commanded, the *Pinta*, and the *Niña*. On Oct. 12, 1492, land was sighted by a sailor, Rodrigo de Triana, aboard the *Niña*.

Rock Island Dam (below), on the Columbia River in central Washington, is one of many dams and water-control projects built to harness the power of the Columbia and its tributaries.
Bob & Ira Spring

His Book of Priviliges, Columbus, Rare Book Division, New York Public Library

A painting by Piombo of Christopher Columbus at the time of his voyages. Above is Columbus' coat of arms, given to him by the king of Spain. It shows a group of islands, and its motto reads "Columbus found the New World for Spain."

Courtesy of The Metropolitan Museum of Art, Gift of J. Pierpont Morgan, 1900

At left is the oldest known world globe. It was made in 1491 and does not show the Americas. Below are the routes taken by Columbus on his several voyages. The first trip, in 1492, established proof that other lands could be reached by sailing west. The second expedition in 1493 had 17 ships and 1500 men. Its primary purpose was colonization. The third voyage, in 1498, expanded the area of explorations and furthered the search for gold and spices. South America was discovered at this time. Realizing the New World was not the Indies, Columbus, in 1502, made a last effort to find a way to them by exploring the coast of Central America.

Warren Clifton Shearman Coll.

This was the island in the Bahamas that Columbus called San Salvador. It is sometimes known as Watling Island. Columbus landed and claimed it for Spain and then sailed to discover other islands. He coasted the northern side of Cuba and of Hispaniola, where the *Santa María* was wrecked. Shortly afterward he sailed for home in the *Niña*. With him he took samples of the wealth of what he believed until his death were the Indies. Ferdinand and Isabella received him with honor and immediately petitioned Pope Alexander VI to draw the famous Line of Demarcation, granting to Spain all lands discovered or to be discovered west of a line 100 leagues west of the Azores.

Columbus made three other voyages. The second one was in 1493, and the third was in 1498, when—near the mouth of the Orinoco River—he sighted the mainland of South America. In 1502, on the fourth voyage, he sailed down the coast of Central America from Honduras to Panama in the hope of finding a passage to India.

For all his labors, courage, and important discoveries, Columbus failed to achieve personal wealth and glory. Colonizing the New World was difficult. The land failed to produce for him the great riches he had imagined. The expeditions were rife with mutiny and dissension. Rumors of mismanagement and misrule reached the ears of the Spanish monarchs and finally led to the withdrawal of Columbus' dignities. Before he could be reinstated, Queen Isabella died, and Columbus passed the last two years of his life in poverty and neglect. He died at Valladolid, Spain.

COLUMBUS is the capital of, and third largest city in, Ohio. It is a commercial, trade, and educational center. The city is located in central Ohio on the Scioto River at its junction with the Olentangy River. The population of the city in 1960 was 471,316.

Points of interest in the city include the State Office Building, the Capitol, and the Columbus Gallery of Fine Arts. Ohio State University is located here.

Industries in Columbus manufacture such diversified items as clothing, electrical and heating equipment, aircraft, and food, paper, and foundry products. The city is also a trade center for an agricultural area. Columbus was settled in 1812, the same year that it became the state capital.

COMA BERENICES, or Berenice's Hair, is a northern constellation between Leo and Bootes. It is visible in the evening sky from midnorthern latitudes between March and August. The visible constellation is an open cluster of faint stars of fifth and sixth magnitudes. However, with an opera glass you can see 20 or 30 stars of the cluster on a clear, moonless night.

The constellation Coma Berenices, or Berenice's Hair, represents the hair of an Egyptian queen, according to legend. Fearing for her husband's safety while he was at war, Berenice cut her hair and placed it in the temple of Venus as an offering. Later the hair disappeared; and, to placate the queen, the royal astronomer told her that it had been converted into the stars of this constellation by the god Jupiter.

COMBUSTION is burning, or a chemical action in which both heat and light are produced. It is a type of oxidation reaction, in which a combustible substance, a fuel, unites chemically with oxygen. The burning of coal, oil, or gas are examples of combustion.

The kindling temperature of a substance is the temperature at which combustion begins in that substance. A substance oxidizes more rapidly at a higher temperature than at a lower one. When a certain temperature is reached, a particular substance will begin to oxidize so rapidly and give off so much heat that the substance burns.

Spontaneous combustion takes place when, without heat being added from outside sources, the oxidation of the substance produces so much heat that the kindling temperature of the substance is reached. Spontaneous combustion of improperly stored oily rags and waste materials is the cause of many fires in homes. Substances that oxidize rapidly should be stored in cool, well-ventilated places.

If a limited supply of oxygen is present during the combustion of fuels such as coal, gas, and oil, a poisonous gas, carbon monoxide, may be formed. Carbon monoxide is the product of incomplete combustion. When a sufficient supply of oxygen is present, complete combustion occurs.

COMEDY. In general, plays that make people laugh and that have happy endings are either comedies or farces. Comedy is distinguished from farce by its tone, which is generally not extreme enough to include the horseplay farce depends upon. Both are vague terms, the lines between them wavering and indistinct, but in comedy, character is often developed at the expense of plot, and some attempt may be made at subtlety.

Comedy arose in classical Greece and probably grew out of Greek festivities (the word itself derives from the Greek word for *festival*). Yet the extant comedies of the great comic poet Aristophanes display a kind of comedy close to farce. Riotous and satirical, it ridicules various Athenian ideas and institutions. (See ARISTOPHANES.) The comedy of Aristophanes is called Old Comedy. The New Comedy of the Greek Menander and the Roman writers Plautus and Terence gave sentimental, but humorous, pictures of contemporary life. Here are seen that set cast of typical figures, such as the irate father and the spendthrift son, that are common in the theater throughout history.

In the medieval miracle play comedy does occur, notably in the *Second Shepherd's Play*, but the chief purpose of these plays is devotional. (See MIRACLE PLAY.) In Elizabethan England two forms of comedy developed. First is the romantic comedy of Shakespeare. This comedy, with its pastoral convention of idealized rustics, was particularly successful in such a play as *As You Like It*. On the other hand there developed the realistic comedy of Ben Jonson, as in *Volpone*.

In the late 17th century the comedy of manners flourished, in France with Molière and in England with the Restoration playwrights, such as Congreve and Wycherley. A distinction may be made between Molière's comedy and that of the Restoration playwrights in that Molière, in such plays as *Tartuffe*, emphasizes character, and the English Restoration playwrights, in such plays as *The Way of the World*, emphasize wit. In the 18th and 19th centuries, sentimental comedy developed, but today this form, as seen in a play like Hugh Kelly's *False Delicacy*, seems a parody of life. Exceptions to this sentimentality are the plays of Richard Brinsley Sheridan, such as *The School for Scandal* and *The Rivals*, both of which are excellent attempts to return to the comedy of Congreve and Restoration.

Realistic comedy is usual on the stage today. Examples are *Major Barbara* by Shaw and *The Playboy of the Western World* by Synge. The comedy of manners survives in the plays of Somerset Maugham, such as *Our Betters* and *The Circle*, and in such plays as Philip Barry's *The Philadelphia Story*. Sentimental comedy is found in Sir James Barrie's *Quality Street* and *A Kiss for Cinderella*. The tradition of French wit is continued in France by Jean Giraudoux and Jean Anouilh. Drama that mixes comedy with tragedy has been done both by Anton Chekhov and Sean O'Casey.

Combustion combines oxygen from air and carbon from coal to form carbon dioxide gas. Continued combustion requires replenishment of oxygen by air circulation. As the carbon dioxide rises, air is drawn in at a lower level, thereby furnishing a constant supply of oxygen.

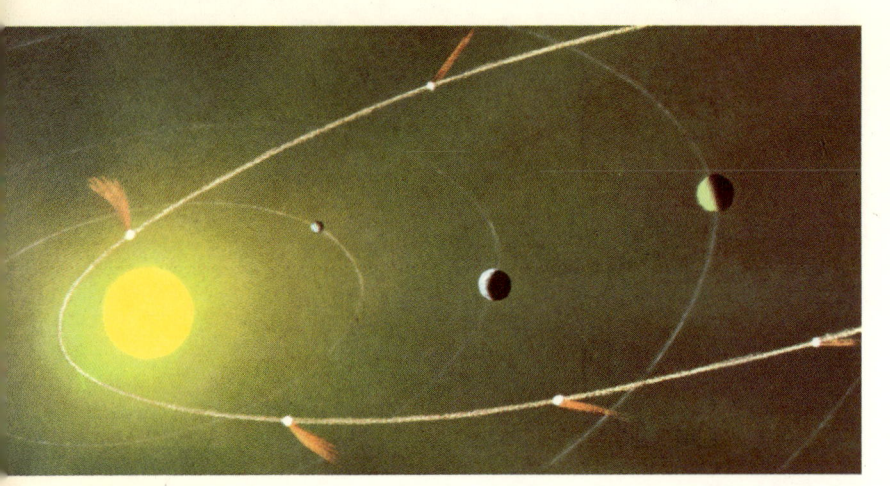

The diagram above shows a comet at a number of positions in its elliptical orbit through the solar system. Its tail, which may be 100 million miles long, is always pointed away from the sun. Only five or six comets in a century can be seen without the aid of a telescope.

COMET, a luminous body in space that passes among the planets in a long, elliptical orbit and often shows a beautiful, streaming tail. According to one theory, comets are made of frozen gases mixed with metallic material. When they come near the sun, their gases evaporate and glow. Radiation pressure from the sun pushes the gases and ejected dust away from the comet, and this material forms the luminous tail. Because of this pressure, the tail points away from the sun regardless of what direction the comet is moving.

Most comets are too faint to be seen with the naked eye, but several are visible by telescope every year. Some of these are new comets, and others have been seen before and are returning. The returning comets move in orbits among the planets and pass near us periodically. Others pass only once and return to space beyond the planets.

We don't know for certain where comets come from. Some astronomers think there is a spherical shell of comet material around the sun far beyond the planets. Nearby stars could disturb some of this material and send it falling toward the sun.

Comets are sometimes torn into several parts when they pass near the sun. This happened to Biela's Comet in 1846. (See BIELA'S COMET.) Some comets are found to be traveling at different places along nearly the same orbit. They are thought to be pieces of a larger comet once torn apart in this way.

Most of a comet is very thin gas and dust, so thin that stars shine right through the tail. The earth passed through the tail of Halley's Comet in 1910, and astronomers could notice no effect at all. (See HALLEY'S COMET.) Parts of the head of some comets could be damaging if they penetrated the earth's atmosphere, but the chances of a collision are extremely rare.

Comets are named for their discoverers. They are also given a number, which includes the year of the comet's discovery and a Roman numeral showing its order among comets that passed nearest the sun that year.

COMIC BOOK, a series of cartoons appearing in one booklet. Though the original comic strips were usually humorous, bestselling comic books have dealt with mystery, adventure, and horror stories. Walt Disney's Mickey Mouse and Donald Duck are favorite characters in the humorous type of comic book. Superman, Batman, and Captain Marvel, invincible men who have fantastic adventures, are among the most popular comic-book heroes.

Several early forms of cartoons in tabloid form began to appear around 1911, but the great flood of comic books did not begin until 1938, when *Superman* first appeared on the newsstands.

Comic books have been accused of lowering American standards of taste. More seriously, they have been attacked as unfit reading matter for children because of their sensational escapism and open display of violence. In 1954 some of the comic-book publishers appointed a censor to control publications.

Educators have taken an interest in comic books as a medium for teaching reading skills and even for teaching subjects in the school curriculum. Such comic books as *True Comics* and *Picture Stories from American History* or *Picture Stories from Mythology* present subjects in appealing cartoon form. *Classic Comics*, one of the most successful of such ventures, presents summaries of the plots of great works of literature in the form of comic books.

COMMEDIA DELL'ARTE, an Italian form of theatrical entertainment that flourished from the 16th through the 18th century. Its chief characteristic was improvisation: The actors were furnished only with a rough outline of a plot, called a scenario, which they acted out according to their own inclinations. This freedom to improvise required great mental agility on the part of the actors, with the result that the *commedia dell'arte* was a most vigorous, lively, thoroughly entertaining style of theater.

Commedia dell'arte was performed by groups of traveling players who wandered all through Italy and, eventually, into other countries as well. Each actor in the company devoted his entire career to a particular role; these stock characters represented definite personality types whose chief characteristics were known to every member of the audience. The most famous was Arlecchino (Harlequin), a servant who was alternately clever and foolish. Others included the Capitano, a braggart soldier; the Dottore, a sort of early version of the absent-minded professor; Pantalone, a constantly deceived old man; Colombina, a clever maid; and Pulcinella (Punch) and Brighella, two vicious and dishonest characters.

While *commedia dell'arte* placed its greatest emphasis on improvised dialogue, it did not depend on that alone for its liveliness. Pantomime, also improvised, held an important place, as did singing and dancing. Performances took place on wooden platforms erected in streets or public squares. Usually the only scenery was a cloth backdrop, representing a street. The costumes, often elaborate, were standardized so that each of the stock characters could be easily recognized.

Many elements of the *commedia dell'arte* passed into other forms of theater. Its influence is particularly evident in the comedies of Molière and in 18th-century Italian comic opera (*opera buffa*). Elements of the *commedia dell'arte* survive in such events as Punch-and-Judy shows, harlequinades, and pantomimes.

These drawings represent (left to right) Arlecchino (Harlequin), Corneto, and Pantalone (Pantaloon), three of the dozen or so stock characters in the *commedia dell'arte*. Since the plots and even the mannerisms of the characters were known by the audience in advance, the success of the production depended on the actors' skill in improvisation.

Columbia Univ. Lib.

COMMERCE. See TRADE AND COMMERCE.

COMMERCE, UNITED STATES DEPARTMENT OF, an executive department of the U.S. government, created in 1903 as the Department of Commerce and Labor. In 1913 the two groups of functions were separated by the act establishing the independent Department of Labor. The purpose of the department is to foster, promote, and develop both domestic and foreign commerce, industry, and transportation.

The department is headed by a secretary, an under secretary, an under secretary for transportation, and three assistant secretaries. Among the department bureaus are the Bureau of the Census; the Coast and Geodetic Survey, charged with the duty of surveying and charting the coasts of the United States, the compilation of aeronautical charts, and other duties; the National Bureau of Standards; the Patent Office; the Weather Bureau, which is responsible for meteorological observations and for weather forecasts; the Bureau of Public Roads; the Bureau of Foreign Commerce; the Business and Defense Services Administration; the Office of Business Economics; and the St. Lawrence Seaway Development Corporation.

The U.S. Department of Commerce occupies this building in Washington, D.C. Models and facsimiles of a number of famous U.S. inventions are on display here.

COMMERCIAL, a paid advertising announcement on a radio or television program. Broadcasting stations in the United States are operated for profit, and the initial costs are paid by private businesses seeking to sell goods or services.

Commercial advertising began around 1920. Various companies offered to supply program material for radio in return for the chance to advertise. Weekly programs of drama and entertainment became an inducement for the public to buy receiving sets, and manufacturers became the financial backers of the majority of stations.

Advertising agencies handle the construction and placement of advertisements. They arrange for television and radio commercials to be announced on a network or spot basis, that is, on several connected stations simultaneously, or at different times on a number of individual stations not connected. Costs are calculated according to the time of day, the number of announcements per day, the length of the program, and the estimated number of listeners. For example, the most expensive advertising time comes on weekday evenings and late Sunday afternoon. Sometimes two or more companies may sponsor the same program on a cooperative basis. Commercials are submitted to their sponsors for final approval. They are also regulated by the Federal Communications Commission.

Live commercials on both radio and television are the most direct and least expensive types of delivery but also the most risky. Electrical transcriptions on radio and films on television are safer and more suitable for the widespread advertising of national products.

Slogans advertising brand names and advertisements in the form of dialogues or dramas were among the earliest radio commercials. In the early 1930's they became more informal and conversational and were often woven into the program of entertainment itself. In 1939, when a song was written advertising Pepsi Cola, jingles and singing commercials flooded the market. Today, this type of commercial makes use of the country's most popular songs and vocalists.

Now television offers more scope for the commercial than radio. The animated cartoon, for example, has been particularly successful.

L. B. Prince

COMMERCIAL REVOLUTION, THE, a slow but continuous change in the pattern of the European economy from the 14th to the end of the 17th century. Although it contained many trends, it was made most evident by the increase of trade and the rise of a capitalistic merchant class.

The spread of double-entry bookkeeping, which was used by progressive Venetian businessmen by the 12th century, was vital to the commercial revolution. Impetus also came from political unification and from exploration and invention. These changes stimulated, and were in turn stimulated by, the commercial revolution.

In the early Middle Ages there was virtually no trade. Under the feudal system each manor was almost entirely self-sufficient. Later the towns began to grow, but their commerce was limited to individual craftsmen, organized into guilds, making goods to order for use in

Treasure mined in Spain's New World colonies was carried back to the mother country aboard such galleons as the one shown.

the immediate neighborhood of the town. Trade between towns and countries was limited to the very few goods that could not be produced locally. Money was not particularly important, most transactions being simply barter. Under such a system no one could accumulate any great wealth, but none suffered to any great extent from poverty.

The commercial revolution was brought about by the increasing realization that many products could be produced more cheaply if they were produced in quantity in one place. In order to establish the sort of large business enterprise that could accomplish this, raw materials and capital goods were necessary, and these were far too expensive for the ordinary medieval craftsman. Consequently a new merchant class arose, consisting of men who were able to finance large projects. These capitalistic merchants also supervised the distribution of the goods, from which they reaped large profits. Eventually they came to control large areas of the European economy, and many attained great wealth. The very nature of their business enterprises demanded that their products be sold over a wide area, and trade consequently increased. This weakened and eventually destroyed the guilds, whose members were generally undersold until forced out of business. This forced them to become employees of the merchants; they were dependent on the merchants for their livelihood and were generally less well off than they had been before.

As trade between cities increased, the importance of money as a means of exchange also increased. The tremendous influx of American gold and silver into Spain in the late 15th century provided a new incentive to the commercial revolution. So, too, did the new trade routes to Asia and the Americas opened by the Portuguese and Spanish in the 14th and 15th centuries.

Eventually the commercial revolution brought about regulation of trade by the various European governments. The economic theory behind these regulations was called mercantilism. (See MERCANTILISM.) The changes wrought by the commercial revolution continued in effect until replaced by the even greater changes of the Industrial Revolution, which began during the 18th century. See INDUSTRIAL REVOLUTION.

COMMISSION FOR TECHNICAL COOPERATION SOUTH OF THE SAHARA IN AFRICA (CCTA), a development plan for African countries. Such a plan was advocated by Prime Minister Kwame Nkrumah of Ghana at a Commonwealth Prime Ministers' Conference in June, 1957. A meeting was held in London in July to discuss the feasibility of Nkrumah's suggestion. The plan was to be designed to associate dependent or independent African countries with European and American nations providing technical aid.

Discussions were held later in 1957 in London. The mutual assistance program was formally inaugurated in Accra, Ghana, in February, 1958. The eight members were Great Britain, Belgium, France, Portugal, the Union of South Africa, the Federation of Rhodesia and Nyasaland, Ghana, and Liberia. The commission planned to draw up bilateral treaties between nations receiving aid and nations giving aid and to furnish advisers, experts, and equipment to African countries.

COMMITTEE MEETING. A committee is a group of people selected from a larger group, called the parent group, for a special purpose. The purpose of a committee may range from setting up a constitution for a new club to preparing a program for a special event. The committee meets as often as its members think necessary or as often as the organization's bylaws require. Most of the time the meetings are held regularly

The work of a committee varies with the nature of the parent group. A large group may rely on its committees to make decisions. A smaller group may rely on the committee to expedite the decisions of the parent group.

A committee should be composed of members who are familiar with the task at hand. For example, a committee to set up a constitution should have some members familiar with law.

The recommendations of a committee should have the approval of the majority of the members. A minority report may be made by the members who do not agree with the recommendation.

The members of a committee should be representative of the total membership of the parent group. In this way all segments of the parent group will remain interested in the work of the committee.

The chairman of a committee may be appointed (usually by the group's president) or elected by the parent group. The committee members are then appointed by the president or selected by the committee chairman.

The committee chairman has the responsibility for getting the work done that the parent group has assigned to the committee. But at the same time he should be aware of the wishes of all the committee members. He should let everybody speak up. In this way everyone will work with the group rather than as isolated individuals.

When a committee meets, the problems to be discussed should be clearly outlined. Each person should understand what the problem is. Each person should also find out as much as he can about the problem —before meetings when possible. Committee members should suggest solutions to the problem or problems and then should discuss the solutions. The committee should try to determine how much work each possible solution would require from members of the committee and also from members of the parent group. When a decision is reached and a program laid out, definite tasks should be assigned to each committee member.

Some committees appoint one member to keep a record of what goes on at meetings. This record then becomes the basis of the committee chairman's report to the parent group.

Committee meetings should be held in a comfortable place. Each person should be supplied with pencil and paper, so that he may jot down thoughts that occur to him during committee meetings. A blackboard in the room is helpful in case a visual record needs to be made of important points. Good communication among all members of a committee and between the committee and the parent group helps keep an organization running smoothly and efficiently.

COMMITTEE OF CORRESPONDENCE, a type of political committee organized and appointed by colonial assemblies in America to mobilize action and opinion against British infringements of colonial rights. The first committee was appointed by a Boston town meeting led by Samuel Adams on Nov. 2, 1772. The committee was to keep in communication with other towns in the colony, send information, and state their case. Between November, 1772, and January, 1773, many more such committees were organized under Samuel Adams' leadership in New England towns. The system rapidly spread, and by 1774 all the colonies except Pennsylvania and North Carolina had established similar organizations. The committees were highly successful in marshaling public opinion against the crown policies, as well as in dictating colonial business dealings with Great Britain and organizing resistance among the colonists.

COMMUNICATION, the process of exchanging ideas, attitudes, and beliefs. Although communication is most often thought of as communication by language, many kinds of communication do not involve language, and many are not even intentional. Much of man's inventive talent has been devoted to developing machinery to facilitate communication. Such machinery has given rise to mass communication, a phenomenon of great importance to the modern world.

Communications may be received by any of the senses or any combination of them. For example, perfume is a means of communication by smell; tapping someone on the back is communication by touch. What we most often think of as communication is verbal communication, which involves speech and other forms of language, such as writing and Morse code. (See LANGUAGE; MORSE CODE; SEMANTICS.) Verbal communication is the most explicit kind of communication and the vehicle for man's literature and most of his history. However, one should not assume that all communication is verbal; much of the important communication in a society is nonverbal.

There are three principal means of nonverbal communication—signs, actions, and objects. Signs, in this sense, are gestures explicitly intended to communicate. They may range from the single gesture of the hitchhiker to complete sign languages, such as the language of the deaf. (See DEAF SPEECH; GESTURE; SIGN LANGUAGE.) Actions include all movements not exclusively intended as signs. For example, the act of eating, though not primarily intended as communication, may communicate much about the eater's background and temperament to a critical observer.

Communication by objects includes both intentional and unintentional display of materials. A person's dress, for example, may communicate information about the person; the arrangement of a room may tell a guest something about how he is expected to act—whether he should ask permission before sitting, for instance. Communication by objects may be relatively permanent, unlike communication by signs or actions. Thus an Egyptian tomb or the writings of an 18th-century scholar, faithfully preserved, may continue to communicate for centuries.

Many animals besides man communicate, for the most part using gestures and inarticulate cries. Warning calls are common among animals. Thus, the Virginia deer, when running from danger, raises its white tail as a signal to its companions; the beaver, sensing danger, slaps its tail on the water as a warning signal. Mating calls are also common among birds and mammals. Among the more complex forms of animal communication are the dances bees use to communicate the location of nectar and pollen.

It has long been believed that no animal besides man possesses articulate speech. However, research with the bottle-nosed dolphin, or porpoise, shows that this intelligent mammal can converse by means of sharp, high-pitched whistles.

The importance of communication to human society is obvious once that society is seen as not a static sum of persons and institutions but an intricate, dynamic system of common understandings. These understandings result from communication. Thus the United Nations does not exist as a concrete object but only as an abstraction from thousands of acts of communication, all having common points of reference.

Communication serves two basic functions in making society possible. It allows for both the development of common ideals and the preservation of those ideals from generation to generation. In short, communication gives both unity and continuity to groups and thus makes society and culture possible.

Since earliest times man has devised methods for communicating farther and faster. Systems using smoke by day and fire by night were employed in the ancient civilizations of China, Egypt, and Greece. News of the fall of Troy in 1184 B.C. was relayed to Greece by means of signal fires. The American Indian developed similar means of communication, the smoke signal. Primitive tribes of Africa communicated by drums, using a specialized language. A semaphore system invented by Claude Chappe was adopted by the French government in 1794. Through a series of signal towers, messages could be sent more than 150 miles in 20 minutes in clear weather. Other European countries, including Russia, adopted similar systems. See SEMAPHORE.

Early attempts at communication by electricity involved static electricity. The discovery by Hans Christian Oersted in 1819 of the relationship between electric current and magnetism made possible the

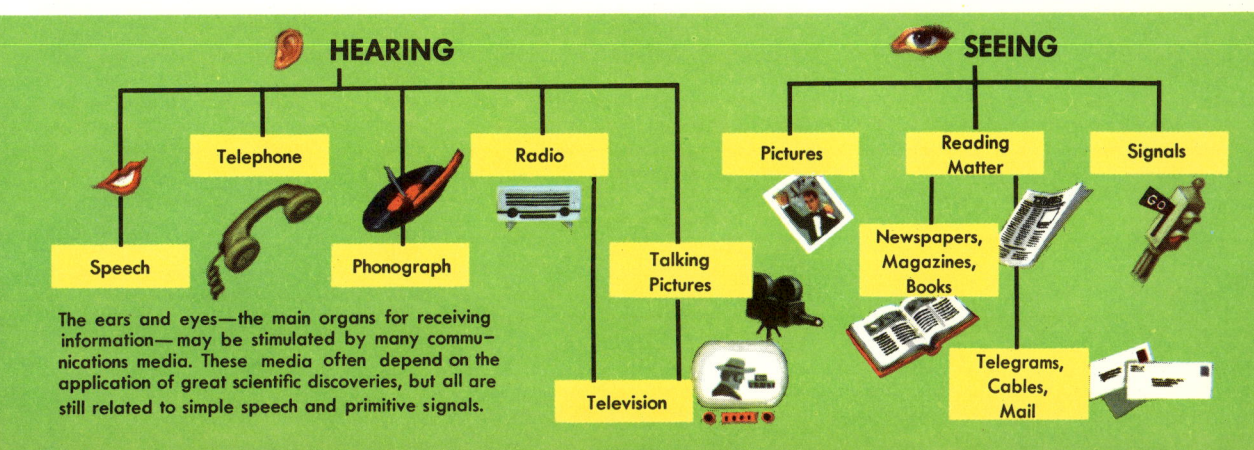

HEARING

Speech — Telephone — Phonograph — Radio — Talking Pictures — Television

SEEING

Pictures — Reading Matter (Newspapers, Magazines, Books) — Signals — Telegrams, Cables, Mail

The ears and eyes—the main organs for receiving information—may be stimulated by many communications media. These media often depend on the application of great scientific discoveries, but all are still related to simple speech and primitive signals.

Although communication is accomplished largely by verbal means, that is, by the written or spoken word, nonverbal means of communication play a significant role in everyday life. Under certain conditions objects can be substituted for verbal instructions or explanations. However, this sort of object language is effective only when objects are familiar and their intended use is known. The traffic barricade, above, when properly placed, warns the motorist or pedestrian of a detour; and the fence, right, warns the passerby to stay out.

electromagnetic telegraph. Early telegraph devices were invented by Karl Friedrich Gauss and Wilhelm Weber in Germany, Charles Wheatstone and William Cooke in England, and Samuel Morse in the United States. The first public telegraph system, using Morse's device, was established between Washington, D.C., and Baltimore, Md., in 1844. Submarine cables, beginning with one laid in the English Channel in 1850, made telegraph communication across rivers and oceans possible. The first "talking telegraph," or telephone, was patented by Alexander Graham Bell in 1876.

In 1887 Heinrich Hertz showed for the first time how an electric spark caused electromagnetic waves. In 1896 Guglielmo Marconi, an Italian, obtained a British patent for a practical wireless telegraph, using the waves discovered by Hertz. Reginald A. Fessenden succeeded in 1900 in transmitting voice by wireless. The vacuum tube, the work of John Fleming and Lee De Forest, made modern radio possible.

An experimental television program was sent by wire as early as 1927. Seventeen experimental television stations were operating in the United States by 1937. Meanwhile, a color television system was demonstrated by John Baird in England in 1928.

Invention of the transistor, announced in 1948, made possible the miniaturization of radio communication devices. The transistor is a vital part of artificial earth satellites, used for communication purposes. See entries on individual communication devices. See TRANSPORTATION.

Improved communication devices permit not only the transmission of messages farther and faster but also the transmission of one message to great numbers of people. This is mass communication.

Because of their wide and often continuous appeal the mass communication media (newspapers, magazines, radio, television, and so forth) offer unprecedented possibilities for influencing public attitudes and opinions. Whoever gains control of the mass media tends to direct all communication toward one end—capturing an audience and influencing its thought. In the United States, for example, the mass media are part of the country's business organization, and they tend to influence people not only toward buying certain products but also toward accepting the values that prevail in the business world.

The question of the control and the influence of mass media encompasses many controversial issues. The pay-TV issue—whether to finance television by viewer's subscriptions or by advertising—points up the matter of control. The influence of mass media is questioned in such issues as the possible effects on children of violence presented through television, newspapers, and so forth.

Recent times have been characterized by continual concern with communication. The mass media, encouraging and exploiting this concern, will continue to change patterns of society, from the family through the United Nations. See CYBERNETICS.

COMMUNISM is a political philosophy and a form of government based on socialism. Like socialism, communism calls for government ownership of all the means of production. In addition, the followers of communism believe in the dictatorship of the proletariat, or the control of the government by the workers. Every man is supposed to work according to the best of his ability and to receive according to his needs. Communists contend that communism will finally lead to a classless society with the disappearance of the state.

The idea of communism is very old. The Greek philosopher Plato described a kind of communist government in his book *The Republic* over 2,000 years ago. The word *communist* has also been used to describe communities of people in which all goods are owned in common. Examples are the various Christian monastic orders and the famous Brook Farm experiment in the United States.

Modern communism draws most of its ideas from the German economist Karl Marx, who lived a hundred years ago. Friedrich Engels, a German political writer and a friend of Marx's, also contributed to communist theory. Together they wrote the *Communist Manifesto*, published in 1848.

Marx's ideas found many followers, but not until after the Russian Revolution was communism established by any government. The Union of Soviet Socialist Republics was the first communist state in the world. See RUSSIAN REVOLUTION; UNION OF SOVIET SOCIALIST REPUBLICS.

The instrument of communism in the U.S.S.R. and throughout the world is the Communist party. There are communist parties in many countries. Although the constitution of the Soviet Union does not mention the Communist party, the party actually controls the government.

After World War II other communist governments arose in Europe and Asia. These included China, Czechoslovakia, East Germany, North Korea, Hungary, Poland, Rumania, and Bulgaria. A communist state different from Soviet pattern was set up in Yugoslavia. See CAPITALISM; DEMOCRACY; DICTATORSHIP; SOCIALISM.

COMMUNIST PARTY, a political organization based on the doctrines of Karl Marx and Nikolai Lenin. According to Marxist-Leninist theory, before the party gains control of a government it is the vanguard behind which the proletariat (working class) unites against the *bourgeoisie* (property-owning class). Once the party controls a government it institutes and dominates, according to theory, the so-called dictatorship of the proletariat. The classic example of this dictatorship is the government of the Soviet Union. Thus, the purpose of the Communist party is to await and assist the collapse of the capitalist system, to seize the leadership of the revolting masses, and to institute the dictatorship of the proletariat in order to attain the goal of a classless society. See CHINESE COMMUNISTS; COMMUNISM; RUSSIAN REVOLUTION.

Prior to the successful revolution led by the Bolsheviks in Russia in 1917 there was but one Communist party, which was international. In 1918 the Bolsheviks became the Russian Communist party. Thereafter, the more militant Socialist groups in Europe and the Second International (a Socialist international formed in 1889) became Communist parties on the basis of their support of the policies of the Russian Communist party. In 1919 the Third, or Communist, International (Comintern for short) was held in the Soviet Union. It was designed to start a worldwide Communist movement in opposition to the less militant Socialists. In the United States the Communist party was formed in 1919 by elements that broke away from the U. S. Socialist party. Other Communist parties were formed in most other nations. The Cominform (Communist Information Bureau), or Fourth International, was formed in Poland in 1947 by representatives of various Communist parties. Nine years later the organization was dissolved.

The Communist parties are controlled by a rigid chain of command that begins with the Communist party of the Soviet Union. Its directives descend through the national parties of other countries to the regional parties and the local parties, then to the basic units, the cells. The parties usually consist of a hard core that is loyal no matter what the policy adopted by the Communist party may be and a less militant membership that cannot be definitely relied upon in time of crisis. The Communist party is the only party in the U.S.S.R. and directs the so-called dictatorship of the proletariat. The party in France, as well as Italy, is a large organization with strong voter support in elections. The U. S. Communist party, which has never been large, was outlawed in 1954. In 1956 at the 20th Party Congress Nikita Khrushchev's denunciation of the excessive repression of Stalin's regime placed Communist parties throughout the world in the embarrassing predicament of having supported without question actions by the party that were revealed as wrong.

COMPARATIVE ANATOMY, the comparative study of the anatomy of all animals and of man. Comparative anatomy may be regarded as a division of both biology and anatomy. In comparative anatomy the external form, the appendages, and the internal organs and organ systems of various animals and of man are compared in order to discover their similarities and differences. The principal method of comparative anatomy is painstaking laboratory dissection. Dissection exposes both large and minute parts of the organs of various animals so that they can be directly compared.

An important project in comparative anatomy is the comparative study of the appendages, musculature, skeleton, circulatory system (heart, arteries, veins), respiratory

Bone structure in corresponding appendages of three vertebrates is compared below.

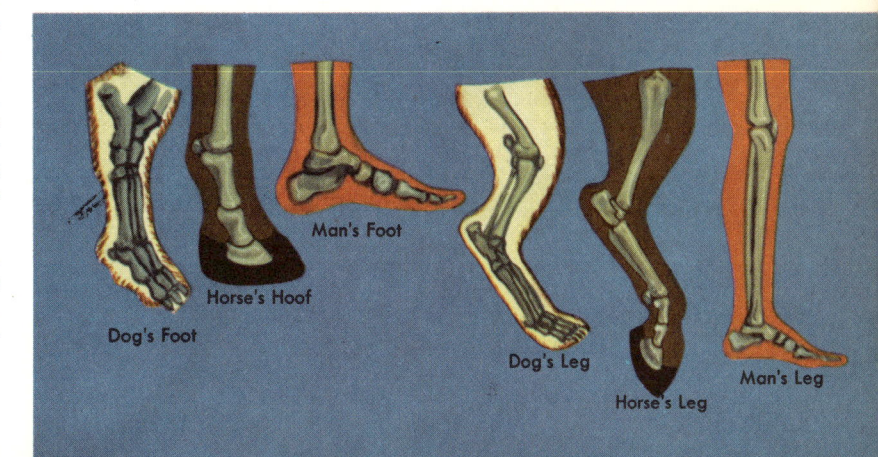

Dog's Foot — Horse's Hoof — Man's Foot — Dog's Leg — Horse's Leg — Man's Leg

system (lungs or gills), nerves, and brain of representative species of each of the seven mammalian classes. The cyclostome to be studied might be a lamprey; the elasmobranch, a dogfish shark; the piscean fish, or true fish, a perch; the amphibian, a frog; the reptile, a lizard; the bird, a pigeon; the mammal, a cat or a human being. By means of this project comparative anatomists have discovered that the organs and organ systems of all mammalian classes are fundamentally similar in structure, despite their apparent diversity. For example, they have discovered that the forelimbs of amphibians, reptiles, and mammals, the wings of birds and bats, the flipper of the whale, and the arm of man have skeletons that are fundamentally similar, even though these appendages are apparently so different in form and function.

The anatomical similarities and differences discovered by comparative anatomists enable them to classify all species of animals in their proper phylum, class, and genus, and to ascertain the evolutionary changes that have occurred in the organs and organ systems of related animals.

COMPASS AND COMPASS DIRECTIONS, means by which people are able to find their destination without the use of landmarks, stars, or the sun. The magnetic compass is the simplest type of the instrument. It consists of a magnetized needle

The compass rose below is designed for use in a specific region—that where magnetic north, the direction of the north magnetic pole, is 11° 45′ west of true north.

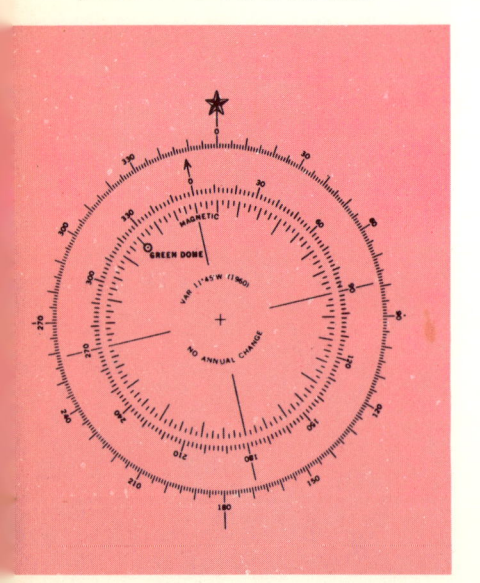

placed on top of a small steel point, or pivot, in the middle of a round card on which are marked the points of the compass (north, east, south, and west). One end of the needle always points toward the North Magnetic Pole of the earth.

The magnetic compass was first used by the Chinese and was carried to Europe in the 12th century by the Arabs. The compass played an important part in the great voyages of discovery by European mariners in the 15th, 16th, and 17th centuries. When steel ships were made, it was found that the metal of the ship became magnetized and caused the compass to be inaccurate. In 1911 a new kind of compass was invented. It is called a gyro compass and is now used on all large ocean liners. It is not disturbed by the large amount of steel in modern ships.

COMPOSER, an author who orders or arranges (literally, puts together) artistic elements to form a whole, but especially a writer of music.

At the outset, the composer is concerned with putting together the simplest musical elements, that is, notes, in a line that forms a melody. He may then write other melodic lines to be played or sung with the first one, a combination resulting in counterpoint. When considered vertically or simultaneously, notes in these lines constitute harmony.

Next the composer puts together melodies and long sections into movements of various kinds. In combination these movements form a musical structure, such as a fugue, sonata, or symphony. The composer must also choose the different kinds of instruments to be played or, if his composition is vocal, the parts to be sung.

Composers do not necessarily write their musical pieces in the order just outlined, but they must consider these musical elements at some point in their work.

COMPOUND (chemistry). See MIXTURE AND COMPOUND.

COMPROMISE OF 1850, a term applied to five laws passed by Congress in September, 1850, in an effort to find a satisfactory solution to the slavery question.

The compromise, between Northern senators who wished to prevent the extension of slavery and Southern senators who feared that an increase in the number of free states threatened the existence of slavery, dealt principally with the future of slavery in territories acquired after the Mexican War. The introduction by Senator Henry Clay of eight resolutions containing the substance of the compromise brought about the greatest debate in congressional history. The compromise was attacked by extremists of both sides, but it was supported by moderates who believed that preservation of the Union without war was of greater importance than unyielding adherence to principles on slavery.

A basic principle of the Compromise of 1850 was that of popular sovereignty or "squatter sovereignty," which left the new territories free to decide for or against slavery at the time of their admission to statehood. Two bills organizing the territories of New Mexico and Utah on this basis were passed. The act organizing New Mexico also provided for payment of $10,000,000 by the United States to Texas, a slave state, in return for abandonment by Texas of claims to part of the New Mexico territory. The other three acts of the compromise were: admission of California as a free state; an act providing for abolition of the slave trade, but not of slavery, in the District of Columbia; and a stringent and more enforceable law for the capture of runaway slaves, the Fugitive Slave Act of 1850.

COMPTON, ARTHUR H. (1892-), American physicist, was born in Wooster, Ohio. He was educated at the College of Wooster and Princeton University. He was professor of physics at the University of Chicago from 1923, being head of the physics department and dean of the physical sciences division from 1940 and director of the metallurgical laboratory from 1942. His discovery that the wave lengths of X-rays change when they are scattered is called the Compton effect and won for him in 1927 the Nobel prize in physics (jointly with Charles T. R. Wilson) and the Rumford Medal. He discovered the total reflection of X-rays and, with others, the complete polarization of X-rays and X-ray spectra from ruled gratings. He directed the world cosmic-ray survey (1931-1934) and discovered the electrical composition of these rays. In April, 1945, he was appointed chancellor of Washington University, St. Louis, Mo. His works include *The Freedom of Man* (1935) and *Human Meaning of Science* (1940). He aided in perfecting the atomic bomb. He resigned from Washington University in 1953 to devote himself to research.

BASE OF 10	100's	10's	Units
	1	0	0
		5	0
			4
Total	1	5	4

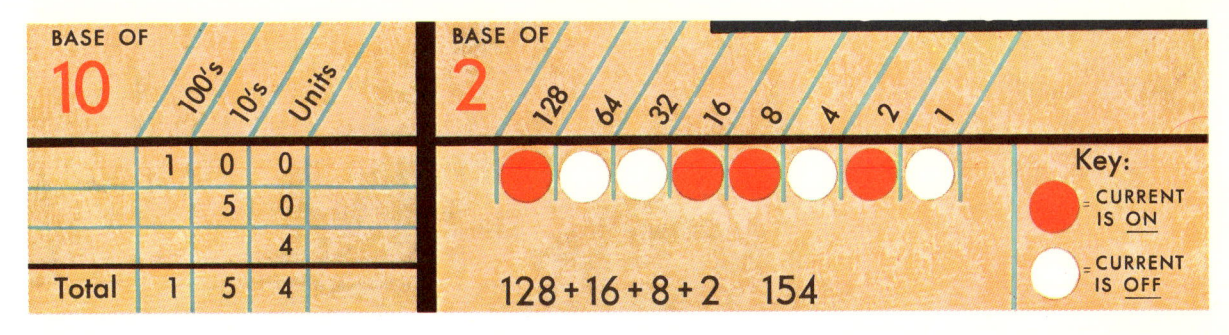

BASE OF 2 — 128, 64, 32, 16, 8, 4, 2, 1

128 + 16 + 8 + 2 = 154

Key:
● = CURRENT IS ON
○ = CURRENT IS OFF

Digital computers work with binary numbers—numbers to the base of 2—instead of decimal numbers, which we ordinarily use. Just as the decimal number 154 is the sum of one 100, five 10's, and four units (left), so the equivalent binary number (right) is the sum of one 128, no 64's, no 32's, one 16, one 8, one 2, and no 1's, or units. This number is handled by the computer as a pattern of ons and offs in an electrical current.

Burroughs Corporation Electrodata

In this computer installation, results are typed out on the electric typewriter at right.

COMPUTER, a machine that solves complex and logical mathematical problems involving many separate operations. The calculations may include addition, subtraction, multiplication, division, integration, and differentiation. (See ARITHMETIC; CALCULUS.) Computers are used to solve problems that would be tedious and time consuming to analyze by ordinary mathematical methods. Computers are also used to solve problems that have no known solution by ordinary methods.

Computers of two types are used —the analog computer and the digital computer. The analog computer uses a changing amount of gear or shaft rotation or a changing amount of electrical voltage to represent a series of numbers. The digital computer uses digits (0, 1, 2, 3 . . .) to represent a quantity. The digits, in turn, are represented by physical quantities in the machine such as the position of an electrical switch or the direction of a magnetic field. Digital computers are more exact than analog computers and can solve more types of problems. Digital computers, however, cost more to build and to operate than analog computers.

The first analog computers were mechanical computers. Electronic analog computers, which have been developed since World War II, are now used.

Electronic analog computers consist of a series of electrical circuits containing amplifiers, resistors, condensers, and various arrangements of wiring. Computations such as multiplying by a constant factor and adding are accomplished by feeding the initial voltage, representing a quantity, through resistors and amplifiers. The resulting voltage represents the answer. Integrating and differentiating are done by feeding the initial voltage through amplifiers, condensers, and resistors. Because the answer found by an analog computer is a changing quantity, the answer is best recorded on a graph. Particular values can be read from the graph.

Analog computers are particularly useful in solving differential equations. Analog computers are also used as automatic controlling devices in chemical manufacturing processes, in flight and navigation control, and in missile and rocket firing controls.

The first digital computer was the Harvard Mark I, an electromechanical digital computer that began operation in 1944. The digital computers now built are electronic.

Digital computers are composed of five main parts: the input unit, the storage unit, the arithmetic unit, the sequence-control unit, and the output unit.

The input unit accepts the numbers used to state the problem and the program instructions for solving the problem. The numerical inputs are usually coded in binary notation, a system that employs a string of only two symbols—0 and 1—to represent all numbers. The coded material is fed into the computer on punched paper tape, punched cards, or magnetic tape. The operating instructions include arithmetic commands, such as "add" and "divide," and logical commands, such as "recognize which is the smaller of two numbers."

The storage, or memory, unit of the computer stores the numbers used to state the problem, the intermediate results of computation, and the final results. The storage unit also "remembers" the operating instructions. A selection system is built into the storage unit so that any number put into the unit can be quickly located when it is needed. Numbers can be copied from the unit or inserted in the unit while the problem is being solved.

The arithmetic unit performs the actual computations. The computations are limited to addition, subtraction, multiplication, division, reference to tables of functions, and selective choice. In a selective choice the machine chooses one of several possible procedures. The procedure chosen may depend on whether a number computed preceding the choice is positive or negative. Mathematical problems must be stated so that they can be solved by the computations the machine can perform. Each sequence of computations may be repeated many times in solving the problem.

The sequence-control unit accepts the operating instructions and causes the various units of the computer to perform their operations in the order needed to solve the problem.

The output unit records the computed results, which are usually stated in binary notation. These computed results may be recorded in typewritten form, on punch cards, on an oscilloscope, or on magnetic tape.

Digital computers are useful in solving ordinary and partial differential equations (analog computers cannot solve partial differential equations), in solving simultaneous algebraic equations, and in computing mathematical functions. Digital computers are used to obtain numerical solutions to scientific problems. Digital computers are used by factories, insurance companies, chains of department stores, aircraft companies, and government agencies to analyze complicated data and to classify and record large quantities of data. Other nonmathematical applications include language translation and the storage and retrieval of data.

COMSTOCK LODE, a large and extremely rich vein of gold and silver in the western part of Nevada, on the east slope of the Virginia Mountains, discovered in 1859. From its discovery until 1879, when its output began to decline, more than 500 million dollars' worth of gold and silver was mined. The lode greatly affected the development of San Francisco, resulting in the establishment of the San Francisco Stock Exchange and of many banks and other businesses.

CONCENTRATION CAMP, in international law, a camp designed to hold prisoners of war or political prisoners. Such camps first made their appearance during the Boer War. Rules as to how prisoners were to be treated in these camps were adopted at the Hague conferences of 1899 and 1907. These rules provided that prisoners must receive food and clothing comparable to a nation's own soldiers and that prisoners must not be confined except when necessary. Some effort was made in World War I to maintain the Hague rules. At the Geneva Convention of 1929 more rules were added to prevent the abuses that had occurred during war. These rules were ignored by the Axis powers in World War II.

With the rise of the Nazis to power in Germany in 1933, a totalitarian government was inaugurated. The concentration camp became a major weapon in the arsenal of a government that sought to dominate its subjects totally. The inmates in these camps were in effect prisoners of war in the battle of the Nazi state against individuals.

Presumably, such camps were to be used to obtain forced labor. The labor, however, was extremely inefficient, for the inmates were dying. Neither the Nazi camps nor those in the Soviet Union under Joseph Stalin (accounts of which were given by Polish survivors in *The Dark Side of the Moon*) paid their way in labor. In Germany the concentration camps were also used to train the new Nazi elite, who were to treat men as things. Indeed, everything in the camps was bent on eradicating the humanity in men. Inmates were carried to the camps in cattle cars. Their heads were shaven, and the clothes were grotesquely fashioned. Inside the camps men were categorized—the Jews were marked for early extermination, the Soviets and Poles were to be eventually exterminated, the French were a doubtful category, and Scandinavians as a group were not marked for extermination, no matter how much they hated nazism. The fate of the inmates was a carefully guarded secret. In effect, they had disappeared from the face of the globe.

The horrors of concentration camps—Auschwitz, Buchenwald, Dachau—have been told by such survivors as the Frenchman David Rousset (*The Other Kingdom*). The point in remembering these atrocities is to prevent their recurrence. There is a danger that they can recur in any modern nation in which the ideal of the worth of the human individual is forgotten.

CONCERTO is a musical composition in sonata form for solo instrument with instrumental or orchestral accompaniment. The piano and violin are the two most frequently used solo instruments.

Roughly speaking, the concerto was composed in two different styles: namely the *concerto grosso* and the classical concerto. The *concerto grosso* as written by Corelli, Vivaldi, and Bach in the late 17th and early 18th centuries consisted of three or more movements. A small group of solo instruments, usually strings, played in alternation with a large group of orchestral strings. Bach's six Brandenburg Concertos are the most famous of this type.

The classical concerto, which was perfected by Mozart, began with a strong first movement, proceeded to a lyrical slow movement, and ended with a bright rapid finale. In this later style of the concerto, the orchestra accompanied the solo instrument or played without it. The romantic composers, however, made solo parts more prominent. In the modern concerto the parts of solo instrument and orchestra are again more closely knit.

CONCORD, capital of New Hampshire, is located on the Merrimack River in the southern part of the state. The city, which had a population in 1960 of 28,991, is a printing and financial center. Concord is also a rail center for an agricultural area. It has electronics, machinery, and handicraft industries. Granite quarries are in the vicinity.

Concord contains some interesting buildings. The Capitol, the state historical society and museum, which is housed in the former residence of Franklin Pierce, and the old Rolfe-Rumford home, built in 1764, are noteworthy. Nearby is the childhood home of Mary Baker Eddy, the founder of the Church of Christ, Scientist. Concord was settled in 1725 and became the state capital in 1808.

CONCRETE as a construction material is suited for many uses. It is durable, sanitary, and fire resistant. The upkeep cost of concrete is low, and it can easily be made attractive in appearance. Because it is plastic when first mixed, it lends itself well to the construction of many objects. On the other hand, perhaps no other material depends so much for its success upon the user. Good materials, accurate proportioning, and careful control in all operations are essential.

A concrete beam bends slightly under a load. The beam will soon break in two unless it is reinforced by steel bars (below).

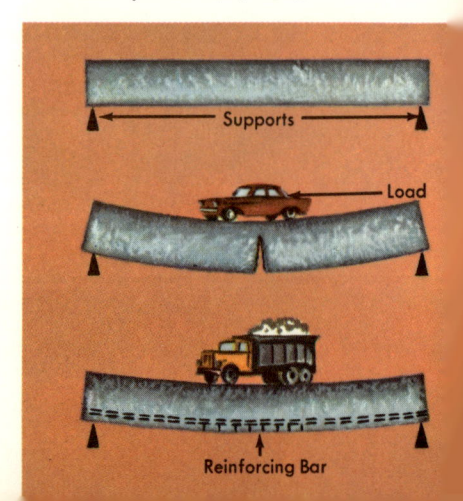

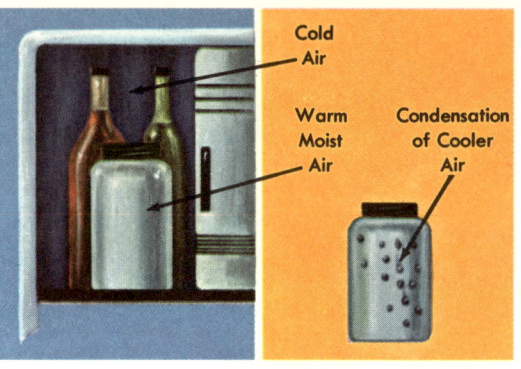

The above experiment illustrates the condensation of water vapor. First, breathe into a warm, dry mason jar. Next, seal it, and place it in the refrigerator near the cooling unit. When the jar is removed (right), droplets of water will have formed in it.

Concrete is a mixture in which a paste of portland cement and water binds fine and coarse materials, known as aggregates, into a rocklike mass as the paste hardens through the chemical action of the cement and water. It is composed of an active material (cement) and inert materials (aggregates). It might also be termed a mass of inert materials held in place by a binder. The binder constitutes the more expensive ingredient. The inert materials are relatively inexpensive. Good concrete has all surfaces of the aggregate thoroughly coated with the paste and all voids filled. The quality of concrete depends upon the quality of materials, the proportioning, and the workmanship. The economy depends upon the manner in which these are combined to secure a dense, compact mass with a minimum of binder.

Concrete has many uses, as in foundations, walls, bridges, dams, buildings, and highways. When necessary a smooth surface can be obtained by applying a second layer of concrete or asphalt on top of the first layer. Since concrete is strong in compression and weak in tension, some type of reinforcement is generally used to give it strength in tension. Generally, within the normal limits for workable mix, the strength of the hardened concrete will increase with a decrease in mixing water, presuming that the amount of cement is being held constant.

Concrete, at the time of mixing, can be made to conform to any desired shape by the use of forms. Forms are the molds or receptacles in which the concrete is placed so that it will have the desired shape when hardened. Concrete lends itself to a variety of finishes and treatments. It can be made in a wide choice of colors, and it can be given special surface treatments for use as architectural or decorative concrete.

CONDENSATION is a general term indicating a change to a denser, more compact form. Condensation usually refers to the change of a gas or a vapor to a liquid or solid. Condensation may also refer to the accumulation of electric charges, the increase in density of a sound wave, or the combination of molecules to form larger molecules.

The condensation of a gas or a vapor to a liquid or solid is the reverse of the process of evaporation. (See EVAPORATION.) Evaporation requires a decrease in pressure or a rise in temperature. Condensation requires a fall in temperature or an increase in pressure. When a liquid evaporates, it absorbs heat. The amount of heat the liquid absorbs per unit of mass is called the heat of vaporization. When a vapor or a gas condenses, it releases heat, and the heat released per unit of mass is called the heat of condensation. For any substance the heat of condensation equals the heat of vaporization. When 1 gram of steam (water vapor) condenses at 100° C., it releases 540 calories of heat and changes to one gram of water at 100° C.

Condensation plays a very important role in the earth's weather. See ATMOSPHERIC CONDENSATION; PRECIPITATION.

CONDENSATION TRAIL, a small stream of clouds left behind airplanes flying at high altitudes or in low temperatures. The cause of these clouds is not completely known, but there are two theories that help explain how condensation trails might be formed.

Sometimes the clouds are formed behind the wingtips of the plane. The airplane, cleaving through the air, leaves a low-pressure area behind it. Air rises to refill this area when the plane has passed. The rising air cools, and its water vapor may condense and form little clouds.

In such a circumstance the clouds are formed in the same way as when they form in the air rising over a mountain.

More often the clouds will develop behind the engine exhaust In this case the water vapor in the air condenses because of the addition of condensation particles in the form of exhaust fumes. The air, of course, must already be at a high humidity, so that its water vapor is just about ready to condense anyway. The additional condensation particles are all that is needed to start the process of cloud formation.

CONDITIONED REFLEX. A reflex is a simple, involuntary muscular contraction or a glandular secretion that occurs in response to a stimulus. An example of a muscular reflex is the blinking of the eyes when a hand is suddenly and quickly thrust near them. The stimulus for the blinking is the approaching hand. An example of a glandular reflex is the secretion of saliva when food, which is the stimulus, is seen, smelled, or tasted. Both the blinking and the salivation occur automatically and unconsciously. Each is the natural, or unconditioned, reflex to its respective stimulus.

Each of these reflexes can sometimes be made to occur to an alien stimulus. A dog can be made to salivate at the sound of a bell if on several previous occasions he heard the bell ring about five seconds before food was presented to him. During the first few trials the dog does not salivate at only the sound of the bell, but after about ten trials, he does salivate when the bell is rung, even if the food is not presented afterward. The dog salivates when the bell is rung because he has learned to associate its ringing with the food. The ringing of the bell is termed the conditioned stimulus; salivation at the sound of the bell alone is termed the conditioned reflex.

The conditioning of a dog's salivary reflex to the ringing of a bell was first accomplished by the Russian physiologist Ivan Petrovich Pavlov. In a series of famous experiments conducted early in the 20th century, Pavlov also conditioned the dog's salivary reflex to such stimuli as a flashing light, a pinprick, and a current of air. That the human salivary reflex likewise can be conditioned is demonstrated by the fact that the mere mention of appetizing food will often cause our saliva to flow when we are hungry. This type of conditioned

CONDUCTION

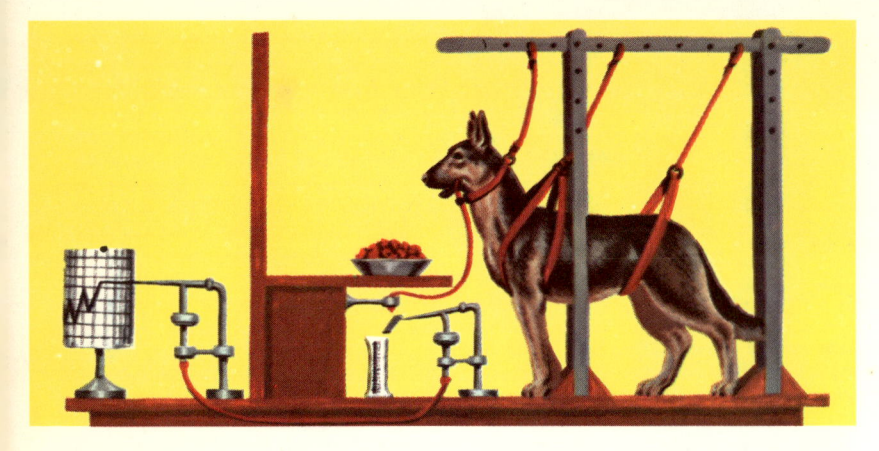

Pavlov's experiments on conditioning the salivary reflex of the dog involved an apparatus similar to that shown here. The rate of saliva flow was continuously recorded on a drum.

reflex results after a number of trials, even though we may not be aware of its development.

Many other human and animal reflexes can be conditioned. If a bell is rung each time a pencil is thrust toward a man's eyes, causing them to blink, they will soon blink when he hears the bell ring by itself. A hungry baby will stop crying when allowed to drink milk from a nursing bottle. In an experiment a buzzer was sounded on several occasions while crying babies were quieted by being allowed to drink from nursing bottles. After several trials the hungry babies ceased crying when the buzzer was sounded, even though they were not given any milk. A man will run from the path of an oncoming car because he has been taught to withdraw his body from a pain-inflicting object.

Some psychologists have theorized that many of man's habitual reactions to his experiences are based upon conditioned reflexes. Conditioned reflexes may be the basis of many of his fears, aversions, preferences, and prejudices (racial and otherwise). Psychologists have also theorized that much of man's everyday behavior consists of diverse conditioned reflexes organized into complex patterns. See REFLEX.

CONDUCTION, CONVECTION, RADIATION. Conduction, convection, and radiation are methods of transferring heat. Heat is a form of energy. (See HEAT.) Some other forms of energy are electromagnetic waves, such as light, and kinetic energy (the energy of motion). Energy can change from one form to another. Energy can change from heat to waves or to motion and from waves or motion to heat. Convection and conduction involve the change of some of the heat in a body to kinetic energy. A radiating body loses heat in the form of waves.

Convection is the transfer of heat from a place of higher temperature to a place of lower temperature by the movement of the heated substance. If a pot containing water is placed over a fire and heated gently, the water at the bottom of the pot is heated more than the water at the top of the pot. The kinetic energy of the molecules of the heated water is increased. When the energy of the molecules is increased, the molecules move faster, and the heated water becomes less dense, or lighter. Cold, heavy water from the top of the pot sinks and displaces the lighter, heated water at the bottom of the pot. When the heated water is forced to the top of the pot, the heated water cools and becomes heavy and sinks. A system of circulation is established that is called a convection current. Heat is transferred from the bottom to the top of the pot because the water itself moves from one part of the pot to another.

Conduction is the transfer of heat within a substance from an area of higher temperature to an area of lower temperature without any progressive motion of the parts of the substance. If one end of a metal rod is held in a fire, heat travels along the rod until all the parts of the rod are hot. The molecules at the end of the rod that is held in the fire begin to vibrate rapidly because some of the heat energy is transformed to kinetic energy. The vibrating molecules knock against adjacent molecules and cause them to vibrate.

Convection currents, indicated by the arrows, are set up in a beaker of water when it is heated at one side. Heat is transferred by the upward current into the air above.

After a while all the molecules in the rod are vibrating rapidly. Some of the energy transferred by the vibrations of the molecules is changed back into heat energy, and the whole rod becomes hot.

All substances do not conduct heat with the same efficiency. Most metals are good heat conductors. Liquids are poor conductors of heat. The exact measure of the heat conductivity of a substance is called its coefficient of thermal conductivity. The coefficient of thermal conductivity of a substance is defined as the quantity of heat that will flow

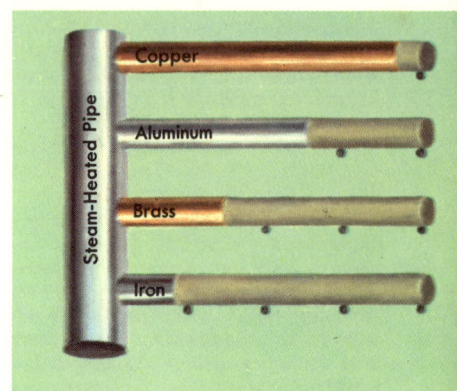

Conduction may be demonstrated and measured by use of a conductometer. The rates at which the paraffin coatings melt indicate the relative conductivity of the metal rods.

through a unit cross section of a bar of the substance in one second when the difference of temperature between the ends of the bar is 1° C. and the bar is 1 centimeter long.

Radiation is the transfer of heat by electromagnetic waves. The heat the earth receives from the sun is an example of heat transferred by radiation. Some of the intense heat of the sun is converted into electromagnetic waves. The waves travel with the speed of light and can pass through empty space. The waves can travel through a medium like

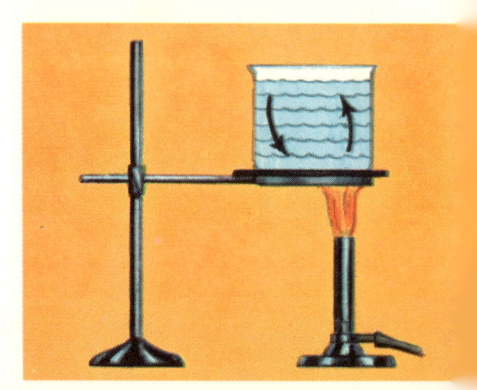

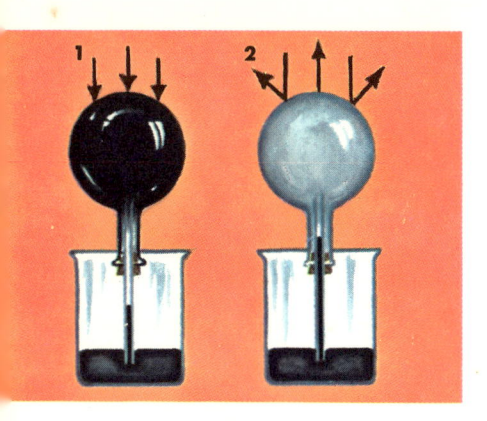

Radiation produces heat in an absorbing body. The darkened flask, 1, absorbs more radiation than the clear one, 2. Heated air expands, forcing the water column down.

air without heating it. When the waves strike a body through which they cannot pass easily, they cause the molecules of the body to vibrate more rapidly, and the body becomes heated.

All bodies, whether they are hot or cold, continuously lose heat by radiation. Hot bodies radiate more heat than cold bodies. Some substances are good radiators and good absorbers of radiation. A poor radiator is also a poor absorber of radiation. In general, rough, uneven surfaces are good radiators and absorbers. Polished surfaces are poor radiators and absorbers.

CONDUCTOR, MUSICAL, the director of a symphony orchestra, a chorus, or a combination of instrumental and choral forces. His job is one of the most difficult in musical interpretation. He must know every aspect of the music to be performed, understand the capabilities and limitations of every instrument and voice, and be an expert in dealing with people. Above all, he must be capable of coaxing his interpretation from a large group of musicians. Such demands help account for the existence of so few good conductors at any one time and for the rarity of great ones.

Present practices of conducting were first fully developed during the late 19th century. Among the most famous conductors of this period were Hans von Bülow, Charles Lamoureux, Sir Hamilton Harty, Gustav Mahler, Arthur Nikisch, Richard Strauss, Hans Richter, and Karl Muck. But the 20th century became the golden age of conducting. Germany and Austria produced such giants as Felix Weingartner, Bruno Walter, and Wilhelm Furtwängler; England, Sir Thomas Beecham; The Netherlands, Willem Mengelberg; Italy, Arturo Toscanini. The great orchestras of the United States became among the best in the world under such conductors as Serge Koussevitzky at Boston, Leopold Stokowski at Philadelphia, Pierre Monteux at San Francisco, Otto Klemperer at Los Angeles, Frederick Stock at Chicago, and Mengelberg and Toscanini at New York. Of these only Beecham and Stokowski were fully active in 1960, although Walter, Klemperer, and Monteux continued to make a limited number of appearances. Among other noteworthy conductors of the period were Erich Kleiber, Fritz Busch, Artur Rodzinski, Clemens Krauss, Ernest Ansermet, Tullio Serafin, and Hermann Scherchen. Mention must also made of Günther Ramin, Fritz Lehmann, and the great cellist Pablo Casals, whose devotion to the music of Johann Sebastian Bach produced excellent results.

After World War II a new generation of conductors, some of whom had been active earlier, became prominent. In the United States the outstanding figures were Fritz Reiner of the Chicago Symphony, Eugene Ormandy of the Philadelphia Orchestra, and Charles Munch of the Boston Symphony, as well as William Steinberg at Pittsburgh, Georg Szell at Cleveland, Paul Paray at Detroit, Antal Dorati (formerly at Minneapolis), Dimitri Mitropoulos (formerly conductor of the New York Philharmonic), and Leonard Bernstein of the New York Philharmonic. Of these only Bernstein was born and trained in the United States. Among the outstanding European conductors of this period were Herbert von Karajan, director of the Vienna State Opera, the Vienna Philharmonic Orchestra, the Berlin Philharmonic Orchestra, and the Salzburg Festival; Eduard van Beinum, conductor of the Concertgebouw Orchestra of Amsterdam, The Netherlands; and Eugen Jochum, Beinum's successor at Amsterdam. Other important European directors were Hans Rosbaud, Georg Solti, Lovro von Matacic, Rudolf Kempe, Rafael Kubelik, Igor Markevitch, Sir John Barbirolli, Sir Malcolm Sargent, and Sir Adrian Boult. Among Russian conductors those best known outside the Soviet Union were Eugene Mravinsky and Kiril Kondrashin. See ORCHESTRA.

CONE, a reproductive organ of an evergreen conifer of the class Gymnospermae. All conifers, such as the pine, fir, and spruce, bear two types of cones. One type, called the staminate cone, produces pollen which is similar to the pollen produced by roses or corn. The other type of cone, called the ovulate cone, produces egg-containing ovules, which lie naked on the inner surfaces of the scales of the cone. If the eggs are fertilized by pollen from the staminate cones, the ovules will develop into seeds. Later the seeds will be released from the ovulate cones, will fall to the earth, and may grow into trees. Unfertilized ovules can never develop into seeds. Each tiny grain of pollen has a pair of wings by which it is borne in the breeze from the staminate cone to an ovule in the ovulate cone. At the time of pollination the scales of the ovulate cones are spread open to receive the pollen, but after pollination they are again closed during the development of the seed. In some species this period from pollination to the ripening of the seeds may be two years.

Staminate cones are small, about ½ inch long, and grow in clusters

The versatile Leonard Bernstein is a composer, pianist, and lecturer, as well as a conductor.
Columbia Records Photo

The first Confederate flag, **1**, was the official one from 1861 to 1863. The battle flag adopted in 1863 as the official Confederate flag, **3**, remained such until the downfall of the Confederacy in 1865. The Confederacy also had other flags, **2** and **4**.

on the lower branches of the trees. Ovulate cones, always larger than staminate cones of the same tree, grow singly or in pairs on the higher limbs. The ovulate cones of various species of evergreen differ greatly in size. Those of pines are the largest, ranging from 10 to 20 inches in length. Spruce and fir cones are from 2 to 6 inches long.

CONE, a solid, funnel-shaped figure. It consists of line segments from all the points of a circle meeting at a single point outside the plane of the circle. This single point at the peak of the cone is called the vertex, **C**. The circular area opposite the vertex is called the base of the cone, **B**. A perpendicular line from the vertex to the base is called the altitude, **A,** of the cone.

If you want to find how much the cone will hold, you must first find the area of the base, using its radius, **D**. (See Circle.) Then multiply that area by the altitude and divide by 3. The volume of a cone is always one-third of the volume of a cylinder with the same base and altitude. See Cylinder.

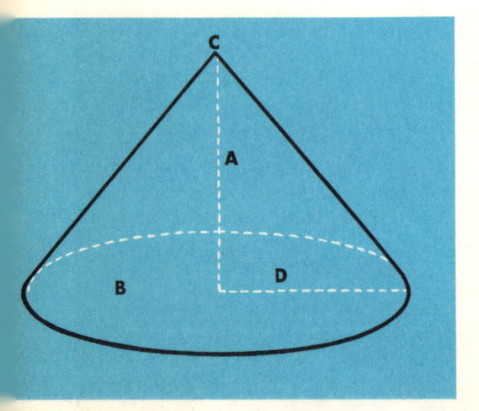

CONFEDERATE STATES OF AMERICA was the name of the organization of states that seceded from the Union at the time of the American Civil War. The confederation was comprised of South Carolina (seceded in 1860) and Mississippi, Alabama, Florida, Georgia, Louisiana, Texas, Virginia, Tennessee, Arkansas, and North Carolina (seceded in 1861). The western counties of Virginia refused to secede and became West Virginia. Delegates from the first six of these states met on Feb. 4, 1861, in Montgomery, Ala. They adopted a provisional constitution, named Jefferson Davis of Mississippi president of their provisional government, and adopted a flag. This flag was later replaced by the favorite flag of the Confederacy—one with a red field with blue diagonal cross bars that held 13 white stars. The seat of the Confederacy was moved to Richmond, Va., in July, 1861. Davis was elected president in November, 1861, and the government functioned at Richmond until toward the end of the war.

During the Civil War (Apr. 12, 1861—Apr. 9, 1865) the government of the South operated under the Permanent Constitution of the Confederate States of America, adopted by the convention of Southern states on Mar. 11, 1861. This document was based upon the federal Constitution of 1787 but with the 12 amendments incorporated in the main text. The right to slavery was guaranteed in the territories. As a special recognition of the rights of the states Confederate officials were made, in certain cases, subject to impeachment by state legislatures. Furthermore, the preamble of this constitution stated that each state was acting "in its sovereign and independent character."

European governments, especially the governing classes of England and France, were partial to the cause of the Confederacy but never recognized its government. The government of the Confederacy came to no formal end. It disintegrated with the surrenders of the Southern armies one after another in April and May, 1865, and the capture of Jefferson Davis near Irwinsville, Ga., on May 10, 1865.

CONFUCIANISM, the system of thought that developed around the teachings of Confucius, China's great sage, and that dominated the social and political life of China until the 20th century.

Confucianism arose from the combination of pre-Confucian writings, called the Five Classics—looked upon as the authentic records of the institutions and traditions of the ancient Chinese—and their interpretations by Confucius in the 5th century B.C., Mencius, and the neo-Confucian scholars of later times.

Confucianism placed particular emphasis on human relationships and on the rules governing the relations between the dead and the living and between father and son, man and wife, old and young, friend and friend, and ruler and subject. The virtue of filial piety, or sons' observance of their duties toward their parents, assumed an almost religious significance and came to be considered as the source of moral conduct. Confucianism maintained that only a dutiful son can serve his country honestly, either as an official in the government or as a soldier on the battlefield.

The greatest contribution of Confucianism lay in education and in the new ideas it introduced into practical government. The two were closely connected because the government officials of the Chinese Empire were for centuries recruited from among Confucian scholars, called the *ju-kiao*, or the school of literati. Confucians believed that the only good government is the one that makes its people happy and prosperous. The governing should be in the hands of the learned and virtuous men, because they alone can check the power of tyrannical rulers in the interest of the common people. Through the centuries high-ranking Confucian scholar-officials tried to put this principle into practice by introducing economic and political reforms for the good of the people as a whole.

Partly because it advocated the stability and the unity of the empire, Confucianism was made the official philosophy and the basis of the government of China in the 1st century B.C. Nevertheless, Confucianism was eclipsed by both Taoism and the newly introduced Buddhism between the 3d and the 7th century A.D., when China was divided politically and experienced frequent periods of social and economic upheaval.

But the Confucian classics continued to be studied, and Confucian scholars enjoyed the imperial patronage again during the T'ang Dynasty (618-906), which unified China. During this period Confucianism became a reform movement against Buddhism. Although Confucian government officials persecuted Buddhist monks and monasteries, Buddhism deeply influenced Confucian thinking.

A new form of Confucianism, called neo-Confucianism, flourished during the Sung Dynasty (960-1279) and was influenced especially by Zen Buddhism. While neo-Confucianism retained the concerns of original Confucianism, striving for an orderly, prosperous, and happy society under a benevolent government, it also acquired a new philosophical and more speculative bent from its Buddhist influences.

Among the neo-Confucian scholars, who founded different schools, the most prominent was Chu Hsi (1130-1200). His commentaries on the Confucian classics became the standard in all schools and in all civil service examinations until 1905.

By their insistence on tradition and on a stable government neo-Confucian statesmen tended to resist changes in Chinese society and, in opposition to the principle of original Confucian doctrine, supported the absolutism of the imperial government.

After the establishment of the Republic of China the attempt to revive Confucianism as the basis of moral teaching and religion in the schools failed. See CONFUCIUS.

This conglomerate was found in New York.

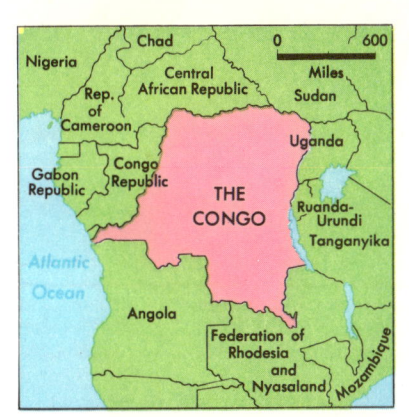

The primitive huts of this village of the Congo Republic are of mud and straw.

CONFUCIUS (551-478 B.C.), a famous Chinese philosopher, was born in the state of Lu to a poor family. When he was 17, he was made inspector of corn markets, and a few years later he started on his career as a teacher. He was made the chief magistrate of the city of Chung-tu and after a successful career was elevated to the office of minister of justice. He and two disciples elevated the state of Lu to a leading position in the kingdom. Eventually he left his office and spent a number of years wandering through the states teaching his philosophy, which was to hold sway in China for many centuries. He then retired to Lu.

CONGLOMERATE, a rock composed of rounded fragments of rocks and minerals embedded in a cement of finer materials. The fragments have been rounded by impact, abrasion, and grinding during transportation by water. The rounded fragments may be as small as a pea or as large as a boulder. The cementing material is usually iron oxide, silica, calcium carbonate, or clay.

This street is in Leopoldville, the capital and largest city of the Congo Republic.

CONGO, an independent state in central Africa. Its area of about 905,000 square miles lies astride the Equator and occupies about two-thirds of the Congo River basin. There is a 25-mile Atlantic coastal strip on the west. The capital is Leopoldville. The Congo republic of the French Community lies to the west, across the Congo River. About 13,000,000 people, most of them Negroes, live in the Congo.

Most of the territory lies in a depression, but in the south is found the Katanga Plateau, and on the east the Ruwenzori Mountains and the elevated great lakes of Africa. The Crystal Mountains lie in the southwest. The Congo River describes a great arc from the Katanga Plateau to its outlet on the Atlantic. The Congo basin is always hot and humid, with heavy rainfall, but in the Katanga and other highlands the climate is more moderate.

A wide strip of tropical rain forest crosses the north, but most of the remainder is park forest grassland, with intermittent equatorial forest areas along the river valleys. About half of the area is forested. Navigable rivers and short railroads to go around falls and rapids are the main arteries of transportation.

The Congo was acquired by the king of Belgium as personal property in 1884. It became a Belgian colony in 1908, after international criticism of exploitation of native laborers. It continued under the administration of the Belgian government after World War II. As a result of nationalist riots throughout 1959, demanding independence, the Belgian government agreed to free the Congo on June 30, 1960. After independence there was considerable disorder and bloodshed in the country. As a result of attacks upon Europeans, the UN intervened.

CONGO RIVER, the great river of central Africa. It is about 3,000 miles long, and although shorter than the Nile, it carries more water to the ocean than all the other rivers in Africa combined. It forms on the Katanga Plateau and flows northward, paralleling the great African lakes. After crossing the Equator it describes a great westward curve, then turns southwest, recrosses the Equator, and flows through the Crystal Mountains to the Atlantic, where it enters a long and wide alluvial estuary at Matadi. It receives the Ubangi and Kasai rivers and many other tributaries and drains an area of about 1,450,000 square miles. It is navigable over long stretches; but intermittent falls, including Stanley Falls and Livingstone Falls, made the building of railroads around them necessary. The Portuguese discovered the Congo between 1482 and 1484.

CONGRESSIONAL INQUIRY, the power of the U.S. Congress to investigate any subject within its competence. There is no specific provision for congressional inquiry given by the Constitution. Congress' powers, however, are implied by its legislative and regulatory functions. In the decision of the case *McGrain* vs. *Daugherty* (1927) the Supreme Court ruled that ". . . the power of inquiry—with process to enforce it—is an essential and appropriate auxiliary to the legislative function." The Supreme Court has also called the investigating committee the "eyes and ears of Congress."

Investigations can be conducted by either house of Congress. Standing, special, or joint committees can investigate. However, these committees can not function as courts, and crime, if disclosed, must be handled by the regular judicial process. Inquiries are held for two main purposes: first, to look into the workings of government departments and discover whether there is any waste or corruption; second, to collect facts with an eye toward new laws. An example of the first function was the investigation into government departments that resulted in the Teapot Dome exposé of 1924. An example of the fact-collecting function was the investigation into the dubious workings of the stock market in 1933. This study aroused public opinion (another important function of inquiry) and bore fruit in the Securities Act of 1933, the Securities Exchange Act of 1934, and the Public Utility Holding Company Act of 1935.

The right of inquiry, like many other governmental ideas, was based on British practice. The British House of Commons won its right to investigate in the 17th and 18th centuries. The first U.S. congressional inquiry was conducted in 1792 to determine why General Arthur St. Clair had been so badly equipped in his ill-fated expedition against Indian tribes on the Ohio border. The blame was laid on the War Department, and a better equipped expedition was sent out. About 1,000 investigations have been conducted since then.

Congressional investigations have been denounced by some critics who feel that they are often conducted at the expense of individual rights. However, critics also admit that investigations have done a great deal of good. For example, the Special Committee to Investigate the National Defense Program looked into war contracts between 1951 and 1954 and saved taxpayers about 15 billion dollars.

CONGRESS OF INDUSTRIAL ORGANIZATIONS. See AMERICAN FEDERATION OF LABOR AND CONGRESS OF INDUSTRIAL ORGANIZATIONS.

CONGRESS OF THE UNITED STATES, the legislative branch of the U.S. government, deriving its powers from the Constitution. It consists of the Senate and the House of Representatives. The powers of Congress are enumerated in Article I, Section 8, of the Constitution.

The Senate is composed of two members from each state. The 535 seats in the House are apportioned on the basis of population, each state being allowed at least one representative. A member of Congress must be a resident of the state from which he is chosen. A senator must be over 30 years old, a representative over 25. Senators are elected for terms of six years; the terms of one-third of the senators expire every two years. Representatives are chosen for two-year terms, the membership of the entire House being determined every two years.

Each house conducts its affairs under its own rules. The real work of legislation is done by committees. There are 20 permanent or standing committees in the House and 16 in the Senate; in addition, temporary or special committees are created to do some specific job. The vice president is the presiding officer of the Senate. He has no vote except in case of a tie. The Senate elects one of its own members to preside in the absence of the vice president or in case of vacancy in the office. The House elects from its own membership a presiding officer, called the speaker. The Senate has power to ratify or reject all treaties and to confirm or reject appointments of cabinet members, federal judges, officers of the military services, and many other appointments made by the president. The House of Representatives has the power to originate all revenue bills.

A bill that has passed both houses is sent to the president, who may sign it, veto it, or do neither; in the last case the bill becomes a law after ten days unless Congress has previously adjourned, in which case the bill dies. A bill vetoed by the president may become a law only after it has been passed by a two-thirds vote of each house. A regular annual meeting of Congress is required by the Constitution; the 20th Amendment adopted in 1933 sets the opening date as January 3. The president may call additional special sessions of Congress.

Both houses of the U.S. Congress are assembled (below) to hear an address by the president.
UPI

CONGRESS SYSTEM, chiefly the idea of the Austrian statesman Prince von Metternich, was the conservative reaction to the Napoleonic Wars. (See METTERNICH, PRINCE VON.) Composed of the Quadruple Alliance of Austria, England, Russia, and Prussia (later the Quintuple Alliance upon France's joining), the congress system was an attempt to maintain the peace settlement of the Congress of Vienna, to act as a repressive force against any European revolutionary movements, and to prevent any member of the Bonaparte family from again attaining the French throne. About the same time a vaguely worded agreement to rule Europe on Christian principles, instigated by Czar Alexander I of Russia and called the Holy Alliance, was signed by all European monarchs except the British prince regent, the Turkish sultan, and the pope. (See VIENNA, CONGRESS OF.) At the first congress, the Congress of Aix-la-Chapelle (1818), the question of French indemnity payments and the allied occupation of France was settled. The reactionary nature of the congress system was emphasized in later congresses.

The second and third of these congresses, held respectively at Troppau (now Opava, Czechoslovakia) and Laibach (now Ljubljana, Yugoslavia), considered what measures were needed to deal effectively with revolutions that had just occurred in Spain, Portugal, and Italy. The antirevolutionary Troppau Protocol, signed by Austria, Prussia, and Russia (England and France abstained), advocated intervention against revolutions considered dangerous to the European peace. In accordance with this protocol Austria overthrew the revolutionary government in Naples, Italy, and restored its former ruler Ferdinand I in 1821.

In 1822 the last congress was held at the Italian city of Verona to consider the revolution in Spain as well as those in Greece and the Spanish colonies in the Western Hemisphere. In Portugal absolutism was revived without interference from the alliance. At this final congress France accepted the principle of intervention and, acting upon this principle, forcibly overthrew the revolutionary government in Spain. Also through this congress Russia failed to support Greece in its revolt against the Ottoman Empire. British prime minister George Canning opposed the action of France in Spain but was unable to stop it. However, he strongly supported U.S. recognition of the independence of the Spanish colonies in South America and the declaration of the Monroe Doctrine. This statement and England's support of it weakened the congress system. See MONROE DOCTRINE.

Through the succeeding years attempts were made by Metternich to revive the congress system. Two factors made the system untenable. The first was the 1827 treaty between England and Russia (joined, shortly, by France) to support Greece in its war for independence. The second was the series of revolutions that occurred throughout Europe in 1830. Revolutions in France, Belgium, Germany, Italy, and Poland resulted in the collapse of the already weakened congress system.

CONGREVE, WILLIAM (1670-1729), an English writer of comedy, was born in Bardsey, a town near Leeds. He was educated at Kilkenny School and Trinity College in Dublin, Ireland. At both he was a fellow student of Jonathan Swift. He studied to be a lawyer but soon gave up law for literature. His first novel, *Incognita*, was published in 1692, and in the following year he wrote his first comedy, *The Old Bachelor*. In 1694 appeared *The Double Dealer* and in the following year, *Love for Love*. His one tragedy, *The Mourning Bride*, was produced in 1697. In 1700 appeared his masterpiece, *The Way of the World*. The poor reception given this last work was supposedly responsible for Congreve's retiring from his successful writing career. He was buried in Westminster Abbey.

CONIFER. See EVERGREEN.

CONJUNCTION is one of the eight parts of speech. A conjunction is a word that joins other words, phrases, or clauses. All of these words are conjunctions: *and, as, both, because, even, for, if, that, then, since, so, but, although, either, neither, except, lest, or, nor, notwithstanding, provided, though, whereas, whether.*

Sometimes conjunctions are used in pairs: *neither—nor, either—or.* Such conjunctions are called correlatives. It may be difficult to tell the difference between a conjunction and a preposition, for both are joining words. If the word really belongs to the word that follows it, so that together they make a phrase, it is a preposition. In the sentence "The present was for me," *for* is a preposition; the words *for* and *me* go together. In the sentence "Apples and milk taste good for lunch," the conjunction *and* doesn't really belong to either the word *apples* or the word *milk*. In the following example *for* is a conjunction: "He enjoyed the lunch, for apples and milk are tasty."

CONJUNCTIVITIS is an inflammation of the conjunctiva, the delicate mucous membrane that covers the exposed part of the eye and the inner surfaces of the eyelids. Infection, irritation by chemicals or various forms of light (klieg lights), and allergy are the main causes of conjunctivitis. The severity of the inflammation may range from mild redness of the eye with itching to severe involvement with the formation of ulcers and the discharge of pus. Pinkeye is the name of conjunctivitis caused by a germ that is carried on the hands and is sometimes transmitted by the use of common towels. Conjunctivitis should be treated by a physician, since common remedies may set up a secondary irritation.

CONNECTICUT, the Constitution State, is a small, historic state which has retained many of the charms of early New England. The capital and largest city is Hartford. Chief cities include New Haven, Bridgeport, Waterbury, and Stamford. Connecticut has an area of 5,009 square miles, which could be contained in Texas about 53 times. It is the 48th state in area. Connecticut measures approximately 90 miles east-west and 55 miles north-south and forms a rough rectangle. The population, according to the 1960 census, was 2,535,234.

Connecticut may be divided into two topographical regions: the east and west highlands and the central lowland. The western highlands include the Litchfield Hills and Bear Mountain (2,355 feet), the highest point in the state. Connecticut is drained by the Connecticut River in the central lowland, by the Thomas River in the east, and the Naugatuck and Housatonic rivers in the west. There are numerous lakes throughout the state. The coastline varies between rocky and sandy beaches. Several good harbors are along the coast. Connecticut has a humid, continental type of climate.

Almost two million acres are classified as forest land in Connecticut, and such species as chestnut, yellow poplar, birch, maple, hemlock, and beech are found. Connecticut is primarily an industrial state, and many persons are employed in specialized

Shown above is the state flower of Connecticut, the mountain laurel. The robin is the state bird. To the right is a view of the Capitol at Hartford.

Courtesy of the Connecticut Development Commission

Photo, Josef Scaylea, New England Council
Fishing vessels (above) are moored to the docks at Stonington, on the seacoast.

Shown above are the flag and the seal of Connecticut, the Constitution State.

Courtesy of the Connecticut Development Commission
Power presses stamp out silver spoons in one of the state's many silverware plants.

industries. Other important occupations are farming and fishing. Many highly skilled craftsmen are required for the numerous precision industries. Leading manufactured products include firearms and ammunition, clocks and watches, brass products, pins and needles, silverware, and textiles.

Most of the people live in urban areas or in the central lowland and along the southern shore. Connecticut's proximity to New York City has given the state a large commuting population.

The New England countryside of the state attracts summer and winter visitors. There are excellent lake and shore resorts. Picturesque towns, with their traditional New England village greens, are found in all parts of the state. Nearly all have places of historic interest. The quaint port at Mystic in the southeast is a major tourist attraction.

The Dutch in 1614 were the first to explore Connecticut. The real settlement of the region began in 1633, when the Dutch colonists from New Amsterdam entered the Connecticut River valley. The church had strict control over the government and was responsible for the famous blue laws. In some instances these laws provided for drastic punishments for certain crimes. The region had an English charter until it became a state. Connecticut in 1788 was the fifth state to ratify the Constitution.

With the decline of shipping during the 19th century the state turned to manufacturing. In the 1840's the building of railroads and the immigration of European workers greatly stimulated and expanded Connecticut's industries, as have the two World Wars since that time.

CONNECTICUT

Nickname: Constitution State
Seal: Three grapevines representing early agricultural pursuits
Flag: State seal in center of shield with ornate border—state motto below—field of flag azure blue
Motto: Qui Transtulit Sustinet (He Who Transplanted Continues to Sustain)
Flower: Mountain laurel
Bird: Robin
Capital: Hartford
Largest cities: Hartford, New Haven, Bridgeport
Area: 5,009 sq. mi. (including 110 sq. mi. inland waters)
Rank in area: 48th
Population: 2,535,234
Chief universities: Yale University, University of Connecticut, U.S. Coast Guard Academy
Chief rivers: Connecticut, Housatonic
Average temperature: Hartford, 27° F. (Jan.), 73° F. (July)
Average annual rainfall: 42 to 48 inches
Chief economic activities: Manufacturing, dairying, poultry raising
Chief manufactures: Firearms and ammunition, airplanes, machinery, ball bearings, electrical equipment, textiles, clocks, fabricated metals
Notable attractions: Fishing villages, ocean resorts
Important historical dates:
  1614 Region explored by Dutchman Adriaen Block
  1633 First trading post established by Dutch
  1635 Hartford settled
  1639 Fundamental Orders (written constitution) adopted
  1662 Under English rule—royal charter granted
  1788 One of original 13 states— fifth to ratify Constitution

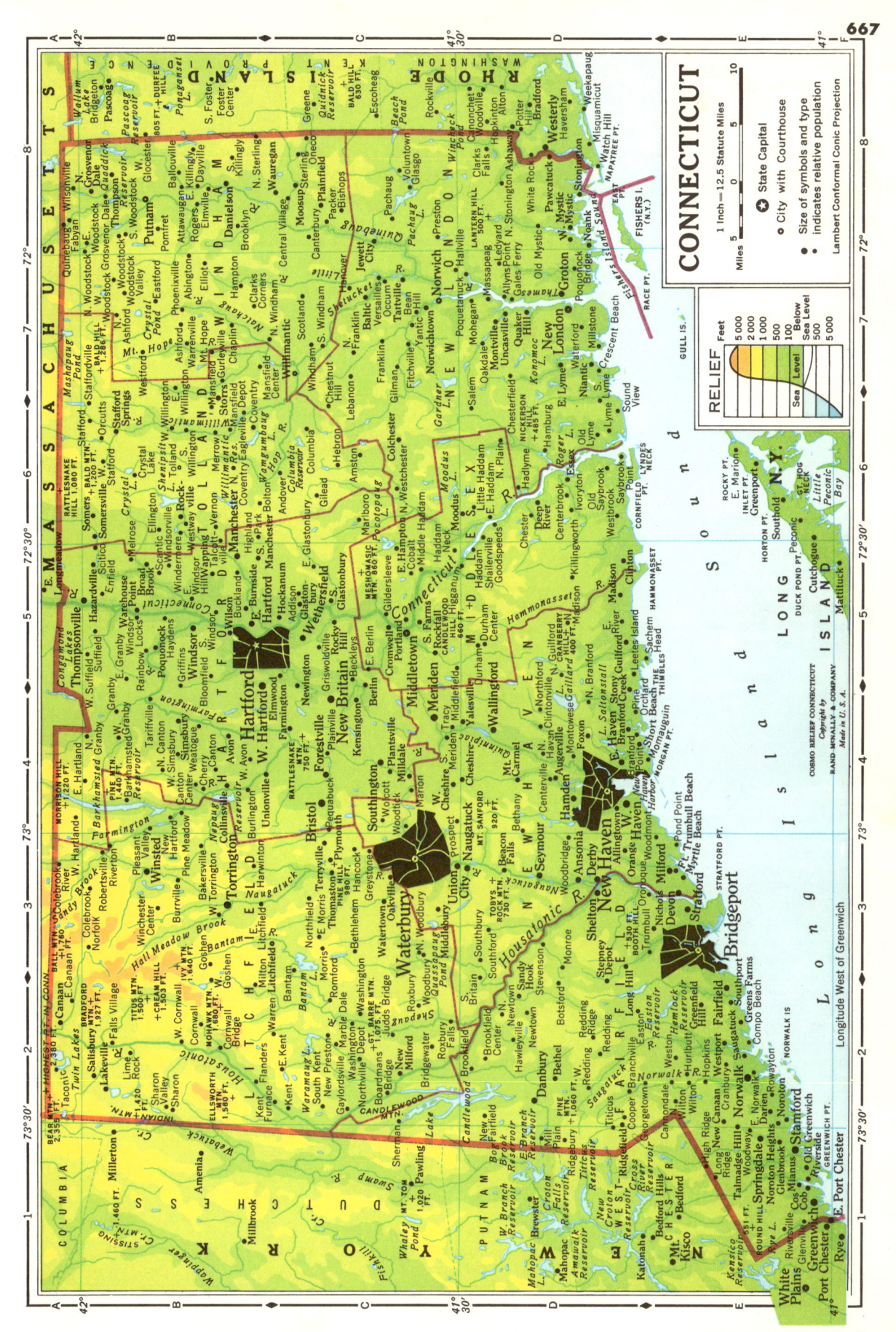

CONNECTICUT

CONNECTICUT COMPROMISE, in United States history, a plan for the organization of the national legislature, presented to the Constitutional Convention of 1787 by Roger Sherman, of Connecticut. This plan was a compromise between the plans presented by New Jersey and Virginia. (See NEW JERSEY PLAN; VIRGINIA PLAN.) It proposed a legislative branch of the government consisting of two houses: the Senate, in which each state would have an equal representation; and the House of Representatives, in which the representation of the states would be in proportion to their populations. This compromise was adopted in a modified form by the convention and was incorporated in the Constitution.

Sherman presented the compromise at a meeting of a convention committee formed to resolve the dispute, between supporters of the New Jersey and Virginia plans, over the manner of representation. This committee was composed of one member from each state represented at the convention.

CONQUISTADOR. The word means "conqueror" in Spanish and usually refers to the Spanish explorers in the New World during the 16th century. The conquistadores conquered and ruled many peoples. Some people have called them the "many little emperors of the New World." Among the most famous were Vasco Núñez de Balboa, Francisco Vásquez de Coronado, and Francisco Pizarro.

The conquistadores contributed many descriptions of lands and peoples in the New World. Hernando de Soto, for example, provided the earliest description of the southern United States.

At first the Spaniards sought a passage by water to the Far East, just as Columbus had done before them. Meanwhile, adventurers from Hispaniola entered the Gulf of Mexico and discovered Yucatan, with its gold and its cultivated maize fields. Two years later, in 1519, Cortes conquered Mexico and confirmed the hopes of riches. Many of the voyages of the conquistadores to the northern part of South America were stimulated by a search for El Dorado, an Indian chief covered with gold dust. The name later came to be applied to the place that was the object of the search. See AZTEC; BALBOA, VASCO NÚÑEZ DE; CORONADO, FRANCISCO VÁSQUEZ DE; INCA; MAYA; PIZARRO, FRANCISCO.

CONRAD, JOSEPH (1857-1924), English novelist of Polish birth and upbringing, was born at Berdichev in the Ukraine. His original name was Teodor Józef Konrad Korzeniowski. After the unsuccessful Polish revolt against Russian rule in 1863 the Korzeniowski family was exiled to northern Russia, from which Józef returned an orphan in 1869. He was educated by tutors and at a high school in Crakow, Poland, which he left in 1874. For three years he served in the French merchant marine and was briefly engaged in smuggling arms into Spain. In 1878 he joined the British merchant marine and rose to the rank of master mariner before retiring from the sea because of ill health 16 years later. In 1886 Korzeniowski became a British subject and changed his name to Joseph Conrad.

Conrad turned to writing only after his enforced retirement from the sea. His first novel, *Almayer's Folly*, published in his 38th year, was followed by many others, most of them based upon his experiences at sea or in the tropics. In his writing Conrad demonstrated his mastery of English. His prose style is not only beautiful but also strikingly original, as perhaps best exemplified in his descriptive passages. His works are also distinguished by acute moral and psychological analyses of a kind not common in English writing but which rather recall Conrad's Polish background. His principal themes—honor, heroism, moral alienation, guilt, expiation of sin—are all present in the short novel *Heart of Darkness*, a tale based on Conrad's knowledge of the Congo River. Among the many other works set on the sea or in the tropics *Youth, Typhoon, Lord Jim, Chance,* and *Tales of Unrest* are best known. Other important works include the novels of European revolutionary intrigue *The Secret Agent* and *Under Western Eyes* and the book of reminiscences *Mirror of the Sea*.

Conrad first achieved wide recognition with the publication of *Chance* in 1914. His popularity declined after his death in 1924 but revived after World War II.

CONSERVATION OF ENERGY. See ENERGY, CONSERVATION OF.

CONSERVATION OF MASS. See MASS, CONSERVATION OF.

CONSERVATION OF MASS-ENERGY. See MASS-ENERGY, CONSERVATION OF.

CONSREVATION OF NATURAL RESOURCES. Since the dawn of history civilizations have ruthlessly exploited the earth's natural resources through expanding human populations, slaughter of wildlife, accelerated erosion, and pollution of watercourses. These problems were intensified by the Industrial Revolution.

The conservation concept was recognized during the latter part of the 19th century and has been extensively developed in the United States. Establishment of Yellowstone National Park, the first in the world, in 1872, set the stage for large reservations of public land to safeguard resources. Presidents Harrison and Cleveland set aside vast forest reserves in the West. These and other reservations became the national forests, which totaled 160,582,000 acres in 1950 and which have been administered by the U.S. Forest Service since it was established in 1905 under the leadership of Theodore Roosevelt and Gifford Pinchot. Game laws were enacted, and at the turn of the century public interest in wildlife preservation led to the protection of habitats as private sanctuaries and federal and state refuges. Overgrazing and other misuse of land, especially in the West, was destroying the range and water resources of the nation, and the principles of reclamation were conceived. In 1908 President Roosevelt called a conference of state governors to discuss various conservation problems.

According to the conservation concept, land should be devoted to its wisest use to ensure perpetuation of renewable natural resources—soils, forests, wildlife, and so forth—and to avoid depletion of such nonrenewable resources as minerals, oil, and coal. Translation of this ideal into practical reality made progress during the first half of the 20th century, although the nation still suffers from wastage of soils and timber, destruction of wildlife habitats, unwisely planned engineering projects that do not consider all aspects of sound land use, and other factors diminishing the natural heritage. The National Park Service administers 24,997,000 acres, including 180 natural and historical areas, of which 29 are full national parks. The U.S. Fish and Wildlife Service (formerly the Bureau of Biological Survey) cooperates with the states on research and has jurisdiction of over 270 refuges. In addition to safeguarding federal timber and grazing resources the Forest Service has especially reserved 14,486,759 acres

CONSERVATION OF NATURAL RESOURCES

This fish (below) is being tagged for future identification. Restocking streams and lakes with hatchery-grown fingerlings is another activity of fish conservation.
Frank Iwen

Courtesy of Oregon State Highway Department
Above is a section of Oregon's rugged seacoast that as yet is in its natural state. Conservationists aim to set aside such areas so that they will never be disturbed and yet will be accessible for the people's enjoyment.

U.S. Soil Conservation Service Photo
Through strip cropping and contour cultivation the farmers of this area (above) are preventing the erosion of valuable soil.

A small metal band is fastened to the leg of a yellow-breasted chat (above). Banding aids the conservation researcher in determining birds' migratory habits.

A continuous yield of timber is possible with a coordinated program of selective cutting and reforestation. The cutover areas in the stand shown at the left will soon be replanted with seedlings.

Courtesy of Allis-Chalmers

as wilderness and wild areas to preserve for future generations extensive examples of undisturbed natural land. The Bureau of Reclamation harnesses streams, and the Tennessee Valley Authority has demonstrated flood control and other water-management benefits on a broad watershed basis. President Franklin D. Roosevelt established the Soil Conservation Service and other conservation agencies and programs, provided forces of young men to work in the parks and forests under the Civilian Conservation Corps, and expanded the national-park and wildlife-refuge programs.

Throughout the world most nations have laws protecting wildlife, and many have established preserves for native fauna. Notable are such vast reservations as Kruger National Park in the Union of South Africa and Kafue National Park in Northern Rhodesia, covering more than 8,000 square miles each, and the Serengeti National Park in Tanganyika, which protects some three million larger animals. Forty-eight nations have national parks; others have large nature reserves.

International treaties include migratory bird treaties for federal protection of species migrating across Canada, the United States, and Mexico; the Convention on Nature Protection and Wild Life Preservation in the Western Hemisphere; the London Convention for the Protection of African Fauna and Flora; whaling treaties; and others. Forestry and soil-conservation programs are spreading into many regions. Overgrazing by domestic livestock is a crucial problem in many parts of the world, and studies are being made to find workable solutions.

Two agencies of the United Nations are working in this field: the Food and Agricultural Organization (FAO), concerned with problems of ensuring food production and the application of efficient practices on land used for economic purposes; and UNESCO, which deals with scientific, educational, and cultural aspects of conservation. The secretary general of the United Nations has directed the Economic and Social Council to establish an evaluated register of the national parks and reserves of the world to encourage and strengthen conservation programs. The International Union for Conservation of Nature and Natural Resources, which was founded in 1946, coordinates the work of scientists, technicians, and officials of all nations. In 1960 this organization launched a special project aimed at conserving the wild life of Africa.

CONSERVATIVE PARTY, BRITISH, is one of the two major political parties in Great Britain.

The party stands, in the main, for free enterprise and generally opposes state ownership of industry and other types of business, but it does support national labor and social-welfare legislation. After the Conservative party gained control of the government in 1951, the government returned the nationalized iron, steel, and trucking industries to private ownership but retained the state-run national health service and all other industries and services nationalized by the Labour government after World War II.

In foreign policy the Conservative party supports the United Nations and British participation in NATO and favors close cooperation between Great Britain and the United States.

The Conservative party is directly descended from the political group called the Tories, which appeared in the 1670's after the restoration of the monarchy. The Tories initially supported royal powers against the Whigs, who supported the powers of Parliament. The Tory group acquired the name Conservative party in 1832; the name indicated that the party desired to preserve political and national traditions as they were. A notable step in party history was taken by Benjamin Disraeli, who turned the party's energies toward protecting labor and gaining and preserving an empire. The interest in empire continued to be important to the party for a long time.

CONSONANT, one of the two main classes of elementary language sounds. Vowels comprise the other main class. (See VOWEL.) A consonant sound is made with obstruction of the stream of breath. When a consonant is combined with a sound that has more sonority, it is considered to be part vowel and is called a semivowel or a semiconsonant. (Y, for example, is a consonant in *yard* and a vowel in *very.*)

The consonants, or consonant letters, are *b, c, d, f, g, h, j, k, l, m, n, p, q, r, s, t, v, x, z,* and sometimes *w* and *y.*

CONSTANTINE THE GREAT (280?-337), a Roman emperor, was born in Upper Moesia at Naissus (now Nis, Yugoslavia). He was the son of Constantius Chlorus, a caesar—or lieutenant emperor—of the western portion of the empire, which at that time was ruled by the two augusti, or emperors, Maximian and Diocletian.

These emperors, however, retired to private life, and the army chose Constantine as emperor. Maximian soon grew tired of being only a citizen, and once more took the title of emperor. Constantine marched against him, took him prisoner, and caused him to be strangled. This brought on a war between Constantine and Maxentius, the son of Maximian. During this war it is said that Constantine saw in the sky a cross of fire bearing the message "By this sign thou shalt conquer." He was victorious, and from that time the sign of the cross was put on the Roman banners.

Constantine made many changes in the government of Rome. He was the first Roman emperor to accept Christianity and to give the Christian Church equal rights with pagan worship. Also, he moved the capital from Rome to Byzantium, which became known as Constantinople (now Istanbul). His new capital was not so much given up to heathen customs as Rome was. In 325 he called the first general council of the Church at Nicaea. He died near Nicomedia in 337, after dividing his empire among his sons, Constantine, Constantius, and Constans.

CONSTANTINOPLE. See ISTANBUL.

CONSTELLATION, a pattern in the sky formed by a group of stars. Long ago men watched the sky and imagined that the patterns of stars were mythical heroes or animals outlined there. The names for these constellations were known to the ancient Greeks, who probably learned them from peoples in Babylonia. Ptolemy, a famous Greek astronomer of Egypt in the 2d century A.D., made a list of 48 constellations visible from his part of the world. The early explorers who voyaged to the southern coast of Africa reported new constellations visible there. Today we have a map of the sky for all directions from the earth. It is divided into 88 constellations.

Even though we no longer think of the constellations as creatures in the sky, their patterns and names are still useful to us. They help us to recognize and refer to different parts of the sky. Since the early 1600's the names of constellations have been part of the names of individual stars. A star's full name gives first its Greek letter and then its constellation (in the Latin genitive case). The Greek letters are assigned in order of brightness within the constellation. The brightest star of a constellation is named Alpha (α), the next brightest Beta (β), and so on. If the stars are of almost the same brightness, they are named by position, like the stars of the Big Dipper. Some stars had a name long before the present system was adopted, so they now have two names—a popular name and a scientific name. For instance, the star Algol is also known as Beta Persei, which tells us it is the star Beta in the constellation Perseus.

In space there are constellations in every direction from the earth, but for several reasons we cannot see all of them at once. The earth itself blocks our view of over half of space at any one time, and the stars in the direction of the sun are

The constellations of the zodiac are shown here as if they were viewed from outside. Sunlight blots out the constellations from the day sky. Only those constellations in the night sky can be seen from the earth. When the earth is in this position, the constellations Scorpius and Libra (and others in the same area of the celestial sphere) will appear each night. However, when the earth has revolved to a position on the other side of the sun, the constellations Taurus and Aries will appear each night.

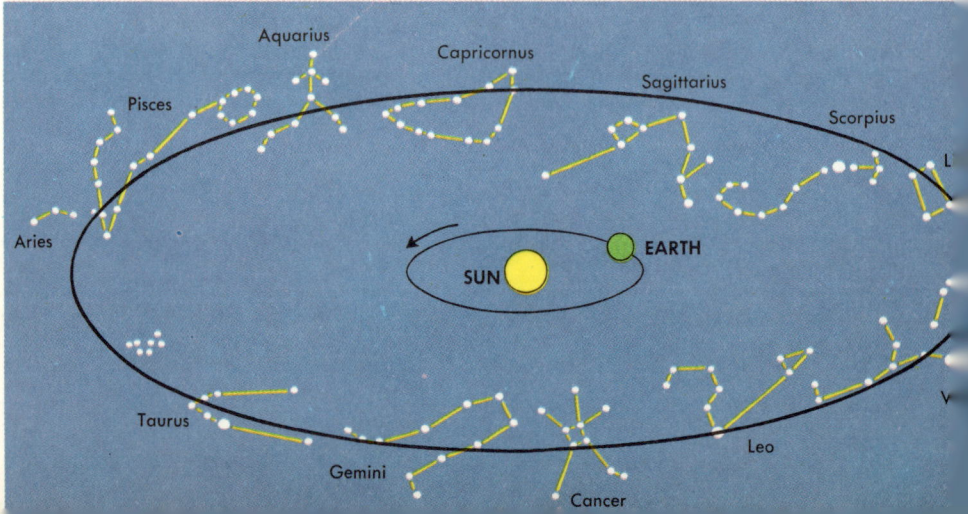

blotted out by its glare. So we are only able to see part of space at night when we are on the shadow side of the earth. Because the earth turns from west to east, stars come into view during the night over the eastern horizon and slip below the horizon in the west. However, some stars are so near the pole we can see them all through the night. The earth does not turn in a north-south direction, so in the Northern Hemisphere you can never see some of the constellations of the southern sky, and in Australia, for instance, you cannot see some of the northern constellations.

The earth also circles around the sun, so the direction of the night sky is slightly shifted every night. In a few months the direction is so different that we see some constellations not visible before, and others have dropped out of view. This is why we speak of constellations of autumn, winter, spring, and summer. It takes a year to see the full circle of space visible from our hemisphere. If the sun did not blind our view during the daytime, we could see the full circle in 24 hours. The individual constellations will be found under separate entries.

CONSTITUTION (ship). See OLD IRONSIDES.

CONSTITUTIONAL ACT, in Canadian history, an act that was passed by the British Parliament in 1791 and that divided the province of Quebec into two new provinces, Upper Canada and Lower Canada. For the first time in Canadian history each province was given an elected legislative assembly.

Until the time of the American Revolution the province of Quebec had been inhabited mainly by people of French origin. Since 1760 the British governors had ruled without an elected assembly because the only people who wanted one were the British, who were a minority. The governors wanted only an assembly they could dominate. The outbreak of the American Revolution caused an influx of loyalists into the province of Quebec from the American colonies, and the demand for an elected legislature increased. Furthermore, the British government wished to make the province pay the costs of its administration, but because of the failure of Britain's attempts to tax the American colonies, the British government decided that the province would have to tax itself. This could not be done without an elected legislature. Because of the size of the province and the sharp differences between the British and French populations, one legislature was impossible. Therefore the province was divided so that Upper Canada was largely British in population and Lower Canada was largely French.

CONSTITUTION OF THE UNITED STATES, a document establishing the union of 13 separate states by providing them with a federal government. The original text of the Constitution was signed on Sept. 17, 1787, by 39 delegates of the Constitutional Convention, after four months of discussion. Less than a year later, on Sept. 13, 1788, the Constitution was proclaimed by the Continental Congress. With the inauguration of George Washington as its first president on Apr. 30, 1789, the new United States was launched.

Even before the declaration of their independence from England and during the Revolutionary War, the states tried to compose their differences and adopt similar ways of action. (See DECLARATION OF INDEPENDENCE.) There was an agreement between Maryland and Virginia on navigation of the Potomac River and Chesapeake Bay. But only five states sent delegates to Annapolis, Md., in September, 1786, to discuss uniform commercial regulations for all the states. The Second Continental Congress, which had operated under the Articles of Confederation since March, 1781, as the Continental Congress, could do nothing without the states' cooperation. The basic weakness of the Articles of Confederation was that they could be freely defied or ignored by the states. Problems of trade and the disturbing state of finances finally forced the states to open the Constitutional Convention in Philadelphia on May 25, 1787. George Washington was unanimously elected its presiding officer.

The sessions of the Constitutional Convention were strictly secret, and for many years afterward nothing definite was known about the proceedings. Finally published in the early 19th century, the secretary's minutes and the journals of most delegates proved fragmentary. But James Madison, of Virginia, had kept complete notes, particularly of debates, and from these notes historians derive most of their knowledge of what took place.

The new Constitution was not a radical document but was the result of practical experience as well as knowledge of political theory and history. It provided for an effective but not an all-powerful central government. The Constitution is the supreme law in two senses: It stands above state laws, and it is higher than any of the laws passed by the Congress. The basic principle of the Constitution is that supreme power resides in the people and is delegated by the people to the government. The government must respect the rights of the people and render an account to them.

At the Constitutional Convention of 1787, 39 delegates signed the U.S. Constitution.

Under the Constitution the powers of the federal government were to be separated and assigned to three branches: the executive, the legislative, and the judicial. Each branch was to have its own powers and as little ability as possible to influence the choice of persons to the other two branches. By this separation of powers and by various checks and balances—the president's veto, Congress' power of impeachment, and so forth—the delegates to the Constitutional Convention hoped to prevent demagogical control of the government by any person or group of persons.

The Constitution further limited the powers of the national government by guaranteeing, in the first ten amendments, certain "natural rights"—freedom of religion, speech, press, and peaceable assembly. (See BILL OF RIGHTS.) The 10th Amendment reserved to the states all powers not specifically prohibited to them or granted to the national government. However, the 14th Amendment forbade the states to "deprive any person of life, liberty, or property, without due process of law." By 1961, 23 amendments, as well as custom and judicial decision, had considerably altered the original content of the Constitution.

CONSTRUCTION INDUSTRY, the building of public and private works, such as roads, bridges, dams, refineries, steel mills, apartment houses, and other large, expensive, and permanently located structures. The construction industries use all kinds of tools, from those found in the individual carpenter's kit to the very largest earthmovers, cement mixers, power cranes, and trucks. A Long Island, New York, builder of a $100,000,000 apartment house will use helicopters and monorail trains to bring material to the construction site.

About a third of the U.S. construction industry (30 billion dollars a year) is financed and directed by the national, state, and local governments. But these projects largely employ local private contractors, who buy, rent, and lease their heavy machinery from other private companies that specialize in the management of construction equipment. Many men get their start in the construction industry by buying a bulldozer or truck and then seeking work on a big job. Less than a third of construction companies survive as long as 11 years, while half of them fail after 3 years. In a recent year, out of 48,282 construction firms filing federal income-tax reports, 18,786, or more than one-third, reported no net profit.

The three million workers below the rank of engineer in the construction industry are almost entirely young men. Their weekly earnings are 30 percent above the average earnings in manufacturing and 80 percent above the average in retail trade. Only bituminous mining, petroleum refining, and some of the printing trades surpass the earning power of construction workers. Most of their skills are learned in on-the-job training during an apprentice period of several years.

CONSUL, the head of a consulate, which looks after the interests of a nation's citizens abroad. The practice of sending consuls to other cities became common in the ancient world as a result of the growth of commerce. In Greece consuls were known as patrons. Diplomatic missions abroad have consular sections attached to them. There are also separate consular offices located in major cities, especially in port cities.

The chief duty of a consul is to protect the interests of the citizens of his own country in the nation to which he is assigned. If a citizen of France, for example, should fall into the hands of the police of another nation, he would contact the French consulate. The consul would endeavor to protect the citizen's legal rights. Consuls are also charged with issuing visas, gathering economic information, checking bills of lading, and supervising the hiring of sailors by the ships of their own nation. To accomplish these tasks the consuls must have the power to negotiate in the name of their government with local officials. The diplomatic mission under the ambassador, however, is the sole official negotiator with the central government. The ambassador usually has under him a supervisory consul general, who coordinates the work of

---

OCCUPATION: Carpenter
NATURE OF WORK: Building, installing, and finishing of wood structures
PERSONAL FACTORS—ABILITIES, SKILLS, APTITUDES: Manual dexterity with tools and good health for outdoor work are needed. Aptitude for arithmetic is also necessary.
EDUCATION AND SPECIAL TRAINING: Apprenticeship program, after high-school graduation, consists of four years of on-the-job training with a minimum of 576 hours of related classroom instruction.
WORKING CONDITIONS:
1. **INCOME:**
   COMPARED WITH OTHER CAREERS WITH EQUAL TRAINING: Average
   COMPARED WITH MOST OTHER CAREERS: Average
2. **ENVIRONMENT:** Outdoor work, in season, April to November
3. **OTHER:** Hourly rate high but employment seasonal; wage rates established by unions; employment opportunities excellent
RELATED CAREERS: Joiners, cabinetmakers, roofers, construction builders
WHERE TO FIND MORE INFORMATION: United Brotherhood of Carpenters and Joiners of America, 222 East Michigan Street, Indianapolis 4, Ind.

OCCUPATION: Plumber
NATURE OF WORK: Installing, altering, and repairing pipe systems.
PERSONAL FACTORS—ABILITIES, SKILLS, APTITUDES: Mechanical aptitude, manual dexterity with hand tools, and good knowledge of mathematics are necessary. Good physical condition is also needed.
EDUCATION AND SPECIAL TRAINING: Apprenticeship program consists of 10,000 hours (five years) of on-the-job training, in addition to related classroom instruction. Some localities require a journeyman's license.
WORKING CONDITIONS:
1. **INCOME:**
   COMPARED WITH OTHER CAREERS WITH EQUAL TRAINING: Average
   COMPARED WITH MOST OTHER CAREERS: Average to high
2. **ENVIRONMENT:** Active, strenuous work, mostly indoors
3. **OTHER:** Union hourly wage rates with fringe benefits; regular hours
RELATED CAREERS: Pipefitter, steamfitter, gasfitter, specialized contractor
WHERE TO FIND MORE INFORMATION: National Association of Plumbing Contractors, 1016 20th Street, NW, Washington 6, D.C.

OCCUPATION: Building Contractor
NATURE OF WORK: Taking full responsibility for the construction of a structure
PERSONAL FACTORS—ABILITIES, SKILLS, APTITUDES: The ability to plan work, to direct others, and to estimate time and materials for a job is needed. A sound knowledge of business practices and financing is also necessary.
EDUCATION AND SPECIAL TRAINING: Sound journeyman knowledge in one of the building trades is the greatest help in assuring success as a contractor. College work in engineering, business management, and accounting is desirable also.
WORKING CONDITIONS:
1. **INCOME:**
   COMPARED WITH OTHER CAREERS WITH EQUAL TRAINING: Average
   COMPARED WITH MOST OTHER CAREERS: Average to high
2. **ENVIRONMENT:** Mostly outdoor work at noisy construction site; wages high but seasonal; union wage rates for 40-hour week
3. **OTHER:** Trade unionization; business easy to enter, though competition usually keen
RELATED CAREERS: Construction foreman, estimator, construction superintendent, trade or vocational school instructor, salesman for building-supply company
WHERE TO FIND MORE INFORMATION: American Federation of Labor and Congress of Industrial Organizations, Building and Construction Trades Department, 815 16th Street, NW, Washington 6, D.C.; Associated General Contractors of America, Inc., 1957 E Street, NW, Washington 6, D.C.; National Association of Home Builders, 1625 L Street, NW, Washington 6, D.C.

the consular section of the diplomatic mission and the separate consulates within the nation to which the diplomatic mission is assigned.

CONTAINMENT POLICY, in international relations, a United States foreign policy designed to check (contain) the expansive tendencies of the U.S.S.R. The containment policy was first outlined in an article in the July, 1947, issue of *Foreign Affairs*. The article was signed "X." "X" turned out to be the career diplomat George F. Kennan.

Kennan supported his policy with several arguments based on his knowledge of the Soviet Union, some of it obtained during his stay there as an ambassador. He first pointed out historical reasons for the feeling of insecurity that he believed the Soviets to have. He felt that Marxist ideology was a buttress to members of an insecure ruling class, and that it helped explain for them the reasons for repression within the U.S.S.R. by picturing other nations as threatening. Moreover the dedication to Marxism meant a patient effort on the part of the U.S.S.R. to advance the cause of the world revolution. To meet this situation, Kennan believed that the United States must pursue a long-range, patient world-wide policy of applying a counterforce wherever the Soviet Union encroached. This was the policy of containment, and it became an important element of U.S. foreign policy in relation to the Soviet Union.

CONTINENT, a large, platform-like mass rising above the ocean basins. Europe and Asia together, Africa, North America, South America, Australia, and Antarctica are all continents. In political geography and in description, Europe and Asia are considered as separate continents, but since there is no natural separation between them, in physical geography they are one. The word *Continent* is also used in speaking of the mainland of Europe as distinguished from the British Isles.

CONTINENTAL CONGRESS, the name of the federal legislature of the American colonies (which later became the United States) during the American Revolutionary period and under the Articles of Confederation. From Sept. 5 to Oct. 26, 1774, at Philadelphia, the First Continental Congress was in session and consisted of a general gathering of representatives of all the colonies except Georgia. It was held to discuss the colonists' grievances against England's colonial policy. An agreement was made not to import goods from England.

The Second Continental Congress gathered on May 10, 1775, and, because of the fighting at Lexington and Concord, was inclined to be more decisive than the First Continental Congress. In accordance with plans of the Congress to form an army against England, George Washington was appointed military commander in chief. The Congress adopted the Declaration of Independence on July 4, 1776. Under the Articles of Confederation, adopted Nov. 15, 1777, but not ratified by all the states until Mar. 1, 1781, the Congress attempted to direct the military strategy and to solve the financial problems of the American Revolution, but it declined both in influence and in quality of personnel.

The Continental Congress was replaced by the present form of government when the new Congress of the United States assembled on Mar. 4, 1789.

Robert D. Bezucha

Independence Pass is the highest automobile pass in Colorado. It cuts through North America's Continental Divide, which here is formed by the Sawatch range of the Rocky Mountains. In the map (left) you can trace the Continental Divide from Alaska down through Canada, the United States, and Mexico. As you can see, the greater part of North America drains into the Atlantic Ocean.

CONTINENTAL DIVIDE is the name given to the ridge of mountain summits that separates the rivers that flow to one side of a continent from those that flow to the other side. In North America the Continental Divide is a great ridge of the Rocky Mountains in the western part of the continent. It divides the rivers flowing east into the Atlantic Ocean from those flowing west into the Pacific Ocean. In the United States it is sometimes called the Great Divide. The divide was a rugged barrier to the early settlers of the southwestern United States.

CONTINENTAL DRIFT, the theory that the continents were once joined together and that they split apart and drifted to their present positions at some time in the distant past. The first man to put forward a theory of drifting landmasses was Antonio Snider about 1865. Nearly 50 years later an American geologist, F. B. Taylor, reached similar conclusions through independent investigations. In 1908 he pointed out that the coasts of Labrador and southwest Greenland run almost parallel for over 400 miles and that the shapes of the two coasts are so much alike that they could fit together like pieces of a jigsaw puzzle. He also noted that the facing coasts of Greenland, Ellesmere Island to the northwest, and Baffin Island to the southwest are all so alike that they would fit together in the same way to form one block of land. Furthermore, Taylor pointed out, the southwestern coast of this block would then fit into the northeast coasts of Hudson Bay and Labrador, making a greatly enlarged North American continent. However, it has been pointed out that the similarity of shapes is much less at the edges of the continental shelf. (See CONTINENTAL SHELF.) Furthermore, the shapes of the continents were notably different in the distant periods when the drift is supposed to have occurred.

At almost the same time, Alfred Wegener, in Germany, came forward with a similar idea about other continents. In 1910, without knowing of Taylor's work, he published a book explaining why the southern continents—South America, Africa, India, and Australia (with Tasmania)—are shaped like triangles. Wegener wrote that they all once formed parts of a great landmass near the South Pole, joined to Antarctica. Later, he said, great cracks appeared in the earth's crust running outward from the pole. Then the parts thus formed split away from Antarctica and drifted toward the Equator and thus moved gradually farther from each other. The idea seems less fantastic now than it once did, but there is much evidence against it, and geologists have not generally accepted the theory.

CONTINENTAL SHELF, the underwater ledge that surrounds all continents. The shelf varies in width from several hundred miles to 10 miles or less. Along the east and west coasts of North America the continental shelf is very wide in the north and becomes rapidly narrower toward the south, all but disappearing at Florida and southern California. The widest shelf in the world is in the Barents Sea off the arctic coast of Europe. It is 750 miles across and from 600 to 1,200 feet deep.

The ocean bottom on the continental shelf slopes gently, but not smoothly, from the shoreline to the outer edge. Figures compiled from contour charts and other examinations in all parts of the world show an average width of 42 miles and an average depth of the flattest portion of 210 feet.

Geologists and oceanographers have only in recent years carried on a systematic study of the continental shelf, and their ideas on its origin are still undergoing modification. The growing evidence indicates that several factors played a part in creating the shelves. The major ones were probably wave cutting, sedimentary deposits, erosion, and glacial action.

The world's richest fishing grounds are located in waters over the continental shelves in various parts of the globe. The North Sea and the Grand Banks of Newfoundland are outstanding examples.

CONTRACT, a type of agreement between two people or groups of people. Those who make a contract agree to do something for each other. An agreement to do something without reward is not a contract. An agreement for the sale of a house can be a contract. An agreement to take care of a friend's dog while the friend is away on a trip is a favor, not a contract. A contract is an agreement that can be enforced in a court of law. If one of the agreers does not carry out his part of the contract, the other one can take him to court.

Almost all business is based on contracts. A person who buys insurance makes a contract with the insurance company. A person who takes a job makes a contract with his employer to do certain work in return for certain money.

Contracts can be either written or oral. A written contract is better

A canyon in the continental shelf off New Jersey runs far beyond the present mouth of the Hudson River. In the Ice Age the ocean level was lower, and part of this canyon may have been a river. Note the sudden drop at the edge of the continental shelf.

because it is easier to make certain, if the matter has to be taken to court, just exactly what the agreement was. In some cases a written contract is required by law. It is not necessary that the things agreed upon be done at once nor that they be done at the same time later on, but the agreement should be clear and definite about the times when things are to be done.

CONVECTION. See CONDUCTION, CONVECTION, RADIATION.

CONVENTION, the act of coming together or assembling; the state of being assembled. Conventions have been important throughout the political history of the United States. It was a constitutional convention held in 1787 that framed the U.S. Constitution. The secession conventions held in the Southern States resulted in the Civil War, and the Montgomery convention of 1861 formulated the Constitution of the Confederate States of America. Constitutional conventions have been called to consider and prepare state constitutions.

The major U.S. national political parties meet in convention every four years to nominate candidates for president and vice president, to adopt a campaign platform, and to elect their national committees. The custom of assembling in convention has extended to affairs other than politics, and many conventions for miscellaneous purposes are held annually.

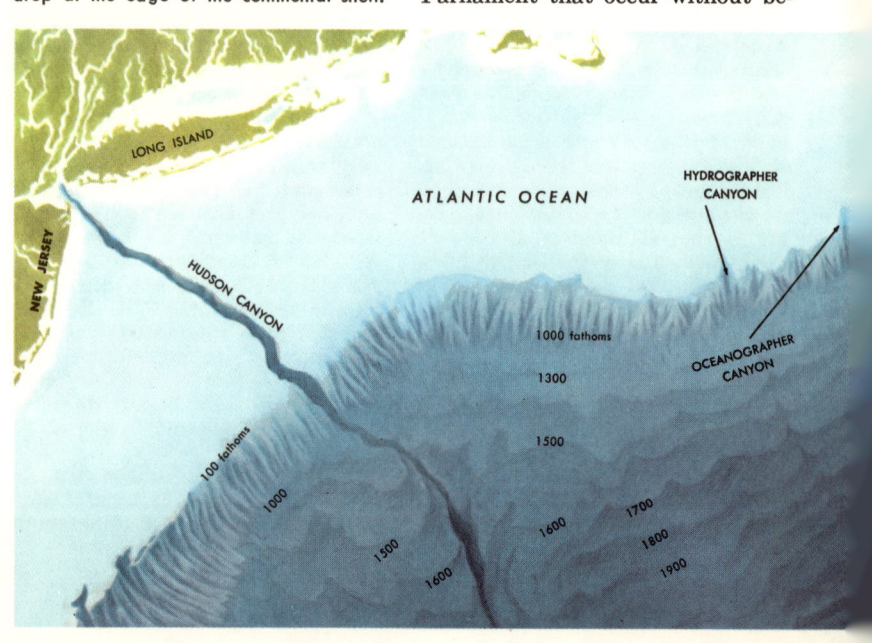

In English history the word *convention* is applied to those extraordinary meetings of the British Parliament that occur without being called by the sovereign or without previous royal consent. Such a meeting would be at a time of national crisis.

In French history the word is applied to what was more fully named the National Convention, which succeeded the National Legislative Assembly on Sept. 21, 1792, and was dissolved Oct. 26, 1795.

In diplomacy a convention is equivalent to a treaty; thus there have been conventions by the United States with the leading nations of the world.

CONVENTION OF 1818 was the major peace settlement between England and the United States after the War of 1812. This treaty settled several problems that diplomats failed to solve during the negotiations for the peace treaty that ended the war.

According to the convention England reopened the Newfoundland and Labrador fisheries to U.S. citizens, though on a more limited basis than formerly; gave up its claims to trade on, and navigation of, the Mississippi; and accepted the 49th parallel from Lake of the Woods to the Rocky Mountains as the boundary between the United States and Canada. The boundary west of the Rocky Mountains was left undefined, and the territory west of the Rockies, the Oregon country, which both countries claimed, was left open to settlement by English and U.S. nationals for the next 10 years. The convention also renewed the commercial treaty of 1815, which had dealt with U.S. commerce in the East Indies.

CONVEYOR BELT, an endless belt, made of layers of rubber, cotton cord, artificial fibers, or steel wire, for moving people and materials. The belt is run over motor-driven pulleys and is supported on rollers, or idlers.

Ordinary conveyor belts handle vast numbers of people (when the belts are installed as moving sidewalks) or quantities of materials like coal, ore, sand, merchandise in stores, and parts in factories. Conveyor belts in the mining industry may use more than 2,500 horsepower on a "flight." Belts may carry up to 6,000 tons of rock or ore per hour at 800 feet a minute. Special belts are built to withstand the effects of water, acids, and materials as hot as 250° F. Trough-shaped conveyor belts for carrying grain, ore, or crushed rock run on flat center rollers and also on side rollers set at an angle of about 30 degrees. Since conveyor belts tend to stretch in use, the slack must be taken up by a screw or weighted device at either end or on the under, or return, side of the assembly.

Conveyor belts can move vast quantities of materials in situations where trucks or railroads cannot operate. According to the Goodyear Tire and Rubber Company, the core of the Anderson Ranch Dam, near Boise, Idaho, was built by moving on a 2-mile conveyor belt more than 8,000,000 tons of clay around a mountain range with grades up to 32 degrees, through tunnels, and over a canyon wall. The belt was 3 feet wide, moved at the rate of 550 feet per minute, and delivered 1,280 tons of clay an hour. Before its installation at the Anderson Ranch Dam, this conveyor belt had already moved 12,700,000 tons of aggregate at the Shasta Dam in California.

CONVULSION, a violent, involuntary contraction of the muscles. Although convulsions are alarming, children frequently have convulsions that have no connection with serious disease. In fact, some children have convulsions almost every time they run a high fever. So try not to lose your head if you are present when a child has a convulsion or spasm. There is no need to be frightened.

During a convulsion a child usually loses consciousness, rolls his eyes up or to one side, and stiffens out. Arms and legs and sometimes face and head twitch violently. Often he holds his breath and turns blue.

When a child has a convulsion, protect him from injury and prevent him from swallowing or biting his tongue by holding a folded wad of cloth (a handkerchief or towel) between his teeth.

Young children frequently have convulsions at the beginning of an acute illness, much as an older person may have a chill. Since a convulsion is always a symptom of some abnormal condition, a doctor's advice should be sought to discover and treat the underlying illness.

COOK, CAPTAIN JAMES (1728-1779), English navigator, was born at Marton, Yorkshire. After a meager education he was apprenticed to a shopkeeper in Staiths, a small seacoast town. With the opening of the Seven Years' War in 1755 he entered the royal navy. In 1759 he was made master of the *Mercury* and performed dangerous services in the St. Lawrence River near Quebec. His advancement was rapid and his sailing of wide scope. As commander of the *Endeavour* he sailed to the Pacific in 1769 to make observations for the government on the transit of Venus. On the *Resolution* he journeyed toward the Antarctic in 1772 until he was halted by ice at 71° S latitude. During this voyage he explored New Zealand and the eastern coast of Australia. His remarkable record of disease prevention aboard ship won him decorations and membership in the Royal Society, as well as advancement to the rank of post captain in the navy and the appointment of captain in Greenwich Hospital.

Sailing in July, 1776, to find whether the Atlantic and Pacific oceans met in the Arctic regions, he explored much of the western coast of North America. He also rediscovered Hawaii (then called the Sandwich Islands), to which he returned in January, 1779. In February Captain Cook set sail for Kamchatka, but he was forced to return to Hawaii because of an accident. There, because of the stealing of a boat by the islanders, Cook seized the king and held him as hostage. This led to hostilities, which resulted in Cook's being killed.

COOKIES. See CAKES AND COOKIES.

The conveyor belt at right is delivering finished comic magazines—printed, cut, and folded—from a high-speed lithography press. The magazines now go to the bindery.

COOKING

At the left a solar furnace, which utilizes the heat from the sun's rays, becomes an effective but somewhat cumbersome kitchen appliance. Scientists are constantly searching for more efficient ways of preparing food. At the upper left a chef and his assistants toil in an early forerunner of the modern kitchen. Although a seemingly simple development, the introduction of manmade vessels to hold food (above) was a crucial step in the advancement of cooking. A double oven and adjacent range comprise a modern cooking center (right). Windows in the oven doors let the cook watch what is baking without having to open the doors.

John Strohm

Courtesy of Whirlpool Corporation

COOKING. Any method of preparing food by the application of heat is called cooking. Cooking modifies food in a number of ways. It postpones the beginning of spoilage, kills disease-producing organisms, changes the nutritive value of food, and makes some food more digestible than it is in the uncooked state. Cooking also changes the flavor of food. This function has become increasingly important with the development of cookery, or the art of cooking.

No one knows how early in history cooking may have originated. Peking men, about one million years B.C., had fires in their caves, but these were most likely used primarily for warmth. The effect of heat on food may have been discovered accidentally, as Charles Lamb suggests in his "Dissertation on Roast Pig."

In ancient Greece cooking became a highly developed art. Master cooks were the highest paid men in the country. Through their contact with Asia, the Greeks learned to make their banquets more and more sumptuous.

The Romans borrowed from the Greeks their achievements in the art of cooking. Favored by its geographical position, Italy remained the center of culinary tradition during the later years of the Roman Empire. The customs of remoter parts of Europe, however, began to assert themselves as the Middle Ages progressed.

Modern cookery began in Italy during the Renaissance. Italian cooks brought about a revival of cookery in France and introduced a cultured simplicity unknown there before. It is to the Italians apparently that later developments in cookery are due.

England followed the Continental fashions, and in addition a distinctive national cookery arose. Flowers were used in dishes—marigolds, primroses, and cowslips. Later, with the Puritan influence, simpler tastes returned, with emphasis on natural flavors and fewer spices.

The culinary art in France was refined under the reigns of Louis XIV and Louis XV. The French Revolution was temporarily a blow to cookery. However, after this time French restaurants began to thrive and attracted many talented cooks. French cooking became a culinary ideal.

Methods of preservation internationalized the use of many foods. In England frozen lamb and mutton were received and consumed in 1878. The processes of canning contributed to the increased use of some foods.

To the cookery of other countries America has added its own foods—potatoes, Lima beans, squash, corn, and tomatoes. Pizza, an Italian dish with a bready crust and tomato-and-cheese paste, is now found in the United States in more forms perhaps than in Italy. The term "melting pot" of the United States applies, among other things, to the cooking pot.

The names given to different methods of cooking are related to the kinds of heat to which the raw materials are exposed. The principal modern methods are broiling, roasting, baking, frying, boiling, and steaming. Other methods are variations or combinations of these six. Broiling is cooking by direct exposure to the radiant heat of coals, electric coils, or flame. Pan broiling is cooking in a heavy metal frying pan without moisture. The fat is poured off as it accumulates. Roasting usually means to cook in an oven by dry heat. It also means to cook by exposure to radiant heat before a fire or in an open oven. Baking is to cook with dry heat under coals, on heated stone or metal, or in an oven. Boiling is to cook by the heat of boiling liquid, usually water. Variations of boiling are scalding and simmering. Water is scalding when large bubbles of gas collect on the bottom and sides of the container. In simmering, the large bubbles of water vapor rise nearly to the surface but break before reaching the surface. (Simmering is preferable for protein foods and specifically for hard-cooked eggs.) Steaming is cooking with water vapor under pressure. If the steam is allowed to escape, the boiling point of water is raised, and temperatures above the usual boiling point can be attained; this is the principle of the pressure cooker. Frying is to cook in a pan or on a griddle with fat. Braising involves browning meat in a small amount of fat, adding a small amount of liquid, covering tightly, and cooking slowly for a long time.

Good cooks plan meals ahead of time. Foods that take longer to cook are prepared first. The cook arranges to serve hot foods well heated by serving them immediately or keeping them in a warm oven or a similar place. Sometimes plates require warming or chilling beforehand. Cold foods must be put in the refrigerator in time. Butter and most cheeses should be left at room temperature for a few minutes before serving.

COOLIDGE, CALVIN (1872-1933), 30th president of the United States, was born at Plymouth, Vt., July 4, 1872. A graduate of Amherst College in 1895, he studied law in Northampton, Mass., and was admitted to the bar in 1897. He was mayor of Northampton in 1910, served in the Massachusetts Senate from 1912 to 1915, and was president of the state senate in 1914. In

Calvin Coolidge, U.S. President

1916-1918 Coolidge was lieutenant governor of the state. He was governor from 1919 to 1920.

The next year his name was placed in nomination at the Republican national convention. When Warren Harding received the nomination, Coolidge was placed on the ticket as vice-presidential candidate. The Republicans won the election, and Coolidge succeeded to the presidency on Aug. 3, 1923, on the death of Harding. In 1924 Coolidge was elected president in his own right, with Charles G. Dawes as vice president.

Coolidge's administration was noted for his prosecution of the Teapot Dome scandal of 1924, for his veto of the agricultural subsidy and price-fixing McNary-Haugen bill, and for the improvement of U.S. relations with Mexico. Coolidge did not desire another presidential term and retired to Northampton, Mass., in 1929.

James Fenimore Cooper

COOPER, JAMES FENIMORE (1789-1851), American novelist, born in Burlington, N.J. He studied at Yale College and entered the American Navy as a midshipman at the age of 18. His three years in the Navy gave him a knowledge of nautical matters and sea characters that he later used in some of his novels. His first success was *The Spy* (1821). With *The Pioneers* (1823) he inaugurated the series of "Leather-Stocking Tales." This group of his most famous books, dealing with the Indian scout Natty Bumppo, included *The Last of the Mohicans*, *The Prairie*, *The Pathfinder*, and *The Deerslayer*. His novels of the sea included *The Pilot*, *The Red Rover*, *The Water-Witch*, *Wing-and-Wing*, *Afloat and Ashore*, and *Miles Wallingford*. He also wrote a *History of the Navy* (1839).

Cooper acted as consul for the United States at Lyons, France, for a short time after 1826. He visited Germany, Switzerland, and Italy and returned home in 1833. For nearly 20 years afterward he continued his literary labors, producing about 30 novels, works of social criticism, and a comedy.

COOPERATIVE, a type of organization that is owned and controlled by people who use goods and services, not by investors. Cooperatives refund to patrons what would be middle-men's profits. They serve both consumers and producers, such as farmers raising crops for market. They set standards of quality and help millions of families become business owners. Cooperatives are generally divided into two main groups, distributing and producing.

Efforts were made to operate cooperatives in Scotland and England before the beginning of the Rochdale Society of Equitable Pioneers in 1844, but few of them attracted much attention. Robert Owen had taught the benefits of the cooperative system earlier, but it remained for 28 poverty-stricken weavers of Rochdale, England, to devise the cooperative fundamentals that have been adopted as guiding principles wherever the movement has spread. Each of the 28 original members subscribed £1 for a single share of stock in the venture. Within 25 years the society boasted about 5,500 members. The cooperative fundamentals laid down by the Rochdale weavers were: membership open to all; limitation of the number of shares to be held by any one member; democracy in government, with officers elected by and responsible to the members, and each member entitled to one vote only, regardless of the number of shares he held; sale of goods at market prices; cash sales; and refunds to each member in proportion to the amount of his patronage in the store. On the basis of these principles the cooperative movement was introduced into nearly every country of the world.

The main cooperative principles have been established in the United States since about 1829. By the middle of the 20th century cooperatives furnished at least 15 million U.S. families with credit, insurance, groceries, farm supplies, electricity, housing, health care, and many other needs.

COORDINATE COVALENT BONDING. See CHEMISTRY.

COOT. See RAILS, COOTS, GALLINULES.

COPENHAGEN, the capital and principal seaport of Denmark, located on the islands of Zealand and Amager off the eastern coast of the country, 18 miles west-northwest of Malmo, Sweden. The Oresund, a channel between the two islands, forms a sheltered harbor, which is crossed by a bridge. The business section stretches westward from the harbor toward the large central squares of the city, Kongens Nytorv and Raadhuspladsen. To the north and south lie the aristocratic quarters, with the handsome Amalienborg Square and its royal palaces. The population is about 800,000, slightly less than the population of Boston.

Through Copenhagen passes about 50 percent of the kingdom's foreign trade. The chief exports are grain, rape seed, butter, cheese, beef, cattle, wool, hides, and grain spirit. Factories in the city make porcelain, pianos, clocks, watches, mathematical instruments, chemicals, sugar, beer, and tobacco.

Among the outstanding historic buildings of the city are the domed Marble Church, begun in 1749; Amalienborg Palace; the 17th-century Rosenborg Palace and gardens; the Polytechnic Institute; Trinity Church, with its 117-foot-high Round Tower; the Royal Library; and the University of Copenhagen (founded in 1479).

About the middle of the 12th century Copenhagen was a fishing village. In 1254 it became a town, and in 1443 King Christopher III made it the capital of the kingdom. It was besieged by the Swedish forces in 1658 and was swept by fire in 1728, 1794, and 1795. The harbor was the scene of a great naval battle in April, 1801, when Horatio Nelson virtually destroyed the Danish fleet. The city prospered during the 19th and early 20th centuries until it was occupied by the Nazis in April, 1940. The Danish underground movement carried out such successful sabotage that the Allies did not bomb the city during World War II. Copenhagen was restored to the Danes on May 10, 1945.

COPERNICUS (1473-1543), or Mikolaj Kopernik, was the father of modern astronomy. Born at Torun, Poland, he studied medicine and theology at the University of Krakow. In 1496 he traveled to Italy and studied canon law and astronomy at Bologna about two years. In 1500 he taught mathematics and astronomy in Rome. When about 30 years old he became a Roman Catholic priest and also received a doctorate in law from the University of Ferrara. After 1505 Copernicus lived in Frauenburg, East Prussia. Besides fulfilling his priestly duties he studied astronomy.

Before his time most people believed in the Ptolemaic system, which held that the stars and planets revolved around a motionless earth. But long before, a few men had realized that this did not agree with the observations of the actual motions of the stars and planets. Copernicus decided to simplify this complicated system. His great book, *De revolutionibus orbium coelestium*, published in 1543, stated that the earth rotates on its axis and revolves with the planets around the sun. However, Copernicus' calculations did not put the sun precisely in the center, because he said that the earth does not describe an exact circle around the sun. He could never explain fully why the earth moves and never realized that it revolves around the sun in an elliptical—and not in a circular—path.

COPLAND, AARON (1900-   ), American composer, was born in Brooklyn, N.Y. After he was graduated from public high school, he went to France in 1921 to study music with Nadia Boulanger. He lectured on music at the New School for Social Research from 1927 until 1937, at the Berkshire Music Center from 1940, and at Harvard from 1935 to 1944. In 1951 he was named Norton professor of poetry at Harvard. Among his compositions are *Dance Symphony*, which won the RCA Victor Award in 1930; *El Salón México*, a clarinet concerto; the ballets *Appalachian Spring*, *Rodeo*, and *Billy the Kid*; and the opera *The Tender Land* (1954). Among his other awards were the Pulitzer prize for music in 1944, the New York Music Critics Circle Award in 1945, and the 1950 award of the Academy of Motion Picture Arts and Sciences for his score for the motion picture *The Heiress*. He also wrote several books on music—*What to Listen for in Music* (1938), *Our New Music* (1941), and *Music and Imagination* (1952).

Native copper (pure copper) occurs in a matrix, which is rock in which the metallic crystals are embedded. Copper may occur in the forms shown at the right: **1,** copper crystal; **2,** native copper in a matrix; **3,** cuprite; **4,** bornite; **5,** chalcocite; **6,** azurite; and **7,** native copper. Copper was probably the first metal to be used by man.

COPPER, a metallic element, symbol Cu. There are three general classes of copper ore: copper sulfides, native copper, and copper carbonates and oxides. Copper occurs in large quantities naturally and is found in combination with several other minerals. It ranks second in the world's use of metals, iron being first.

Native copper is an isometric mineral, with a hardness of 2.5-3.0 and a characteristic red color on fresh surfaces. Chalcopyrite, malachite, and azurite are other minerals that provide a source for copper smelting. Chalcopyrite is the chief ore that is mined in Africa, Canada, Chile, England, Spain, and the United States. A large deposit of native copper is found in the Lake Superior region around northern Michigan. The United States is the leading producer of copper in the world. Other great producers are Chile, Canada, Peru, the Congo, and the U.S.S.R., with Mexico and Japan also producing some.

There are two methods used in the extraction of copper from its ores: pyrometallurgy, or furnace smelting, and hydrometallurgy, in which the copper in the ore is dissolved in a leaching solution and then usually extracted by electrolytic deposition. The copper extracted by either of these methods is then refined either electrolytically

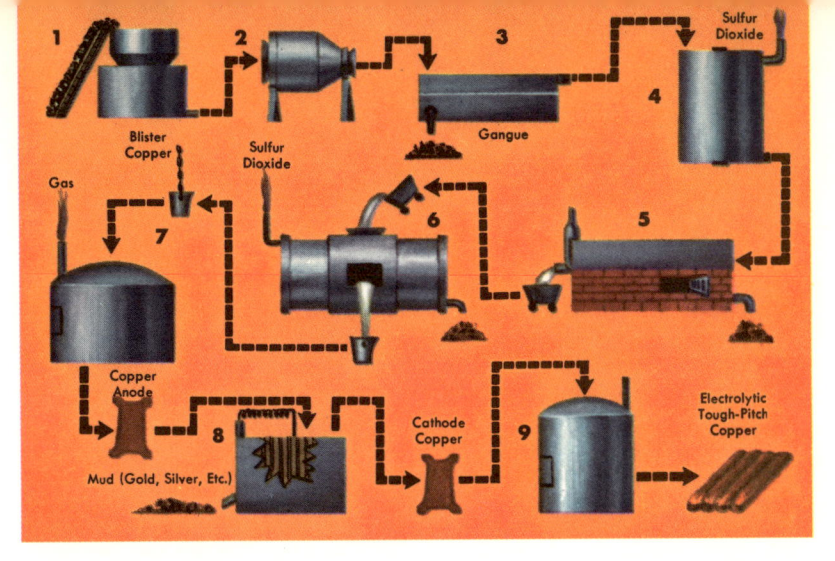

The principal steps in producing pure copper from the sulfide ore include 1, the crusher; 2, ball-mill pulverizer; 3, flotation concentrator; 4, roaster; 5, reverberatory furnace; 6, converter; 7, fire refinery; 8, electrolytic refinery; and 9, fire refinery.

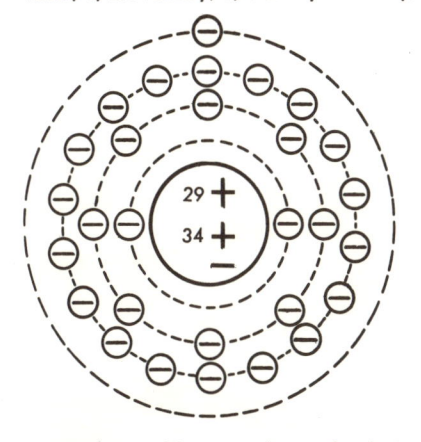

Copper (at. no. 29, at. wt. of most abundant isotope 63) has 29 electrons (−) around a nucleus of 29 protons (+) and 34 neutrons.

or by a furnace-oxidation process. Copper is red in color, malleable, and ductile and has a bright metallic luster. In company with oxygen it forms cuprous oxide and cupric oxide. Copper conducts heat easily, being second only to silver in heat conductivity. Copper wire, because of its high degree of electrical conductivity, is the most widely used form of the metal. Copper is also used in alloys, such as bronze (copper and tin), brass (copper and zinc), and Monel metal (copper and nickel).

COPPERHEAD, a poisonous pit viper of North America, with a range from New England to Florida and west to the central plains and the Big Bend National Park in Texas. It is a variegated, reddish-brown or coppery hue and reaches a length of 3 feet. Not vicious in temper, the copperhead rarely bites unless molested. Its usual food is small animals, such as mice.

COPYRIGHT AND PATENT. The definitions and purposes of the copyright and the patent were well stated by the writers of the United States Constitution. In Article I, Section 8, they wrote that Congress has the power "to promote the progress of science and useful arts, by securing for limited times to authors and inventors the exclusive right to their respective writings and discoveries." The copyright, however, is also given to promote the production of literary, artistic, and educational works.

Only published works can be copyrighted. Published works include books, magazines, newspapers, lectures, plays, musical compositions, maps, works of art, reproductions of works of art, photographs, and motion pictures. Usually the publisher rather than the author obtains the copyright. The copyright is given for 28 years and can be renewed for one additional term of the same amount of time. The holder of a copyright is the only one who can print, publish, or sell the copyrighted work or who can perform it if it is a play or music. Of course, the holder of a copyright can give someone else permission to do these things. However, if someone does these things without permission, the copyright owner can obtain a court order to prevent the person from continuing and can sue him for money. In the United States, copyrights are issued by the Copyright Office, which is part of the Library of Congress. Though each nation has its own copyright system, there are several international treaties that protect in other countries a work copyrighted in any one of them.

Patents are issued on new products, new machines, new manufacturing processes, new improvements on these, and on new designs. Plants (newly developed hybrids) can also be patented. Ideas cannot be patented. Because a patented object must be completely new, securing a patent is more complicated than obtaining a copyright. The Patent Office in Washington, D.C., must conduct much research to ensure that the object is really new before it issues a patent. Because of the complexity of the application process the Patent Office suggests that people have the help of patent lawyers when they apply for patents. The inventor applies for the patent, although he may have given or sold his rights to someone else. Most patents are issued for 17 years. No patent may be renewed except by a special act of Congress. A patent gives its owner, or patentee, the exclusive right to manufacture, use, or sell the patented object. The patentee can sue for damages someone who violates the patent, can obtain a court order to stop the violation, and sometimes can make the violator hand over any profits made from the sale of the patented object. A U.S. patent does not give protection in foreign countries; a patent must be obtained in each country where protection is desired.

The copperhead is a poisonous pit viper. The heat-sensitive pits, located between nostril and eye, help the snake locate its prey.

CORAL

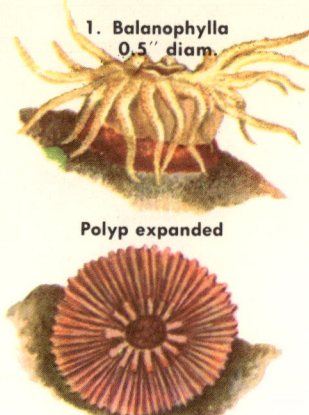

The coral called the sea fan resembles the tinted fan of a lady of bygone times.

This coral polyp, 1, is called Balanophylla. Its skeleton, 2, is seen from the top.

CORAL, the hard, limy skeletons of numerous little sea animals called coral polyps. They are found in all tropical and subtropical seas. They are simply made creatures, their bodies being scarcely more than little sacs, with the upper end open and surrounded by a number of little tentacles, or arms. These wave in the water, creating currents that bring in food. Usually the polyps live in colonies of enormous numbers, their skeletons joined onto one another. Sometimes the colonies take the form of big, branching, treelike structures. Many rocks contain bits of fossil coral, which show that coral must have existed on earth millions of years ago.

The coral used in jewelry is found chiefly in the Mediterranean, Japanese, and Red seas. It is usually red, but there are also pink, yellow, white, and black corals. Precious coral is found in deep water, and its branches usually extend out like those of an unsupported vine. It is obtained by diving and by dredging for the better grades, which usually are in water too deep for diving. The making of coral into beads and cameos is an important industry in many Italian and Japanese towns. See CORAL REEF.

CORAL REEF, a ridge or mound of limestone. The limestone is made up of the hard parts of coral polyps, algae, mollusks, Foraminifera, worms, and other marine organisms that lived, or are still living, on the reef. The corals provide the framework for a growing reef, but much of the reef material is the product of other organisms. See CORAL.

Coral reefs grow only in waters at least as warm as 68° F. The reef-building organisms live in shallow (less than 150 feet deep), clear water where there is plenty of light and food. The top of a growing reef is just a little above low-tide level. Living organisms occupy the top and sides of a growing reef. Many of the organisms cement their skeletons to the existing reef structure. When those organisms die, others build and anchor their skeletons on top of the old ones. Loose shells and hard parts of dead organisms work downward and block up cracks and crevices in the framework until the reef is a massive and solid structure. The reef organisms are always trying to build upward and outward. However, the action of waves and currents, muddy water from nearby land, and the level of low tide limit the growth of reefs.

Coral reefs have three forms: fringing reefs, barrier reefs, and atolls. A fringing reef is built on a shore. There is no space of water between the land and the reef. Most fringing reefs are only a few hundred feet wide. A barrier reef is separated from land by a space of water called a lagoon. Barrier reefs often surround islands in the Pacific and Indian oceans. Barrier reefs may be thousands of feet wide and miles long. The most famous barrier reef, the Great Barrier Reef, parallels the northeast coast of Australia for over a thousand miles. Atolls are ring-shaped reefs without islands in the center of their lagoons.

Several hypotheses exist about the formation of atolls and barrier reefs. Charles Darwin, the famous naturalist, originated the hypothesis that barrier reefs and atolls form when an island with a fringing reef gradually sinks below sea level. As the island slowly sinks, the coral reef builds upward. First, a barrier reef is formed when the island is partly submerged. When the island is completely submerged, only the ringlike reef, which grew straight up as fast as the island sank, remains near sea level.

A coral snake is ringed with colored bands.

CORAL SNAKE, a small, venomous snake of the same family as the cobra. It occurs from the southern United States to South America. Its very small mouth makes it less dangerous than it would otherwise be. The usual color is rich red with black and yellow transverse bands.

Artha Hornbostel

At the right is a portion of the coral atoll that constitutes Wake Island. Below are various types of coral reefs: The upper two have an island in their lagoon, whereas the lower one does not.

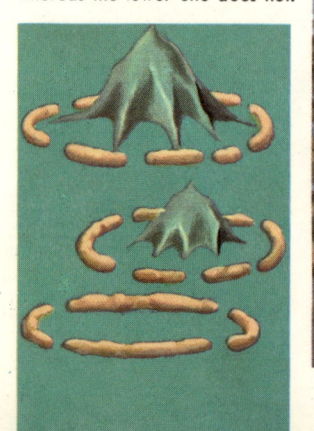

CORBETT, JAMES J. (1866-1933), U.S. boxer and heavyweight champion of the world from 1892 to 1897, was born in San Francisco.

After winning a few amateur events, Corbett entered professional boxing in 1884. He won over opponent Joe Choynski and fought a 61-round draw with Peter Jackson. His big match came with John L. Sullivan in 1892 in New Orleans. He defeated the Irishman in the 21st round. Corbett defended his title until 1897, when Robert Fitzsimmons knocked him out in the 14th round.

Known as "Gentleman Jim," Corbett perfected the straight-hitting style of boxing during the 1890's, the Golden Age of the Prize Ring. This style was an attempt to use the body weight in every blow. Fighters hit with their bodies and used their arms merely as the vehicle of force.

Corbett's last fight occurred in 1903, when James Jeffries knocked him out in the 10th round. He was the first heavyweight champion to win under the Marquis of Queensberry rules. He appeared on the stage and radio and in the motion picture *Gentleman Jim*.

CORK, the outer layer of the bark of an evergreen oak, which grows chiefly on poor, rocky soil in the countries along the Mediterranean. Spain and Portugal are the great centers of cork production. The tree is also cultivated in India and in the United States on plantations in California, New Mexico, and Arizona. The cork oak is generally a small tree of irregular shape. It is very slow-growing, and it usually takes 20 to 30 or even 50 years for the trunk to reach a diameter of 5 or 6 inches. Not until then is the tree considered large enough for the first stripping of the bark. As a rule, the trees are stripped every 8 or 10 years. Many trees live for 100 or 200 years. The layer of cork varies in thickness from $\frac{1}{2}$ inch to over 2 inches.

Cork is used for bottle stoppers and in making life preservers, lifeboats, artificial limbs, soles for shoes, penholder tips, fishing-rod handles, and fishing floats. It is also used for insulation in refrigerators and for covering steam kettles. Cork waste is ground to a flour and used in making linoleum and floor tiling.

These large semicircular strips of bark were taken from cork oaks growing in Portugal. Commercial cork will be made from the bark.

CORMORANT, the common name of a family of dark, long-necked water birds. Two of the thirty species have been trained to assist men with their fishing, and two species are commercially important as producers of vast quantities of a rich fertilizer known as guano.

Cormorants, related to anhingas, gannets, and pelicans, are almost worldwide in distribution. Fossil remains from the Eocene period have been found in California and Florida. Unlike most water birds, cormorants do not have water-resistant feathers. Around a wharf these birds often sit upright in a spread-eagle pose on pilings or rocks while drying their plumage. Their blackness and the continual twisting of their snakelike necks give them a sinister appearance, which may account for Milton's description of Satan as a cormorant.

The two species trained to fish are found in India, China, and Japan. The birds are held on leash while they pursue fish through the water, catch them, and bring them to the owners. Sometimes a tight collar is placed around the bird's neck to prevent its swallowing the fish. The collar is removed when it is time for the bird to feed.

The famous guano producers are the Peruvian, or guanay, cormorants, sometimes called the world's most valuable wild birds. Huge colonies have nested for years on islands off the western coast of South America; their droppings, rich in nitrogen, have accumulated into immense deposits, which the Peruvian government has sold for over a century at millions of dollars annually. Off the southern coast of Africa are other important guano-producing cormorants.

The double-crested cormorant, which is the common cormorant of North America, dries its wings by outspreading them in the sun.

The common North American cormorant, the double-crested, is found on inland lakes and rivers and in the coastal areas. A glossy bird about 35 inches long, it has an orange throat pouch and in breeding plumage is adorned with black and white tufts above the eyes. Its crude nest of sticks or weeds is placed on a cliff, in a tree or bush, or on the ground.

CORN, the most important of all grains grown in the United States and ranking only after rice and wheat in world production. A well-known annual member of the grass family, common field corn, is known also as maize, or Indian corn, and is widely grown throughout most of the temperate and subtropical regions of the world. It is believed to have originated in Mexico or South America and was cultivated in the New World long before the time of Columbus.

The plant may vary from 3 to 15 feet in height, depending on the

Ed Drews—Photo Researchers

variety, with a heavy pithy stem, long tapering leaves, and fibrous underground roots, which are supplemented by coarse prop roots that develop as the plant increases in height. The ears are borne as a fleshy axis emanating from the axils of the leaves and are pollinated by wind-borne pollen originating in the ripened male flower, or tassel, at the top of the stalk. The female inflorescence, or ear, is covered by protecting leaves, or husks, and terminates in a style, or silk, which receives the wind-borne pollen.

Corn is best produced on loamy, well-drained soil in regions where summers are warm and rainfall is abundant. Planting usually takes place in May, in a well-prepared seedbed, followed by cultivation, which is continued until the corn is large enough to discourage weed growth. If the crop is to be harvested as grain, it is husked late in October and November, mechanical pickers being used in commercial production. However, corn for ensilage is cut before full maturity and while still green. Six types of corn are recognized: pod, pop, floury, sweet, flint, and dent, all of which belong to the same species. By far the most important of all types is dent, which makes up the great annual yield of field corn that is fed to livestock and used by mankind for corn meal and other food products.

A major development in corn production has been the adoption of hybrids, produced by crossing pure strains, which the plant breeder calls inbred lines. Hybrid corn has a higher yield, is more resistant to drought, insects, and diseases, and produces ears of more uniform quality. The planting of hybrid corn has resulted in an increased yield of from 20 to 30 percent over old varieties of corn. Hybrid corn was developed by plant geneticists in the United States, and for 15 or 20 years almost all commercial corn grown in that country was hybrid. In Italy, the U. S. S. R., India, and other countries, however, hybrid corn is a recent innovation and was introduced through close cooperation with American plant scientists.

Among the insect pests that attack corn are the chinch bug, the corn borer, the cutworm, the corn maggot, and the corn-ear worm.

Principal corn-producing states are Iowa, Illinois, Minnesota, Indiana, Nebraska, and Ohio. More than half of the world's corn is grown in the United States. Other leading producers are Brazil, Argentina, the U. S. S. R., Mexico, the Union of South Africa, and Italy. More than two-thirds of U.S. corn is consumed by livestock on the farms where it is grown.

CORN BELT, an important agricultural area in the north-central plains of the midwestern United States. The acreage of corn (about 50 million acres) in this region is greater than the acreage of any other crop. The belt stretches westward from western Ohio through Indiana, Illinois, and Iowa into Nebraska, and it includes neighboring parts of Missouri, Kansas, South Dakota, and Minnesota. Iowa and Illinois lead the nation in corn production. The long summers, adequate annual rainfall, and deep soil found here favor corn cultivation.

CORNEILLE, PIERRE (1606-1684), French dramatist, was born at Rouen. He was educated as a lawyer. *Mélite* was an early work of his, which was performed in Paris. From 1633 to 1635 he wrote a series of comedies, which include *La Suivante* and *La Place Royale*. Corneille was one of the five dramatists who wrote under the direction of Cardinal Richelieu. From 1634 to 1636 came *Médée*, his first tragedy; *L'Illusion comique*, a comedy; and in 1637, *Le Cid*. This last work was severely criticized, in a judgment handed down by the French Academy, on points of both grammar and style.

In 1640, however, Corneille began writing his great series of tragedies —*Horace*, *Cinna*, and *Polyeucte*. In 1643 his comedy *Le Menteur* appeared, and in either 1644 or 1645 his tragedy *Rodogune*. Later works of Corneille include *Don Sanche d'Aragon*, *Pertharite*, and *Oedipe*. In his last years Corneille wrote a verse adaptation of the *Imitation of Christ*.

CORNET, a modern brass or silver wind instrument of the trumpet kind. It was first introduced into France. The cornet is now seldom used in a symphony orchestra. It has a melodic tone and is effective as a solo instrument in bands. It is unusually flexible in tone, with a range about the same as that of the trumpet.

The cornet is played like other wind instruments of the brass family. The lips are applied to the mouthpiece and communicate vibrations to a column of air in the tube of the instrument to produce the sounds and determine the pitch. The three valves are operated by finger pressure on one or more pistons and make possible a complete range of notes.

CORNWALLIS, CHARLES (1738-1805), English general and administrator in India, was born in London and was educated at Eton and Cambridge. Upon finishing his education, he served in the army and later was a member of Parliament. In Parliament he opposed the government in its action against the then American colonies. When the colonies revolted, however, he went with his regiment to America, where he served as a major general and with distinction. He routed Gates at Camden, New Jersey, and defeated Greene at Guilford Court House, North Carolina. With his defeat at Yorktown, Virginia, by American and French troops, however, the English cause in America fell.

In England Cornwallis escaped censure for his defeat at Yorktown, and in 1786 he was made governor general in India and the commander in chief at Bengal. He inaugurated a series of reforms, notably in the judicial system, which were known as the Cornwallis Code. (See BRITISH EAST INDIA COMPANY.) In 1793 he returned to England and served in the Cabinet. He was made viceroy of Ireland in 1798. In this office

The yellow tassel atop the corn plant consists of flowers that produce pollen. An ear of corn becomes fertilized and can mature after the yellow silk at its tip has received pollen from the tassel of another plant.
Courtesy of the Ford Motor Company

he was moderate and attempted to pacify the Protestants and the Roman Catholics. In 1802 he was a plenipotentiary, negotiating the Treaty of Amiens between England and France. He went again to India as governor general in 1805, but he died shortly after his arrival.

CORONA, the outer atmosphere of the sun. It is a very thin mixture of gas and dust and extends for millions of miles out from the sun, possibly as far as the earth and beyond. It is visible during a total eclipse of the sun. Then the moon blocks out the direct light from the sun so we can see the light from the corona. This light includes partly sunlight reflected by electrons and dust particles and partly light emitted by ionized atoms at very high temperatures.

The corona is thinner than any vacuum we can produce on earth, but its gas is still much denser than that of interstellar space. The temperature at the surface of the sun is only 6,000 degrees Kelvin, but in the corona about 25,000 miles above the surface the temperature is estimated at 2,000,000° K., and it may be as high as 100,000,000° K. during solar flares.

CORONA, in the atmosphere, a small rainbow-colored ring produced in a thin cloud veil over the sun or moon. The corona looks as though it surrounded the sun or moon, but its source is really in the cloud cover. Sometimes the corona is only a luminous area (aureole) bounded by a brownish-red ring, or it may have two or more rings outside the aureole. These rings are bluish on the inside and reddish on the outside. This color pattern is just the opposite of that in a halo. See HALO.

The corona is formed by the diffraction of light by tiny drops of water in the cloud cover. The bigger the drops of water, the smaller will be the corona formed. A corona gives a clue about the weather to the shrewd weather prophet. If the weather observer sees a corona becoming smaller, he knows that the tiny water drops in the cloud veil are increasing in size. The air must be becoming more humid. So the weather prophet can predict a possible storm.

CORONA BOREALIS, or the Northern Crown, a northern constellation lying between Hercules and Bootes. It is visible in the evening sky from midnorthern latitudes between April and October.

Although the sun is always surrounded by its rainbow-colored corona, the corona is visible only during a total solar eclipse. At other times it is obliterated by the sun's glare.

CORONADO, FRANCISCO VÁSQUEZ DE (1510-1554), Spanish explorer, was born in Salamanca. In 1535 he came to New Spain (Mexico) as part of the retinue of Antonio de Mendoza, the first viceroy. In 1538 he was named governor of the province of Nueva Galicia, whose capital city, Guadalajara, he did much to improve.

The Spanish had discovered great wealth in Mexico and were eager to find more. Mendoza accordingly appointed Coronado commander of an expedition in the north, about which there were many rumors—including those of the Seven Cities of Cibola, whose streets were alleged to be paved in gold. Coronado's expedition set forth in February, 1540, and returned over a year and a half later. From the Spanish point of view it had been a failure, for the great cities had failed to materialize. The expedition was nonetheless tremendously important. Among its discoveries were the Colorado River, the Grand Canyon, the upper reaches of the Rio Grande, and the Pecos River. After spending over a year in what is now New Mexico and Arizona, Coronado moved northeast to a point near the present site of Wichita, Kan. None of this territory had previously been seen by white men, and the expedition's records are of great importance as the first accounts of the Indian Pueblo civilizations and the Great Plains.

After his return to Mexico Coronado was reinstalled as governor of Nueva Galicia but in 1544 was removed from office because of neglect of his duties and cruelty to the Indians. He returned to Mexico City, where he spent his remaining years as an official in the city government.

The constellation Corona Borealis is so named because its seven stars lie in a semicircle that suggests a crown. In Greek mythology this crown belonged to the maiden Ariadne.

CORONA BOREALIS

CORONAGRAPH, a telescope adapted for viewing or photographing the sun's corona. Before the coronagraph was invented in 1930, the corona could be seen only during a total eclipse of the sun while the moon exactly blocked out light from the sun's surface. The coronagraph achieves the same effect by placing a disk in the telescope tube. The disk exactly blocks light from the sun's surface but leaves the light from the corona visible.

A corporation is organized around four groups—stockholders, directors, officers, workers.

CORPORATION, a business association created and treated by the law as an artificial person. Although a corporation is legally a responsible body, it is owned by those who hold shares, or stock, in it. The corporation is a necessary form of business organization, considering the size of huge modern industrial operations.

The process of creating a corporation is interesting. Those who want to establish a corporation meet and discuss their plans. They draw up articles of incorporation. These articles set forth the purpose of the corporation, its name, how long the corporation intends to do business, what kinds of stock are to be issued, the stock subscribed for by the incorporators, and where the corporation is to be located. The people intending to create the corporation then apply to the proper state officials for a charter. The officials examine the intentions of the incorporators and decide whether or not they will issue a charter to them. If the charter is issued, it will record the articles of incorporation and state the government laws concerning corporations. The corporation is now ready to start business. To obtain the money it needs, it sells stock to those interested in sharing ownership, or issues bonds to those interested only in lending money at interest to the corporation. See STOCKS AND BONDS.

The main advantage of the corporation over most other forms of organization, such as the general partnership and the single proprietorship, is that in case of business failure only the corporate body, the artificial person recognized by the state, must pay the debts it has incurred. The shareholders are liable only for the amount they have invested in it. Since the shareholders enjoy this limitation on their liability, the corporation is able to bring together much larger sums of money than either a partnership or a single proprietorship could. See BUSINESS ORGANIZATION.

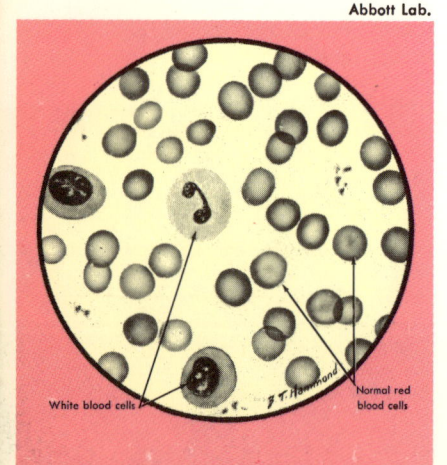

CORPUSCLE. A corpuscle is one of the tiny cells making up the formed parts of the blood. (See BLOOD.) There are two kinds of corpuscles: red and white. Red corpuscles number about 5 million per cubic millimeter. White corpuscles number about 7,000 per cubic millimeter.

The two kinds of corpuscles, or blood cells, appear at left as seen through a microscope.

The red corpuscles are round, concave disks, with large edges thinning toward the middle. The white corpuscles are more spherical and of different shapes and are capable of independent motion. The corpuscles originate in the marrow of the long bones and in lymph tissue. The red corpuscles contain hemoglobin and function in the transport and exchange of oxygen and carbon dioxide in the lungs and tissues. The white corpuscles function chiefly in combating disease and infection.

CORROSION is the slow destruction of materials, particularly metals, by chemical agents. The chemical agents that cause corrosion can be placed in four groups: oxygen and oxidizing chemicals, acids, salts, and alkalis. Corrosion usually refers to the destruction of materials exposed to air or water.

A familiar example of corrosion by oxygen is the rusting of iron. Iron exposed to a humid atmosphere is attacked by oxygen, and the surface of the iron is changed to an iron oxide.

High humidity and air pollution greatly increase the rate of atmospheric corrosion of materials. Many

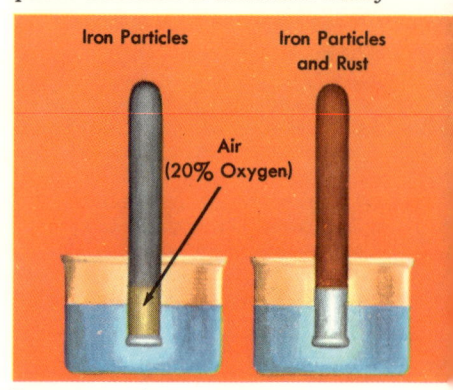

The corrosion of iron in air consumes part of the air, as the experiment above shows. A test tube is coated inside with iron particles and inverted in water, 1. Rusting consumes oxygen from the air inside the test tube, and the water rises in the tube, 2.

chemicals that pollute air unite with water to form acids. Acids rapidly corrode many metals and building stones.

Materials in coastal installations and in boats and ships are corroded by sea water. The salts in the sea water partially dissociate to form acids that do the actual corroding.

Several metals that are resistant to corrosion by acids are rapidly corroded by alkalis. Alkaline chemicals are present in the polluted air of some industrial districts.

The most common method of combating corrosion is to coat non-resistant materials with resistant materials such as paints or varnishes. Easily corroded metals may be plated with corrosion-resistant metals. An effort may be made to remove the acids and the excess oxygen from the water to which materials are exposed.

CORTES, HERNANDO (1485-1547), the conqueror of Mexico, was born in Medellín, Spain. After the discovery of America by Columbus, numbers of young Spaniards, seeking adventure or gold, settled in the West Indies. Among these was Hernando Cortes, who became the owner of an estate in Cuba. The Spanish governor of the island fitted out an expedition against Mexico, which had just been discovered, and gave the command to Cortes. Reaching Vera Cruz, Cortes burned his fleet. This forced his followers to conquer the land or die. He marched boldly into Mexico, seized Montezuma, the ruler of the Aztecs, and obtained from him a quantity of gold. The governor of Cuba was so jealous of Cortes that he sent out a force, under another Spaniard. Leaving some of his men in Mexico, Cortes went to meet the expedition and took its leader prisoner. On his return to Mexico Cortes learned that Montezuma had been killed by his own subjects and that the Spanish troops had been driven out of the city. The battle of Otumba was fought, the Aztecs defeated, and Mexico made a Spanish province. Cortes was very badly treated by some of his countrymen in Spain, and it is said that he boldly charged Emperor Charles V with ingratitude because he did not protect him.

CORTISONE, also called compound E (17-hydroxy-11-dehydrocorticosterone), a hormone of the cortex of the adrenal gland. It has life-maintaining properties in animals from whom the adrenal glands have been removed. Thus it has specific therapeutic value in adrenal-cortical insufficiency (Addison's disease).

Cortisone has also been found to relieve symptoms, often with dramatic rapidity, in such diseases as rheumatoid arthritis, rheumatic fever, allergic diseases of the eyes, skin, and mucous membrane, and colitis. However, the relief is often maintained only as long as the cortisone treatment is continued, and relapses occur when use of the drug is discontinued.

Infectious processes and acute

Mexican Consulate
Hernando Cortes conquered Mexico for Spain.

surgical conditions may be undetected while a patient is undergoing cortisone treatment, and the hazard of the stress-producing experience of a surgical operation is increased. Anyone receiving cortisone should make the fact known to the surgeon before undergoing an operation.

CORUNDUM, Al_2O_3, aluminum oxide, is a common mineral found in metamorphic rocks, in igneous rocks, and in soils and stream sands. Large crystals of corundum are found in some pegmatites. Corundum is a hard mineral; only diamonds are harder. Corundum is heavy for its size. Crystals of corundum are often barrel shaped. Some crystals are marked with horizontal lines. Crystals are transparent or translucent and are found in many different colors. The transparent varieties comprise certain gem stones, for example, ruby (deep red) and sapphire (blue). A dark, granular mixture of corundum, magnetite, and hematite is called emery. See EMERY; RUBY; SAPPHIRE.

CORVUS, or the Crow, is a small southern constellation between Virgo and Hydra. It is visible in the evening sky from midnorthern latitudes between April and June. The two stars in the Crow's wings point behind it toward the bright star Spica in Virgo. Spica can be used to help locate Corvus in the sky.

Corvus, the Crow, is linked in legend to Crater, the Cup, and Hydra, the Sea Serpent, two constellations near it. Apollo sent a crow to fetch a cup of water for a sacrifice to Jupiter, but the crow stopped at a fig tree to wait for the fruit to ripen. He returned carrying a water snake and pretended the snake had delayed him. Apollo saw through the lie. To punish the crow he placed him in the sky next to the cup but ordered the snake never to let him drink.

COSMETICS are preparations designed to be applied externally to beautify and improve the body. As aids to beauty they have an ancient history.

The Chinese have long been experts in the use of cosmetics. Early Egyptians placed alabaster vases of cosmetics and unguents in their tombs. Cleopatra attained a high degree of art in the embellishment of the eyes with kohl. The formulas for powder, paint, bleach, henna, perfume, and lotion were centuries old when Cleopatra used them. The ancient Hebrews were pupils of the Egyptians. Trade in perfume and balm was a profitable business for the Ishmaelites. The Bible refers to Jezebel, the wife of Ahab, as a painted woman. The Romans received the custom from the Greeks. A treatment in a Roman bath included an application of fragrant oils and perfume. Roman ladies of the 1st century had quite an array of cosmetics—white lead to whiten the skin; kohl for the eyelids and lashes; rouge for the cheeks and lips; pumice stone for whitening the teeth; depilatories; cures for skin eruptions; and bleaches and hennas for the hair. The Japanese developed the tattoo to a high level as an adornment. Thousands of miles away the North American Indians also tattooed their bodies, and war paint became the symbol of hostile tribes.

Baths of wine and milk were taken by the ladies of the 17th-century English courts. Both sexes adorned themselves with paint, powder, and patches. However, Puritans of the Commonwealth had such a distaste for artificial beauty aids that a law was passed against their use. It stated that any woman who beguiled a man into marrying her by the use of such aids would be punished and the marriage would be declared null and void. The courts of France and Italy favored the use of cosmetics. Napoleon I was susceptible to the artistic refinements of his time, and Josephine ran up a cosmetic bill that would

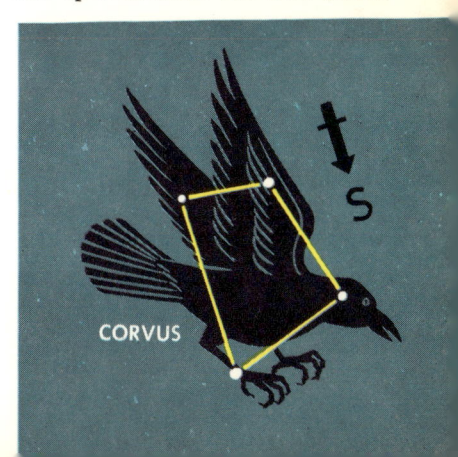

CORVUS

be staggering even today. During American colonial times the use of cosmetics varied from Puritan New England to cavalier Virginia. Victorian standards sharply cut down the application of powder and paints. The 20th century, however, has seen a great expansion in the use and variety of beauty aids.

The cosmetic industry in the United States has a retail sales volume approaching one billion dollars a year. On the market are diversified preparations for improving and beautifying all parts of the body—shampoos, tints, and grooming lotions for the hair; powders, shaving lotions, cream makeup, rouge, lipsticks, and eye makeup for the face; toothpastes, mouthwashes, and enamel cleaners for the mouth; depilatories, deodorants, perfumes, oils, powders, tanning lotions, and softening creams for the hands, feet, and body; and lacquers, hardeners, lacquer removers, and creams for the nails. Cosmetics appear in varied forms. Many may be purchased in liquid, cream, ointment, or powder form and under a variety of brand names. Selection of a cosmetic product is often on a trial-and-error or personal-preference basis.

Cosmetics are essentially beauty aids, although they are often used to alleviate such conditions as dry or chapped skin and to provide protection from exposure. They cannot be expected to bring about marked physical changes when damage has been done by dissipation, age, excessive exposure, or disease.

Cosmetic advertising has sometimes tended to be extravagant, and some cosmetics have contained injurious ingredients. Modern cosmetic firms, however, spend millions of dollars each year in research and testing to make their products safe and appealing. In addition, the manufacturers must meet certain government requirements.

COSMIC DUST is a very thin mixture of gas and tiny solids drifting in space among the stars of a galaxy. The gas consists mostly of hydrogen atoms, and the solids are tiny specks of frozen gas or metals about $\frac{1}{10,000}$ millimeter thick. Cosmic dust is spread so thinly throughout space that there is on the average only one atom per cubic centimeter. Even the best vacuum we can produce on earth is denser than this. But the space between stars is so vast that the total mass of cosmic dust in a galaxy is about equal to the mass of the stars in the galaxy. Through the millions of light-years separating galaxies from each other, there are no stars and very little cosmic dust.

In many places in our galaxy the dust is concentrated in clouds, called nebulae, that reflect light from nearby stars (See NEBULA.) Other clouds stop the light from stars behind them and show as black "holes" in the sky. Some astronomers believe that stars may be forming inside these dark clouds of gas.

COSMIC RAY, a form of very high energy particles constantly falling on the earth from every direction in space. Some of the radiation comes from the sun, but most of it is from interstellar space. Since it was first detected early in the 20th century, scientists have tried to learn what it is and what causes it. At first all they could learn was that the particles are electrically charged. Next they found that the charge is mainly a positive one. They now believe the radiation is made up mainly of protons and the nuclei of many kinds of atoms. These particles are of great interest because they have more energy than any other atomic particles known. They travel at enormous speeds and strike the nuclei of atoms in the earth's upper atmosphere in violent atomic explosions. Only recently have physicists been able to duplicate some of these collisions in experiments.

The fragments of the collisions are called secondary cosmic rays, and include such particles as neutrons and mesons. They receive part of the enormous energy of the original particles, which are called primary cosmic rays. Some of the fragments penetrate the atmosphere down to the surface of the earth and many hundreds of feet beneath it. They can penetrate up to 18 inches of lead.

We do not yet know for sure what causes the primary cosmic rays. They may come from other stars, but how they reach such great speeds has not been explained.

At the right is shown how cosmic rays cause ionization. A positively charged cosmic ray (dotted line) knocks a negatively charged electron from an atom, leaving the atom positively charged. The electron joins another atom, making it negatively charged.

Hugh Anderson

Instruments for measuring cosmic rays are sent as high as 100,000 feet above sea level by means of weather balloons. Physicists have launched balloons from points all over the globe to learn what forces affect cosmic rays in the vicinity of the earth.

COSMOLOGY is the study of the universe as a whole in order to understand its order. It depends, of course, upon what kind of information is available, but often the same information fits two or more different pictures of the universe, and rival cosmological theories, or models, arise. New information may cause one model to be rejected in favor of another; it may force a revision of a widely accepted model; or it may even require that an entirely new model be found.

Early cosmologies were based upon men's unaided observations of earth and sky and were often interwoven with fantasy. Most of them shared the conception of the earth as the stationary center of the universe with the sun, moon, and stars as relatively small objects.

Certain Greek thinkers over 2,000 years ago changed this picture through their knowledge of geometry and certain observations. They realized that the earth is a sphere and estimated its size rather accurately. They also gained some idea of the distance from the earth of the moon and sun. However, much of this information was ignored or lost.

The cosmology of Ptolemy, an Alexandrian astronomer, was accepted for about 2,000 years. It placed the earth at the center of the universe. The stars, sun, moon, and planets circled around the earth. The complex motions of the planets were described by means of combinations of circles. Although the Ptolemaic system was not completely successful, it was able to predict the positions of celestial objects with surprising accuracy.

Copernicus introduced the idea of a rotating earth traveling around the sun as one of the planets. The rotation of the earth explained the apparent motion of the stars, and for the first time it became possible to think of the stars as at a great distance. Galileo's invention of the telescope helped confirm Copernicus' system and opened a great stream of new information.

Within the past 50 years order was discovered among the stars. The sun was found to be a part of a huge revolving spiral of billions of stars called the Galaxy. Then the universe was found to be strewn with billions of such galaxies separated by enormous distances. The galaxies themselves have now been found to occur in clusters.

Today's cosmology confronts the fact that these clusters of galaxies are apparently all spreading away from each other, so that the universe of matter is expanding in all directions. At least two major cosmological models attempt to explain this expansion, as well as other conditions observed in the universe, but not enough information is yet available to confirm either model. The concern with this expansion illustrates the emphasis in present-day cosmology on describing the development of the universe as well as its present structure. For a discussion of the present models of the universe, see UNIVERSE.

Some of the cosmologies that have prevailed in men's thinking are illustrated here: **1**, the world as described by Thales; **2**, cutaway view of the crystal spheres, a popular conception before Copernicus; **3**, Copernicus' view, with planets revolving around the sun; and **4**, the modern conception of a vast universe containing billions of galaxies.

COSSACKS, a group of Russian people characterized by their adventurous and freedom-loving way of life. Under the czars the Cossacks became a special military caste whose service gained them land and other privileges.

Historically, the Cossacks were located on the vast steppes of southern Russia. There, in the 15th century, they settled along the banks of the Dnieper, Don, Ural, and Terek rivers. This was the Wild West of Russia—a region far from the fortified security of Russian civilization. In many ways the Cossacks were like America's frontiersmen. Their name comes from a Tatar word meaning "free adventurer."

To protect themselves from Tatar bands, who roamed freely after the crumbling of the empire of the Golden Horde of Genghis Khan, the Cossacks formed democratic military societies. All Cossacks had a vote in the general assembly, which elected a headman (hetman) of the Cossack Host. In wartime the word of the hetman was law. In peacetime he served only as the president of the assembly. All men, regardless of nationality, were free to join the Cossack Host, provided they swore allegiance to Cossack law and to the Eastern Orthodox Church. The Cossacks lived by fishing, hunting, war booty, and, on occasion, robbing caravans. They were skilled horsemen and were trained to the use of sword, lance, and gun. You might like to read Nikolai Gogol's *Taras Bulba*, which is an exciting book about the Dnieper River Cossacks.

Cossacks played an important part in Russian history. The unruly outlaw Cossack Ermak Timofeev led his Don Cossacks to conquer Siberia in the 16th century. In 1670 Stenka Razin, supported by oppressed peasants, led his Cossacks in a revolt against Russia that shook the foundations of that nation. The bearded, proud, resourceful Razin took one garrison after another along the Volga River. Razin finally was defeated and executed, but his fame was proclaimed in the vigorous songs of the Cossacks.

The Cossack guards refused to fire on the people of Petrograd (now Leningrad) during the first days of the Russian Revolution of 1917, but they fought against the Communists to keep their privileges.

The Cossacks fought once more against the Germans in World War II. Their regiments were mechanized, but contingents still battled on horseback.

COSTA RICA

COSTA RICA is a republic of Central America. Because of a high rate of literacy, widespread land ownership, and the absence of army domination, it has enjoyed greater political stability than the other Central American republics. Its area is estimated to be about 20,000 square miles. The Costa Rican people number more than 1,000,000.

San José is the capital of Costa Rica and its most important commercial center. Cartago, Heredia, and Alajuela are other important cities near San José. The two chief seaports are Limón, on the Caribbean coast, and Puntarenas, on the Pacific coast. Quepos and Golfito are Pacific ports from which bananas are shipped.

The interior of Costa Rica is crossed from northwest to southeast by part of the Central American mountain chain. The highest peaks reach some 12,000 feet. In the middle of the country is the fertile central plateau, where most of the people live. This tableland is the heart of the nation, containing San José and other leading cities. North of these cities rises a line of four volcanoes. Poás has one of the world's largest craters. Earthquakes sometime occur.

There are lowlands along both the Caribbean and Pacific coasts. The Atlantic coastline is regular and about 130 miles long. The Pacific coastline is indented and is almost five times as long. Costa Rica has many rivers. The most important is the San Juan River, which flows into the Caribbean and forms part of the country's boundary with Nicaragua.

Climate varies with the altitude. The lowlands are tropical, the central plateau is temperate, and the upper highlands are cool. Rain falls almost every day on the Caribbean lowlands, supporting thick tropical forests. The Pacific coast is much drier. Like the central plateau, it has dry and rainy seasons.

Costa Rica is an agricultural country with relatively few mining and manufacturing industries. Coffee and bananas are the principal money crops, accounting for the bulk of the country's exports. Cacao accounts for much of the rest. Much of the foreign trade is with the United States. Most of the coffee is grown on the central plateau. Bananas are produced on both the Caribbean and Pacific coasts, mainly on plantations owned by companies in the United States. Sugarcane, tobacco, corn, beans, rice, and potatoes are among crops grown mainly for home consumption. Beef cattle are raised on the lowlands in the northwest. On the plateau dairy cattle are important.

It has been estimated that forests cover three-fourths of Costa Rica's area, but the forest resources are only partly exploited. Mining activities have never been large. Gold, mined on the Pacific slopes, is the chief mineral worked. Aside from the processing of coffee and cacao for export, the principal industries are those that produce goods for local use.

The people of Costa Rica are mainly of unmixed Spanish ancestry. This fact makes the country somewhat different from the other Central American republics, where most of the people are mestizos (mixed Spanish and Indian) or Indians. Spanish is the national language. Roman Catholicism is the prevailing religion. A small group of Negroes lives on the Caribbean coast. Negroes were brought to Costa Rica from Jamaica to work on the banana plantations.

Christopher Columbus discovered the Costa Rican coast in 1502 on his fourth voyage. The first permanent settlement was Cartago. The region was part of the captaincy general of Guatemala. In 1821 the captaincy gained its independence from Spain without difficulty. Two years later Costa Rica and the four other former Spanish provinces formed a federation called the United Provinces of Central America. Civil war caused the breakup of the union in 1838, and a few years later the federation was dissolved. The history of Costa Rica as an independent republic has been generally uneventful.

COSTA RICA

Area: 19,690 sq. mi.
Population: 1,000,000
Capital: San José
Largest cities: San José, Alajuela, Cartago, Puntarenas
Highest mountain peak: Chirropó Grande (12,533 feet)
Chief river: San Juan
Climate: Hot in lowlands, temperate on plateau, cool in highlands—heavy rainfall on Caribbean coast, seasonal rainfall elsewhere
National flag: Five horizontal stripes of blue, white, red (wider than others), white, blue
National anthem: *Noble patria, tu hermosa bandera* (Noble Fatherland, Thy Beautiful Flag)
Form of government: Republic
Unit of currency: Colon
Language: Spanish
Chief religion: Roman Catholic
Chief economic activity: Agriculture, including livestock raising
Chief crops: Coffee, bananas, cacao, corn, rice, beans
Chief mineral: Gold
Chief exports: Coffee, bananas
Chief imports: Manufactured goods, machinery and vehicles, chemicals, food, petroleum products

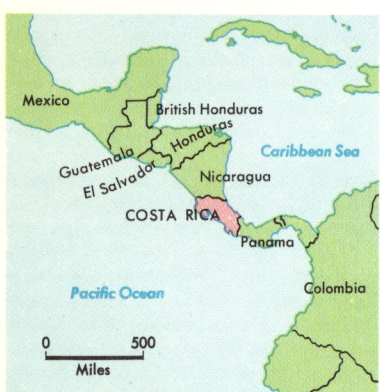

Courtesy of the Pan American Coffee Bureau

The red stripe in the center of the Costa Rican flag is twice the width of the other stripes.

Costa Rica's coffee plantations, unlike those of Brazil, are very small—usually less than 25 acres.

These Costa Rican girls pose with their colorfully painted oxcart, typical of their country.
Courtesy of Pan American Airways

COST OF LIVING, the amount of money needed to pay for all goods and services in maintaining a given standard of living. "Cost of living" is a relative concept, used most frequently to compare present and past conditions. The Consumer Price Index is a useful, though imperfect, measure of changes in the cost of living in the United States.

"Cost of living" has meaning only in relation to a given standard of living and a given environment. Therefore the cost of living for moderate-income city families cannot be applied to high-income or farm families. Cost of living varies also from city to city and from region to region. Accessibility of a city to centers of trade may affect prices, and the climate of a region may affect need for clothing and heat; both factors, in turn, may affect the cost of living.

The Consumer Price Index (CPI), compiled and published by The Bureau of Labor Statistics of the United States Department of Labor, was originally intended to measure changes in cost of living and was called the Cost of Living Index. However, in 1945 it was found that, because the index did not allow for changes in spending habits and quality of goods, it no longer measured changes in the cost of living; the name of the index was changed in that year. Nevertheless, the CPI is often used as an imperfect indicator of changes in the cost of living.

The CPI measures the average change in prices of goods and services purchased by moderate-income families in large cities. Index numbers are assigned in relation to prices in a base year (or average of years), the base year being assigned the index number 100. An index number of 127 for a given year would mean that prices of the goods and services measured averaged 27 percent higher than in the base year.

COTTAGE CHEESE, a soft white cheese made from skim milk. The milk is first pasteurized and cooled. The curd-formation process is started by the addition of lactic acid, rennet, pepsin, or a combination of these in small amounts. The milk is held at about 72° F. until it has a continuous-gel consistency. Then the product is cut, both horizontally and vertically, into small particles by wire cheese knives. Some of the whey flows off in the cutting, but the rest of the whey must be extracted by heating the product to about 90° F., by gentle stirring, and by washing with either water or steam. The cheese is salted and packed in paraffined paper boxes or in glass jars.

Ordinary cottage cheese contains about 1 percent salt. Creamed cottage cheese contains about 4 percent butterfat, because a small amount of cream is mixed with the finished curds. Compared with sirloin steak by weight, cottage cheese is about equal in protein, lower in fat, nine times as high in calcium, and higher in phosphorus.

COTTON is a plant that belongs to the same family as the hollyhock and okra. In addition to providing fiber for cloth, the cotton plant provides cottonseeds for oil and meal. The cellulose in the cotton plant is also used for a variety of products including cellophane.

The cotton plant is handsome, with long-stemmed, lobed leaves and large white or cream-colored flowers, which soon turn pink. The egg-shaped green bolls open when ripe and expose a snowy mass of white hairs attached to the seeds.

Cotton is picked by hand or by machine. After it is picked, the fiber has to be separated from the seeds. This work was done by hand until the invention of the cotton gin by Eli Whitney in 1793.

Cotton is the world's most important fiber crop. India had a cotton industry as early as 1500 B.C. Explorers found cotton growing in the West Indies, in Peru, and in Mexico. The ancient tombs of the Incas have yielded beautiful fabrics woven from cotton thread.

Cotton has a growing season of about 200 days. Seeds planted after the last frost in the spring will produce plants that will yield cotton from September to November. During this long growing season the plant requires a high temperature.

COTTON PROCESSING

Cotton processing begins in the field with the application of chemicals to wither away the leaves of the cotton plant. After the open cotton bolls are stripped off the plant by hand or by machine, the bolls are delivered to the gin for the separation of fiber from seeds. The fiber with a small percentage of trash and leaves is pressed and bound into 500-pound bales and shipped to the cotton factory.

Spinning, weaving, and finishing are the three basic processes in the conversion of raw cotton into fabrics. These fabrics range from heavy sailcloth to the sheerest organdy. Each of the three basic processes is subdivided into many detailed processes, each of which has its own machines and chemical treatments.

When the bales of cotton are opened in the factory, the cotton is graded as to length of fiber. Cotton of similar fiber length is fed into the blending machine for cleaning. Then the loose cotton passes to the carding machine, which pulls the fibers in one direction, shapes them into a wide, thin, loose web, and turns them out as slivers. Slivers are soft, round, ropelike strands about 2 inches in diameter. The slivers are cleaned, refined, and compressed to size for the spinning frames. The spinning frames twist and wind the yarn onto bobbins. The yarn, which at this stage is also called thread, is now ready for weaving. See CLOTH.

From the weaving department, the gray goods go to the finishing department. There, by singeing, shearing, bleaching, and drying, the cloth is prepared for dyeing and printing. Sometimes dyeing is the first process after the cotton bale is

Cotton is being picked by machine on this southern farm. Formerly it was picked laboriously by hand.

This cotton was grown by irrigation in a dry region of the African Sudan. The water was from the Nile River.

The cotton boll is the seed pod of the plant. The cotton fibers are attached to the seed within the boll. When the boll ripens, the cotton within it bursts out (lower right). The world's chief cotton-growing regions are shown on the map.

Eli Whitney constructed this model of his laborsaving cotton gin before 1793.

opened, and sometimes the cotton is dyed as yarn or as thread.

Among the many methods of printing cotton cloth are block, roller, and photographic. The ultimate finish of the cloth comes from its being stretched, starched, filled, and calendered. Cotton cloth can be processed so it is soft or stiff, porous or water repellent, and nonflammable. It can be made substantially shrink resistant.

Some cotton fabrics are produced by knitting instead of weaving. They are elastic, form fitting, and absorbent and do not wrinkle easily. Whole new "families" of cotton cloth have been developed by matting and bonding with a resin.

COTTONSEED PRODUCTS

Cottonseed is the eighth most important cash crop of the United States. Cotton is generally the most important cash crop, and of this crop about three-fifths by weight is cottonseed. Even though the cotton fiber is worth ten times more than the seed, the 3,500,000 tons of seed at $42 a ton amount to almost $150,000,000.

Cottonseed as it comes from the gin yields four major products: oil, meal, hulls, and linters. The oil is used for shortening, cooking oil, salad oil, and margarine. The meal makes a high-protein food supplement for cattle. The linters, which are the short fibers that cling to the cottonseeds, are used for absorbent cotton and for stuffing for furniture. They are also used in the manufacture of rayon, photographic films, and varnishes. A ton of cottonseed yields about 339 pounds of oil and about 942 pounds of cattle meal.

COTTON BELT was a name applied to a large farming region in the southeastern United States where cotton was the principal crop. In this area more acreage was devoted to cotton than to any other crop. The region mainly extended from the Carolinas through Georgia, Alabama, Mississippi, Louisiana, and eastern Texas. Following the Civil War the area stretched to other parts of Texas, New Mexico, Arizona, and California.

Although cotton cultivation is still important, especially in the irrigated regions of the West (Texas is the nation's leading producer), great advances have been made for diversified agriculture in the old Cotton Belt states. Now cotton is the principal crop in only very restricted areas.

COTTON KINGDOM. See PLANTATION LIFE IN THE SOUTH.

COTTONWOOD, a stout tree of the willow family, growing up to 90 feet tall. The quaking, dull-green leaves are from 5 to 7 inches long and somewhat heart shaped at the base. They are fastened to the stems in such a way that they will quiver in the slightest breeze. The male and female flowers grow on separate trees, and both are borne in tassels, called catkins, which bloom before the leaves unfold. The fruits are attached to silky white parachutes, called cotton, which often float so profusely in the air as to give the appearance of a gentle snowfall. The tree is forbidden in some cities because the roots tend to clog sewers. It grows rapidly, and its wood is soft and porous and tends to warp. It is used in making cheap boxes and crates. It is also used to some extent as pulpwood. Cottonwoods are native to the United States east of the Rocky Mountains and prefer rich, moist soils. They grow thickly in the valleys of rivers and streams and in low places in meadows.

These are cottonwood leaves and blossoms.

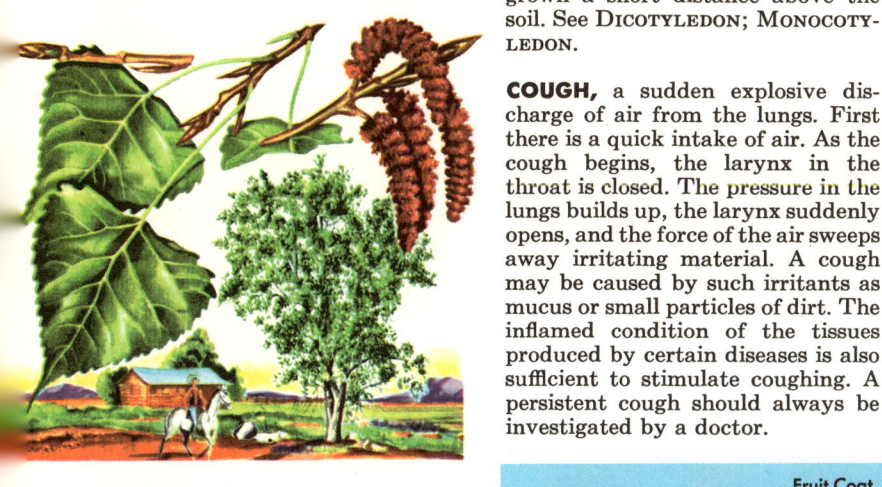

COTYLEDON, a small leaflike organ that nourishes a young angiosperm plant for a while after it has germinated. The cotyledons develop within an angiosperm seed as part of the tiny embryonic plant that is enclosed by the seed. As the embryonic plant germinates and grows upward from its seed, the cotyledons are attached to the lower part of its stem. The cotyledons are called seed leaves because in many plants they resemble small green leaves. Cotyledons are really modified leaves, whose primary function usually is the storage of food for the young plant, which will develop from the seed.

Stored within the cotyledons are proteins, starch, and oils, which nourish the tender young plant during the first stages of its growth. The cotyledons obtained these foods from the parent plant and stored them—sometimes for many months—while the seed lay dormant in the earth during winter. The cotyledons nourish the young plant from the time it begins to germinate until it has developed true leaves, which can manufacture their food by means of photosynthesis. The cotyledons wither and fall from the stems of most plants soon after their true leaves have developed and have begun photosynthesis.

Only angiosperms have cotyledons. All angiosperms are divided into two large subclasses on the basis of whether they have one or two cotyledons. Monocotyledonous angiosperms, such as corn and wheat, have only one cotyledon, while dicotyledonous ones, such as beans, oaks, and sunflowers, have two cotyledons. The small, green, leaflike cotyledons of many plants can be seen on the lower part of their stems as soon as they have grown a short distance above the soil. See DICOTYLEDON; MONOCOTYLEDON.

COUGH, a sudden explosive discharge of air from the lungs. First there is a quick intake of air. As the cough begins, the larynx in the throat is closed. The pressure in the lungs builds up, the larynx suddenly opens, and the force of the air sweeps away irritating material. A cough may be caused by such irritants as mucus or small particles of dirt. The inflamed condition of the tissues produced by certain diseases is also sufficient to stimulate coughing. A persistent cough should always be investigated by a doctor.

COULOMB, CHARLES DE (1736-1806), a French scientist, was born in Angoulême. He was famous for his experiments on friction and for the invention of a torsion balance to measure the force of magnetic and electrical attraction. In early life he studied engineering. In 1779 he gained a Royal Academy of Sciences prize by a work on magnetic needles and again two years later by his "Theory of Simple Machines." For speaking critically about a projected canal in Brittany, he was imprisoned for some time, but he earned the hearty approval of honest Bretons as well as of his own conscience. The coulomb, quantity unit in electricity, was named for him. He was elected to the French Academy in 1782.

COUNCIL OF CONSTANCE, a council of the Roman Catholic Church held from 1414 to 1418 in the town of Constance, then a free city of the Holy Roman Empire and now a city of southern Germany. The council was called by the papal claimant John XXIII with the support of the Holy Roman emperor Sigismund. Its main object was to end the Western Schism, a situation in which three different persons had come to be recognized as pope by different parts of the church—John XXIII, Gregory XII, and Benedict XIII. Gregory XII is now considered to have been the true pope at that time. The council was also called to bring about reforms within the church, an important aim of Sigis-

The longitudinal section of a sunflower seed (upper left) shows the cotyledons folded within it. After the sunflower plant has grown a short distance above the soil, its two cotyledons unfold and can be observed.

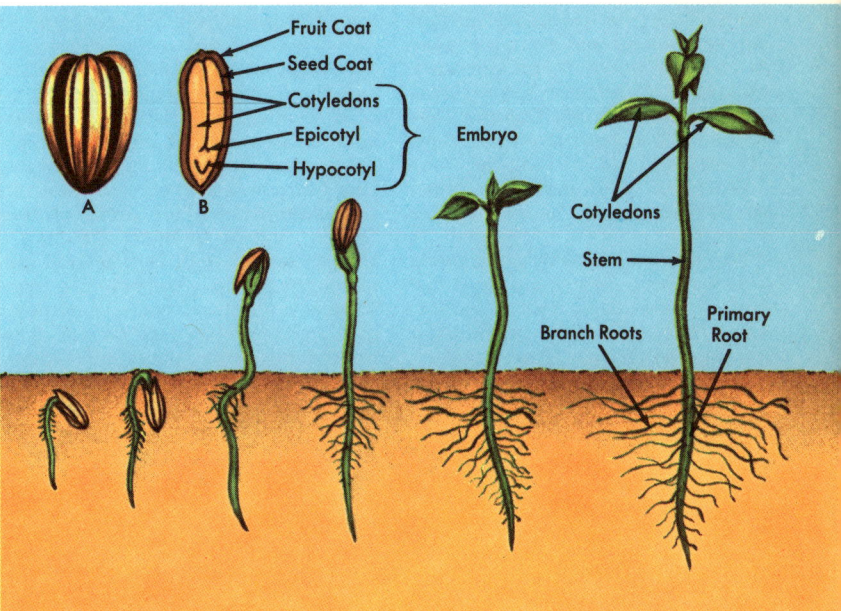

mund, and to suppress heresy. Many thousands of persons attended the council, including John XXIII, Sigismund, 29 cardinals, 3 patriarchs, 33 archbishops, hundreds of bishops and abbots, and thousands of monks, princes, noblemen, ambassadors, and professors and doctors of theology and canon law. Gregory and Benedict sent envoys but did not attend in person.

The council agreed to vote by nations instead of by individuals, an unprecedented procedure that decreased the importance of the large Italian delegation accompanying John XXIII. The nations voting were Italy, Germany, France, England, and a late arrival, Spain.

The council early decided that the only feasible way to resolve the schism was to obtain the abdication of all three papal claimants. John promised to resign but later fled secretly to Austria. This action threatened to dissolve the council; but Sigismund held the council together. It finally declared that its power was derived directly from God and that even the pope was bound to obey the council's decisions. This doctrine is now considered to have been illegal. However, John was seized, imprisoned, and deposed, and he finally bowed to the decision of the council. Gregory abdicated with dignity. Benedict secluded himself in an impregnable castle at Peñíscola on the coast of Spain, where he died without giving up his claim to be the true pope. The council, however, deposed him in 1417.

The council then decided that those voting for a new pope should include not only the cardinals but an additional group of six representatives from each of the five participating nations. The pope was then to be elected by a two-thirds majority of the cardinals and of each of the national groups so that his election would be unanimously supported. After three days of voting, Cardinal Ottone Colonna was chosen. His coronation took place Nov. 21, 1417, and he took the name of Martin V. This ended the Western Schism, which had lasted for 40 years.

The reforms made by the council were few because it considered the election of a pope first in importance. The council did require the new pope to promise to make extensive reforms after taking office.

The council's action against heresy resulted in the burning of John Huss and Jerome of Prague. (See HUSS, JOHN.) It also condemned the doctrines of John Wycliffe.

COUNCIL OF EUROPE, an organization to stimulate and unify the economic, social, cultural, scientific, and legal policies of European nations. The Council of Europe was the idea of the consultative council of the Brussels Treaty Organization. It was created in 1949 by the foreign ministers of Belgium, Denmark, France, the Republic of Ireland, Italy, Luxembourg, the Netherlands, Norway, Sweden, and the United Kingdom. Turkey, Greece, the German Federal Republic, and Austria joined the council later. The organization held its first meeting at Strasbourg, France, in 1949.

The Council of Europe purposes to protect the common heritage of its members and to facilitate economic and social progress. This aim is pursued by discussions, agreements, and concerted action on matters of common concern. The members are bound to respect the principle of the rule of law and to safeguard the human rights of their citizens.

Normally, each member is represented on the Committee of Ministers by its foreign minister. The committee passes resolutions concerning the aims of the council and procedural matters. Action on important matters requires the unanimous affirmation of all members voting. A Consultative Assembly debates matters of concern to the council and makes recommendations to the Committee of Ministers. Members of the assembly are chosen by the parliaments of the member nations. The assembly meets for a period of about a month each year. The administration of the council is handled by the Secretariat headed by a secretary general appointed by the Assembly. In 1958 the council created a European Court of Human Rights.

COUNCIL OF NICAEA, FIRST. This was the first ecumenical, or churchwide, council of Christianity. It was held in Nicaea (now Iznik, Turkey) in the summer of A.D. 325. Constantine I summoned representatives of the church from all parts of the Roman Empire to the council, with the consent of Pope Sylvester I. He had only recently gained rule over the eastern provinces of the empire, and unity within the empire was one of his main concerns. Consequently, news of continuing religious controversy over the doctrine of Arianism distressed him. It was to settle this controversy and restore religious unity to the empire that Constantine called the council.

Arianism, named after its founder, Arius, denied the full divinity of Christ by asserting that Christ had been created by God. At the council the opponents of Arianism, led particularly by Athanasius, deacon of the bishop of Alexandria, persuaded the council to condemn Arius' teaching and to expel Arius and his followers from the church.

The council then defined an orthodox doctrine of Christ as God the Son, coeternal and coequal with God the Father, being of the same substance with the Father. It published a profession of faith afterward known as the Nicene Creed, established the date of the celebration of Easter, and adopted 20 canons regulating other church matters.

COUNSELOR, a person who advises others on educational or vocational goals. School counselors may teach classes, advise pupils, help plan programs for pupils, consult with teachers and parents, maintain good relations between the school and the community, and assist pupils in solving their personal problems. The counselor does not simply tell persons what to do. He may listen to people discuss their own problems and encourage them to solve these problems through their own initiative. He aids persons in the discovery of their own talents.

In elementary schools the counselor may work with children who have problems in social and personal adjustment. However, counseling is being recognized as important for all children, and especially for the very bright children. The high-school counselor helps pupils find part-time jobs and suggests vocations for those pupils leaving school. The college counselor helps students prepare for the jobs and professions for which they are especially suited. The counselor tests students and interprets the results of these tests.

Government agencies also use counselors, especially in connection with work with veterans. Counselors work for the U.S. Employment Service, the Vocational Rehabilitation Service, and the Veterans Administration. Unions such as the United Automobile Workers also operate counseling programs. Counselors are employed by organizations such as the YMCA and the YWCA.

Many people feel that because they "know what they want," counseling is unnecessary. However, it is sometimes hard to decide just what jobs a person can do until he is

> **OCCUPATION:** Counselor
> **NATURE OF WORK:** Directing the judgment or conduct of others through advice or instruction
> **PERSONAL FACTORS—ABILITIES, SKILLS, APTITUDES:** An ability to convey ideas clearly and simply, to deal with people effectively, and to inspire confidence and a well-adjusted personality, an even temper, and emotional stability are essential.
> **EDUCATION AND SPECIAL TRAINING:** A bachelor's degree with teaching experience is the basic requirement. An M.A. and a Ph.D. are necessary for advanced positions. A school counselor must have a state teaching certificate.
> **WORKING CONDITIONS:**
>   1. **INCOME:**
>   **COMPARED WITH OTHER CAREERS WITH EQUAL TRAINING:** Average to high
>   **COMPARED WITH MOST OTHER CAREERS:** Average
>   2. **ENVIRONMENT:** Variable — camp, school, college, hospital, industry, and business
>   3. **OTHER:** Usually regular hours; fringe benefits; excellent opportunities
> **RELATED CAREERS:** Personnel worker, psychologist
> **SPECIALIZATION:** Camp counselor, school, college, or university vocational counselor, rehabilitation counselor, counseling psychologist in industry and in health agencies, domestic relations counselor
> **WHERE TO FIND MORE INFORMATION:** American Personnel and Guidance Association, 1605 New Hampshire Avenue, NW, Washington 9, D.C.; U.S. Department of Health, Education, and Welfare, Office of Education, Washington 25, D.C.

adequately tested. The counselor will also be able to suggest the proper school curriculum for those who know what they want. Students may not be aware, for example, that four years of English may be very important to, say, a businessman. The counselor will also be able to suggest innumerable job possibilities of which the student or veteran is unaware, and he will give students information about scholarships and specialized schools.

A counselor must have a college degree with work in such subjects as psychology, education, tests and measurements, biology, economics, community relations, social sciences, and counseling techniques. Experience in business and social work is also valuable. The school counselor, of course, needs a teaching certificate. He also needs a master's degree or a year's postgraduate work in education, psychology, or sociology. Counselors at the university level may need a doctor's degree. The personal characteristics of a good counselor include fairness, a well-balanced philosophy of life, emotional stability, an ability to get along with people, broad cultural interests, and an extensive knowledge of employment conditions and economics. A counselor will earn as much as the better paid teachers. Moreover, counselors have the satisfaction of helping people achieve the most in life.

COUNTERFEITING, producing false copies of something of value. Money, of course, is the favorite subject for counterfeiting. The counterfeiting of money is a crime dating at least from the reign of the Roman emperor Nero. Marco Polo discovered that Kubla Khan issued notes printed on mulberry paper. The counterfeiters of this paper money were punished with death. In the United States, Americans lose large sums of money because of clever counterfeits.

To detect a counterfeit bill a person must be familiar with the money he handles. Then he will notice the differences in the bills that are counterfeit. A counterfeit one-dollar bill, for example, may have a flat, lifeless portrait of George Washington; an uneven, darker background behind the portrait; indistinct lines on the border of the bill; blunt, uneven saw teeth on the treasury seal; or a badly spaced serial number. Counterfeit money looks bad because it is printed on cheap paper by defective plates and is usually made by poor engravers.

Counterfeiters are traced by the U.S. Secret Service, a division of the Treasury Department. The service maintains a card index of all the counterfeit bills that have been made since the size of the bills changed in 1929. Convicted counterfeiters face a fine of up to $5,000 and a prison term of up to 15 years.

Akin to counterfeiting is forging. Forgeries have been made of famous paintings; for example, Hans van Meegeren, a Dutch painter-forger, fooled noted authorities on art with his paintings in the style of Jan Vermeer.

There have also been many forgeries of political documents. An example is the *Protocols of the Elders of Zion*. These *Protocols* pretended to show a scheme by the "leaders of Zion" to overthrow all governments and rule the world. A trial held in Bern, Switzerland, in 1934 established the fact that the *Protocols* were admitted to be forgeries by those who first used them, the secret police of czarist Russia.

COUNTER-REFORMATION, or Catholic Reformation, a movement of reform within the Roman Catholic Church during the 16th and 17th centuries. Its major phase lasted from about 1560 to the end of the Thirty Years' War in 1648, but the entire movement extended before and after these dates.

The name of the movement implies that it arose solely in reaction to the Protestant Reformation. However, movements for reform had been under way in the Catholic Church well before the Protestant

Below are shown a genuine and a counterfeit bill. The arrow on the counterfeit (right) indicates one of several areas where deviation from the genuine article is apparent.

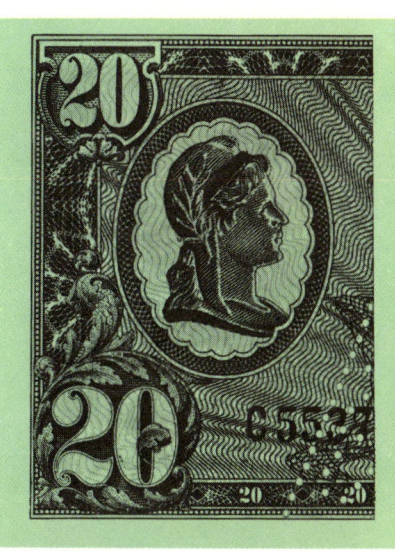

Reformation. The Counter-Reformation was therefore not just a response to the Protestant Reformation but a development of Roman Catholic reform movements under the stimulus and challenge of Protestantism.

Important features of the Counter-Reformation were the succession of three reforming popes, the expansion of the newly formed Jesuit order with its great missionary zeal, the definition of doctrine and adoption of reform laws at the Council of Trent, and the recovery of Poland and southern Germany to the Catholic faith.

In 1560 the situation of the Roman Catholic Church had become quite bleak. The Protestant Reformation had swept through much of Europe. Only in Spain did the hold of the Roman Catholic Church seem secure, and even there certain defections to Protestantism had occurred. On his deathbed in 1559 Pope Paul IV lamented, "From the time of St. Peter there has not been a pontificate so unfortunate as mine." The most astute diplomats of the time saw no likelihood of a change for the better. However, the church did shortly find the necessary vigor within itself both to reform and to meet the challenge of the Reformation.

Three reformist popes won new respect for the papacy. St. Pius V set a needed example of asceticism. Gregory XIII enthusiastically encouraged education. Sixtus V strengthened the finances of the church.

The Jesuit order, or Company of Jesus, which had been approved in 1540, infused the Catholics with great confidence and extended its missionary and educational work throughout Europe and into Africa, Asia, and America. St. Vincent de Paul worked zealously among the poor of the Paris slums. Among laymen a new religious feeling centered upon a reverence for the sacraments.

The Council of Trent, held between 1545 and 1563, was one of the most important of all the church councils. It defined many doctrines of the church that were disputed by the Protestants, among them doctrines on the Scriptures and tradition, original sin, justification, Christian marriage, and indulgences. It also introduced reforms of the monastic orders and the clergy. The fact that the reforms were faithfully carried out shows that a genuine revival of religious feeling had occurred as a consequence.

Both Protestants and Catholics vied for control of the governmental apparatus of the states and cities. Where Protestants controlled the government, Protestantism was enforced. Where Catholics controlled the government, Catholicism was enforced. Religious wars, especially the terrible Thirty Years' War, resulted in definition of national religious affiliations. As a result of these, southern Germany and Poland were returned to the Catholic faith.

COUNTRY DANCE, a kind of dance that originated in rural England. Two country dances, Sellenger's Round and Greensleeves, eventually became children's games.

The first country dances in England were probably processionals or rounds. The dancers danced around a tree or a sacred object. Later the dances found their way into the ballrooms and the court.

The country dances of the 17th and 18th century reflected the exaggerated courtesies of the period. Jane Austen's heroes and heroines performed their dances in sets. The country dance spread to the Continent, especially to France. There it was called the *contredanse*. It became more polished and less boisterous and returned to England.

The English country dance was popular because it allowed each couple in the room to join in its evolutions. In the Roger de Coverley, an English country dance, the dancers changed places, moving backward and forward, parting and uniting again. The music was in two-four time or six-eight time, and the steps were smooth and gliding. This dance was similar to America's Virginia reel. Other country or folk dances were Scotland's Highland fling and Ireland's jig.

Morris dancers continue an English country dance tradition more than 500 years old.
B.I.S.

COURAGE, the attribute of those who brave or endure physical or mental pain to uphold an ideal. There are a great many varieties of courage. Physical courage is only one kind, and it is sometimes overstressed to the detriment of other types of courage. Courage is not the monopoly of any group, nation, or philosophy. Indeed, courage has been frequently displayed by people fighting for an unjust cause.

Sheer physical courage might be represented by the colossal Ajax, a hero of Homer's *Iliad*. He was second only to the mighty Achilles in strength and bravery. Ajax feared no man, and he once engaged Hector of Troy in single combat. It was Ajax who recovered Achilles' body from the Trojans. Courage of this type might be displayed in defense of any cause. It represents man's ability to overcome his fear of death.

Moral courage is another type. It was shown by Samuel Sewall, who had presided over the witchcraft trials in Salem in 1692. Several years later Sewall handed his minister a confession, which the minister read to the congregation of his meetinghouse. As Sewall stood in his pew, the congregation listened to his admission of guilt and error in his judgment of the Salem "witches."

There is another, more subtle, type of moral courage that is displayed at times. Sometimes it passes almost unnoticed. It is displayed by people like Anne Frank, who in the midst of the horrors of World War II had the courage to write: "In spite of everything I still believe that people are really good at heart."

COURT, a public body responsible for the administration of justice. The term *court* refers more exactly to the tribunal than to the place where justice is administered. When a court is in session it is comprised of the plaintiff, the defendant, and the judicial power.

Courts may be courts of record, in which judicial proceedings are formally recorded. Some inferior (lower) courts are courts not of record and keep no record of the proceedings. Courts may also be divided into courts of general jurisdiction, which hear all cases of a particular type, and courts of limited jurisdiction, which may hear pleas of a limited nature or may hear cases only within a certain territory. The nature of a court's jurisdiction also distinguishes it. Actions may be

COWBOY

commenced in courts of original jurisdiction. Courts of appellate jurisdiction, however, hear only those actions appealed from other courts. Courts of intermediate jurisdiction may have original jurisdiction or hear cases appealed from lower courts. Criminal courts are courts convened to try crimes, acts that violate a law and render the offender subject to prosecution of the state. Civil courts handle subjects that are not considered criminal. Special types of courts include courts of admiralty, having jurisdiction over civil and criminal maritime cases, and courts martial, or military courts. See JUDGE; SUPREME COURT OF THE UNITED STATES.

In Great Britain civil cases are brought before county courts or before a court of the high court of justice, which includes the queen's bench division, the chancery division, the probate, divorce, and admiralty division, and the assize courts. Magistrates at petty sessions may hear summarily (without a jury) cases of a minor criminal nature. On indictment (the formal accusation by a grand jury) the magistrate sends more serious criminal cases to be heard at quarter sessions or assize courts. Cases may be appealed to the House of Lords, the judicial committee of the privy council, the court of appeal, the court of criminal appeal, and, in cases of court martial, to the court martial appeal court.

The Supreme Court of Canada is the chief Canadian appellate court in civil and criminal cases. It also advises the governor in council on questions submitted to it and the Senate and House of Commons on private bills. Claims by or against the crown are heard in the exchequer court, which also hears admiralty cases. Miscellaneous courts have jurisdiction over particular types of cases, such as income tax, bankruptcy, and farmers' credit. All Canadian provinces have minor courts, which hear minor criminal and civil cases, and county and district courts. Each province has a superior court with almost unlimited jurisdiction. This court is called a supreme court, a court of queen's bench, or a superior court. The provinces also have courts of appeal.

The High Court of Australia, while it has some original jurisdiction, hears mainly appeals. Other Australian courts with commonwealth jurisdiction are the federal court of bankruptcy and the industrial court, which is charged with settling industrial disputes by arbitration, setting the basic wage, and so on. Each state has its own judicial system, consisting of lower, or magistrates', courts, which are limited to minor civil and criminal cases, and high, or judges', courts, which deal with more serious offenses and important civil cases. In nonfederal cases appeals can be made from state courts to the privy council.

The Federal Republic of Germany had to reestablish its court system following World War II. The judicial system had been subordinated to the purposes of the Nazis, so that a trial to determine guilt or innocence was not possible—the courts decided cases to further Nazi policy. The Law to Restore Legal Uniformity was enacted in 1950. It set up a level of civil and criminal courts including the local courts, which handle small civil cases and minor criminal actions; the district courts, which handle civil and criminal actions of greater importance and appeals from the local courts; the courts of appeal, which hear those cases appealed from the district courts; and the Supreme Federal Court, which is the court of last resort for civil and criminal jurisdiction and decides the constitutionality of the government's actions.

The basic courts in the U.S.S.R. are the people's courts, which hear civil and criminal cases. Appeals from these courts may be made to territorial, regional, or area courts and to the courts of the autonomous regions and national areas. All of these courts hear the more serious criminal and civil cases. The supreme court of an autonomous republic or a union republic tries civil and criminal cases within its jurisdiction, hears appeals from the lower courts, and supervises the courts within the territory. The Supreme Court of the U.S.S.R., the highest judicial organ of the country, supervises the entire court system, hears appeals from lower courts, and tries the most important of both criminal and civil cases.

COVALENT BONDING. See CHEMISTRY.

A covered wagon travels to new land.

COVERED WAGON. The original covered wagon was the Conestoga wagon, designed in the Conestoga Valley of Lancaster Co., Pennsylvania, in 1755. It was boat shaped and had slanted ends, with a sag in the middle, both crosswise and lengthwise, so that shifting loads would settle toward the middle. The heavy back wheels were as much as 6 feet across. It was usually drawn by a six-horse team, and its sturdy construction made it ideal for fording streams and traveling over rough ground. The Conestoga was used as far west as the Mississippi, but for the prairie trips and the gold-rush days there were important modifications, especially in size, that led to the development of the prairie schooner.

The prairie schooner had six or seven arching bows over which a canvas cover was stretched. It came into common use after 1821. Drawn by oxen or mules, it was both a means of transportation and a home for the pioneer family journeying west.

COWBIRD. See BLACKBIRDS, GRACKLES, COWBIRDS.

COWBOY, a worker on the Great Plains ranches that prospered in the 19th century. Mounted and colorfully dressed, his job was to guard, protect, and drive to market the huge herds of cattle that grazed on the unfenced pastureland.

The cowboy's job was created by changing conditions in Texas and elsewhere on the western prairies. When the railroads reached Kansas and cattle could be shipped to eastern markets, it became profitable to raise cattle on the open pastureland, left vacant by the extermination of the herds of bison. Cattle grazed freely on the open range; when ready to be sold, they were driven in herds of 2,000 or 3,000 to towns along the railroads.

The cowboy at left is shown rescuing a calf from starvation on the snow-covered range.

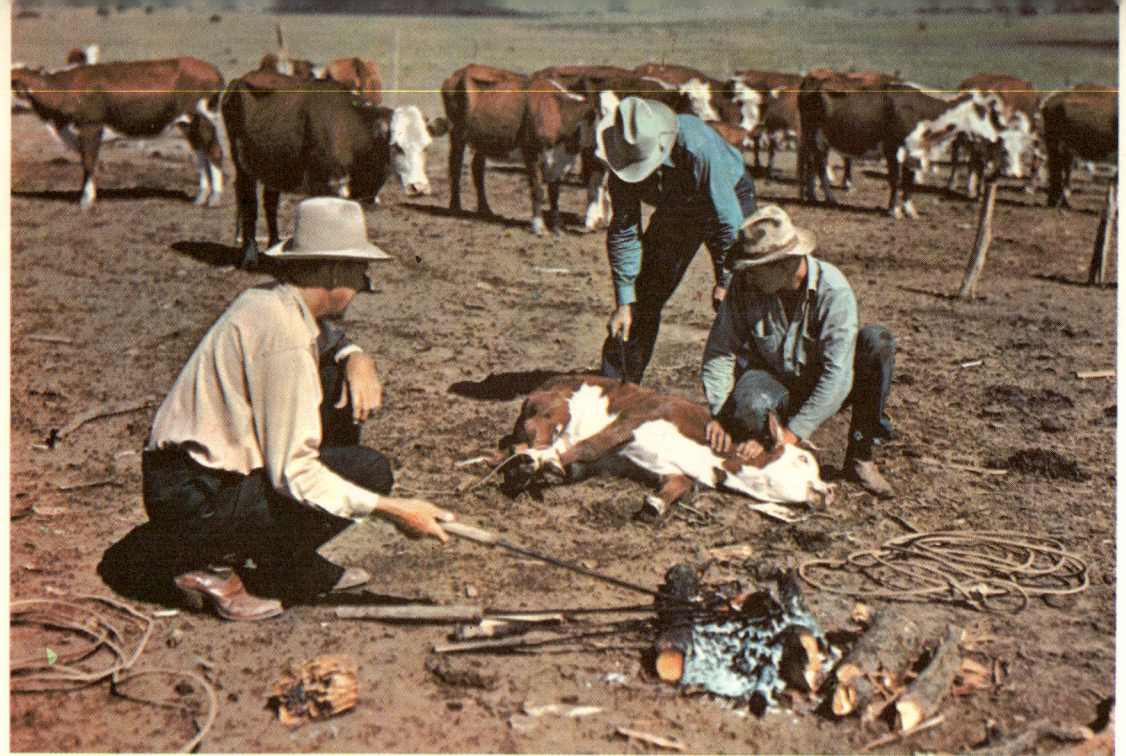

These cowboys are heating a branding iron with which they will brand the calf. The brand affixed upon a calf is usually either its owner's initials or some symbol adopted by the owner. The brand will identify the owner of a calf throughout its life.

The cowboy's job was to protect the cattle from Indians and wild animals, to prevent their straying from the herd, and to drive them across hundreds of miles of range to market. His work kept him almost always outdoors, usually on horseback, and forced him to develop much courage and resourcefulness.

His appearance made him a colorful person. He always carried the necessary tools of his trade: lasso, whip, revolver (usually called a six-shooter), and spurs. His clothing was both picturesque and practical: The narrow, high-heeled boots were designed not for walking but for stirrups. The broad-brimmed hat served both as a shade from the sun and as an umbrella. The handkerchief around his neck could be pulled over his face during duststorms. The buckskin gloves protected his hands from the reins and the lasso. The chaps protected his legs from branches and thorns, yet allowed cooling air to circulate beneath them.

The cowboy's heyday was from about 1865 to about 1885. After that time overcrowding of the grazing land caused a serious decline in ranching, and the fencing of the open range led to an increasingly diminishing role for the picturesque **cowboy of early times.**

COYOTE, a kind of small wolf, known also as the prairie wolf, found chiefly in the Great Plains and desert region of the West. It looks a good deal like a gray wolf but is somewhat smaller, averaging about 40 inches in length. Its color is usually dull yellowish gray with black cloudings on the back and sides and dirty white below. The hair is coarse; the tail is bushy, tapering, and tipped with black; and the ears are erect. The coyote lives in burrows, which it digs in the open plains, or in washouts or deep holes in the banks of rivers. A mother coyote gives birth to from five to seven puppies each May or June.

A coyote is considered to have slinking and stealthy habits. It lives on rabbits, chipmunks, mice, and small birds, and it often prowls about ranches in quest of young pigs, lambs, and poultry. Coyotes frequently hunt in packs, uttering high-pitched, yelping cries and bloodcurdling yells, which seem half howl and half bark. The coyote is not really dangerous to man, however dangerous its cries may sound.

Coyotes frequently utter a series of long, shrill howls soon after sunset.

CRAB, a crustacean with a short, broad body and ten legs, the front pair of which is generally larger than the others and has strong, pincer-like claws. It usually walks sidewise, and it swims either sidewise or backward. Crabs and other crustaceans belong to the phylum Arthropoda. Like all arthropods, crabs have an external skeleton and jointed, paired appendages.

Some crabs are much used for food. The blue crab is an important food along the Atlantic and Gulf coasts of North America, as are other crabs along the Pacific coast. If caught just after it has shed its shell and before the new one has hardened, the crab is known as a soft-shelled crab. It is usually fried or broiled and is delicious. Hard-shelled crabs—which are the crabs after their new shell has hardened— are much less valuable.

The hermit crab sticks the hind end of its body, which is soft and unprotected, into a snail shell or other empty shell and drags it around wherever it goes. As the crab grows, it changes the shell from time to time for a larger one. The male of the fiddler crab has one claw very much enlarged. When disturbed, it holds it up and saws back and forth with it, much as a bass-viol player does with a bow. Crabs 10 to 12 feet across are sometimes found off the coast of Japan. The oyster crab is a very tiny crab that lives inside an oystershell. It is sometimes encountered in oysters stews if the oysters have not been looked over thoroughly.

Between one and five million tiny eggs are sometimes laid by a single female crab. Crabs hatch from their eggs as tiny larvae that swim freely. They soon undergo anatomical changes and enter a second larval stage, during which their adult form gradually develops. Many species molt their shells weekly or monthly as they grow. Some species increase their size by one-third each time they molt. They cease molting after reaching maturity during their second or third year.

CRAB, THE (constellation). See CANCER.

CRAFTS are skills in making things with your hands. A knowledge of one or more crafts provides hours of pleasant relaxation and results in feelings of real accomplishment. Crafts work can also save you money and, in the case of a particularly good craftsman, can provide a means of earning a living. However, the satisfaction of a job well done always outweighs any desire for money in the mind of someone who is a true craftsman.

Crafts exist in such variety that anyone can find one to suit his needs and tastes. If you want to help with household repairs, you may choose from among carpentry, electrical work, furniture repair, tile craft, and concrete work. If you are interested in homemaking, you should investigate such crafts as baking, home canning, sewing, knitting, or interior decoration. If you are inclined to try something artistic, you might consider modeling, etching, carving, glassblowing, beadwork, or leatherwork. If you would like to learn a trade, you can get a good start from automobile mechanics, welding, cabinetmaking, printing, or metalwork.

In this encyclopedia you will find entries on all these and many more crafts. Few spare-time activities can provide as much satisfaction as you will receive from the achievements of craftsmanship.

Hermit crabs use empty snail shells as portable habitations.

The edible blue crab is a scavenger that during summer inhabits brackish water near river mouths.

The Pacific kelp crab inhabits tidal pools and beds of kelp.

The stone crab (above) has a hard shell. The male fiddler crab (right) has one large claw.

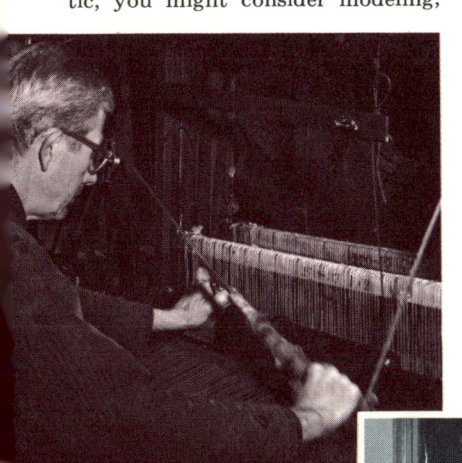

About 3"

The hindmost pair of legs of the calico crab (above) is flattened and otherwise modified for swimming.

The nine-lined spider crab (above) has long, thin legs and resembles a spider.

Clarke Coll.

Chamber of Com. Inc., Asheville, N.C.

A craftsman (above) is weaving fabric on a hand loom. These girls (right) are displaying the earthenware vessels that they made in a ceramics studio at Clarke College, Dubuque, Iowa.

CRAMPS are sudden, uncontrolled muscle contractions. They may be simple twitches or strong, painful contractions of one or more muscles. Tense people tend to have cramps of the muscles of the eyes, the face, and the calves of the legs. Such cramps may be helped by the application of heat, the use of massage, and the taking of a drug such as aspirin.

Cramps are also caused by mineral poisons, such as lead, arsenic, and mercury. Infections, plant and animal poisons, and snake venom are other agents causing cramps.

In warm countries a deficiency of ordinary salt, lost through perspiration, is a common cause of cramps. Many types of abdominal pain from various causes are referred to as **cramps**, such as menstrual cramps.

CRANBERRY, a vinelike plant, found in Asia and Europe as well as in North America. The American cranberry is cultivated in bogs for its valuable fruit. The plant has thick evergreen leaves, pinkish flowers, and a bright red berry about $\frac{1}{2}$ inch in diameter. Special climatic conditions and soils are needed for successful cranberry cultivation. Proper climates for commercial cultivation of cranberries are provided in such states as Massachusetts, New Jersey, and Wisconsin. Acid lowland soils are essential. The berries are used for sauces, salads, and pies.

CRANE, STEPHEN (1871-1900), an American writer, was born in Newark, N.J. In 1895 he published a war novel called *The Red Badge of Courage*, which at once made him famous. He was a newspaper correspondent in the Greco-Turkish War of 1897 and in the Spanish-American War of 1898. Among his other books were *Maggie: A Girl of the Streets, George's Mother, The Little Regiment and Other Episodes of the American Civil War,* and *Active Service,* a satire about war correspondents. He went to Europe in 1899 after contracting tuberculosis; he died the next year in Germany.

CRANE, a tall, stately bird with a long neck, long legs, and a powerful voice. These are characteristics of all of the 14 species of the widely distributed family of cranes. North America has two species, the whooping crane and the sandhill crane. Cranes from foreign lands are often seen in American zoos, for these birds live and breed well in captivity.

Sandhill cranes are extremely wary birds. Though more numerous than whooping cranes, sandhills are greatly reduced in numbers.

Cranes engage in an elaborate courtship ritual, in which the two birds bow ceremoniously to each other and jump high with wings outstretched. Cranes are often said to mate for life; in some countries it is believed that if a crane is killed, its mate will die of a broken heart. In Asia the killing of a crane is supposed to bring bad luck. Cranes feed on insects, small marsh animals, and roots and tubers of marsh plants. They migrate in long lines or in V-shaped flocks. The nest contains only two eggs, and only one family is raised yearly. Chicks leave the nest the day they are hatched but cannot fly for several months; the parents feed and care for them until they are about six months old.

The sandhill crane is gray or light brown, with a red crown, which is brighter at breeding time. The bird stands about 4 feet high. It ranges from Alaska to California, Texas, Louisiana, Florida, and Mexico. In migration it sometimes appears in huge flocks, but it is not a common bird.

The whooping crane, one of the rarest birds in North America, is also the tallest. It stands almost 5 feet high, weighs from 8 to 17 pounds, and has a wingspread of $7\frac{1}{2}$ feet. The adult is white with black wingtips and a red crown. Its name comes from its sonorous call, which carries for several miles. This loud call is due to its unusual windpipe, which is 4 or 5 feet long and is coiled into large loops.

In the early 1800's the whooping crane was a common bird, but encroaching civilization reduced its numbers. By 1923 it was thought to be extinct, but each year a few birds appeared. In 1937 an area of 47,000 acres of Texas swampland was set aside as the Aransas National Wildlife Refuge, and the whooping cranes now winter there. In 1940 the species numbered 32, and the annual migrations had become matters of popular concern. For years the breeding grounds were the object of an intensive search. Finally, in 1954, a few whooping

Marcus J. Clark

Cranes are sometimes mounted on the backs of trucks. Such cranes are quickly and easily moved from one job to another.

A magnetic crane handles scrap iron at a steel mill. The magnetic crane is merely a rotary crane carrying a large electromagnet rather than a hook or shovel. The crane operator picks up and drops the load of iron by turning an electric current on and off.

cranes were spotted from a helicopter near Great Slave Lake in western Canada. In 1955 a party went in on foot and located the breeding grounds, 2,400 miles north of the Texas wintering grounds. By 1957 the cranes numbered only 24. News of the tally of returning birds each fall was eagerly awaited, even by persons with no other interest in birds. North America had already seen the extinction of three or four species in the 20th century (the passenger pigeon, heath hen, Carolina parakeet, and possibly the Eskimo curlew), and the possible passing of this species was the cause of much concern by many people. In 1958 there were 32 wild whooping cranes, but in the fall of 1959 only 31 returned to Aransas, and only one of those was a young bird. Six additional birds were in captivity—a highly publicized pair (Josephine and Crip) and three offspring in a New Orleans zoo and a crippled bird in San Antonio, Tex.

CRANE, a machine for lifting loads and transferring them from one place to another. Cranes may be operated by hand or by steam, electric, hydraulic, or pneumatic power.

Traveling cranes are beams supported at the ends by wheels running on overhead tracks. If they are operated by hand, the span is limited to 40 feet and the load to 50 tons. Electrically operated, they may have a capacity of 200 tons with a span of 125 feet. Gantry cranes are similar except that they have supporting legs at the ends that travel along ground tracks. They are also called bridge cranes. In both types the hoist is operated from a tracked carriage traveling along the top of the beam.

Rotary cranes operate from fixed pivots or from vertical columns or pillars. They may be permanently located or mobile, as on crawler trucks or flat cars. The rotary motion may be limited or may be over an entire circle. In the jib type of rotary crane, the jib may rise or fall in part of the lifting action furnished by cable and pulley at the end of the jib, or it may be fixed to swing horizontally. A yard jib crane is strongly guyed and carries a horizontal jib having a track. A hoisting carriage operates along this track. A column jib crane operates much in the same manner except that it is of smaller capacity and is manually operated, being essentially a shop crane. Derricks are little different from cranes, usually being built of timber, with a rotating table and post that can be easily moved.

CRANK, a bent arm that is turned to set a shaft in motion. It is commonly used in internal-combustion engines, steam engines, pumps, and other machinery to convert rotary motion into reciprocating motion or vice versa. In an automobile engine the reciprocating, or up-and-down, motion of the piston is transmitted through a connecting rod to the crankshaft, which imparts turning motion to the wheels. The bell crank is a lever that transmits motion by means of a central, fixed pivot and right-angled arms with hinged connections.

Beautiful Crater Lake is seen here from one of the high cliffs that overlook its shoreline. The lake has no inlet or outlet but is kept at a constant level by fall of rain and snow. Wizard Island, in the foreground, is a cinder cone produced by eruptions after the main crater had collapsed.

CRATER, or the Cup, is a small southern constellation west of Corvus and north of Hydra. It is visible in the evening sky from midnorthern latitudes between March and June. It somewhat resembles a goblet tilted toward Corvus.

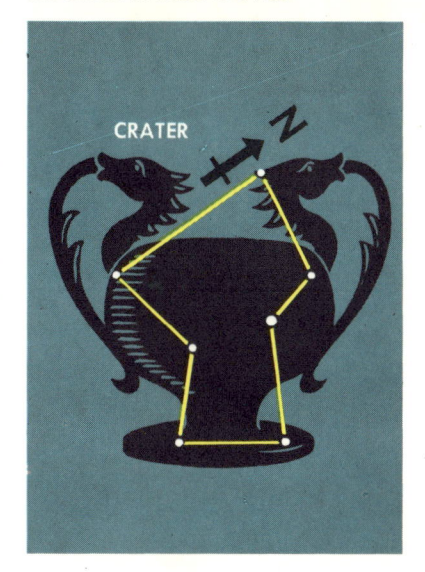

Crater, the Cup, has been variously pictured as belonging to Apollo, Hercules, Achilles, Dido, Medea, Bacchus, Icarius, and even Noah. According to one ancient story, Apollo punished Corvus, the Crow, by placing him in the sky next to the Cup but ordering Hydra, the Water Snake, to guard the Cup and never to let the Crow take a drink.

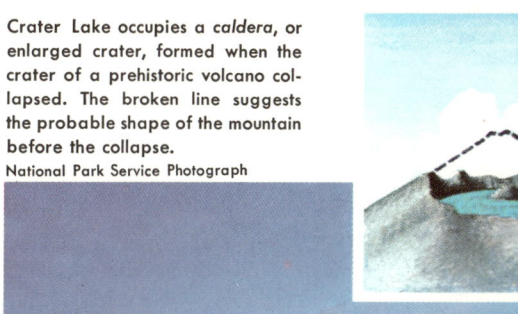

Crater Lake occupies a *caldera*, or enlarged crater, formed when the crater of a prehistoric volcano collapsed. The broken line suggests the probable shape of the mountain before the collapse.
National Park Service Photograph

CRATER LAKE NATIONAL PARK   699

A crater a quarter of a mile across formed within a week after the volcano Paricutín rose from a Mexican cornfield in 1943.

CRATER, the central opening of a volcano, from which are ejected lava, fragments of rock, dust, vapors, and steam. The crater is usually less than a mile wide and not more than a few hundred feet deep. The basin-like hollow of a crater is formed by the accumulation of volcanic products about the opening.

CRATER LAKE NATIONAL PARK is in the Cascade Range of southwest Oregon. The park's most notable feature is Crater Lake, which is situated in a pit at the summit of Mt. Mazama. It is remarkable for its deep-blue color. The park covers some 250 square miles and contains many beautiful volcanic peaks, including Mt. Scott (8,938 feet) and Cloudcap (8,070 feet).

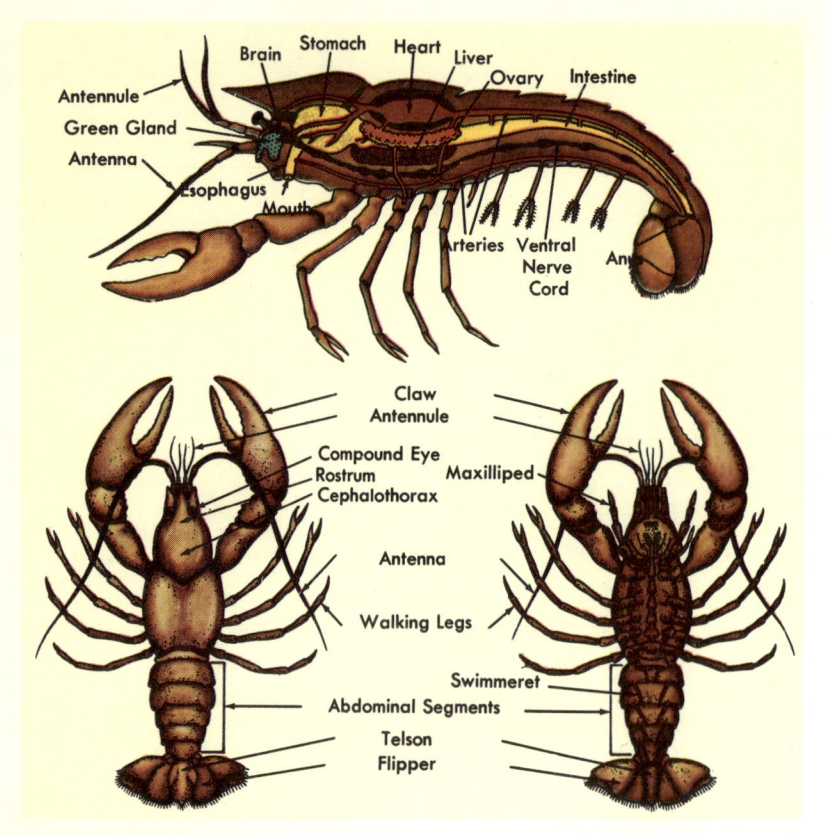

The external anatomy and the many complex internal organs of the crayfish are shown above.

CRAYFISH, a common fresh-water crustacean that resembles a small lobster. Crayfish inhabit lakes, streams, and rivers. They can swim in water, crawl along the bottom, and burrow in the mud of the shore. During the day they usually hide under rocks or logs but stick out their antennae so they can detect the approach of prey or enemies. At night they creep forth to feed on any decaying animal bodies or vegetation that can be found.

Crayfish may attain a length of 6 inches. Their first pair of legs is equipped with large, powerful pincers for seizing occasional live prey. The other four pairs of legs are used for crawling backward and forward. They swim, always backward, by flapping a fin at the end of the tail. They also have four pairs of legs by which they crawl both backward and forward. Crayfish breathe through fishlike gills while under water or in the air. Their long, slender antennae, which can be waved about, are sensitive organs of touch. Crayfish hatch from eggs that, after being laid, are glued with a sticky secretion to small appendages, called swimmerets, that lie beneath the mother's abdomen. The newly hatched crayfish cling to their mother's body for about two weeks.

Crayfish are native to most temperate and tropical regions of all continents except Africa. In some European countries they are considered a table delicacy and are raised by the millions for market. In the United States they are used as fish bait.

CRAYON. Crayons are a kind of pencils for drawing. They are made of chalk, pipe, gypsum, or charcoal and are of all colors. The materials are ground up into a paste, with some gum, starch, wax, soap, sugar, and so forth, to make them hold together; they are then molded into little rolls of the proper size. The paste is colored with different pigments, such as Naples yellow, indigo, vermilion, umber, and carmine, according to the color wanted. Black crayons are made of black chalk or of charcoal. Crayons vary in hardness, the soft being used by means of a stump, a roll of soft leather or cartridge paper on the end of which the crayon is rubbed, while the hard ones are used just like an ordinary pencil.

There are four general kinds of crayons: wax-molded, in which pigments are mixed with liquid wax; wax-extruded, in which the mixture is extruded like a plastic; wax-impregnated, in which the mixture is extruded and dipped in wax; and chalk crayons, which are of two types. In the first type powdered chalk is used in a doughlike mixture that is extruded, cut, and dried; in the second type color and plaster of Paris are mixed with water, poured into molds, and dried.

CRAZY BONE. See FUNNY BONE.

CRAZY HORSE (1849-1877), great Indian chieftain of the Sioux Confederacy. His Indian name was Tashunca-Uitco. He received the name Crazy Horse because, at the time of his birth, a wild pony dashed through the village.

The Oglala tribe, led by Crazy Horse, scorned village life and made frequent raids against other Indian tribes and white men. The Sioux ignored the government order that all roving tribes must be back on their reservations by 1876. An army unit, headed by Colonel J. J. Reynolds, attacked and destroyed Crazy Horse's village near the Little Powder River. Crazy Horse resisted stubbornly. He joined forces with Dakotan chief Sitting Bull and wiped out General George Custer's command in the Battle of the Little Bighorn. Attacked by other units, Crazy Horse surrendered to authorities after many of his people deserted him. He was shot while trying to escape from Camp Robinson, in Nebraska.

CREAM SEPARATOR, a machine for the separation of cream from whole milk. The machine uses the principle of centrifugal force. (See CENTRIFUGAL FORCE.) Cream is lighter than milk; when whole milk is allowed to stand, the cream will rise to the top. For mechanical separation the whole milk is poured into a closed bowl. Within this bowl are a number of cream-separator blades, which are turned up at the edge and fit one over the other. They revolve at a high speed and set the whole milk in motion. This movement leads to the separation of the heavier skim milk from the lighter cream and its accumulation at the outer edge. The outer part of the bowl is connected with a skim-milk outlet, while the inner part is connected with a cream outlet. The skim milk and cream emerge from the container by separate outlets and then run into containers that have been designed for each of the liquids.

CREDIT, the receiving of goods, services, or money on the basis of a promise to pay for them in the future. Credit implies that the person extending it, the creditor, trusts the debtor to pay at a specified time in the future. So that the creditor will be willing to part with his goods for a promise to pay in the future, credit demands that there be a surplus of wealth over immediate needs.

Credit makes the currency elastic. By manipulating credit regulations purchasing power can be increased or decreased as necessary. Credit allows long-distance payments to be made safely, and through it accumulated funds in banks are extended to productive enterprises. However, if used unwisely, it may encourage extravagance.

One form of credit is personal credit, by which an individual can secure consumers' goods in the present and pay for them in the future. The charge-account system of department stores is an example of this type of credit.

Credit is also commonly extended by businessmen to one another. This is done by means of such credit instruments as the open-book account, an entry on the books of the creditor charging a buyer of goods the price of the merchandise; the promissory note, a written promise to pay for goods delivered at a specified time; the trade acceptance, an order from the creditor to the buyer ordering him to pay for goods delivered at a certain time; and a bill of exchange, which is similar to the trade acceptance except that it does not record that the debt grew out of the sale of goods.

Bank credit is the ability of a bank to secure or extend funds on credit. Among the credit instruments used by banks are the bank draft, an order from one bank to another to pay a specified amount of money; the bank acceptance, a draft upon a bank to which the bank drawn upon agrees by accepting the draft; and the bank note, a written promise to pay. Federal reserve notes, which comprise most of the paper money of the United States, are promises to pay issued by the federal reserve banks. Banks may extend credit by such means as the overdraft, which allows a customer to withdraw more money than he has in account at the bank; the loan account, which is opened for the customer at a rate of interest; and traveler's letters of credit, which allow the holder to draw foreign money abroad up to the limit of his domestic account. Travelers' checks are a form of the traveler's letter of credit.

Investment credit consists of long-term loans made to business entrepreneurs, who expect to repay the loans out of future earnings. (See STOCKS AND BONDS.) Public credit is obtained by government units, which acquire funds in return for promises to pay—government bonds or paper money. Agricultural credit is obtained by farmers through the mortgage of their real estate. See CHECK; MONEY.

CREDIT UNION, a cooperative organization in which members save by buying shares and make loans to each other for good purposes at low interest. Members must have a common bond of association, such as employment in the same office or factory or membership in the same church. The credit union encourages thrift. Most loans are made on character, although the law requires other security for larger loans. Members run the credit union on a nonprofit basis, and all officers serve without pay except the treasurer, who may be paid.

Credit unions are chartered under national or state laws. In the United States half operate under the Federal Credit Union Act of 1934, which is administered by the Bureau of Federal Credit Unions, in the Department of Health, Education, and Welfare.

The Credit Union National Association (CUNA) was founded in 1934 to develop and promote credit unions. In 1940 it expanded membership to all in the Western Hemisphere, and in 1958 it became a worldwide association. The main office is in Madison, Wis.

Most credit unions are in the United States and Canada, but by 1960 the movement had spread to 45 countries with about 25,000 credit unions and 14,000,000 members. Each year people in more countries begin credit unions. For instance, the Fiji Islands have about 250 credit unions.

Credit unions in the United States hold about 2.8 percent of the money that is in personal savings accounts and 8 percent of the installment loans. Membership in the 20,000 U.S. credit unions was 11,300,000 at the beginning of 1960. See COOPERATIVE.

CREOLE, a name applied to certain people of Latin descent born and raised in the Americas. In the United States the name usually refers to those inhabitants of Louisiana directly descended from the original French settlers of New Orleans. In Latin America the name is given to the descendants of the Spanish and Portuguese colonizers.

A high percentage of the population of New Orleans, Louisiana's largest city, is Creole. Although Louisiana has been part of the United States since 1803, the Creoles preserve many customs of their ancestors, including use of the French language. Characteristic of Creoles is devotion to family life and to Creole society.

In Louisiana the Acadians (Cajuns), French-speaking inhabitants of the bayou country, are considered a distinct group and are not to be confused with the Creoles.

Latin American Creoles were leaders in their countries' fights for independence. Their dissatisfaction with Spanish rule, under which they were allowed few important governmental positions and little voice in national affairs, was one of the principal causes of the Latin American revolutions.

Courtesy The De Laval Separator Company
After whole milk is poured into the separator, its revolving blades separate the cream from the skim milk. The cream and the skim milk then drain from different spouts.

CRETE is a Greek island in the Mediterranean Sea. Mountains, once covered with forests, run through the whole length of the island. Mt. Ida, or Mt. Psiloriti, is the highest peak, rising about 8,000 feet. Crete covers 3,200 square miles and has about 500,000 people.

Greek mythology made Crete the scene of many adventures of the gods and heroes. Here Zeus was born, and here his son King Minos reigned. The legends of Greece told of a great civilization that had flourished on Crete many, many centuries ago. In the early 20th century excavations uncovered the ruins of great palaces built in prehistoric times. These discoveries proved that the legends were based on fact. The Minoan civilization, as it is known, lasted some 1,500 years, from about 3000 B.C. to about 1400 B.C.

In later times Crete belonged to the Romans, the Byzantines, and the Saracens. It was sold to the Venetians in 1204 and was ruled by them until it was conquered by the Turks in 1669. Finally, after many insurrections, Crete was united with Greece in the early 1900's.

Pierre M. Martinot

The people of Crete have always been known as skilled artisans. The fresco above was done long before the Christian Era. Right, two contemporary potters work.

CRIBBAGE, a game for two players who use a regular deck of cards and a board with pegs and holes for scoring. There are several varieties of the game, but six-card cribbage is the most popular. After the cut for the deal, the dealer deals six cards to his opponent and six to himself. Each player then discards two cards. They form the crib, which is counted later as a part of the dealer's hand. Next the nondealer cuts the deck, and the dealer turns up the top card. If this card, the starter, is a jack, the dealer moves one of his pegs two counts on the board for "his heels." It is also later counted as if it were part of both hands and of the crib. In scoring, kings, queens, jacks, and tens each count 10; the other cards count their face value, with the aces counting as one.

The play begins with the nondealer, who lays down one of his cards, on his side of the cribbage board, face up. The dealer then plays one of his cards. If the two cards add up to 15, the dealer pegs, or scores, two points. The players continue to play cards in turn, and each time the value of the card is added to the total of the cards previously played. Whenever a card brings the total points to 31 exactly, the player of that card pegs two. When neither player can play a card without bringing the total above 31, the count starts again at zero. The first player who cannot play under 31 says "go," and his opponent then scores one and continues the play until he cannot play under 31. If he can play to exactly 31 (with one card or more) he pegs two points.

In the play whenever the last two or more cards make certain combinations, the player who plays the last card scores. A player who can play a card of the same rank as the last previous one played pegs two for a pair. For three cards of a kind, the player pegs six. For four

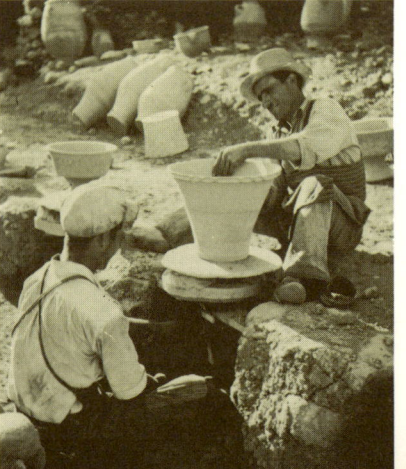

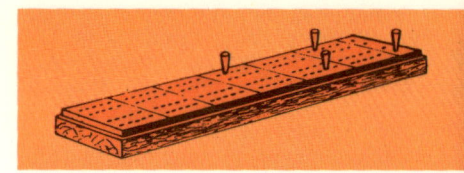

Ministry of Inf., Greece.

The cribbage board has a double row of 30 holes on each side and a game hole at each end. Each player has two pegs and moves them from hole to hole to record the score.

cards of a kind, the player pegs 12. For a run the player pegs the number of cards in the sequence. The score for game is either 61 or 121.

After all the cards have been played out, each player counts the scoring combinations of his own cards and pegs those points. The nondealer's points are pegged first, then the dealer's cards, and finally the crib.

Above is the North American field cricket.

CRICKET, a small insect related to the grasshopper. It has long feelers, wings that fold flat on the back when not in use, and long, strong hind legs, fitted for jumping. The male makes a shrill noise, known as a chirp, by rubbing his wing covers together.

The European house cricket, which is about an inch long, lives in the cracks of walls and floors. It hides away during the day and comes out at night in search of food. Its chirp, which is a call to its mate, is usually begun at twilight and continued until daybreak. This cricket has been introduced into the United States but is seldom found here.

The mole cricket is so called because its forefeet are adapted for digging, like those of the mole. The insect burrows in the moist earth near streams and ponds. It makes underground galleries and sometimes does a great deal of damage to vegetation by cutting off roots that obstruct its path.

CRICKET, the national summer game of England, played also throughout the British dominions, especially in Australia, India, South Africa, and the West Indies. It has been played in England since the 13th century. Originally the ball was bowled along the ground, and only an underarm motion was permitted. Sidearm bowling began in 1826 but was not officially allowed until 1844. The present rule allowing overarm bowling was adopted in 1864. The Marylebone Cricket Club of London, so named in 1787, has remained the recognized rulemaking body for the sport all over the world.

The game is played between two teams of 11 men each. Two wickets, 22 yards apart, are defended by two batsmen of the same team. Each wicket consists of three round stumps in a row with two pieces of lighter wood, called bails, on the top. The entire wicket is 28 inches high and 9 inches wide. The ball is leather covered and weighs $5\frac{1}{2}$ ounces. A full-sized bat is 38 inches long and $4\frac{1}{2}$ inches across at its widest part. The bowler pitches the ball with a full overarm motion, trying to hit the wicket and knock off the bails on the first bounce of the ball. If he does this, the batsman is out. In defending his wicket, the batsman naturally tries to hit the ball for a run. The batsman can be put out in several other ways. He can be out by having a flyball hit by him caught by a fielder; by hitting the wicket with his bat; by a fielder's hitting the wicket with the ball while the batsman is outside the safety zone behind the wicket; by the wicketkeeper's hitting the wicket with the ball; by being hit on the leg by a pitched ball when his leg is in front of the wicket; and by deliberately hitting the ball twice except in defending the wicket.

The defending team is credited with a run if the bowler delivers the ball with an illegal motion (called a no-ball) or when he is out of proper position (a wide).

Bowling takes place alternately from each wicket, in a series of six pitches. The series is called an over. A maiden over is one in which no runs are scored. A run is scored by a hit far enough to allow the batsman to change places with his partner at the other wicket. At the end of each over, the fielders change positions, and the bowler at the opposite wicket continues the attack. When a batsman is put out, the next man of his team takes his place at the wicket, and this continues until all of the 11 men have batted. This completes an inning, and the other team takes its turn at bat. The game usually allows two innings to each side. A match may last as long as five or six days, but the average club match lasts a day or a day and a half.

The high point of each season is the England-Australia Test Matches, which date from 1877.

Cricket matches in Australia are popular and draw large crowds of enthusiastic spectators.

CRIMEAN WAR (1854-1856), in which Turkey, France, Britain, and the Italian kingdom of Sardinia defeated Russia, is so called because almost all its action was limited to the Russian peninsula of Crimea in the Black Sea. The first major war between any European powers since the fall of Napoleon (1815), the Crimean War marked the beginning of a series of conflicts that by 1871 had drastically altered the map of Europe.

For centuries Russia had hoped to conquer Constantinople and thereby gain a foothold on the Mediterranean Sea. Both the British and French governments believed that such a development would be against their own best interests. Russia also claimed the right to protect Orthodox Christians within the Turkish Empire and had a longstanding dispute with France over the custody of the holy places in Palestine. To enforce its claims Russia invaded Turkey in 1853. France entered the war on the side of Turkey and was soon joined by Britain. Sardinia, whose only concern was unifying Italy under its own leadership, joined the war only in order to gain favor for its cause with the French government. Although almost exhausted by internal warfare, Austria also mobilized an army that moved to, but did not cross, the Russian border.

After the British navy had blockaded Russian ports in both the Baltic and the Black seas, the British and French armies invaded the Crimea. The main action of the war was an allied attack on the principal Crimean port, Sevastopol, which fell after an 11 months' siege had thoroughly exhausted the resources of the defending Russians. Meanwhile Czar Nicholas I had died, and after the fall of Sevastopol his successor, Alexander II, sued for peace.

The peace treaty was signed at Paris in 1856. Its principal feature was a pledge by the signing powers to refrain from further attempts at taking territory from Turkey. Three sections of European Turkey were established as self-governing principalities; two of them soon merged to form the kingdom of Rumania, while the third eventually became the nucleus of what is now Yugoslavia. As a result of the war Austria was so weakened that it was unable to prevent the subsequent unifications of Italy and Germany. To placate his subjects the new Russian czar, Alexander II, had to initiate widespread reform, culminating in the freeing of the serfs (1861).

CRIMINOLOGY, scientific study of crime, criminals, and criminal law. Criminology is part of the study of human behavior; knowledge is drawn from such areas as law, medicine, religion, education, social work, and public administration.

In early times many people believed that crimes were committed by people who were possessed by devils. The witch hunt of Massachusetts in the late 17th century was a result of belief in the power of demons to possess, or enter into, people. Since then many explanations for crime have been suggested: radio, television, and comics and children who no longer respect their parents.

According to one theory, heredity plays a part in criminal behavior. Some people believe a special set of physical characteristics is to be found in criminals. Sometimes mental retardation is considered characteristic of a criminal.

Since little is known about body type and its relation to crime, and since criminals are found with all types of physical characteristics, other causes for criminal behavior are investigated. It is part of the criminologist's work to take a person's environment, background, and all possible causes of crime into account.

Criminologists study penal institutions and judicial systems. They see them in relation to the total society, including its politics, customs, conflicts, divisions of labor, and social changes. They study attitudes toward law as well as the behavior and the background of criminals.

A criminologist may study a person, a nation, an institution, a family, or an incident. He finds out all he can about it. This is called a case study. He can also make a statistical study, which deals with masses of facts. This involves finding what facts are typical and recurrent and how they are related to other facts. A question you could study statistically is, "Is there any relation between life in big cities and crimes against property?"

With mental disease being more and more recognized as a basic factor in criminal behavior, psychiatry is playing an increasingly important part in the treatment of the criminal, and many juvenile and criminal courts are using the services of psychiatrists and behavior clinics. Increasing use of probation, indeterminate sentencing and parole, special laws for habitual criminals, and improved penal institutions shows the growing influence the new theories in criminology are having on the courts and on the U.S. public. In many large cities police departments have set up crime-prevention bureaus whose function is to establish adequate playground facilities and in other ways eliminate conditions that breed crime.

Criminology involves not merely experts but all citizens. Understanding crime is part of preventing it.

Criminologists believe inmates of prisons should be given vocational training so that they will be able to find employment when they are released.

Federal Prisons

Adapted from Inst. for Hand Knitting

The basic crochet stitches are the chain stitch, **1**, the single crochet **2** and **3**, the double crochet, **4**, the triple crochet, **5**, the increasing, **6**, and the decreasing, **7**, stitches, and the slipstitch, **8**. These can be combined to form a variety of patterns. All crochet work begins with a chain, the length of which is determined by the number of chain stitches it contains. Stitches **5** and **6** increase or decrease the length of succeeding chains. The slipstitch joins chains and serves as an invisible stitch.

CROCHETING is a kind of handwork done with a hooked needle and thread or yarn. With the hook a chain of loops is made of a desired length and other chains are joined to it in various ways.

Many kinds of articles may be made in crochet, ranging from lace trimmings for lingerie to heavy wool afghans and thick cotton rugs. Garments may also be made, as well as hats, bags, gloves, and accessories. The type of article to be made determines the size of the hook and the thickness of yarn or thread to be used. Steel hooks and fine cotton or silk threads are used to crochet delicate trimmings, doilies, tray cloths, and the like. Bone or plastic hooks and woolen yarns are more suitable for making wool hats and afghans. For cotton rugs large wooden hooks are used.

Crocheting is thought to be an ancient art, although there is no definite record of its origin before 1672 when it was displayed at an exhibition in Dublin, Ireland. When fine cotton threads were brought into Europe, crocheting became an important handicraft for nuns, who made decorative altar fronts and other pieces for the church. During the Irish famine of 1846, nuns in Ireland made lace patterns in crochet and sold their work to help feed the starving populace. They developed several beautiful patterns based on natural objects, the shamrock and rose among others.

Later in the 19th century, crocheting became established on the Continent as a ladylike occupation for women. In the United States it is now regarded as an enjoyable and inexpensive hobby. Some women even turn to crocheting as a way of earning money at home.

CROCKETT, DAVID (1786-1836), better known as Davy Crockett, American pioneer, Indian scout, politician, and humorist, was born in Limestone, Tenn. He spent a shiftless youth until his political career began with his appointment as a justice of the peace. He relied on common sense rather than on a law education. He believed this was the reason none of his decisions was reversed. After he had been twice elected to the state legislature he accepted a proposal that he run for Congress. To his surprise he was elected twice. Crockett's associates in politics made him a backwoods hero with stories about his humor, shrewdness, intelligence, and pioneer spirit. Crockett dressed the part by wearing leather clothes and a squirrel-skin hat. When he was defeated for re-election, he left Tennessee to serve in the War of Texan Independence. He died at the Alamo in San Antonio. Crockett was credited with writing his *Autobiography*, *The Life of Martin Van Buren*, and *Colonel Crockett's Exploits and Adventures in Texas*. These books had Crockett's robust manner and contained good examples of the farce and the exaggerated tall story.

CROCODILE, a large, lizard-like reptile that spends part of its time in the water and part of it basking or sleeping in the sun at the water's edge. Crocodiles are found only in tropical rivers and lakes. The crocodile is an ugly creature, 10 to 30 feet long, with flattened body and head, short powerful limbs, and a long thick tail, all covered with horny, armor-like scales. It is dark green or olive green, often with darker spots. The head has a long snout and an enormous mouth, its strong jaws containing many long, sharp-pointed teeth. The animal can move fairly rapidly on land but is ungainly. It swims with great ease, however, its tail acting as a propeller.

Some crocodiles are ferocious and much feared. They live on fish, other water animals, and land animals that come to the water's edge to drink. Sometimes crocodiles attack people and kill or mutilate them.

The common crocodile of Africa was sacred to the ancient Egyptians, who built temples in its honor at Thebes and other places, worshiped it in life, embalmed it in death, and laid its body away in sacred catacombs. Thousands of embalmed crocodiles have been found, and some are now in museums. These sacred crocodiles were adorned by the priests with precious stones, rings, and bangles and were fed on sacred food.

Crocodiles are related to alligators. A principal difference is that the fourth tooth of the lower jaw of the crocodile fits into a notch in the upper jaw, whereas the same tooth in the alligator and caiman fits into a pit in the upper jaw.

CROCUS, one of the earliest of the spring garden flowers. It belongs to the iris family and was brought to North America from the Old World. Each crocus plant, which is from 3 to 8 or 10 inches tall, bears a single, goblet-shaped flower. The flowers are of many colors: white, yellow, orange, rose, lavender, purple, and blue. Some are of solid colors, while others are striped or variegated.

Most crocuses bloom in the spring, although there are also fall-blooming varieties. The crocus is the familiar harbinger of spring, for it bursts into bloom shortly after the last snows have melted and not infrequently before. Crocuses are often planted in lawns, which make a good background for the bright-colored flowers. They are also planted in flowerbeds and borders and are often raised in greenhouses or as house plants.

CROESUS (flourished 560-546 B.C.), the last king of Lydia, a state in western Asia Minor, was the first to introduce pure-gold coins as currency. Croesus, known in antiquity as a fabulously wealthy king, inspired the saying: "rich as Croesus." He had friendly relations with the Greeks of Asia Minor, who supported him against the Persians. However, the Persian King Cyrus captured Croesus' capital, Sardis. Croesus' fate is uncertain. Some legends say that he was slain by the Persians; others, that he was saved by the god Apollo and became a friend of Cyrus.

The crocodile is known as a cold-blooded reptile because it derives virtually all of its body heat from outside sources. The temperature of its blood is environmentally determined.

Crocuses are most beautiful if they blossom when there is an abundance of moisture.

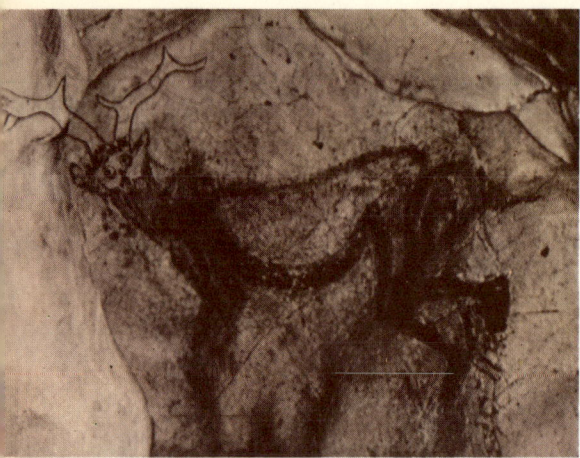

Above is a deer drawn on a cave wall by a Cro-Magnon artist. The smudges at lower center are caused by the smoke of torches that supplied light for drawing. Paintings of mammoths and bison also have been found.

Cro-Magnon man was often over 6 feet in height. He was skilled in making weapons and other artifacts.

Cromwell, the anti-Royalist commander

A head based on Cro-Magnon skull structure
Courtesy of the American Museum of Natural History

A Cro-Magnon skull, showing modern structure
Courtesy of the American Museum of Natural History

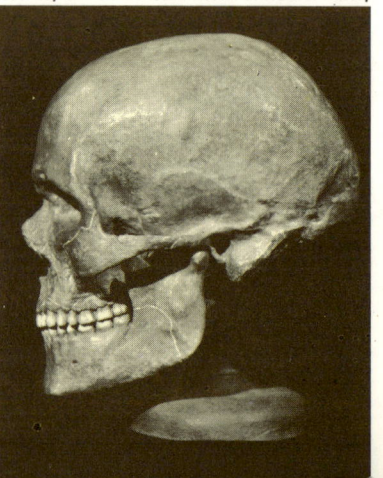

CRO-MAGNON MAN. About 35,000 years ago, at the beginning of the second phase of the last glaciation, modern types of men lived in Europe. They looked like many people we see today. We know this from the bones that have been discovered. One of the main types of these modern men was Cro-Magnon. Cro-Magnon man is the name given to fossil remains of man found near the cave of Cro-Magnon near Dordogne in southern France. Similar fossils of man who lived somewhat later than Cro-Magnon, during a late phase of the Ice Age, called the Magdalenian, were found near them. Cro-Magnon people were tall and had big bones, large brains, and long heads.

Cro-Magnon men were among the first people to go far into the caves. Archaeologists have found their paintings—mostly of animals—on almost inaccessible cave walls. Cro-Magnon men also modeled animals in clay. Scientists believe that the drawings and models of animals were made for ritual purposes, possibly to insure good hunting.

CROMWELL, OLIVER (1599-1658), English political and military leader, was born at Huntingdon, the son of a gentleman farmer. In early manhood he experienced a religious conversion and became a convinced Puritan. His religious beliefs included a conviction that he was obliged to further God's will with all his powers; they also carried the assumption that he knew exactly what God's will was.

Cromwell entered Parliament in 1628. Before the English Civil War he attracted little attention outside his native district. Although he had had no previous military experience, when the war broke out in 1642, he raised a troop of cavalry for Parliament and led them with such success that in two years he was a lieutenant general and second in command of the Parliamentary army. His New Model Army was largely responsible for the brilliant victories at Marston Moor and Naseby. See CIVIL WAR, ENGLISH.

In 1649 Cromwell was a member of the court that tried Charles I and sentenced him to death. England was then declared a commonwealth, a republic to be ruled without a king or a House of Lords. The House of Commons became the ruling power, and the Council of State, of which Cromwell was a member, was appointed to carry on the government. As leader of the army Cromwell was the principal leader of the new government.

Almost immediately he was forced to put down an uprising in Ireland, which he did with great severity, and to defeat a Royalist uprising in Scotland. Aside from these uprisings, Cromwell faced many problems in ruling England. He was pressed by radical Puritans on one hand and by conservative elements on the other and was unable to agree even with Parliament. Accordingly he abolished Parliament and on Dec. 16, 1653, assumed the title "Lord Protector of the Commonwealth." As such he was an absolute ruler, a king in all but name. In an effort to return the government to something resembling constitutional principles he ordered elections for a new Parliament. Since he could not agree even with this Parliament, it was soon dissolved, and before long the government was nothing more than a puritanical military dictatorship. Cromwell was not happy with the situation, but he could find no satisfactory alternatives. After his death in 1658 the government rapidly disintegrated, and in 1660 the monarchy was restored. See CHARLES II.

CROP ROTATION. Crop rotation is the changing, in successive seasons, of crops grown on the same soil. It has as its purpose the improvement of the soil and the balanced withdrawal of plant food. Different crops take different substances from the soil, but crop rotation slows down the depletion of its various elements. This principle has been practiced since the days of the Egyptians, but only in recent times has it been done scientifically. Crop rotations vary with types of soil; few methods are adhered to rigidly. Corn is usually rotated with wheat or oats and a leguminous crop such as clover, soybeans, or alfalfa. In some regions corn is planted twice before the soil is put to another crop. Where corn can be harvested early, winter wheat is sometimes planted immediately after it. Cotton and tobacco are frequently rotated with legumes. Leguminous crops are valuable because they replenish the nitrogen in the soil; frequently they are plowed under to make the soil even more fertile. Much of the wheat grown on semiarid land is rotated with other crops or grown after the land has lain fallow for one or two years to conserve moisture.

Below are crop rotations for various areas. By changing successive crops, the buildup of diseases and insects peculiar to a certain plant is prevented, and the nutrient balance of the soil is better maintained.

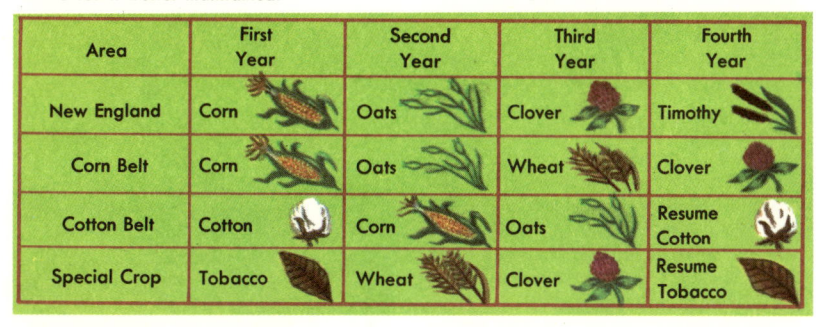

Area	First Year	Second Year	Third Year	Fourth Year
New England	Corn	Oats	Clover	Timothy
Corn Belt	Corn	Oats	Wheat	Clover
Cotton Belt	Cotton	Corn	Oats	Resume Cotton
Special Crop	Tobacco	Wheat	Clover	Resume Tobacco

The farmer below is mowing a field of legumes planted in a crop rotation to rebuild a soil after its depletion by a cash crop.
Courtesy of the Ford Motor Company

Below is an example of a cash crop, which is planted after legumes are plowed under to supply nutrients for it.
Courtesy of the Ford Motor Company

CROQUET, an open-air game played with wooden balls and mallets on either a closely clipped lawn or a specially prepared court. The game is basically a revival of the old game of pall-mall, which gave its name to the well-known London street. The object of the game is to drive the ball through nine wire arches in proper order. Beginning at a post at the end of the court, each player must drive his ball to a post at the other end and return it to the starting place. Each arch gone through earns the player another shot. He may receive two shots by hitting another ball but must drive his ball through an arch before he can hit that ball again. The game is usually played by two to six persons.

CROSSBOW, the weapon that on the continent of Europe was known as the arbalest. It was used throughout the 12th and 13th centuries.

It was a bow, in the sense that it fired an arrow or bolt. When it was unstrung, it resembled a cross, for it consisted of a stock, or shoulderpiece, shaped like a modern rifle butt, and a crosspiece well up along what would be the barrel on a rifle. The cord of this strong stiff bow was caught over a hook and was drawn back by a ratchet wheel worked by one hand. In front of the trigger was a groove, in which was put a quarrel, or bolt, a short, stout piece of wood, pointed with iron and having four narrow feathers to keep it on its mark.

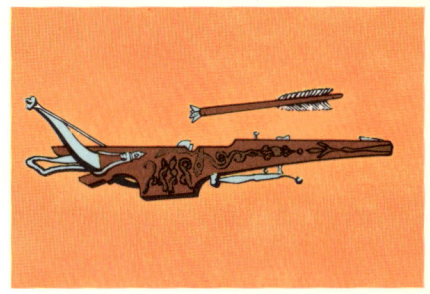

Some of the larger crossbows were so heavy and stiff that after a man had fired one, it took him some minutes to bend and load again. Largely because of this slow action, though they were very powerful weapons, they were replaced by the long bow, which was much lighter, was easily carried, and could fire as many as four shots a minute in the hands of a skillful archer.

The crossbow made its reputation during the crusades. Because of greater accuracy and heavier missiles, European crossbowmen proved superior to the Asian horse archers whom they battled.

Ornamental crossbow and bolt, or arrow

CROSS-EYE. A young baby does not have control of his eye muscles, and sometimes his eyes look in different directions. Most babies develop muscle control during their first year; after that time their eyes work as a team.

Once in a while a baby cannot make his eyes work together because there is a defect in the working parts. This condition is called cross-eye, or squint.

It is not always easy to know during the early months whether a baby's eyes are really crossed or not. If by the time a baby is 3 months old his eyes are not straight most of the time, a doctor should be consulted. If the baby's eyes still look crossed sometimes when he is 6 months old, the doctor will probably suggest that the baby be taken to an eye specialist.

The earlier treatment is started, the better the chances of good results. Even a baby can wear a patch over one eye to strengthen the other and keep what he sees from being blurred. The baby may also be fitted with glasses.

Sometimes a simple operation is necessary a little later, and eye exercise may be advised. Only the eye specialist can decide what treatments are best for a child, as cross-eye has several different causes.

CROUP. Sometimes when a child gets laryngitis, he has a harsh, barking cough. When he has this type of cough, he is said to have the croup. The doctor will be able to prescribe drugs that will fight the germs causing the laryngitis. A child with the croup feels better if he breathes warm air moistened with plenty of steam. An old-time method of making the steam was called the croup kettle method.

CROW. See JAYS, MAGPIES, CROWS, RAVENS.

CROW, THE (constellation). See CORVUS.

CROWBAR, a tool used as a wedge or as a lever in moving heavy objects. It is a round iron bar several feet long, often pointed at one end and flattened like a wedge at the other. Some crowbars are made with a nail claw at one end. To move a rock, the end of the crowbar is inserted under a corner of the rock. Then, by applying force to the other end of the crowbar, the rock is easily moved out of its position. See LEVER.

CRUELTY TO ANIMALS, PREVENTION OF. Although some say that the dog is man's best friend, many persons treat dogs and other animals with neglect and cruelty. Sometimes dogs and horses are not fed or sheltered properly. A few cowardly people beat or torture dogs or other animals in order to work off anger that they dare not direct toward other persons. In the days before the automobile, when vehicles were pulled by horses, drivers often overworked their horses or beat them in order to make them go faster. During past centuries in England and America animal fights and the torturing of animals were witnessed as pleasurable shows. Roosters, or cocks, would be made to fight each other with sharp spurs fastened to their claws. Bullfights still take place in Spain and Latin America. In bearbaiting a blindfolded bear was tied to a stake, and dogs were incited to attack and enrage it.

Organizations for the prevention of cruelty to animals were first formed in England and the United States during the early 1800's. The American Society for the Prevention of Cruelty to Animals, the ASPCA, was started by Henry Bergh and was incorporated in the state of New York in 1866. Later such societies came to be known as humane societies. They were a part of the widespread 19th-century humanitarian movement that advocated charitable treatment of poor people, orphans, industrial workers, criminals, and the insane. Humane societies succeeded in passing laws that forbade all forms of cruelty to animals. It became illegal for the owners of animals to neglect to feed and shelter them properly, to overwork them, or to treat them cruelly. Violators could be tried and punished. Humane societies in cities now feed and shelter unwanted, homeless animals and painlessly put to death sick and injured ones.

CRUSADES, THE, were waged by the Christian peoples of Europe against the Turkish peoples of Mohammedan faith who, from the 11th century, occupied the Holy Land (Palestine) and the city of Jerusalem. Christians venerated this city as the place where Christ lived, died, and was buried, and they could not let the Mohammedans rule over it. Between the years 1096 and 1291 Christian kings and princes led eight crusading armies for the reconquest of the Holy Land. Famous leaders of the crusades were Peter the Hermit, Richard the Lionhearted, and St. Louis. In the Children's Crusade in 1212, 50,000 children were disbanded in Italy or lost. Some of the Crusades were temporarily successful in repelling the Mohammedans, but after 1271 the Holy City remained permanently in Mohammedan hands.

Also during the Middle Ages Christian peoples in the country now called Spain fought other Mohammedans for over 200 years for possession of the Iberian Peninsula. This was the only crusade with lasting results in favor of the Christians.

The Crusades were also fought for other than religious reasons. By the 12th century Europeans had a flourishing trade with Asia in spices and silk. This trade was cut off or at best seriously threatened by the push of the Turkish peoples who occupied the trade routes leading to Asia. Another reason for the Crusades was the effort of popes and kings to send the rebellious nobles away from home. While the nobles were fighting in the Crusades, these popes and kings hoped to restore their own power in Europe.

The only positive result of the Crusades was that Christians became better acquainted with the habits, beliefs, and ways of life of other peoples. This made Europeans less complacent about themselves and their achievements.

CRUSTACEAN. The crustaceans include the lobster, crab, shrimp, crayfish, sow bug, water flea, and barnacle. They are characterized by a body divided into two parts—the cephalothorax (a fusion of head and thorax) and the abdomen—and by numerous pairs of appendages. The chief economic importance of crustaceans is the value of some species as food.

Most crustaceans are marine, although many live in fresh water and a few live on land in damp places. Lobsters, crabs, and shrimps swim through the ocean with a backward motion and also crawl along the bottom. Barnacles attach themselves to such objects as ship hulls or piers. Crayfish live in fresh-water lakes and streams and in holes along the banks. Water fleas appear in swarms in fresh water. The pill bug, a kind of sow bug, is often found in moist places under logs or rocks.

Crustaceans have no internal skeleton but rather an external skeleton, or exoskeleton. Many of them have large, clawlike pincers used for seizing prey, for fighting, and for swimming. The abdomen carries smaller jointed appendages and ends in a horizontal fin, or telson, used in swimming. Crustaceans have compound eyes and two sets of antennae, which are equipped with organs of touch, taste, and smell. They breathe by means of gills.

Lobsters, shrimps, and some crabs are considered delicacies. Although formerly plentiful, the lobster has been caught in such large numbers along the New England coast of the United States that it now has to be protected by law. Smaller crustaceans are important as food for fishes. Barnacles have long been a nuisance because of the way they foul ship hulls.

In 1095 Pope Urban II exhorted the fighting men of Europe to join the First Crusade.

CRUSTACEAN

Gooseneck Barnacles

Sow Bugs

Giant Spider Crab

Rock Barnacles

Fresh-Water Shrimp

Fairy Shrimp

Blue Crab

Cyclops

Ostracods

Fish Louse

Hermit Crab (in shell)

Crayfish

Hermit Crab (out of shell)

Ghost Crab

American Lobster

Fiddler Crab

Mantis Crab

Rock Crab

Crustaceans are classified with insects and arachnids in the phylum Arthropoda. The anatomy of crustaceans and insects is fundamentally similar. Both have externally segmented bodies, paired jointed appendages, a hard external skeleton containing chitin, and sensory antennae. As young crustaceans grow, their external skeleton is molted and regrown several times.

CRUTCH, a support to aid in walking. In walking with crutches, a person must learn to support his weight with his shoulders and arms. All crutch walkers should learn at least two gaits: a fast one for making speed across streets and a slow one for crowded places. If a walking cast can be used to immobilize a broken bone in the leg, using a crutch may be unnecessary.

A victim of polio, below, walks on crutches.
Courtesy of The National Foundation

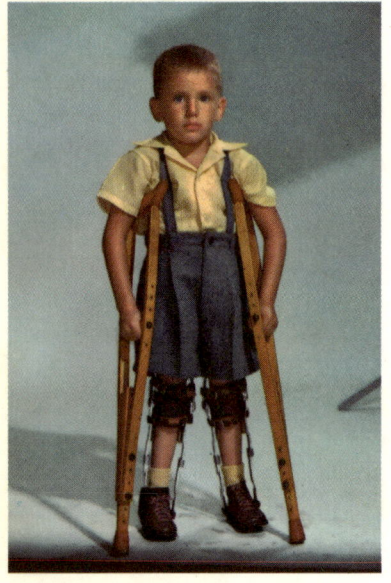

CRUX, or the Cross, is a small southern constellation lying south of Centaurus and north of Musca. It is not visible at any time of the year from midnorthern latitudes. Four of its stars form the well-known Southern Cross.

Four brilliant stars of the constellation Crux lie close together and form the famous Southern Cross. Three of them are between first and second magnitudes, while a third-magnitude star completes the cross.

Gacrux
CRUX
Beta Crucis
Acrux
S

CRYING, a profuse flow of tears. Such a secretion of tears can be brought about by pain or by such emotional states as grief, disappointment, and anger. Just how emotional tension causes crying is not known, although it is fairly well recognized that crying helps to relieve the tension.

Tears are a clear, watery, slightly salty solution with the usual function of lubricating and cleansing the eye. The tears are secreted by the lachrymal gland, which lies above and toward the outer part of the eye and under the upper eyelid. Tears pass through small lachrymal ducts into the eye and normally flow into the nose through ducts at the inner corner of the eye. If the tears are secreted too fast, they overflow the lower eyelid and run down the cheeks.

Crying is the only signal a baby can give about his wants. It does not necessarily mean that he is hungry or in pain. It may simply mean that he is not sleepy and wants companionship. While prolonged or frequent crying is not good for a baby, crying that goes on for five or ten minutes several times a day is nothing to be alarmed about. Even though you may not know just what a baby is crying about, you can help him feel he can rely on you by picking him up and soothing him.

CRYSTAL, a solid matter in its most highly developed and organized form. It is composed of molecules, atoms, or ions arranged in an orderly sequence peculiar to that particular substance. It is bounded externally by plane faces arranged in a definite geometrical scheme, and it is a homogenous solid in which the arrangement about every molecule is the same as that about every other molecule. Thus, in a diamond, every carbon atom is symmetrically surrounded by four other carbon atoms.

Arrangement of the faces of crystals shows a definite symmetry that permits the grouping of crystals into distinct classes and systems. There are 32 classes of crystals, belonging to 6 (or 7) systems defined in terms of the general shapes assumed by the crystals of various substances.

The isometric, or cubic, system includes all crystals having three axes of equal length perpendicular to each other. The hexagonal system includes all crystals that have four axes. Three equal horizontal axes intersect each other at angles of 60 degrees, and the fourth, of different length, is perpendicular to the plane of the other three. In the tetragonal system, the three axes are perpendicular to each other but are of unequal length. The horizontal axes are of equal length, but the vertical axis may be either longer or shorter than the other two. The orthorhombic system includes those crystals having three axes perpendicular to each other but all of unequal length. Crystals of the monoclinic system have three unequal axes. Two of these are inclined to each other at an oblique angle, and the third is perpendicular to the plane of the other two. The triclinic system includes all crystals having three unequal axes intersecting each other at oblique angles.

Crystals have the peculiar property of being susceptible to cleavage. They can be split in some directions more readily than in others. Cleavage surfaces are always parallel to crystal faces or to possible crystal faces.

Crystals, except those of the isometric system, possess also the property of double refraction, because light is transmitted by the crystal with different speeds in different directions.

Some crystals, such as quartz, show the property of pyroelectricity. Under proper temperature conditions positive and negative charges of electricity develop simultaneously on different parts of the same crystal. If quartz is heated to about 100° C., it will, on cooling, develop positive charges of electricity at three alternate prismatic edges and negative charges at the three other edges.

Another property of some crystals (quartz, for example) is that of piezoelectricity, development of an electric charge under pressure. This characteristic makes such substances useful in physical laboratory experiments and in the manufacture of the microphones employed in radio broadcasting.

Little is known about the causes of crystal formation or why some substances assume crystalline form while others do not. In a suitable environment a crystal will grow, and if a broken crystal is placed in a suitable solution, it will quickly repair the break and assume again a perfect crystalline form.

A tiny grain of sand containing silicon dioxide (the chemical name of quartz) may blow about the earth for years unchanged, but if it should fall into water containing the right solution of silicon dioxide, it will begin to form new and perfect crystals in a short time.

CRYSTAL SET

Above are crystals of galena, a lead mineral, and halite, common salt. Both form isometric crystals. Both galena and halite have excellent cubic cleavage. The crystals of these substances have three axes that are of equal length and are at right angles to one another. Garnets, which may be of gem quality, also form isometric crystals.

Below are crystals of quartz, one of the commonest minerals in the earth's crust, and calcite, a common carbonate mineral. These crystals belong to the hexagonal system, in which three axes of equal length are arranged in one plane at 120-degree angles to each other, while a fourth axis of a different length is at right angles to them. Another such crystal is that of beryl.

Above are crystals of epidote, a common silicate of aluminum and calcium with water, and augite, a complex silicate (a pyroxene). These crystals belong to the monoclinic system, which has three unequal axes, two of which meet at right angles and the third of which is oblique to one of the others. Epidote is common in metamorphic rock.

Above are crystals of zircon, a mineral sometimes of gem quality, and rutile, a titanium dioxide sometimes used in rings. These crystals are tetragonal. They have two horizontal axes of equal length and a vertical axis that may be shorter or longer than the others. All three of the axes are at right angles to each other.

Shown below are crystals of sulfur and staurolite, an iron-aluminum silicate. These crystals are orthorhombic. They have three axes, all of different length and all at right angles to one another. Staurolite is frequently found as twinned crystals, which may form a perfect cross, or the twinning may be at an angle of 60 degrees.

Above are crystals of Amazon stone, a mineral sometimes of gem quality, and rhodonite, which may also be used as a gem stone. These crystals belong to the triclinic system, in which all the axes are of unequal length, and none forms a right angle with another. Albite, some of which is cut as moonstone, also has triclinic crystals.

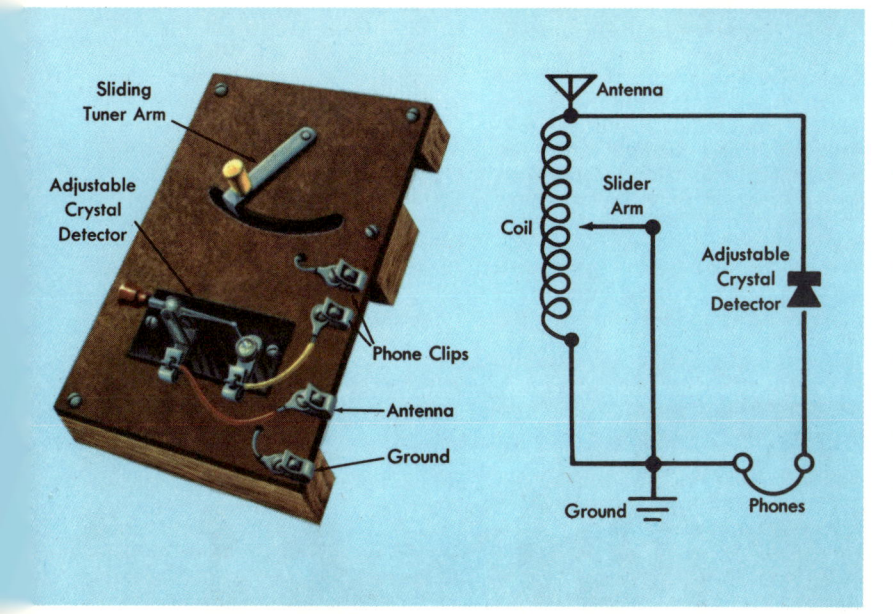

A crystal set, above left, is easy to make. It is built on a wood panel raised by two wooden cleats. A sliding tuner arm contacts a coil wound on a block beneath. At right is the schematic circuit diagram. The receiver works well on strong local stations.

CRYSTAL SET. Early radio receivers had no tubes. Most of them used crystals as detectors. For this reason they were known as crystal receivers or crystal sets. Usually the crystal that was used was a galena crystal, but silicon, carborundum, and certain other crystals were also used. Crystal receivers were superseded by vacuum tubes because they were not very sensitive and they lacked the amplifying power of a tube. They could receive only local stations, and even then headphones were needed to hear the programs. They had the advantage of being inexpensive to make, and they are still constructed by radio enthusiasts intent on studying the principles of radio reception.

The crystal has returned to prominence in radio technology in the form of transistors and semiconductors. Since the crystals used for this purpose are far superior to the early galena crystals, transistors are able to do the same job that the vacuum tubes do in a radio. See TRANSISTOR.

CUBA

CUBA is a republic occupying the largest island of the West Indies. It is the leading sugar-producing country in the world. Havana is Cuba's capital and the largest city in the Caribbean area. Other large cities are Santiago de Cuba, Camagüey, and Santa Clara. The island is 760 miles long with an area of more than 44,000 square miles, nearly the size of Pennsylvania. About 6,500,000 people live in Cuba.

Approximately two-thirds of the island consists of level or rolling land. The three chief mountain ranges are the Sierra de los Organos in the west, the Sierra de Trinidad in central Cuba, and the Sierra Maestra, which is the highest, in the east.

Coral reefs and mangroves line the 2,000-mile coastline, but there are a number of fine harbors, such as Havana, Santiago de Cuba, and Guantánamo (where the United States has a naval base). Extensive swamps lie on the southern coast. Of the many offshore islands, the largest is the Isle of Pines. Cuba's rivers are short. The Cauto River in the east is the longest.

Cuba's climate is warm all year. The winter months have average temperatures in the low 70's. The summer months are slightly warmer. Unfortunately, hurricanes often strike the island in the late summer. Rain falls mostly in summer. The winter is dry.

Agriculture is the country's most important industry. Sugarcane is by far the leading crop. Sugar, with such byproducts as rum, molasses, alcohol, and sirups, provides most of the national income. Tobacco, grown chiefly in the western part of the island, is the crop second in importance. Pineapples and winter vegetables (mostly tomatoes and cucumbers) are exported in quantity. Rice, citrus fruits, bananas, coffee, cacao, corn, beans, and hemp are among crops grown mainly for home use. There are huge cattle ranches in the eastern half of the island. Cuba's foreign trade was mostly with the United States before the Fidel Castro revolution.

Cuba has good deposits of iron, copper, nickel, manganese, and chrome. Its forests yield mahogany and other valuable cabinet woods as well as cedar for cigarboxes. Manufacturing activity is for the production of consumer goods for the country's own needs. Coastal deep-sea fishing is excellent.

The Cuban people are largely descendants of the Spanish settlers who colonized the island. There is a large group of mulattoes and Negroes, whose ancestors were slaves brought from Africa during colonial days to work on the sugar plantations. Spanish is the national language.

Christopher Columbus discovered Cuba on his first voyage in 1492. The Spanish settled the island in 1511, conquering the native Indians. It became an important part of the Viceroyalty of New Spain. Pirates frequently raided and occupied the towns along the coast. Except for a short period of British occupation (1762-1763) the island remained under Spanish control until 1898.

Cuban revolutionary activity against Spain came to a head in 1898 when the U.S. battleship *Maine* was blown up in Havana Harbor, sparking the Spanish-American War. Losing the war, Spain gave up all rights to Cuba and to the Philippine Islands and Puerto Rico. After a short U.S. military government, Cuba became an independent republic in 1902. Since then revolutions and dictatorships have been common. In 1959 pro-Communist Fidel Castro overthrew the Batista dictatorship. Anti-Castro exiles plotted to retake control. An abortive invasion took place in 1961.

This is a street scene in Guantánamo, Cuba. A United States naval base is near the town. — Thomas E. Bachorz

CUBA

- Area: 44,206 sq. mi.
- Population: 6,500,000
- Capital: Havana
- Largest cities: Havana, Marianao, Santiago de Cuba, Camagüey, Cienfuegos
- Highest mountain peak: Pico Turquino (about 6,500 feet)
- Chief river: Cauto
- Climate: Warm throughout the year—summer rainfall
- National flag: Three horizontal blue stripes separated by two white stripes—large red triangle with white star next to pole
- National anthem: *Al combate corred bayameses*
- Form of government: Republic (?)
- Unit of currency: Peso
- Language: Spanish
- Chief religion: Roman Catholic
- Chief economic activities: Agriculture (including livestock raising), mining
- Chief crops: Sugarcane, tobacco, coffee, cacao, rice, corn, vegetables, fruits
- Chief minerals: Nickel, copper, manganese, iron ore
- Chief export: Sugar
- Chief imports: Foodstuffs, machinery and vehicles, fuels, manufactured goods

Cuban boys, disregarding danger, play along the many railroad tracks throughout the island. — Thomas E. Bachorz

713

The Roman Catholic church shown at the left is one of the many such structures in Cuba. Because Cuba was formerly a Spanish colony, it has the language and many of the traditions of Spain. Like the Spaniards, most Cubans are Roman Catholics. The man in the picture below is helping to harvest Cuba's sugarcane, the country's most important crop. Raw sugar, to be refined abroad, is Cuba's principal export. Although sugarcane is grown throughout the country, the greatest production comes from the eastern half of the island.

Thomas E. Bachorz

Although machinery is used on some Cuban farms, this farmer still plows his land with oxen, as has long been done.
Lisl Steiner

Courtesy of the United Fruit Company

This monument to Máximo Gómez, Cuban revolutionary leader, stands on Havana's waterfront. In the background is the Presidential Palace.

Cuban Tourist Comm.

CUBA AND THE WEST INDIES

1 Inch = 95 Statute Miles

- ⊕ National Capital
- ☆ Divisional Capital
- • Size of symbols and type indicates relative population

Oblique Conic Conformal Projection

715

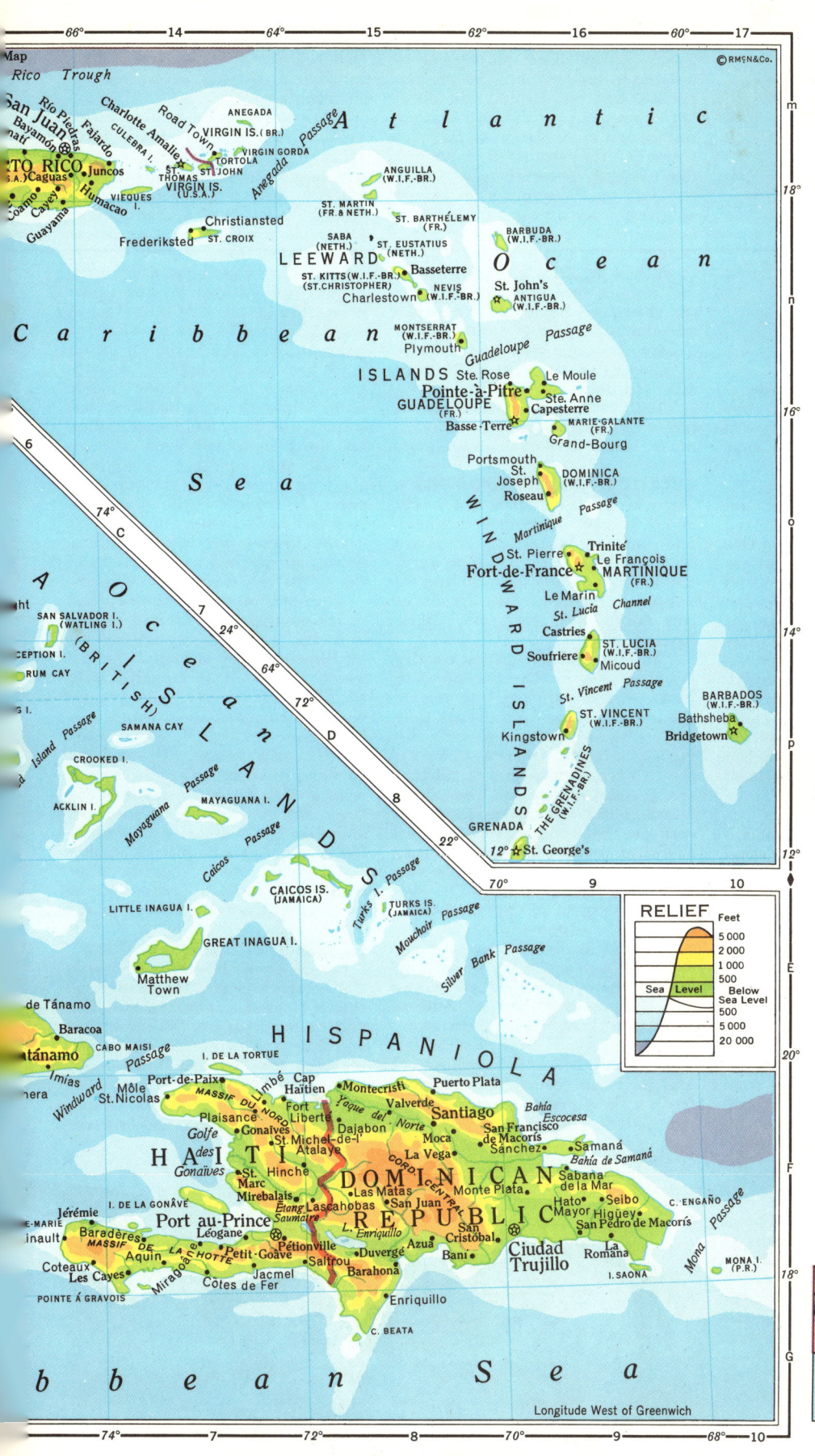

Illustrated above is a Cuban airmail stamp. The Cuban government owns and operates the postal system, which includes telegraph services as well. There are nearly 11,000 miles of telegraph lines located throughout the country.

The Cuban national coat of arms, above, was designed by the same man who designed the national flag. The key symbolizes Cuba as the key to the Gulf of Mexico. The stripes in the lower left of the arms are from the national flag.

The flag of Cuba was designed in New York City by poet Miguel Teurbe Tolon, a patriot in exile from Cuba, more than 50 years before that island gained its independence. The triangle stands for strength and order. The star on the triangle symbolizes a beacon lighting the way to independence.

Location map

For map index, see Volume 20.

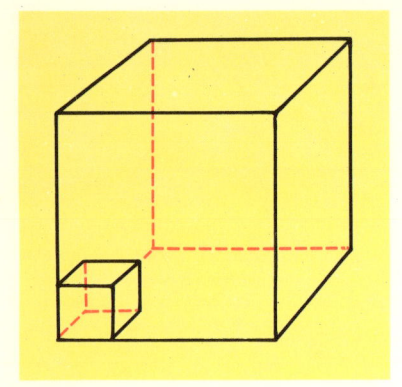

The volume of a cube increases rapidly as an edge is lengthened. The drawing shows a 1-inch and a 4-inch cube. The volume of the small cube is 1 cubic inch; the large cube, 64 cubic inches (4 by 4 by 4).

CUBE, a solid with six identical square sides. The sides are arranged like the walls, floor, and ceiling of a room. All of the angles in a cube are right angles, that is, angles of 90 degrees. All the edges are the same length, so length, width, and height are equal. You could multiply these three together to find how much the cube holds. Because they are equal, you can simply multiply the length of one edge times itself and times itself again. From this fact we get the idea of saying a number is cubed if the number is multiplied by itself and by itself again.

CUCKOO CLOCK, a clock that announces the hours in sounds that imitate the cuckoo, often with the appearance of a wooden cuckoo that bows and opens its beak as the hour is struck. The cuckoo notes are sounded by a pair of organ pipes set in motion by bellows.

Cuckoo clocks were first made in the Black Forest of Germany in the middle of the 18th century. They were probably invented by Franz Anton Ketterer, who supposedly got his idea for the cuckoo clock from the medieval tower clock of a church in southern Germany. When this clock announced the hour, music sounded, and moving figures of the Three Wise Men bowed before the Virgin and Child.

Clockmaking in the Black Forest region started about the middle of the 17th century. It began as an offshoot of woodcarving, which families did during the winter months in place of work on the farm. The first cuckoo clocks were plain rectangular structures, made entirely of wood, with an arched top. The clock face was painted on the front, and floral patterns were painted in each corner. The wooden cuckoo was put behind the door.

Cuckoo clocks of the 19th century were much more elaborate and picturesque; they were often shaped like cottages or farmhouses with a gable on top. The four sides served as a frame for an oil painting of a landscape or a rural, sometimes legendary, scene in the center. A pair of antlers or other imitation hunting trophies were often carved above the clock face. Some of these clocks added another bird to announce the quarter hours or even had a built-in music box that began to play after the hours were struck.

The Black Forest is still a manufacturing center for cuckoo clocks, music boxes, and mechanical toys.

CUCKOOS, ANIS, ROADRUNNERS. These birds are members of a family of 128 species, many of which have odd behavior patterns. They are found worldwide, especially in warm and tropical lands; several species are in North America. Fossils of this family date from the Upper Eocene period.

The Old World cuckoos usually lay their eggs in the nests of other birds, who are tricked into raising the foster nestling even though they neglect their own young while doing so. In North America, however, the two common species of cuckoos—the yellow-billed and the black-billed—build their own nests and care for their young. Both species are slim, brownish, thrush-sized birds with light under parts and long tails. The yellow-billed has large white spots on the tail, reddish wings, and a yellow lower mandible. The black-billed has less white in the tail, a black bill, a red ring around the eye, and no red on the wings. It calls "coo-coo" and is sometimes known as a rain crow. Both species nest in central North America and winter in South America. Both are beneficial, for they feed on insect pests, especially fuzzy caterpillars, which most birds avoid. One yellow-billed cuckoo was seen to devour 47 tent caterpillars in six minutes.

The two anis in the United States—smooth-billed and groove-billed—are found in the southern states. The smooth-billed ani nests in Florida; the groove-billed, in the Rio Grande Valley. Both are long-tailed, glossy-black birds that look rather loose jointed. They resemble grackles except for their bills, which have a high horny ridge on the upper mandible. It is difficult to see whether the bill is smooth or grooved, but their voices distinguish the two species; the smooth-billed has a high, whining double note, while the groove-billed has softer notes. They build large, bulky, leaf-lined communal nests in which several anis lay eggs. They also share the incubation, several often sitting on the nest at the same time. Anis feed in flocks and are often near cattle, feeding on insects on the ground or perched on the backs of the cattle while picking off ticks.

The roadrunner, a ground cuckoo of the southwestern United States, is a shy, amusing, strange-looking bird about 2 feet in length, half of which is tail. It is streaked with olive brown and white above and has white under parts, short wings, and long, powerful legs. It likes desert and semiarid regions with scattered cover, where it walks and runs more than it flies. Often it strides along the roadside, swinging its long tail and raising its great, rough crest. Its food consists of insects, snakes (even rattlesnakes), lizards, scorpions, and small animals such as rats. It preys occasionally on young quails and quail eggs, but it is rated as a very beneficial bird because it feeds largely on insects that destroy crops. Its large stick nest is concealed in a tree or shrub, and its nestlings are fed on snakes and lizards. New Mexico claims the roadrunner as its state bird.

The odd-looking roadrunner feeds on small animals and many kinds of harmful insects.

Species of cuckoos vary greatly in size, but all have a long, graduated tail. The yellow-billed, above, is a North American species.

CUCUMBER, a vegetable widely used in salads and for pickles. It is the fruit of the cucumber vine, an annual belonging to the same family as the melon, squash, and gourd. The plant is probably native to Asia and Africa, but it has been in cultivation for thousands of years. It was known to the ancient Greeks and Romans and is said to have been introduced into China about 150 B.C.

It has a trailing, or sometimes climbing, stem, which is rough and hairy and bears tendrils. The cucumber is usually prickly when young but sometimes becomes smooth when older. The flesh is greenish white to white. The skin is green and sometimes striped, becoming yellow as the fruit ripens. The cucumber is a favorite in home gardens. It is also raised commercially on a large scale for sale as a truck crop and for pickles. A single plant may bear as many as 100 cucumbers.

CULTURE. In popular usage a cultured person is a person who is versed in the fine arts and who has a refined manner. Culture, in this sense of the word, can occur only in a civilization. The anthropologist's definition of culture refers to the entire set of traditions and ideas of human beings.

The traditions are handed down through the generations, and their imprint is found in all the handiwork of men and women. Included in culture are the technological developments, the economic system, the educational system, the political system, the religion, the arts, the folklore, and the fashions of people. The number of choices a person has in his actions is limited by the culture in which he grew up. In this sense, culture includes civilization.

Culture is an attribute of man and no other animal. It cannot be explained in terms of biology. An animal, no matter where it is born and where it grows up, will utter basically the same cries and make the same motions. If a human child's parents are Chinese, and he is raised in England, he will learn to speak English and to dress like an Englishman. He will acquire a large part of English culture.

The word *culture* refers to all of human activity and tradition. Persons who study culture as a whole find things that are common to all groups of people. For example, they find that culture changes gradually as it is passed on from generation to generation. They find that a person's personality is formed and limited by the traditional set of understandings with which he grew up. The personalities in turn form the culture of the next generation. The type of family that one finds in a society is largely determined by the rest of the culture. See FAMILY.

The word *culture* also refers to individual sets of traditional understandings. Thus we can speak of Italian culture, European culture, or Western culture, depending on the number of distinguishing traits that we include. Persons who study individual cultures tend to bring out the uniqueness of each culture. They might delineate an area in North America in terms of traits found there. (See ANTHROPOLOGY.) They might also trace the development and spread of a trait among various cultures through time.

CUMBERLAND ROAD, also called the National Road, was one of the first highways built by the U. S. federal government to help people who decided to move westward. By 1818 this important road was opened as far as Wheeling, Va. (now in West Virginia), where water transportation on the Ohio River was available. In 1833 its extension reached Columbus, Ohio. When completed, the Cumberland Road connected Baltimore, Md., with Vandalia, Ill.

After the War of 1812 the western frontier of the United States extended to the Mississippi River. For the next 50 years this newly acquired territory, especially the Northwest or Great Lakes area, was overrun by settlers from the southern and eastern states. Year after year, thousands of frontiersmen from the Carolinas, Virginia, Maryland, and New England trekked westward along the Cumberland Road. By 1830 the wooded hill country of southern Indiana and Illinois was filled with newcomers. After the building of the Erie Canal in 1825, however, the importance of the Cumberland Road diminished.

Besides playing an important role in the history of westward migration, the Cumberland Road also caused political discussion. Who should be responsible for the repair of the road? Some politicians thought it was the duty of the federal government to levy toll charges and use the money for repair. But President James Monroe, supported by the majority, successfully recommended a national system of internal improvements. So many people were moving westward that the General Survey Bill was passed by Congress. It empowered the president to start surveys for roads and canals. These roads and canals helped to keep those people who were settling the Northwest in touch with their countrymen in the eastern part of the nation.

CUNEIFORM is a type of writing used by ancient people. *Cuneiform* means "wedge shaped." This writing was so named because it is made with combinations of signs in the shape of wedges. The wedge is pointed toward the right, downward, or at a slant. The slanted wedges separate the words.

The Sumerians, who were the first people known to use cuneiform writing, drained their land from marshes. They used much mud and clay, and they wrote mostly on clay. They wrote with a pointed wooden instrument called a stylus. The stylus made the wedge-shaped impression.

Babylonian cuneiform had about 600 symbols. Writing and reading became much simpler with the invention of the alphabet, in which each symbol stands for one sound.

The first cuneiform words to be deciphered were from Persian texts: "Darius . . . great king of kings . . . son of Hystaspes . . . Xerxes, great king of kings . . . son of Darius." Sir Henry Creswicke Rawlinson, one of many scholars in this field, made contributions to the research, beginning about 1835. He found and studied a rock at what is now Behistun, Iran, that contained the same inscription in three languages. Scholars were then able to decipher Persian, Scythian, and Babylonian cuneiform.

CUP, THE (constellation). See CRATER.

CUPBOARD, originally a board or shelf for dishes. It first developed as part of the sideboard, with special shelves for cups and dishes. Cupboards became increasingly popular, beginning in the 17th century in Europe, among the upper classes. The finest woods were used, and they frequently were ornately carved. In modern times the name applies to a closet with shelves for dishes, such as a kitchen cupboard for kitchenware as well as the more handsome cupboards for the best dishes.

CUPID, in Roman mythology, the god of love. He was the son of Venus, and he constantly attended her. With his bow and arrows, Cupid pierced the hearts of the gods and mortals whom he wished to inspire with love.

One time Cupid shot a gold-tipped arrow into the heart of Apollo. The god promptly fell in love with the nymph Daphne. She, however, was pierced with a lead-tipped arrow. This produced just the opposite effect. Running from the god, Daphne asked for help. She was turned into a laurel tree.

Once Cupid shot an arrow into his own heart by mistake. He immediately fell in love with the beautiful Psyche. Venus was so jealous of her son's love that she made Psyche perform three supposedly impossible tasks. When the tasks were completed, the lovers were reunited.

In Greek mythology Cupid was called Eros, the personification of love.

The Curies, Pierre and Marie, above, were two of France's most gifted scientists.

CURIE, PIERRE (1859-1906), and **MARIE** (1867-1934), French scientists and the discoverers of radium. Pierre was born near Paris. Marie was born at Warsaw. She was a pupil of Pierre at the Sorbonne, where he was a professor of physics. After their marriage the Curies continued their work together. In 1898, while investigating the Becquerel radiations from uranium, they came across samples of pitchblende, the substance from which uranium was extracted, and found that it possessed four times the radioactivity of metallic uranium. They concluded that the radiations were caused by some unknown element in the pitchblende sample and began a search for it. A substance was discovered that closely resembled bismuth in its chemical characteristics.

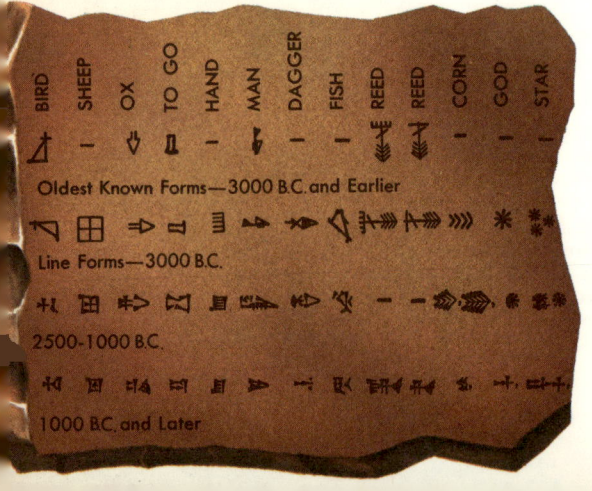

The piece of clay shown above bears a message written in the wedge-shaped signs of cuneiform. Also shown is a stylus, the implement used to impress the signs into the clay.

The evolution of 13 cuneiform signs is traced at the left. This system, originated nearly 6,000 years ago, was used until shortly before the beginning of the Christian Era.

BIRD | SHEEP | OX | TO GO | HAND | MAN | DAGGER | FISH | REED | REED | CORN | GOD | STAR

Oldest Known Forms—3000 B.C. and Earlier

Line Forms—3000 B.C.

2500-1000 B.C.

1000 B.C. and Later

Madame Curie named it polonium in honor of her native Poland. During the same year (1898) the Curies conducted further experiments with the pitchblende and succeeded in isolating a second substance from it, associated with barium, which they called radium. They both received the Nobel prize for physics in 1903, along with Antoine Henri Becquerel. After the accidental death of Pierre Curie in Paris in 1906, Marie Curie continued her work with radium, and she also succeeded her husband at the University of Paris. She received the Nobel prize for chemistry in 1911, the only person ever to receive two such awards.

CURLING, an ancient sport played with large stones on ice. It is the favorite sport of Scotland, where it originated. It is first mentioned in the 16th century, when stones were picked up from the nearest riverbed. The game has been standardized, and the stone used now is a smooth, circular stone with a handle attached to the middle of the top. The game is played by two four-man teams, each player having two stones. The stones are aimed and shoved along the ice toward a "tee," the center of a large circle marked on the ice at each end of the rink. The stone stopping nearest the tee scores one point. If two or more stones of the same team stop closer to the tee than any stone of the other team, one point is scored for each stone. Each team has a captain, called the "skip," who instructs his players on exactly how to deliver the stone for the greatest advantage of the team. The players carry regular brooms, with which they sweep the ice in front of the stone to make it slide farther.

CURRANT, a highly valued small fruit borne in drooping clusters. Currants, which cannot endure hot or dry summers, will thrive in regions too chilly for the growing of most fruit trees. Currants are most commonly red, but there are also white, striped, and black currants. They are borne on smooth-stemmed bushes, which have thick, stocky branches and simple, roundish, often scallop-edged leaves. The flowers are small and are yellowish green with some purple. The currant is related to the gooseberry.

Currants are eaten raw or cooked or are made into jelly and jam. The dried currants used in fruit cake and mincemeat are not currants but a kind of dried grape.

Currier & Ives—Museum of the City of New York, the Harry T. Peters Collection
Reproduced above is a lithograph originally published by Currier & Ives. A rare Currier & Ives print may command a price of hundreds or even thousands of dollars.

CURRIER & IVES, the imprint on popular American lithographs published by two partners during the 19th century. Nathaniel Currier was born in Roxbury, Mass., in 1813. He learned the process of lithography as an apprentice and in 1835 established his own shop in New York. In 1850 James Merritt Ives, born in New York in 1824, joined Currier. After he became a partner in 1857, all lithographs published by the two men were marked with the firm's famous imprint, Currier & Ives. Although Ives himself made some of the prints, the partners usually hired specialists to do the artwork. The completed picture, transferred to stone by lithographic workers, produced black-and-white prints, which were often brightly colored by hand.

Currier & Ives prints, during the last half of the century, satisfied the desire for illustration now supplied by picture magazines. When, for example, an important fire occurred, a Currier & Ives print depicting the disaster was ready within a few days, at a price ranging from 15 to 20 cents. The prints became collectors' items, both for their intrinsic charm and for their value as well-executed pictorial records of the railroads, clippers, steamships, the California gold-rush days, sports, costumes, and many other aspects of expanding America. Nathaniel Currier died in 1888; James Merritt Ives, in 1895.

CURRY, JOHN STEUART (1897-1946), American painter, was born in Dunavant, Kan. He studied in Chicago, New York, and Paris, worked for some years as a magazine illustrator, and then became known for his earthy, objective pictures of Middle West life and his murals of historical subjects. Among his murals were "Western Migration" (Justice Building, Washington, D.C.), "Oklahoma Land Rush" (Interior Building, Washington, D.C.), and a series executed for the Kansas Capitol. Typical of his dramatic easel paintings were "Baptism in Kansas" and "Tornado." During the last ten years of his life Curry was resident artist at the University of Wisconsin.

CURTAINS AND DRAPERIES are fabric window hangings, gracefully arranged. They control the amount of light entering a room, afford privacy, and adorn the room. Curtains (often called glass curtains), draperies, or both may be used, according to personal tastes and desires.

Hangings, the forerunners of modern draperies, were originally

Flowers of some of the species of the currant change from yellow to red.

used over glassless window openings to keep out the elements; early drapery functioned as doors, room dividers, and bed hangings. In modern times curtains and draperies have served primarily as window coverings, although draperies are sometimes used to cover a wall.

Curtain materials include cotton, linen, rayon, plastic, synthetics (such as nylon, Dacron, and Orlon), and combinations of synthetic and natural fibers. The fabric—printed, embroidered, or plain—may be sheer or heavy. Curtains, ruffled or unruffled, may be hung in cottage sets, one for each window. Curtains may be tiered or full length and may be tied back or tailored to hang straight. They may be hung with or without shades or blinds and may be combined with draperies, valances, or cornices to create a decorative effect. Each window or group of windows presents a specific problem of arrangement, style, and color, which should be considered with the total decorative scheme.

Draperies may be the keynote of a room or merely a decorative accessory. Curtains admit some light and provide a view of the outdoors, but draperies may offer more privacy and may cut off the natural light. Drapery fabrics include those used for curtains and also many heavier fabrics. Draperies may complement or contrast with other colors and textures in the room. Lined or unlined, they may be hung alone on a window or over blinds, shades, or curtains; like curtains they may be combined with valances and cornices. Again the arrangement, style, length, color, and texture depend on individual tastes and preferences.

The hardware or fixtures, usually of sturdy metal or plastic, are placed according to the effect desired. Curtain-rod brackets are usually placed on the outside of the window frame so the curtain will cover the opening and the frame. The rods may be simple round bars, from which the curtain hangs on rings, affording a certain mobility. Or they may be of the flat, hollow, extensible variety, holding the curtain in a more permanent arrangement.

Draperies may be hung from rings, a traverse rod, or a crane. A traverse rod is a flat, hollow rod containing a pulley device. Cords at one end of the rod are pulled to move the draperies across the window. A crane is a swinging arm attached to the wall or window frame; it allows the draperies to swing away from the window but not to be pulled across it.

Custer's Last Stand, or the Battle of the Little Bighorn, was part of a war caused by corruption in the Indian Bureau and encroachment on the Sioux's lands. Custer (left) had been sent with his regiment to help capture or disperse Indians who, faced with starvation, had flouted Indian Bureau orders and left their reservations to hunt buffalo.

CUSTER, GEORGE ARMSTRONG (1839-1876), a U.S. army officer, was born in New Rumley, Ohio. He was graduated from West Point in 1861 and took part in the Civil War. He was on General George McClellan's staff during the Peninsular campaign and in 1863 led a brigade of Michigan cavalry in Alfred Pleasanton's corps. His brigade distinguished itself against "Jeb" Stuart at the Battle of Gettysburg and in 1864 he aided Philip Sheridan on his raids. In 1864 he was made commander of the 3rd division of cavalry and won the Battle of Woodstock. Custer received the Confederate flag of truce, which led to the surrender at Appomattox Courthouse. In 1866 he was made lieutenant colonel of the 7th Cavalry. Custer took part in Indian campaigns and in 1874 led an exploring expedition to the Black Hills. During the campaign of 1876 against the Sioux, his regiment formed part of Alfred Terry's column. Custer was sent out to locate the enemy, while Terry and John Gibbon continued up the Yellowstone River. The Indian encampment was found on the Little Bighorn River. Custer decided to attack and divided his force into three parts. He and his own command of 264 were surprised by an overwhelming number of Sioux and annihilated, June 25, 1876.

CUSTOMS, in government, duties placed on imports and exports. Customs may be specific or ad valorem. Specific duties are customs levied on imports and exports according to number or bulk. Ad valorem duties are placed on goods according to their value. The effect of customs is to raise the price of goods. This increase in price is passed on to the consumer.

In colonial America certain trade was denied the colonists. The customs administrators, royal governors, and resident officials spent most of their customs-collecting time trying to control smuggling operations. Later the collection of duties became the responsibility of revenue officers. In Massachusetts the job of collecting customs was given to agents, who earned a certain percentage of all they collected. In spite of heavy penalties against evading customs and a system of paid informers, the 18th century witnessed a great increase in smuggling in the colonies. The Constitution gave Congress the power "to lay and collect taxes, duties, imposts, and excises." Customhouses were placed under the control of the Treasury Department. The functions of the U.S. Bureau of Customs include the collection of duties on imports, the prevention of smuggling, and the enforcement of tariff laws. A state may levy customs only for the purpose of financing the execution of its inspection laws. See TARIFF.

CUT, a break in the skin. If there is bleeding from a cut, cover the cut with a clean cloth or gauze bandage and apply pressure over the area with your hand. Cuts of the tongue or mouth should be treated promptly by a doctor. All severe cuts, deep puncture wounds, and wounds into which dirt has entered should also be treated by a doctor.

Small cuts should be washed out well with soap and water, and a sterile bandage or a clean, freshly ironed piece of cloth should be applied. Large cuts should be covered with sterile gauze. Press the gauze firmly over the wound to control bleeding, and hold it in place until the doctor comes. Do not use strong antiseptics on small cuts. Soap and water make an excellent antiseptic.

CUVIER, GEORGES, BARON (1769-1832), was a French naturalist, statesman, and philosopher. He was born in Montbéliard and educated at Stuttgart, in Germany, and at Paris. In 1800 he was appointed Louis Daubenton's successor as professor of natural history at the Collège de France, and in 1802 he was appointed to the chair of comparative anatomy at the Garden of Plants. Cuvier examined the skeletons of both living and fossil animals. Thousands of species were compared and their similarities noted. Cuvier's *Lessons in Comparative Anatomy* and *Animal Kingdom* raised him to fame among scientists. He was a councilor of the Imperial University and a councilor of state under Napoleon and Louis XVIII.

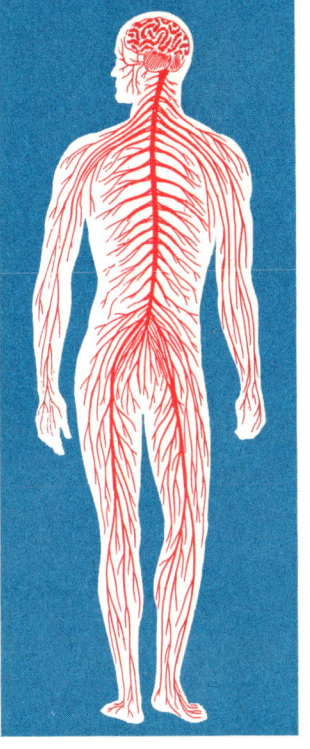

CYBERNETICS, a neo-Greek expression coined by Norbert Wiener and an associate in 1947 to designate the study of control and communication in the animal and the machine. Cybernetics seeks to find the common elements in the functioning of the human nervous system and automatic machines and to develop a theory of control and communication in living organisms and machines. This theory rests upon the similarities noted between complex activities of the human brain and the computing machine: Modern computing machines are capable of memory, association, choice, and other functions similar to those of the human brain.

The central concept in cybernetics is the feedback mechanism, which in response to messages received through the system, feeds back to the system particular messages that modify its operation. Positive feedback increases what the system is doing in direction and magnitude; negative feedback inhibits the activity of the system. An example of negative feedback in machines is the governor of a steam engine. In its original form the two balls attached to pendulum rods swing on opposite sides of a rotating shaft and control the opening of a steam valve by means of a mechanical linkage attached to a collar about the shaft. The opening is reduced when the balls rise (increasing speed) and widened when the balls fall (decreasing speed). The system therefore tends to reach an equilibrium point. Consequently, the engine operates uniformly at the prescribed speed with a given load. Changes in the load would cause an initial corresponding change in the system until an equilibrium is reached again.

The nervous system of the human organism also exhibits a negative feedback mechanism: In order to pick up a pencil, certain muscles have to be moved that do not depend entirely upon a conscious act of the will. In the act of picking up the pencil, the motion of the arm proceeds in such a manner as to decrease by successive stages the amount by which the pencil is not picked up. In this normal response a report by means of sensations is given to the nervous system, which indicates the amount by which the pencil is not picked up until the pencil is actually picked up. If the sensations are wanting, the hand is unable to pick up the pencil. Excessive feedback causes just as serious a handicap: The muscles involved overshoot their mark.

Cybernetics deals with similarities between certain elements of automatic machines, such as the data-processing system at left, and elements of the human nervous system (right).
Courtesy of International Business Machines Corporation

This analogy between machine and human organism can be discovered in many other phenomena. For example, the whole adult brain with its store of memories may be compared with the physical structure of the computing machine together with the instructions given it at the beginning of a chain of operations and the additional information gained from outside in the course of its operation.

CYCAD, an ornamental evergreen plant that resembles a fern or a small palm tree. The cycad, however, is not a fern or a palm but a gymnosperm that bears conelike structures. Seeds are produced between the scales of these structures. Cycads are native to Asia and Australia. Two species of cycad are grown outdoors in Florida and southern California and are cultivated in greenhouses and conservatories in other regions of the United States. One of these species is popularly known as the sago palm.

The sago palm and the other cultivated species of cycad have sturdy, unbranched trunks that grow from 6 to 12 feet tall. Their leaves are confined to a large, dense crown that grows upward and sideways from the top of the trunk. The stiff, glossy-green leaves, which are from 2 to 8 feet long, are divided into many rigid, pointed segments, so that they resemble huge feathers. In the United States the leaves of the sago palm are often made into funeral wreaths.

Cycads belong to a gymnosperm family whose fernlike and palmlike members dominated the earth's vegetation millions of years ago.

The cycad zamia, **1**, has an underground stem from which its leaves arise in a loose clump. The sago palm, **2**, is a cycad whose leaves arch upward and outward from the top of the trunk. The fern palm, **3**, is not a palm but a treelike cycad whose maximum height is 15 feet.

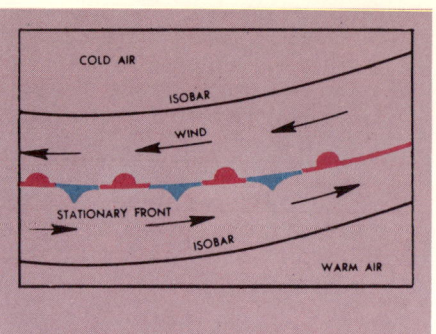

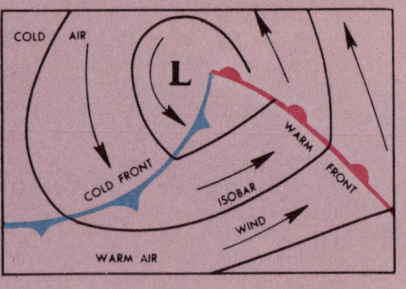

CYCLAMEN, a plant of the primrose family, native to central and southern Europe but grown in the United States as a greenhouse plant and valued for its brilliantly colored, curiously shaped, inverted flowers. These are white, rose, purple, or lilac and are plain, streaked, or blotched. They are borne singly on long stalks, which, like the long-stalked, heart-shaped or kidney-shaped leaves, rise from the surface of a flattened tuber, or corm. Sometimes the petals are fringed or crested. The leaves are thick and are often beautifully marked and mottled. Cyclamens are raised from seed and blossom about 15 months after planting.

CYCLING, or riding a bicycle, is useful transportation to many people and a pleasant recreation or exciting sport to others. In modern cities such as Amsterdam, The Netherlands, one sees hundreds of thousands of bicycles in dense, silent traffic. In Copenhagen, Denmark, major boulevards have bicycle paths between the sidewalks and the street, separated on both sides by beautiful colonnades of trees. Throughout Europe youths may use a widespread system of overnight hostels located about a day's cycling distance apart. (See Hostel.) Bicycle racing reaches a peak of excitement every summer when the Tour of France—a 3,000-mile race lasting almost a month—is held.

Cycling is less popular in the United States, where use of the automobile is widespread. However, bicycles are sometimes more practical than automobiles in small towns. Great numbers of public school students bicycle between home and school. Recreational cycling for adults has gained some popularity with the introduction of three-speed gearshifts and through the influence of young adults who have cycled through Europe.

Cycling became popular in the 1870's after bicycles first came out with rubber tires, metal spokes, and pedals. These were the high-wheeler type, with front wheels over 5 feet high. A fall from one could be somewhat dangerous. The "safety" bicycle with a chain drive, equal-sized wheels, and air-inflated tires made cycling the great adult recreation of the 1890's.

The diagram above shows one of the steps in the life cycle of a cyclone. Warm air pushes against a cold airmass to produce a warm front, while cold air pushes into a warm airmass to create a cold front.

CYCLONE, a roughly circular area of low atmospheric pressure, around which the winds blow counterclockwise in the Northern Hemisphere and clockwise in the Southern Hemisphere. A cyclone may be from 500 to 1,500 miles across. It originates along the boundary separating converging air currents of differing characteristics. It is the opposite of the anticyclone. Cyclones are of two types: the mild cyclone, which creates much of the weather in middle latitudes, including the United States; and the tropical cyclone, which is a small, violent storm. See Hurricane; Typhoon.

Since cyclones are low-pressure storms, they are sometimes called lows. They move eastward across the United States in the mainstream of the prevailing westerly winds. Cyclones are like the whirlpools left behind a boat as you row it. But cyclones are also very large and sometimes cover as much as one-third of the United States.

A cyclone travels about 20 to 30 miles an hour and makes the journey across the United States in from three to six days. As it journeys, winds spiral into it in a counterclockwise direction. This would fill up the low-pressure area, except that air in the center of a cyclone tends to rise. Because of the direction in which the winds swirl into a cyclone, there is a tendency for cold winds to be drawn in from the north and west, while warm, humid winds are pulled in from the south and southeast. As a result, cyclones are the meeting place for cold and warm air. They are factories of weather.

These masses of air of different temperature result in several types of cloud cover and precipitation. The center of a low, where air meets and rises, does not usually have much cloud cover. But to the north and northeast the warm air tends to glide over the cold air to form a warm front. Here there is a dull, gray, overcast sky, with drizzly rain. To the southwest of the low, the cold air generally pushes into the warm air mass and creates a cold front. Temperature in a cyclone tends to be higher than usual in the winter and lower than usual in the summer. The cyclone is one of the many things a weatherman watches for when he attempts to predict the weather. See ANTICYCLONE; COLD FRONT; WARM FRONT.

CYCLONE CELLAR, a place of shelter in areas visited by tornadoes. It is usually a secure underground cellar or room, with an entrance protected by a stout door. The force of a tornado is so great that very little above ground can withstand it. About the only safe place to hide from a tornado is below the ground. Farmers in areas where tornadoes are frequent have learned to take cover in tornado caves. These cellars below the ground are also convenient storage areas for canned fruits and vegetables. The cyclone cellar is usually close enough to the farmhouse to furnish refuge on short notice. But it is far enough from buildings so that the persons inside it will not be injured by the debris left by the tornado. The cyclone cellar is a feature of many midwestern farms. See TORNADO.

CYCLOPS, in Greek mythology, one of a race of one-eyed giants. Two major traditions exist, of which the one presented in Homer's *Odyssey* is the more familiar.

According to Homer, the Cyclopes were cruel, savage creatures who lived in a remote land where they were subject to no government or laws. During the course of his wanderings Ulysses visited them, and he and his men were imprisoned in a cave by one of the Cyclopes, Polyphemus, who each day ate four of Ulysses' men. Ulysses got his captor drunk and blinded him; he and his men then escaped from the cave, whose entrance Polyphemus was guarding, by clinging to the undersides of rams that Polyphemus was letting out to pasture. Polyphemus' prayer of vengeance to his father, Neptune, god of the sea, was responsible for many of Ulysses' later difficulties.

According to Hesiod there were three Cyclopes, named Brontes, Steropes, and Arges. They were excellent craftsmen, manufacturers of (among other things) fortifications and thunderbolts, and often appeared as workmen for Vulcan, the god of thunder. Sons of earth and heaven, they resembled the gods except that each had but one eye.

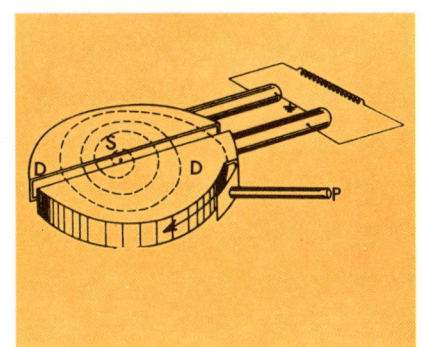

Univ. of Calif.

CYCLOTRON, a machine used by nuclear physicists to accelerate nuclear particles for the bombardment of atoms. It was the first of several devices popularly called atom smashers. The cyclotron was invented by Ernest O. Lawrence of the University of California in 1930. The heart of the cyclotron is a large, circular vacuum chamber, inside of which are placed two hollow semicircular electrodes called dees because they are shaped like the letter D. The dees are given a high-frequency alternating potential difference. In the center of the vacuum chamber, between the two dees, is mounted a tungsten filament to furnish electrons for the purpose of ionizing the gas in the chamber. The entire chamber is placed in a horizontal position and at right angles to a vertical magnetic field between the poles of a powerful electromagnet. The magnetic field causes electrified particles (such as protons or helium nuclei) to move in a semicircle. The charges of each dee are reversed in successive steps (several million times a second), from positive to negative, and the charged particle is yanked across the openings between the dees with ever-increasing speed. While the particle is in the interior of the dee, its speed remains constant. But after it has described a semicircle through the dee, it reaches the gap, or opening, between the dees, where its speed greatly increases. Once the particle is in the interior of the other dee, the speed no longer increases but remains constant until it is again increased at the gap. By this process the particles reach tremendous speeds. Finally, a deflecting plate, charged to a high negative potential, pulls the charged particle out of the dees entirely, so that it can be used to bombard any desired material. See NUCLEAR REACTOR, EXPERIMENTAL; RADIOACTIVE ISOTOPE.

Shown at left is the 184-inch cyclotron at the University of California in Berkeley. The diagram, above left, shows how the cyclotron imparts speed to nuclear particles. Ions from the source, **S,** are caused to travel in a horizontal circular path by the vertical magnetic field produced inside hollow circular electrodes, **D.** These electrodes (called dees) alternate in electrical potential and thereby gradually increase the speed of the particle, which is pulled back and forth between them. The deflecting plate, **P,** draws the particle out of the dees. The dees are contained in an evacuated chamber, and targets may be bombarded either in the chamber or outside it.

CYGNUS, or the Swan, also called the Northern Cross, is a northern constellation lying south of Cepheus and between Andromeda and Lyra. It is in the Milky Way at a point where the Milky Way divides into two great branches, so that the center and bottom parts of the cross lie between the two branches. Cygnus is best visible from midnorthern latitudes from June to December. The first-magnitude star Deneb is the constellation's brightest star and forms the top of the cross. The faint star known as 61 Cygni is interesting because it was the first star for which a measurement distance was obtained (in 1838). Deneb forms a prominent triangle in the sky with two other brilliant stars of nearby constellations—Vega in Lyra to the west and Altair in Aquila to the south.

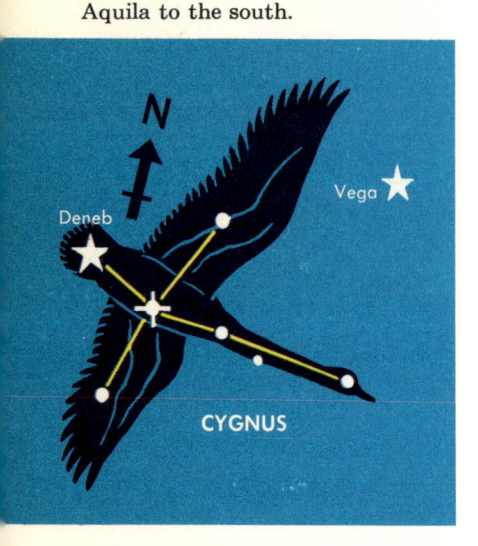

According to one of several legends Cygnus represents Orpheus, who was turned into a swan at his death. Others held that Cygnus was the swan into which Jupiter changed himself or the swan into which Apollo changed Cygnus, son of the king of the Ligurians.

CYLINDER, a solid round tube, flat across each end. Its surface is made up of a set of parallel lines all extending from the points of a circle and ending in another circle of the same size that is in a plane parallel to the plane of the first circle. The surface also includes the area of both circles. The perpendicular distance from one circle to the other is called the altitude of the cylinder. The area of either one of the two equal circles is called the base. To find how much a cylinder holds, you must first find the area of the base, using its radius. (See CIRCLE.) Then multiply the area of the base times the altitude.

CYMBALS, musical instruments of percussion (striking), used usually in pairs and consisting of circular bronze or brass plates, concave in the middle, played by being struck together, one being held in each hand by means of leather straps. They give a sharp, ringing clang if struck together, but they are often only rubbed hard on each other.

Their size varies from little metal finger cymbals to large orchestral cymbals used with the big drum. Experiments have been made, without much success, to make them produce tones of a regular pitch, but their chief uses are to mark tempo or rhythm and to give emphasis. They give a harsh, decided, and barbaric touch to music when freely used. They are very ancient instruments and were used by the Greeks and Romans and by most Eastern nations. Ancient cymbals were more like bells or clips in shape and probably had a more bell-like tone than those in use nowadays.

CYPRESS. There are two quite different groups of trees known as cypresses, both of which belong to the large group of pine relatives. The bald cypress is found chiefly in swampy regions in the southern United States and in Mexico. It is a very tall tree, occasionally 150 to 170 feet in height, with a broad crown, often 100 feet across. All around the trunk are little pointed stumps, called cypress knees, which spring up from the roots. They are spongy inside and serve as breathing organs for the roots, which otherwise would not be able to get air when completely under water. The tree has fine, soft, feathery, light-green needles. The wood is used for cabinetwork and interior decoration.

Quite different from the bald cypress is the Pacific coast cypress. The famed Monterey cypress is a beautiful tree and is much used in California for hedges and windbreaks and as a street tree.

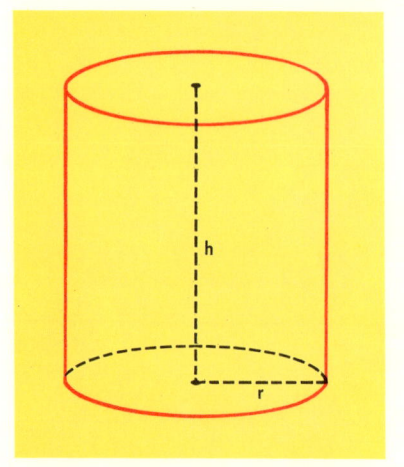

Both the volume of a cylinder and the area of its surface are dependent upon its altitude, h, and the radius, r, of its base. The cylinder may be defined as the solid generated by revolving a rectangle, with sides r and h, about side h as an axis.

The bald cypress thrives in swampy places. Its wood is very resistant to rotting.

CYPRUS is an island in the eastern Mediterranean Sea, south of the Turkish coast. In ancient times it was a major source of copper. The word *copper* is derived from the Greek name of Cyprus. About four-fifths of the people are of Greek extraction. Most of the rest are of Turkish ancestry. Cyprus is about 3,500 square miles in area and has more than 500,000 inhabitants.

Two mountain ranges lie astride a fertile depression, which is the main farming area. The climate is mild with a shortage of rainfall in summer. Agriculture and mining are the chief occupations. Citrus fruits, carobs, and wheat are among the exports. The principal minerals are

CZECHOSLOVAKIA

iron pyrites, copper pyrites, asbestos, gypsum, umber, and chrome.

Cyprus has belonged to many nations, including Phoenicia, Greece, Egypt, Persia, and Rome. King Richard I of England took it from the Saracens in 1191. For nearly 300 years afterward, until taken by the Venetians, it had kings of its own. The Turks captured Cyprus from the Venetians in 1571 and in 1878 gave it to Great Britain.

A movement for union with Greece arose among the Greek Cypriotes. The movement, opposed by the Turkish Cypriotes, resulted in much violence in 1955 and 1956. In 1959 it was agreed that Cyprus should become an independent republic.

These Czechoslovak farmers are still using horses, but they are also using farm machinery to thresh their grain. Machinery is slowly taking the place of hand labor and work animals. Most farms in Czechoslovakia are collective farms like the one here. The farmers do not own their land. Collective farms are formed by combining small private farms. They are worked by the farmers according to a plan developed by them and approved by the government. The farm products are sold to the government, and the income is divided among the workers according to the kind and amount of work each person is assigned.
John Strohm

CZECHOSLOVAKIA is a republic in the heart of Central Europe. The country's population is made up chiefly of Czechs and less than half as many Slovaks. Although the two peoples were separated politically for many hundreds of years, they are of the same Slavic race and speak similar Slavic languages. The Czechs are known as one of the most culturally advanced people in Central Europe. The capital city, Prague, is one of the most beautiful in Europe. Other leading cities are Brno, Ostrava, Bratislava, and Pilsen. Czechoslovakia's area of about 50,000 square miles supports over 13,000,000 people.

The western part of the country, called Bohemia, is surrounded on all sides by mountain chains. In the center of Czechoslovakia lies Moravia, a lowland area bordered by mountains on the north. In the east is Slovakia, a region of rugged hills and low mountains, which are a part of the Carpathian Mountains. The country as a whole has a typical continental climate, with cold winters, and hot, rainy summers. Three fertile plains make the country agriculturally rich. In Bohemia, along

Steel is made in Ostrava, Czechoslovakia, an industrial city near Silesia's coal mines.
Eastfoto

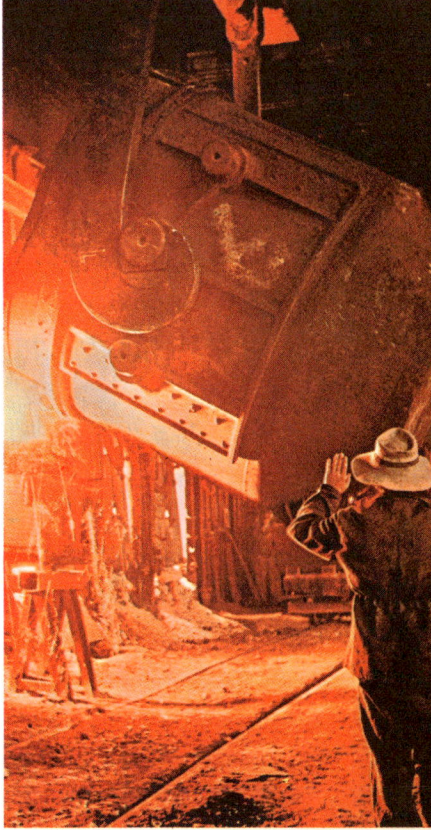

the valley of the upper Elbe River, rye, oats, and barley are grown. Hops are grown for use in making the famous Pilsen beer. The plains of southern Moravia, watered by the Morava River, also grow cereals, legumes, flax, and hemp. The lowlands of southern Slovakia, along the Danube River, are especially suitable for sugar beets and corn. In Czechoslovakian livestock farming cattle, pigs, and poultry are most important.

The country's longest river, the Moldau, cuts across the Czecho-Moravian plateau, which occupies the western interior of Czechoslovakia. Prague is built along the Moldau. West of Prague are located the famous Czech watering places, or spas, of which the best known is Carlsbad. In the east the Carpathian Mountains in northern Slovakia are the skiers' paradise, and many tourists visit the ice caves found there.

Czechoslovakia is rich in coal and iron deposits, but it also has other ores, such as lead, mercury, and uranium. These raw materials helped to make the country a highly industrialized nation. Products of its light industry (shoes, textiles, glass, and china) are outstanding. The Czechoslovaks have an expanding automobile industry, the best known plant being Skoda.

The Czechs and Slovaks organized their first state in the 7th century A.D. where Moravia is today. They accepted Christianity from two Greek missionaries who introduced the Old Slavic language, instead of Latin, into church services in 863. From 1000 until 1918 the Slovaks lived under Hungarian rule. The Czech kingdom of Bohemia was independent until 1620, when it became part of the Hapsburg empire.

After World War I Czechoslovakia became an independent republic. In 1939, however, Nazi Germany occupied the country. In February, 1948, the Communists gained control of the government. This government increased the country's industrial production and mechanized its agriculture. Formerly, Czechoslovakia traded with all parts of the world, but trade under the Communist government shifted to the Soviet Union, its satellites, and a few other countries, such as the United Arab Republic.

Long a residence of emperors and kings, the Czechoslovak capital of Prague (below) is today a major industrial center.
Eastfoto

CZECHOSLOVAKIA

Area: 49,381 sq. mi.
Population: 13,000,000
Capital: Prague
Largest cities: Prague, Brno, Bratislava, Ostrava, Pilsen
Highest mountain peak: Stalin Peak, formerly Gerlachovka (8,737 feet)
Chief rivers: Elbe with Vltava (Moldau), Danube with Morava and Vah
Climate: Hot summers, cold winters—more equable in shielded plains—rainfall mainly spring and autumn—heavy winter snow in mountains
National flag: Upper half white, lower half red—large blue triangle next to pole
National anthem: *Kde domov muj?* (Where Is My Home?) combined with *Nad Tatru sa blyska* (Lightning over the Tatra)

Czechoslovak Socialist Republic flag and seal

Form of government: Communist people's republic
Unit of currency: Koruna
Languages: Czech, Slovak
Chief religion: Roman Catholic
Chief economic activities: Agriculture (including livestock raising), manufacturing, mining, forestry
Chief crops: Wheat and other grains, potatoes, sugar beets, hops
Chief manufactures: Iron and steel, chemicals, fertilizers, paper and pulp, textiles, glass and china, shoes
Chief minerals: Coal, lignite, iron ore, uranium
Chief exports: Machinery and equipment, bicycles, motorcycles, textiles, shoes
Chief imports: Fuel, raw materials, food products

DAHLIA

D is the fourth letter of the English alphabet and of most cognate alphabets. As a Roman numeral D stands for 500. In chemistry D is the symbol for deuterium, or heavy hydrogen, an isotope of the element hydrogen. In mathematics lowercase D (d) is the symbol for differential. D is the second tone of the normal major scale in music.

DAEDALUS AND ICARUS, in Greek mythology, a father and son who fled the wrath of King Minos of Crete by making wings out of feathers and wax. Icarus flew too close to the sun's heat, fell into the sea, and drowned. Daedalus continued to Sicily, where he offered his wings to Apollo. Before Daedalus and Icarus incurred the wrath of King Minos, they were in difficulties in Athens. Daedalus personified the beginning of the arts of sculpture and architecture. He was the grandson of Erechtheus and the son of Metion. Daedalus was jealous of his nephew Perdix and his skill in inventing the saw and potter's wheel. Daedalus threw him off the Acropolis. Condemned to death, Daedalus and his son fled to King Minos' court on Crete. There Daedalus made a cow disguise for Pasiphaë and erected a labyrinth for the Minotaur. Because Theseus escaped the maze, Minos imprisoned Daedalus and Icarus. Works of art were freely ascribed to Daedalus in Greece, Italy, Libya, and the Mediterranean islands. His name was applied to the earlier painted and gilded wooden statues of the gods.

DAFFODIL, a sturdy, single-blossomed or double-blossomed plant whose hybrid forms now include many garden varieties. It is similar in appearance to the jonquil and the narcissus. The large flower of the daffodil has fused petals forming the trumpet, or bell, located above a frill of colored sepals. The flower is pale yellow or golden yellow. The slender, flat leaves, 12 to 18 inches long, are attached to the stem at a point beneath the surface of the ground. The visible part of the tall flower stem has no leaves attached to it.

DAGGER. A dagger is a sharp-pointed knife. It is a very ancient implement of warfare and is represented in modern equipment by the bayonet, a steel dagger-like implement that is attached to a rifle at the muzzle. It is used by infantry.

During the Middle Ages soldiers fought with the sword or rapier in the right hand and the dagger in the left. The Filipinos and the Moros have many varying forms of the dagger. Other forms are the Indian khuttar, the American bowie knife, the Malay creese, the poniard, the stiletto, the misericord, and the anlace.

The golden-trumpeted daffodils shown below are of the Selma Lagerlöf variety.
Gottscho-Schleisner

These gold and copper daggers, which predate the Christian Era by many centuries, were unearthed on the site of the ancient Mesopotamian city of Ur. Even at such an early date the dagger had a high degree of development. The craftsmanship of the sheath (center) is exceptionally fine.

Florists estimate that there are over 10,000 popular varieties of the dahlia, one of the most widely grown garden flowers.

DAHLIA, one of the most beautiful and popular of the fall-blooming plants. It is a native of Mexico and was one of the plants that attracted the attention of Francisco Hernandez, who in 1570 was sent from Spain to Mexico to study the resources of that country. It was more than 200 years later, however, before seeds were carried to Europe and the first European dahlias were raised. At once they became the ob-

Iraq Directorate Gen. of Antiq.

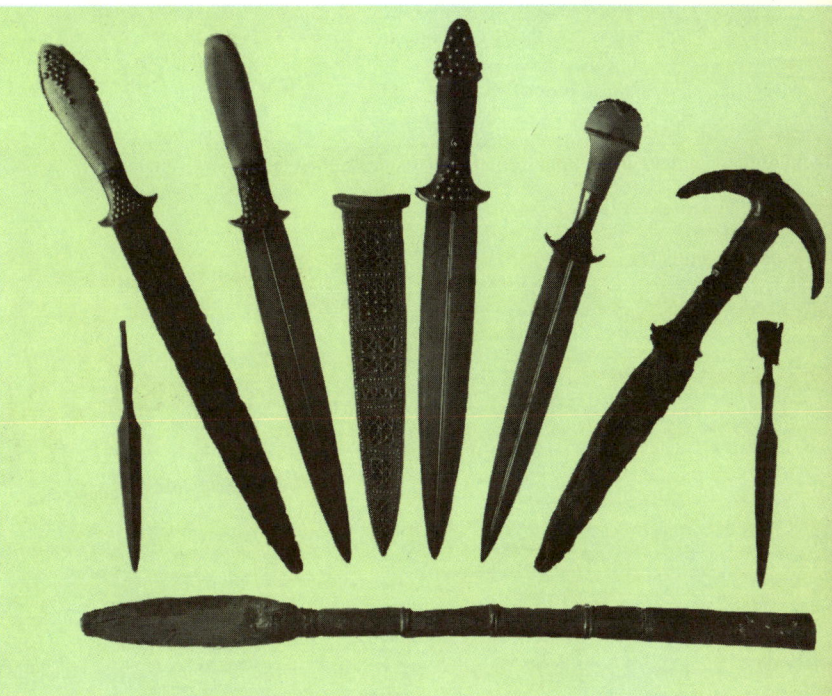

ject of great interest, and soon people began to experiment with them, both in Europe and in America, developing new types, colors, and tints. Now more than 10,000 varieties are known.

Dahlias range in color from royal purple to pale lavender, from scarlet to pink or white, and from brown to gold and cream. They range in width from 1 inch to more than 1 foot. The daisy and dandelion belong to the same botanical family as the dahlia. The dahlia plant grows from 18 inches to 6 or 7 feet high or, in the case of tree dahlias, to 20 feet.

DAIMIO, a member of a class of feudal lords that arose in Japan in the 14th century, came to dominate the land, and survived until the 19th century.

The rise of the daimios was hastened by the increase of the warrior class. Formerly the warriors were loyal to the Hojo family, which ruled Japan, but they became too numerous for the family to control. Instead, during a period of intermittent civil war they shifted their loyalty to various lords, or daimios. These lords grew so in importance through the succeeding two centuries that by the 16th century the daimios' domains formed the natural political divisions of Japan. The daimio ruled in his territory like an absolute monarch. However, the daimios' power to make war among themselves in order to dominate Japan was soon limited by the rise of the Tokugawa family as the ruling power in Japan.

The daimios retained their domains until shortly after the Restoration (the almost bloodless revolution in 1868 that marked the beginning of Japan's rise as a modern world power). In 1869 the daimios were persuaded to give over their domains to the imperial government. Thus feudalism was officially destroyed. The daimios first served as governors of their old territories, but in 1871 these were redivided into new political units called prefectures. The diamios were eventually reimbursed by the government.

DAIRY CATTLE are cattle specially bred to give large quantities of milk. Many countries and regions have their own breeds or strains of dairy cattle. Some of the breeds of England, Scotland, The Netherlands, and Switzerland have become famous all over the world.

The dairy cattle of the United States are derived from imported stock. The five most important breeds of dairy cattle in the United States are the Ayrshire from Scotland, the Brown Swiss from Switzerland, the Holstein (or Holstein-Friesian) from The Netherlands, and the Guernsey and the Jersey, both from islands in the English Channel.

The dairy breeds common in the United States are also popular in Canada. Milking Shorthorns, a breed that originated in England, are important dairy cattle in Canada. Two other breeds used as dairy cattle are the French Canadian and the Red Polled. The French Canadian is a dairy breed that was originated in Quebec. The Red Polled is an English hornless breed. It is used for the production of both milk and beef.

In Great Britain the Ayrshire, Jersey, Guernsey, and Milking Shorthorn are popular dairy breeds. The Red Polled, Dexter, and South Devon dual-purpose breeds are also used in dairy farming. Dual-purpose cattle are used for producing either milk or beef. Another breed is the Kerry. Kerries are small dairy cattle of Irish origin.

In the United States dairy cattle are known as purebred (registered) or grade. The purebred cattle have their pedigrees recorded with their breed association offices, and the annual production of each cow may be registered. A grade cow may have a purebred sire (father) or dam (mother), but her pedigree and production are not registered.

DAIRYING is the business of producing milk on a farm or ranch. The farmer takes care of the cows that produce the milk; he may sell it to a city dairy, where it is pasteurized and bottled for drinking. Milk is also used to make butter and cheese. Some may be made into cottage cheese or ice cream.

Health departments, working with the industry, take the steps needed to ensure the health of the dairy cow and the safety of her product. Dairy farms are inspected for their cleanliness, and the milk that they produce is tested often for its quality. The highest standards are in effect on dairy farms producing milk for use in drinking.

The dairy farmer's ranch or farm is of varying size. On it he keeps as many cows as he can care for, house, and feed. Some may have 10 cows; others, 1,000. A fair average is 30 head per farm. A dairy farmer tries to grow enough hay, grain, and fodder for his herd and to have pasture too. He may buy

Courtesy of the Ford Motor Company

The cattle shown above represent five of the world's major dairy breeds. By changing animals through carefully controlled selection and mating over succeeding generations, these and other breeds were developed in order to suit local needs and conditions.

some feed he cannot grow. A dairy cow weighing 1,400 pounds will eat 4 tons of hay and 1½ tons of grain and will be on pasture five months of each year. In cold areas the farmer must have warm stables. All dairy farms need good milking and cooling equipment.

The dairy farmer's help may come from his family or from hired hands. They care for and milk the cows and grow the needed food. They also keep the farm machinery and buildings in good condition.

The dairy farmer must know about the different breeds of dairy cattle and choose the one best suited for his farm and his market. (See DAIRY CATTLE.) Many farmers raise the calves born to their cows and so replace losses and maintain herd numbers. The dairy farmer must know something about the care of calves and the diseases that can cause illness or death in his herd.

Many dairy farms are highly mechanized. On such farms electricity is used to run the machines that milk the cows, chill the milk, and keep it cold. Some farms have a "milking parlor"—a special room to which the cows walk to be milked. It takes about five minutes to machine-milk a cow. By use of a machine for milking, one man can milk four times as many cows in an hour as can be milked by hand.

Courtesy of Massey-Ferguson, Inc.

The dairyman in the milking parlor shown at the left is pouring fresh milk into a portable canister, which is connected by a flexible tube to a cooling tank nearby. This arrangement eliminates time spent in carrying and reduces the time needed by the dairyman to complete the job. Below is a cutaway diagram showing the interior of a much larger milking parlor. Here the entire operation is mechanized. Machine milking is both faster and more sanitary than hand milking. Milk drawn from the cows by means of suction cups passes through a tube to the overhead pipe and hence to a cooling tank in the adjoining room (foreground).

Courtesy The DeLaval Separator Company

DAISY, a perennial flowering herb of the composite family. The daisy is related to the chrysanthemum, sunflower, aster, marigold, and dahlia. The oxeye and English daisies grow abundantly in Europe, North America, and parts of Asia.

The flower of the oxeye daisy, known also as the white daisy and whiteweed, is not a single blossom but a flat head made up of many tiny flowers. These form a small yellow disk surrounded by 20 to 30 white ray flowers. This daisy is a perennial that grows from 1 to 3 feet high. It is a native of Europe but was introduced into the United States 200 or more years ago and is now one of the commonest weeds in the eastern states. It is particularly abundant in meadows and pastures in broken or mountainous land and often carpets them with bloom in June or July. This daisy is seldom cultivated, but its flowers are gathered in great quantities for use in homes and churches and for wedding decorations. The daisy chains at the Vassar College commencement are made of this daisy.

The English daisy is a low plant, often not more than 3 to 6 inches high. Its rays are white, pink, or purple and sometimes so numerous they almost hide the yellow disk. It is grown in gardens and lawns and is also much used as a border plant. The Shasta daisy, with its very large white flower heads, has been developed by gardeners from a daisy of the Pyrenees.

DALI, SALVADOR (1904-   ), Spanish painter, was born at Figueras in Catalonia, reared there, and educated there, in Madrid, and in Paris. As a student he became keenly interested in the latest trends in modern art, philosophy, and science and particularly in Sigmund Freud's theories of dreams. After moving to Paris he became an enthusiastic exponent of the theories of surrealism, the artistic and literary movement that sought to express in concrete terms the "reality beyond reality," the newly discovered realm of the subconscious, with all its illogicality.

Unlike most surrealist painters Dali chose to represent familiar, easily recognizable objects, but these objects were distorted and placed in wildly illogical contexts. Famous examples include the limp watches in "The Persistence of Memory" and the burning giraffe and the human figure who is at the same time a chest of drawers in "Giraffe on Fire." His peculiar juxtapositions and reversals of normal functioning are even indicated by some of his titles, such as "The Weaning of Furniture-Nutrition" and "A Chemist Lifting with Precaution the Cuticle of a Grand Piano." In many quarters Dali's efforts have been greeted as highly original and significant art; in others he is considered a charlatan. Even his most vehement detractors must admit the brilliance of his draftsmanship; on the other hand, even his most fervent admirers must admit that Dali has been unusually successful at advertising himself.

In 1940 Dali settled in the United States, and shortly thereafter his work underwent a marked change. He very publicly repented his past in the autobiography *The Secret Life of Salvador Dali* and turned to painting religious subjects, which he treated in an almost entirely realistic manner. Well-publicized examples include his "Crucifixion" and "Sacrament of the Last Supper." Dali has also produced stage designs, exotic jewelry, book illustrations, tie designs, commercial art, and surrealist films.

DALLAS, a large city in northeastern Texas, on the Trinity River, 30 miles east of Fort Worth. The 1960 population was 679,684. Dallas is a commercial, industrial, and financial center, serving a rich farming and oil-fields region. The chief manufactured goods are cotton textiles, aircraft, chemicals, leather goods, and processed foods. It is the seat of Southern Methodist University, the University of Dallas, and the dental college of Baylor University. The city has three airports, one of which is the site of a U.S. naval air station. The new Memorial Auditorium provides facilities for conventions and exhibitions. Dallas has an excellent system of parks, a symphony orchestra, and many museums.

Dallas was settled in 1841 and was incorporated as a city in 1871. In 1936 the city held the Texas Centennial Exposition. World War II brought a large expansion of industries and population.

DALTON, JOHN (1766-1844), English scientist, born in Eaglesfield, the son of a weaver. In 1793 he was appointed professor of mathematics and natural philosophy at New College, Manchester. He resigned in 1799 to work on his own research.

Dalton became best known for his atomic theory, which he wrote about in detail in his *New System of Chemical Philosophy*. His hypothesis that elements combine in weights proportional to small whole numbers is known as the law of multiple proportions. Another law that he formulated, called Dalton's law, deals with the partial pressures of gases in mixtures. Dalton's name was also given to a form of color blindness from which he suffered; it is called Daltonism. An interest in meteorology led him to keep a daily record of weather changes from 1787 until his death. In 1822 Dalton was elected a fellow of the Royal Society.

DALTON BROTHERS, a gang of American desperadoes who terrorized Kansas and the Oklahoma Territory in the 1880's and 1890's.

Robert Dalton, leader of the gang, was born in Cass Co., Missouri, in 1867. He was related to the Youngers, another outlaw family. In 1882 he, with his six brothers and one sister, moved to Coffeyville, Kan. For a time he served as a deputy United States marshal in the Indian Territory. However, he gave up his career of law and order after he murdered a rival in a love affair. With his brothers Grattan and Emmet, he organized a band of horse-thieves, which operated around Baxter Springs, Kan. The brothers moved to California in 1890, where they held up a Southern Pacific railroad train. Grattan was captured and sentenced to 20 years. He escaped on his way to prison.

The brothers returned to the Oklahoma Territory and started robbing trains. For some time they kept one foot ahead of the authorities at such places as Red Rock and Adair in the Oklahoma Territory. Prompted by a desire to outdo the James gang's record, Dalton and his brothers made a raid on a bank at Coffeyville, Kan., in 1892. On October 5 the entire gang was killed except Emmet. He was captured and sent to prison. Upon his release he became a law-abiding citizen.

DAM, a bank or mound of rock, earth, concrete, or other material constructed across a stream for the purpose of controlling the water's flow, for creating reservoirs of water, for flood control, for power or irrigation, and for navigation. The material and the type of construction of a dam depend on its location on a river and on the water pressure. For streams that are broad and deep, strong materials are needed, for example, concrete reinforced with steel or stone and concrete mixed. The common forms of a dam are: across a stream in a straight line, diagonally across in one or two straight lines, and in an arc with the convex side toward the current.

Because of the care exercised by competent engineers during the building of the large modern dams, there have been comparatively few cases of failure. To prevent failures outlets are placed at proper inter-

Illustrated below are four of the commonest types of dams: the earth-fill dam (in cross section), the multiple-arch dam, the concrete-arch dam, and the solid-gravity dam.

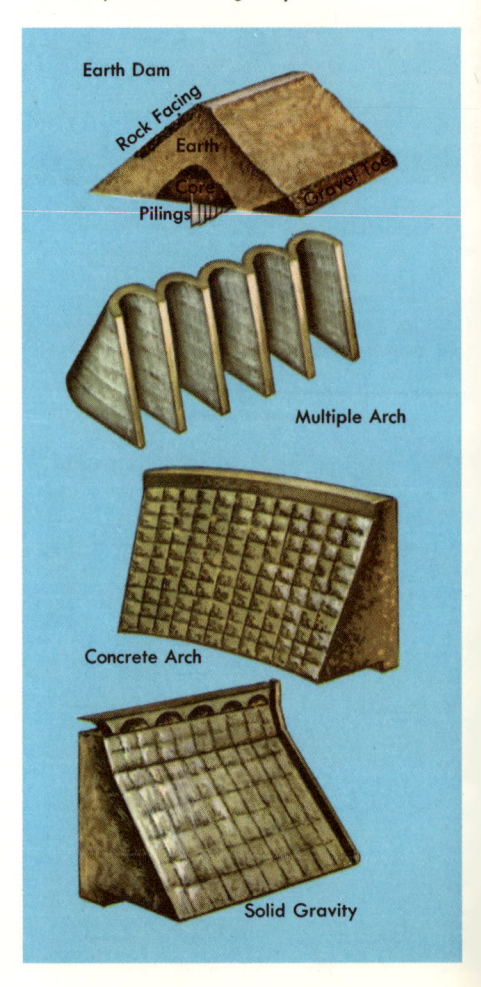

DAMASCUS

This dam (above) is a multiple-arch type.

Before a dam can be constructed, the site must be unwatered. This diversion process, a challenge in itself, usually is accomplished by means of cofferdams and tunnels.

Below is a bird's-eye view of a poured-concrete dam of single arch construction.

vals through the dam or around one end, or the tops are made movable to allow water to spill more easily over the crest and into the stream below.

There are several types of dams. The earth-fill dam, as the name indicates, is made of earth. The upstream portion is of dense material, while the lower is very porous. In the center is usually placed a concrete wall to retain a certain amount of rigidity. Rock-fill dams are made with a concrete slab or face on the upstream side, with loose rock behind. Steel-plate dams consist of triangular steel frames to which steel plates are riveted on the upstream side. Concrete dams are constructed in various forms, such as gravity, single arch, multiple arch, buttressed slab, and overflow. All these types involve advanced engineering designs. They may be built entirely of reinforced concrete, or they may have concrete binding over large quarried stones.

One of the highest dams in the world is Hoover Dam, on the Colorado River at the Arizona-Nevada border. Completed in 1936, it is 1,244 feet long at the crest and is 726 feet high. It has a hydroelectric generating plant. Backed up behind it is the reservoir, Lake Mead, 115 miles long, with a capacity of approximately 31 million acre-feet of water. Hoover Dam is a combination gravity and arched type of dam.

Other high dams are Vajont (840 feet high) in Italy and Mauvoisin (745 feet high) in Switzerland.

Dams often create artificial lakes (below).

DAMASCUS, capital of Syria, a Mohammedan holy city where pilgrims assemble and separate on their way to and from Mecca. It claims to be the oldest city in the world in continuous existence.

Damascus is situated on an extensive plain about 180 miles southwest of Aleppo. The streets are narrow, crooked, gloomy, and dilapidated. As in many eastern cities, windows do not open to the streets but into hidden courtyards away from the streets. The city is divided into Moslem, Jewish, and Christian quarters. The most noteworthy place is the bazaar, made up of streets lined with shops, stalls, and cafes. In the center of the bazaar is the Great Khan, where purchases and sales are made. The Great Khan is a high, vaulted building with a cupola on top, built partly of alternate layers of black and white marble. The gate is one of the finest specimens of Moorish architecture in the world. The most important street is the famous street called Straight, mentioned in the Bible in connection with the conversion of St. Paul. The population of Damascus is about 400,000.

Damascus remains as the center of trade routes across the Syrian Desert. Chief exports are inlaid wood and furniture, silks and cottons, goldwork and silverwork, saddlery, attar of roses, perfumes, and carpets. The celebrated Damascus steel is no longer made here.

The city may have existed 4,000 years ago. History records that at different times Jews, Assyrians, Persians, and Romans ruled Damascus. After St. Paul's visit Christianity spread in and around it. It was the capital of the Arab caliphate from 660 to 753. In 1401 the Tatars sacked it. It was under Turkish rule from 1516 to 1918. Emir Faisal was made the ruler of Syria in 1920, with the capital at Damascus, but he ruled under French supervision. In October, 1925, the Druses, a fierce tribe from the mountains, invaded the city, where an uprising against the French took place. The revolt was quelled by French bombardment. The French left the city in 1945.

DAMIEN, FATHER (1840-1889), real name, Joseph Damien de Veuster, a Belgian missionary and priest, was born at Louvain. After receiving his education at the University of Louvain, he joined the Order of Sacred Hearts of Jesus and Mary in 1863. He was sent to Molokai, one of the Hawaiian Islands, for missionary work. On the island was a colony of lepers, or persons with Hansen's disease. These people had been neglected, and Father Damien, a man of energy and resourcefulness, undertook to improve their condition. He did everything he could for their bodies as well as their souls. Under his care they were well provided with food and shelter. He built schools and a church, doing much of the work with his own hands. A few years before his death he was stricken with Hansen's disease himself.

DAMON AND PYTHIAS. Throughout history there have been various examples of noble friendships. That of David and Jonathan was one, but yet more prominent was that of Damon and Pythias. Both were Syracusans of the 4th century B.C. Dionysius I, the tyrant, condemned Pythias to death but allowed him to go home to arrange his affairs. Damon agreed to take his place. Pythias was delayed, and Damon was led to be executed. Pythias did arrive in time to save his friend, and Dionysius was so pleased by this display of friendship that he pardoned Pythias.

Photo by Myra Armstrong
This man and woman, dressed in bright native costume, are performing a Spanish dance.

DANCE, an expression of emotion or ideas by rhythmic movements of the body or limbs, or both, in unison with rhythmic sounds, such as music or handclapping. Dancing may be a religious rite, a theatrical entertainment, a form of social amusement, or a form of art. From the earliest times dancing has been a means of expression of people the world over. The dances of the American Indians illustrate the ceremonial purposes of the primitive dances. The war dance informed the gods of victory and thanked them for it. Dances of exorcism were performed by medicine men to expel evil spirits. Dances of invocation requested the help of the gods in war, harvest, and various other tribal undertakings.

The art of dancing dates from the time of the early Egyptians, who ascribed that invention to their god Thoth. Among the ancient Jews David danced in procession before the Ark of God. Religious processions went with song and dance to the temples. The Cretan chorus, moving in measured pace, sang hymns to the Greek god Apollo, and the Muse Terpsichore was the patroness of the dance. The Phrygian Corybantes danced in honor of Cybele, and the festivals of Ilia at Rome were also accompanied by wild dances. The Spartans practiced dancing as a gymnastic exercise and made it compulsory for all children. The Romans in general considered it disgraceful for a free citizen to dance except in connection with religious rites. They willingly witnessed the performances of professional dancers of Egypt and India. The early Christians practiced choral dances, while the Puritans saw deadly sin in promiscuous dancing.

OCCUPATION: Dancer
PERSONAL FACTORS—ABILITIES, SKILLS, APTITUDES: Physical stamina and agility, perseverance, versatility, and talent are essential.
EDUCATION AND SPECIAL TRAINING: High-school graduation is essential, and college work is helpful. Training in a school of dance and music, with the fundamentals of both classical and modern dance, is necessary. Period of training may be indefinite, for "a dancer never stops learning."
WORKING CONDITIONS:
1. **INCOME:**
   COMPARED WITH OTHER CAREERS WITH EQUAL TRAINING: Low
   COMPARED WITH MOST OTHER CAREERS: Low
2. **ENVIRONMENT:** Mostly indoor work; long hours of rehearsals; irregular working hours; strenuous life
3. **OTHER:** No established fringe benefits; costs for arrangements, wardrobe, agent; performers' union
RELATED CAREERS: Choreographer, ballerina, dancing teacher
WHERE TO FIND MORE INFORMATION: Actors and Artistes of America, Associated, 226 West 47th Street, New York 36, N. Y.; American Guild of Musical Artists, 247 West 46th St., New York 36, N. Y.; Juilliard School of Music, 120 Claremont Avenue, New York, N. Y.

Many of the medieval dances were solemn and stately in character, like the *danses basses*, which were danced to psalm tunes at the court of Charles IX of France. The galliard and the lavolta were introduced from Italy by Catherine de Médicis.

The minuet became popular in France around 1650 and remained in vogue for about a century. Then came the courante, the saraband, the gavotte, and the quadrille. The galop and the waltz were brought in from Germany. The cotillion was fashionable in the 1820's. The polka was first danced at the Odéon, in Paris, in 1840 by a dancing master from Prague. The schottische was a modified form of the polka.

Certain conventions developed at the balls of the European nobility in the 19th century have come down to us today. At these balls it was customary for the orchestra to play music for several different dances. The order in which they were to be presented was printed on a program. Early in the evening the men would request certain dances with the ladies of their choice, and to indicate their choice of partners they would sign the lady's program next to the particular dance they had claimed. The custom eventually spread to formal dances in America and elsewhere. Programs are still printed for formal dances. Today, however, it is customary to dance almost exclusively with one's companion, and the programs serve principally as souvenirs of the evening.

The era of ballroom and exhibition dancing began around 1910 with such grotesque inventions as the turkey trot, bunny hug, and grizzly bear. From 1912 to 1916 many dance fads appeared, and some died. Popular among these were the tango, the hesitation waltz, and the maxixe, a Brazilian importation. The foxtrot, however, became a kind of standard pattern for rapid social dancing. The Charleston was the most popular of all the newer temporary forms, and it enjoyed an enormous vogue between 1925 and 1927. This was followed by the short-lived black bottom.

In the 1930's came the jitterbug, the shag, and the big apple—dances marked by extreme activity and nervous force. The jitterbug dances were accompanied by a style in jazz music, popularly called swing, that was hailed by some music critics as a vital expression of the American spirit. Meanwhile the Latin American dances, especially the rhumba and conga, became popular. Concurrently, but in lesser degree, three dances of England—the Lambeth walk, the chestnut tree, and the boomps-a-daisy—were in vogue.

In all countries people preserve their own folk dances, stamped with a distinct mark of nationality. Representative of these are the Basque *muchikuok*, the Spanish fandango and bolero, the Italian tarantella, the Polish mazurka and polonaise, and the Scottish reel and Highland fling. In the Orient dancing is chiefly pantomimic and is executed by trained dancers.

Other dances that rose from the folk spirit were the American square dance, the tap dance (which had its beginning in the Irish clog dance and the free dance expressions of the American Negro), and the cakewalk. Beginning in 1940 the American public revived its interest in the square dance. It had been gradually declining in popularity in the rural areas when suddenly city dwellers discovered it. The square-dance craze was as intense and widespread as were the crazes for

A group of costumed maidens (above) performs a classical Greek dance at the ruins of the ancient music theater that was built by Herodes Atticus in Athens.

Norwegian children dressed in gay costumes do a folk dance in a meadow near Hardanger Fjord.

South African gold-mine workers forget their daily toil in the excitement of tribal dances.

Latin American dances. About 1953 the mambo, from Brazil, became a favorite dance at parties.

The trend toward Latin dances started in 1946 and became well established within the next ten years. The cha cha reached the apex of its popularity. Because of its slow and steady beat, the dance was adaptable to practically anything from a jig to a lurch.

For several centuries dancing on the stage has developed along quite different lines of its own. See BALLET.

DANCE, AFRICAN. See AFRICAN DANCE.

DANDELION, a plant that seems especially well adapted to withstand the attacks that man is constantly making upon it in an effort to keep it out of his lawns. The word *dandelion* comes from the French name for the plant, *dent de lion*, or "lion's tooth." It was probably so named because of the dandelion's toothed leaves.

The dandelion has a long straight root that goes deep into the ground and that, once established, is not easily killed. Its deeply notched leaves lie so close to the ground that they wholly or partially escape the blades of the lawnmower. The bright yellow blossom is not a single flower but a head usually made up of more than a hundred tiny flowers. While in bud, the head is bent to the ground, raising itself only when ready to burst into bloom. After blooming, it is again bent over while the seeds are being ripened. Then the hollow stem straightens itself once more, lengthens rapidly, and the head again opens. But this time it is a white, fluffy ball, covered with seeds, each one of which has a little parachute of white hairs that carries it on the breeze.

The leaves, the composite flower, and the downy seeds of the dandelion are shown here.

DANILOVA, ALEXANDRA (1907-), Soviet ballerina, was born in Petergof (now Petrodvorets). After she was graduated from the Imperial Ballet School in Petrograd (now Leningrad), she became a member of the *corps de ballet* at the Maryinsky Theater. In 1924 she left the U.S.S.R. to dance with George Balanchine and Tamara Geva in a tour of Germany. Later she was a member of Sergei Diaghilev's company until his death in 1929. From 1933 to 1938 she was ballerina in Colonel de Basil's Ballet Russe and then prima ballerina with the Ballet Russe de Monte Carlo. In 1954 she toured the United States with her own company. She also danced in the operetta *The Great Waltz* and the musical *Song of Norway*. She appeared notably in *Gaité Parisienne*, *Le Beau Danube*, *Coppélia*, *Swan Lake*, *The Nutcracker*, *The Sleeping Beauty*, and *Scheherazade*. In 1958 she appeared in the Broadway musical *Oh Captain!*

DANTE (1265-1321), Italy's greatest poet, was born in Florence. He belonged to the Alighieri family, a line that had been well-to-do, though not noble, for generations. His father was an esteemed lawyer in the city. Dante's education was thorough and rigorous. He studied mathematics, the sciences, history, and philosophy, read all the Latin poets, and wrote poetry himself. He was also skilled in drawing and had a keen appreciation of music. He was a gay and exuberant youth, capable of strong feelings. When he was 26, he married Gemma Donati and by her had four children.

In his early twenties Dante had become involved in the bitter struggles among the Italian city-states. His family had traditionally supported the papal party, or Guelphs, and he fought with them against the state party, the Ghibellines. In 1302, while he and two other representatives of the Guelphs were in Rome, Dante was banished by an extreme faction within his own party because of his opposition to the policies of Pope Boniface VIII. Later, in his *De Monarchia*, Dante stated his final position on the Guelph-Ghibelline controversy: that the pope and the emperor, having separate functions on earth, should also have separate powers. At any rate, he was threatened with death at the stake if he returned to Florence. Accompanied by his two sons, Dante spent several years wandering through northern Italy, where he remained under the protection of various nobles. Angry and embittered at the charges of corruption in office that the Florentines had trumped up against him, he remained contemptuous throughout his life of their later offers to let him return on conditions of fine and penance.

It was during these years in exile that Dante wrote his *Commedia*, an allegory in verse that envisions his journey through Hell and Purgatory before reaching Paradise. As he explained in his treatise on language and poetry, by *comedy* Dante meant a play or narrative that began unpleasantly and ended happily. Later commentators added the adjective *divina*, so that his poem is now called the *Divine Comedy*.

The great love of Dante's life was a lady named Beatrice Portinari, whom he first saw when he was a boy. In all, he saw her only once or twice before her death when he was 25. But she became a central figure in the *Divine Comedy*.

Dante was the first of the Italian poets to write a major work in colloquial Italian, for Latin was the official language for all such compositions until his time. He died at Ravenna.

New York Public Library

Dante's *Divine Comedy* is an allegorical representation of the theology and moral philosophy that prevailed in medieval Europe.

DANTON, GEORGES JACQUES (1759-1794), a noted leader in the French Revolution, was a lawyer in Paris when the troubles between King Louis XVI and the people began. He at once took the side of the people, and his brilliance as a speaker made him one of their favorite leaders. In 1792 he led the mob to attack the Tuileries, the palace of the king. The whole power was soon in the hands of Danton, Marat, and Robespierre. A Committee of Public Safety was appointed, which had the power to judge and sentence to death anyone it chose. Thousands of innocent people were tried and sent to the guillotine. Those days, which were so marked with blood, have ever since that time been called the Reign of Terror.

At last Danton, having gained all he wished, was anxious to stop the bloodshed. Robespierre was not. He was jealous of Danton and determined to get rid of him, and Danton was soon arrested and tried by the committee that he had helped to set up. Danton defended himself so well at his trial that it was feared that the public would prevent his execution; therefore he was not allowed to complete his defense. He was guillotined when he was 35 years old.

DANUBE RIVER, of central and southeastern Europe, originates in two streams in the Black Forest of southwestern Germany. It borders or passes through Germany, Austria, Czechoslovakia, Hungary, Yugoslavia, Rumania, Bulgaria, and the Ukrainian S.S.R. From its source to its mouth at the Black Sea it is about 1,725 miles long. It is the second longest river in Europe and drains an area of approximately 300,000 square miles.

More than 300 streams and rivers enter the Danube. Most of the country through which the river flows is flat. Near its mouth it widens and forms a large delta. The Danube's course to Vienna is particularly beautiful. Many historic and literary associations are found here.

The International Danube Commission, created by the Versailles Treaty (1921), maintained liberty of navigation and equal treatment of all flags of the Danube along the navigable course from Ulm in Württemberg to Braila in Rumania. Germany ended the commission in 1940 and took full control of the river in 1941.

The Soviet bloc and Yugoslavia, in the Belgrade Conference in 1948, substituted riparian rights for international control of the Danube. These countries formed the Danube River Commission, over the protest of the United States, Britain, and France. In following years the Soviet Union relaxed its control, and agreements which were made among the bordering countries gave freedom of navigation.

DARDANELLES, the ancient Hellespont, is a narrow and strategic strait within Turkey. It connects the small Sea of Marmara with the Aegean Sea. At this particular point it separates Europe from Asia. The strait stretches northeast and southwest and is about 37 miles in length, varying in breadth from about 1 to 4 miles.

The Dardanelles, with the Bosporus strait, controls navigation between the Black and Mediterranean seas. The Bosporus lies at the eastern end of the Sea of Marmara. On an inlet of the strait known as the Golden Horn stands Istanbul. The Dardanelles and Bosporus have always been the object of international dispute.

The Treaty of Lausanne in 1923 provided freedom of the straits for all during peace and for neutrals when Turkey was at war. From the ten signatories of the treaty Turkey obtained permission in 1936 under the Montreux agreement to remilitarize the water route and to assume control. Turkey closed the straits to belligerent warships during World War II.

DARE, VIRGINIA (1587- ?), the first English child born in America, was born at Roanoke Island, off the coast of what is now North Carolina. Her parents, Ananias and Ellinor Dare, were members of Sir Walter Raleigh's colony there. This was the famous Lost Colony, which disappeared between 1587 and 1591.

DARIUS I (about 548—about 485 B.C.), king of ancient Persia, attained his throne in 521 B.C. To do so he was forced to oust the usurper Gaumata, who was masquerading as the son of the great king Cyrus.

Cyrus, who died in 529 B.C., had conquered an empire stretching from India to the Mediterranean. To this, Darius added little new territory; instead he concentrated on consolidating his widespread empire. In the first years of his reign he was forced to put down many revolts by subject peoples. He waged several wars, notably in India, the Caucasus, and what is now the Ukraine, by which he strengthened the frontier defenses of the empire. Darius was a fervent adherent to the religion of Zoroaster, but he did not force his religion upon his subjects; it was he who released the Jews from their Babylonian captivity and allowed them to return to Jerusalem and rebuild the Temple. Darius organized the empire so well that, in spite of a series of weak kings, it survived almost 150 years.

In 492 Darius began a war against Greece, which had encouraged rebellion by the Greek cities in Asia Minor, a part of his empire. The first expedition was shipwrecked; the second was decisively defeated by the Athenians at the Battle of Marathon in 490. Darius died before a third expedition could be undertaken. He was succeeded on the throne by his son Xerxes.

DARTS, a game of skill played with pointed, feathered darts and a target board. No one knows when or where the game was first played, but in its modern form it began in English inns. At first, the customers threw the darts at the round ends of barrels as a pastime to enliven the evening hours. The present-day dartboard is usually placed about 9 feet from the thrower, and the bull's-eye in the center is about 5 feet 8 inches above the floor. On the board are painted several circles. Darts placed in the outer circle count the least number of points, and those in the smallest circle count the most, with the count for the bull's-eye the highest of all.

At its northernmost point the Danube flows placidly past the town of Regensburg, Germany.
Artha Hornbostel

Charles Darwin
Lady Barlow

DARWIN, CHARLES (1809-1882), was an English scientist famous for his theory of evolution, an explanation of the origins, development, and relations of different types of plant and animal life.

Darwin showed little promise of future greatness during his youth. He did poorly in school and spent most of his time at outdoor sports. However, while attending college he became interested in botany and geology. The turning point of Darwin's life came when, at the age of 22, he became the official naturalist on a five-year voyage of exploration on the ship *Beagle*.

His observations on this trip gave Darwin the basic material for his theory of evolution. Before he put forward his theory, most people believed that all the species of plants and animals had been separately and independently created. Darwin, on the *Beagle*, visited the Galápagos Islands off the coast of South America. There he noticed that the animals on each of the islands and on the South American mainland, though very similar, were not the same. He returned to England convinced that all these species had developed, or evolved, from common stock.

Darwin worked for 23 years on his theory before publishing it in 1859 in his best known work, *On the Origin of Species by Means of Natural Selection*. In this book he attempted to show that different kinds of animals and plants descended from one another or from other kinds that lived ages ago. The theory of evolution did not originate with Darwin, but he found a cause for the changes in appearance and structure of plants and animals shown in the stages of evolution. The cause was natural selection, or the survival of the fittest. Darwin said that all animals and plants had a tendency to change in some very slight way and that only those that actually changed to fit the geographic or climatic conditions survived; the others became extinct. Only certain plants and animals could survive, Darwin said, because in any generation of plants there were too many for the amount of food or other sustenance available. The theory of natural selection was developed independently by Alfred Russel Wallace, a contemporary of Darwin's, and papers by both on the subject were presented jointly at a meeting of a British scientific group before the publication of Darwin's book.

Darwin's ideas were violently attacked at first, but they were later accepted by most scholars. After spending his entire life in scientific research, Darwin died at Down, Kent, England, at the age of 73. See EVOLUTION.

The date, shown above singly and in a bunch, together with a date palm, is a food staple in northern Africa and western Asia.

DATE, the fruit of the date palm. This is a beautiful palm tree, which grows to a height of 60 to 80 feet. It has a straight, round trunk, at the top of which is a crown of 40 to 80 huge, shining, feather-like leaves, often 8 to 10 feet long. From among the leaves the fruit hangs in great bunches.

The date palm has been cultivated in the hot desert regions of the Old World for 4,000 or more years. In Arabia it is the chief source of the country's wealth. The tree was introduced into southern California by the early Spanish missionaries, not for its fruit, which does not mature near the coast, but for its leaves, which were used for the Palm Sunday services of the church. About 1890 the U.S. Department of Agriculture began experiments to see if date growing could be developed in the Southwest. Men were sent to the date-growing regions of the Old World to study conditions of soil and climate and methods of growing in order to obtain material with which to experiment in this country. As a result, there are now commercial plantings in desert valleys in both California and Arizona. The date palm was the species of plant in which man first recognized the existence of separate male and female plants, for in this species are male trees that bear only pollen and female trees that bear only fruit. Plantations of female trees fail to develop fruit because of the lack of male trees for pollen.

DATING, participation of a boy and a girl together in a social activity. Such participation is called a date. Usually, but not necessarily, the boy asks the girl to go on a date. The activity can range from sports to motion picture shows, parties, and other entertainment.

There is no set age when people begin dating. Dating usually begins when young people are in their teens. Before this time boys usually prefer to stay with groups of boys, and girls prefer the company of other girls.

Dating usually puts a financial burden on the boy. If he does not have enough money, he may supplement his allowance with a part-time job. It is always wise for him to state frankly his financial limits to the girl he is dating.

Teenagers sometimes "go Dutch," which means that the girl pays her own way. However, the boy usually likes to pay for a special date. If a girl wishes, she may invite a boy to dinner or supply tickets to an event.

Authorities do not agree on the advisability of "going steady," the limiting of dating company to one person. It might not be advisable to date only one person at first. Most teenagers use this period as a way of becoming acquainted with many types of people.

To make a date, a young man should first find a girl he really likes. He should invite her well in advance. The girl should reply promptly. If she accepts, she should be sure that she has all the information as to time, date, and occasion.

The best way to enjoy a date is to relax and to take a sincere interest in the people and situations encountered. Young people should be well groomed. However, dazzling dress and appearance are not necessary. In dating, it is well to look for basic neatness and a pleasant personality rather than for superficial glamor.

DAVID (? -960? B.C.), the second king of Israel and the first king of a united Israel, was the son of Jesse of Bethlehem. One story of David describes him as a shepherd boy who was summoned to heal with his music the melancholy of King Saul. Another tells of his gaining fame by slaying the giant Goliath. At any rate, David did join Saul's court, where his friendship with Saul's son Jonathan, symbolized by their exchange of weapons, became the prototype of all such friendships.

Because of David's growing popularity, he was banished by Saul. To secure himself against Saul, David placed himself under the protection of the Philistines. When Saul died, David pushed north and conquered Jerusalem. Abner, the commander of the forces of Saul's son Ishbosheth, was defeated by David, and as a consequence Abner transferred his allegiance to David.

Throughout his long reign David fought and defeated the various tribes of Israel and succeeded in unifying the nation. In his old age David was saddened by the revolt led by his son Absalom. David's lament for his son is a widely known biblical verse. After his death David was succeeded by Solomon, his son by Bathsheba.

DAVIS, JEFFERSON (1808-1889), president of the Confederate States of America during the Civil War, was born in Kentucky. He was graduated from West Point in 1828 and served in several Indian wars. In 1835 he married the daughter of General Zachary Taylor, future president of the United States, and became a cotton planter in Mississippi. Unfortunately, his wife died three months after their marriage. He remarried ten years later. In the Mexican War he distinguished himself in the battle of Buena Vista. Prior to the Mexican War he had served in the House of Representatives. From 1847 to 1851 he was a U.S. senator, and from 1853 to 1857, secretary of war. He again became senator in 1857, but in 1861, when the Southern states seceded, he left the Senate. He became president of the provisional government and was later elected president of the Confederate states.

During his career in the national government, Davis opposed prohibition of slavery by Congress in newly organized territories of the United States. He favored federal acquisition of new territory to the south, such as Cuba and the Yucatan peninsula in Mexico, and to the west. He thought that such gains would enlarge the slaveholding section of the United States and would benefit that section economically. He was partially responsible for the Gadsden Purchase of territory from Mexico.

Davis had many difficulties as president of the Confederacy. He was ill, his illness made him irritable, and his irritability made it difficult for him to gain the cooperation of various Southern leaders. The Confederate Congress passed 37 out of 38 bills over his veto. Some of the Confederate states, claiming that the Confederate government had no more right to dictate to them than the former national government had, refused to contribute their quotas of troops. President Davis was also handicapped by his attempt to direct both the army and the government, a task too great for any man.

Davis fled after the surrender of Lee at Appomattox Courthouse but was quickly captured at Irwinville, Ga. For two years he was imprisoned at Fort Monroe in Virginia. He was held in irons until his health was greatly impaired. He was released on bail in May, 1867. Mississippi would have sent him to the Senate, but he refused to ask for the federal pardon without which he could not be seated. He died in New Orleans.

Meserve Col., N.Y.
Above is a photograph of Jefferson Davis and his second wife, Varina Howell Davis.

DAVIS CUP MATCHES, annual tennis competitions open to amateur teams of all the nations belonging to the International Lawn Tennis Federation and other nations approved by them. Each year, in a series of elimination matches, a team is selected to meet the team of the nation that won the trophy the preceding year. The trophy that the winning nation receives (the Davis Cup) was donated in 1900 by Dwight F. Davis, an American player. From 1900 to the beginning of World War I the United States, England, and Australia had a monopoly on the cup. Then France developed first-rank players and won the cup each year from 1927 through 1932. Great Britain regained the cup in 1933 and held it until 1937, when it was recaptured by the United States. Since 1937 the trophy has been held by either the United States or Australia. During the years of World War II no matches were played.

DAVY, SIR HUMPHRY (1778-1829), English chemist, was born in Penzance, Cornwall. After having received the rudiments of a classical education, he early developed a taste for scientific experiments. In 1798 he discovered the effect of inhaling nitrous oxide, or laughing gas. This discovery enhanced his reputation. Associated with London's Royal Institution for ten years, Davy was appointed chemistry professor in 1802. He was professor of chemistry for the Board of Agriculture. Among his important discoveries were the isolation of sodium and potassium by electrolysis and the demonstration of the elementary nature of chlorine. The numerous accidents arising from explosions in mines led him to make a series of experiments on the nature of the explosive gas. The result was the invention of the miner's safety lamp. He was knighted in 1812 and was created a baronet in 1818.

Sir Humphry Davy

DAWES PLAN, a plan of payments adopted in 1924 to enable Germany to pay the reparations it incurred in World War I. Germany was reluctant to pay reparations, and its attempt to do so resulted in heavy borrowing and inflation. To allow Germany to stabilize its economy, and thereby its political situation, a group of economists under the American banker Charles G. Dawes devised a plan of payments based on Germany's capacity to pay. The plan was adopted by the Reparation Commission Committee and accepted by the Germans in 1924.

The Dawes plan arranged an American loan of 200 million dollars to allow Germany to base its currency on a gold standard. It then established annual reparations payments that were to increase until 1928. Thereafter, payments were to be made on the basis of Germany's economic prosperity. Reparations stopped abruptly in 1932 as a result of the depression. While it was in operation, the Dawes plan probably helped stave off an immediate European economic collapse.

DAYDREAMING, sometimes called fantasy, is the achievement of satisfactions through imagination rather than through real experience. Since daydreaming requires little effort, it is one of the most common methods people use to achieve a feeling of self-satisfaction. It occurs most frequently when the person is bored by his surroundings or frustrated by not achieving something he desires. In most daydreams the individual pictures himself as a conquering hero who performs great deeds or obtains things he desires.

On the positive side daydreaming sometimes helps a person to think creatively and to avoid making mistakes in the real world. On the negative side daydreaming takes time from real living and may actually hinder the person's ability to achieve real goals.

DAYLIGHT-SAVING TIME, the idea of "saving daylight" by setting the clock ahead one hour in spring and setting it back one hour in the fall. The result of daylight-saving time is that people rise earlier and work in the early morning hours and leave work while the sun is still relatively high in the sky. The people of cities benefit from daylight saving by having several hours of daylight to use after they leave work. The idea, in fact, is of a particularly important value in an urban, industrial society.

Daylight-saving time was first thought of by Benjamin Franklin, who wrote about it from Paris in 1784. Not until 1907, however, did the idea gain a vigorous advocate in William Willett of England. In the United States daylight-saving time was advanced as a war measure in 1916, and Congress passed a daylight-saving time act in 1918. This law required people to put the clock ahead one hour on the last Sunday in March and to set it back to standard time on the last Sunday in October. The law was opposed by farmers and was repealed by Congress over President Woodrow Wilson's veto in 1919. However, daylight-saving time continues to be used in many U.S. cities.

DAY NAMES. We no longer know why the week has seven days. However, the myths from which the days received their names survive.

Sunday is from the Anglo-Saxon *Sunnandaeg,* meaning "sun" and "day." Some people believe it is a remnant of sun worship. This first day of the week is called *dimanche* in French and *domenica* in Italian. This is from the Latin *Dominus,* meaning "the Lord." It was so named because the Resurrection of Jesus Christ was on this day.

Monday is from the Anglo-Saxon *Monandaeg* (moon day). The moon was once worshiped as the wife of the sun.

Tuesday is named for Tyr, the old Norse god of war. Its Norse name was *Tiwesdaeg.* The French name for Tuesday is *mardi,* derived from the old Latin name for the god of war.

Wednesday is named for the Norse god Odin, or Woden. It was *Wodnesdaeg* in Anglo-Saxon. Odin was the father of Tyr and the god of storms.

Thor, the Norse god of thunder, is the reason for *Thunresdaeg,* Anglo-Saxon for Thor's day, or Thursday. Thor was the strongest of the gods.

Friday is named for Freya, wife of Odin. Since Odin and her son Thor each had a day, the ancients named a day for her as well. Otherwise, they thought, she might be jealous and work evil.

Saturday is named for the old Roman god Saturn. He presided over the sowing of the seed. His festival, the Saturnalia, followed the winter sowing in December.

DDT. See INSECTICIDE.

DEAD SEA, a salt lake of southeastern Palestine, is on the border of Israel and Jordan. It is about 14 miles east of Jerusalem. The lake is about 49 miles long and up to 10 miles in width. It covers an area of 405 square miles. The Jordan River, its principal tributary, enters from the north. The Dead Sea has no outlet.

The Dead Sea's surface is 1,292 feet below sea level. It reaches 1,300 feet in the north. The waters are intensely salty and have several times the salt content of the ocean. The eastern and western shores are high and rocky. There are little vegetation and animal life.

By the ancients the Dead Sea was called Asphalt Lake, from the asphalt found near it. Later it was named the Dead Sea. In the Bible it is called the Salt Sea and the Sea of the Plain.

A part of the Israeli Dead Sea potash works at Sodom is shown here. Potash (potassium chloride) is commercially the most important of the various salts found at the Dead Sea. It is widely used as a fertilizer.

Photo, I.S.I.

DEAD SEA SCROLLS, fragments of biblical scrolls found near the Dead Sea in 1947, when Bedouin shepherd boys in the sun-baked hills of the Wadi Qumran west of the Dead Sea discovered a cave containing broken pottery. Eight clay jars were unbroken, and within them were scrolls wrapped in linen. Most of the scrolls, written in Hebrew, were sold to the metropolitan of a Syrian monastery at Jerusalem. Three of the scrolls were sold by a merchant to the Hebrew University in Jerusalem. Eventually, all the scrolls were purchased by the state of Israel and deposited in a museum in Jerusalem. Meanwhile, the search for fresh discoveries continued, and in 1951 more manuscripts were uncovered. By the end of 1955 many caves had been found, one of them with so many fragments of ancient manuscripts that it appeared to be covered with autumn leaves.

With painstaking skill archaeologists placed the fragments together. The result was a group of manuscripts from almost every part of the Old Testament and one complete manuscript of Isaiah. These are the oldest Hebrew manuscripts of the Old Testament in existence. Another group of manuscripts were the *Manual of Discipline*, the *Commentary on the Prophet Habakkuk*, and the *War Between the Children of Light and of Darkness*, all of which were Essene (or Zealot according to some scholars) writings. The discoveries of the Dead Sea Scrolls amount to one of the greatest archaeological finds since the Renaissance.

The scrolls, archaeologists found by excavations, had probably been written by the Essenes, a Jewish monastic group that existed from about 150 B.C. to A.D. 70. The place where the scrolls had been written was discovered, as well as the graves of the scribes. The manuscripts had been sealed in the caves, which served as libraries, to preserve them from destruction by the Romans. The Romans, however, destroyed the monastery in A.D. 68, and the scrolls remained in their vaults until 1947. Later fragments included documents from the second Jewish revolt against the Romans.

The fragments of the Old Testament showed that the present version of the Bible is quite accurate, a testimony to the care of later scribes. A few changes, however, were introduced in the Revised Standard Version of the Bible on the basis of the scrolls. The Essene writings have not been fully appraised. At least one scholar suggested that they presaged all the main doctrines of Christianity. Others thought that the writings dated from after A.D. 66 and were the work of Zealots rather than Essenes. Meanwhile, controversy and research continue on the interpretations of the light shed by the Dead Sea Scrolls on both Judaism and Christianity.

DEAFNESS is the absence or loss of hearing. Some persons are totally deaf, and others are only partly deaf. Deafness has many different causes. But each cause of deafness in some way interferes with the conduction of sound waves to the inner ear. (See EAR.) A simple obstruction of the ear with earwax can cause deafness. Other causes are infection, injury, poisoning, old age, and excessive noise.

Deafness can be relieved if the cause can be eliminated. For example, the removal of earwax can restore a person's hearing if obstruction with earwax was the cause of his hearing loss. Some kinds of deafness can be relieved with a hearing aid. A special type of deafness caused by otosclerosis (a disease of the bone of the inner ear) may be cured by an operation known as the fenestration (window) operation. When a deaf person cannot be benefited by medical or surgical treatment or by a hearing aid, he may learn lipreading.

There are several ways to guard against deafness. A person should always have wax or foreign matter removed from the ears by a doctor. To avoid ear infection one should always blow his nose with the nostrils open and should have a doctor examine at once an aching or discharging ear.

This is the manual alphabet for the deaf. A deaf person can speak 130 words per minute with it. Most deaf people are taught the oral method of speech, but for those with speech difficulties the manual alphabet is very useful.

DEAF SPEECH. For most of us, learning to speak takes no effort at all. Those of us who can hear simply learn to speak by imitating the sounds around us, somewhat like parrots. But deaf children live in a world of silence, unaware that sounds exist, and they must be taught to speak.

In the oral method of teaching the deaf, the teacher must teach the language to a person unable to hear it. The first stages in the oral method are hard, but the effort is worthwhile.

The first step in teaching a deaf child is to show him that when the lips move something important is happening. This is done by having the child touch the teacher's throat to feel the voice vibrations. At the same time the deaf child learns to lipread the word he feels. Then the pupil and teacher stand before a mirror. The teacher forms a word, and the child tries to imitate him. Gradually, the child develops a vocabulary.

The next step is for the child to learn to speak in sentences. Those of us who hear put words together in sentences automatically. The deaf, however, must learn to create sentences out of the single words learned by lipreading. Once speech and language are mastered, however, deaf children can attend school along with those who hear.

In the United States there is an institution devoted to knowledge about deafness. It is called the Volta Bureau and is located in Washington, D.C. It was founded by Alexander Graham Bell. Most people remember Bell because he invented the telephone and forget that he was also a great teacher of the deaf.

DEATH is the end of life. (See LIFE.) Every species of living thing has a particular life span, or normal length of life. For example, the life span of sheep is 15 years. If a sheep does not die as a result of accident or disease or injury before the end of the life span, death may be expected to occur close to the end of the 15-year period.

Death occurring normally at the end of a creature's life span is called a natural death. It is the final stage in the long process of aging—a gradual slowing down of life processes after maturity. For example, when a bird reaches a certain size, it stops growing, but it continues to change. Finally, the bird grows old, loses its strength, and gradually fails because it cannot replace the parts of its body that are worn out. When the bird's vital processes, such as breathing and circulation, stop altogether, the bird dies. Natural death occurs among all animals except those that reproduce by splitting (binary fission). Among such animals, most of which are one celled, the offspring are always merely halves of the parent. Death of these animals can occur only by accident.

When the organism dies, the complicated parts of its body begin to decay. They are changed into the same chemical substances as those from which the food came that kept the organism alive. Thus when death occurs, nothing is really destroyed. The process is somewhat like the melting of the snow-man. The snowman disappears because the snow is changed into water.

DEATH RITE, a ceremony performed in connection with the burial of the dead. Death has always inspired people with sorrow, awe, and sometimes fear. But most societies have also felt that death is not the end of a person's existence. Therefore, especially among primitive peoples death rites were performed with two ends in view: first, to prevent the spirit of the dead person from roaming the earth, and second, to aid him in reaching the dwelling place of the dead.

Tibetan death rites sometimes lasted for 49 days, for the spirit of the dead was thought to have a long, journey. He was aided in this journey by prayers and incantations chanted by Buddhist priests. Friends of the dead person gave offerings of food and tea to sustain the spirit in its journey. The idea that the spirit of the dead needed food and belongings in his other life is very old.

Death Valley was named in 1849 by gold prospectors who tried to cross it. Some of them died of heat and thirst. The average annual rainfall in Death Valley is only 1.4 inches. Although summertime there is unbearably hot, the winters are mild and pleasant.

Graves from the Stone Age contain flint tools, weapons, and marrow bones that were buried with the dead.

The ancient Egyptians had very elaborate death rites. The dead person was buried with food and many of his belongings that the Egyptians thought he would need in the next life. Models of people, houses, and ships have been found in Egyptian tombs. In fact, these tombs provide much of our knowledge about ancient Egypt. The dead Egyptian was also provided with a Book of the Dead, a long papyrus roll that gave him complete instructions on how to reach his destination. So important was the Nile River in the lives of the Egyptians, that they believed a river lay between them and paradise. Their hearse for the dead was shaped like a ship, complete with oars. This was to take the spirit across the river. The vikings, men of the sea, also provided boats so that their dead could sail to Valhalla. In Lapland the dead person was given a reindeer.

In modern times death rites are not usually so elaborate. Friends and relatives pay their last respects to the dead person, and a religious ceremony is performed to honor the dead.

DEATH VALLEY, a desert region in California. It is situated near the border of Nevada, between the Panamint Range on the west and the Amargosa Range on the east. Including its northwest arm, sometimes called Lost Valley, it is about 140 miles long and varies from 4 to 16 miles in width. It was formerly the bed of a salt lake. Immense borax deposits, commercially valuable and formerly mined, are located here. Most of it is 160 feet below sea level, and the lowest part is about 280 feet below sea level. Much of it is covered with a white salt deposit. There is very little vegetation. Of animal life there are only snakes, lizards, and horned toads. Water springs are rare, and people crossing the valley have suffered much. The temperature in summer is very high, sometimes more than 120° F. in the shade. The maximum recorded temperature is 134° F. Sandstorms are frequent.

DE BARY, HEINRICH (1831-1888), a 19th-century German scientist who contributed much to the advancement of botany. De Bary, born at Frankfurt am Main, studied medicine and botany at German universities. He began his researches by studying and classifying the fungi, a large group of plants that includes mushrooms and toadstools. His work on fungi, accomplished while serving as professor of botany at three German universities, established the science called mycology. He then studied epidemic diseases that attack wheat, potatoes, and other plants and discovered effective means of combating them. His most important book, published in 1866, was about the anatomy and physiology of fungi. De Bary received the honor of being named to the rectorship of the University of Strasbourg.

DEBATE, argument for or against a proposition. Debate is essentially a practical art. In our society it plays an important part in legislation, in politics, in business, in law, and in education.

In a legislative body, debate serves to bring out a full analysis of the merits and shortcomings of a bill and to sway undecided members of the body. Joint debates during political campaigns enable voters to hear opposing candidates attack and defend party platforms and past records in office. The Lincoln-Douglas joint debates in the senatorial campaign of 1858 in Illinois are well-known examples of political debates.

In business, debate is used by boards of directors and executive committees in reaching decisions on policy. In law courts, lawyers present the issues, the evidence, and the reasoning in a case by means of debate. Finally, in high schools, colleges, and universities debate has become an important means of education for both the participants and the audience.

Debate may be classified according to form, purpose, and method. Different types are parliamentary debating, cross-examination debating, and formal debating. Parliamentary debating is used in legislative bodies, cross-examination debating has developed in the law courts, and formal debating is based on the conventions of the joint political debate. All three varieties are used in contest debates, or debates in high schools, colleges, and universities.

Formal contest debating originated during the last century at Oxford University, England, in an organization known as the Oxford Union. At each meeting of the union, teams of speakers debated a topic picked in advance. Literary societies modeled after the Oxford Union were organized within a few years at most American colleges and universities. Formal debates were the most important element in the weekly programs.

Early literary-society debates differed widely from formal contest debates of today. "Resolved, that Lincoln was a greater man than Washington" was a typical proposition. Little proof was used; arguments were based rather on the speakers' own opinions, and the judges' decision was based almost entirely on delivery.

Many important changes have been made in contest debating. Law-court practices have been gradually introduced. The use of proof, of testimony, and of rebuttal, or the attacking of opposing arguments, are some of the innovations. Also, the burden of proof has been placed on the affirmative. Topics of debate have changed considerably, too. Today, questions dealing with current political, social, or economic problems are most commonly used.

HOW TO DEBATE

The first steps in contest debating are selecting the topic and wording the proposition. One topic is usually selected for a whole semester or school year. If you should have an opportunity to help select the topic, you should make sure that it is timely and controversial. It should be of interest to your audiences, yet within the ability of the debaters. The proposition should be worded clearly, concisely, and affirmatively. It should state a single, specific proposal without bias and should place the burden of proof on the affirmative team.

The debater should first of all make sure he understands the proposition. He should analyze it to discover the major issues, and he should determine what other issues will be relevant to the debate. A knowledge of the history of the problem is usually essential.

Without thorough research no amount of skill in public speaking will enable a debater to be convincing. The debater must not only do a complete job of research to begin with, but he must keep his research up to date. He must be able to change his arguments in the light of current developments.

In order to organize his case effectively, the debater should prepare a brief. The brief records in outline form, but in complete sentences, the debater's analysis of the proposition. It should contain all supporting material—testimony, statistics, and the like—for both the affirmative and the negative. The brief should place every aspect of the problem in exact relation to every other aspect.

From his brief the debater must derive two kinds of speeches: the constructive speech and the rebuttal. Both kinds, but especially the rebuttal, must be kept flexible so that they can be altered to answer directly the arguments of the opposition as the debate progresses.

Usually there are two debaters to a team. The first speaker from the affirmative team begins the debate, giving the background of the problem and defining any special terms. He is followed by the first negative speaker, who may reinterpret the background if he thinks it incomplete or biased. The second affirmative and the second negative speakers, in that order, offer further arguments and summarize their teams' cases.

These speeches should be constructive. They will be timed, so the debaters must divide their case so as to avoid repetition. The debaters must also plan their individual speeches to use only the allotted time. Eight to twelve minutes is usually allotted for a constructive **speech by each debater.**

The first negative speaker gives the first rebuttal and is followed by the second affirmative speaker. The second negative and first affirmative speakers conclude the debate. Time allotted for rebuttals is usually about half of that for constructive speeches. No new constructive arguments are permitted in a rebuttal. The speaker should analyze his opponents' case and refute their major points as effectively as he possibly can. He should also demonstrate the strength of his team's case as a whole.

DEBS, EUGENE (1855-1926), a founder of the Socialist party of the United States and a labor leader. He contributed to the idea of large industrial unions in preference to trade unions. Debs, one of ten children of Jean and Marguerite Debs, was born in Terre Haute, Ind. He quit school at 15 to work on a railroad. Eventually, he became a locomotive fireman, the secretary of his city's Brotherhood of Locomotive Firemen, and an editor on the *Firemen's Magazine*. He became the national treasurer and secretary of the union in 1880, and in 1885 he was elected to the lower house of the Indiana legislature.

The American Railway Union (ARU) was founded in 1893 in accordance with Debs' views on industrial unionization. Debs became president of the union and led it in a successful strike against the Great Northern Railroad in 1894. Later in the year Debs and the ARU supported the Pullman strike in Chicago. The strike was crushed by federal troops sent by President Grover Cleveland, and Debs spent 1895 in jail. In 1900 he helped found the Socialist party of the United States, and in 1905 he became one of the founders of the Industrial Workers of the World (IWW), although he soon withdrew because of disagreement with some of the organization's methods. He contributed articles to the Socialist *Appeal to Reason* and conducted speaking tours throughout the nation. In 1912 he ran for president (for the fourth time) and received almost a million votes.

Though in prison as a result of an antiwar speech in 1918, Debs ran for president in 1920, polling almost a million votes again. He was released by order of President Warren Harding in 1921. Debs returned in declining health, without his citizenship rights, to a Socialist movement split into many powerless **and contending factions.**

DEBT. When a person (a debtor) has received money or goods from another person (a creditor) whom he must repay later, he is said to be in debt. Everyone at one time or another is in debt.

Properly managed, debt can be a great help to the operation of a complex industrial society. Credit, the counterpart of debt, supplements the hand-to-hand currency and makes possible a vastly increased scale of business activity. Whenever people buy things on credit, they incur debts to the business firms from which they make the purchases. Banks are in debt to their depositors, and these depositors may draw checks on their deposits to pay their own debts. Business firms and governments—city, state, and federal—are in debt to the people from whom they have borrowed money by selling them bonds. Such debts and the mortgage debts many people incur to buy houses are not repayable immediately but over a long period of years. Sensible individuals and business firms try to keep their debts small enough to pay what they owe out of their income if necessary. If the debt of a government were owed to other nations, the burden of debt would be comparable to the burden of the debts of an individual. The national debt in many countries, however, is an internal one, the repayment of which does not involve a national loss of goods and services. See CREDIT; STOCKS AND BONDS.

There are times when an honest debtor cannot pay his debts. Until 1869 a person in England could be put in debtors' prison if he could not meet his obligations. Charles Dickens wrote about people who were put in debtors' prison. Today when someone cannot pay his debts, he can file a petition of bankruptcy in the courts. The courts will then assign his wealth, if any, to his creditors. This done, the former debtor can begin his economic life again, free from debt.

DEBUSSY, CLAUDE (1862-1918), a French composer, was born in Saint-Germain-en-Laye. In 1884 he received the Prix de Rome from the Paris Conservatory for his cantata *L'Enfant prodigue*. In creating a music of mood and impression he was influenced by the symbolist poets and impressionist painters. Both his harmonic forms and manner of using them aroused considerable controversy, although some works, such as the *Prelude to the Afternoon of a Faun*, were instantly popular. His great musical contributions were in expanding the range of the piano and the technique of its performers and in creating a new opera form in *Pelléas et Mélisande*. Other works were a string quartet, *Nocturnes* (*Nuages*, *Fêtes*, and *Sirènes*), *La Mer*, *Iberia*, the cantata *La Demoiselle elue*, songs, and piano music.

New York Public Library
Stephen Decatur was a U.S. naval hero.

DECATUR, STEPHEN (1779-1820), a U.S. naval officer, was born in Sinepuxent, Md. He became a midshipman in 1798 and rose to the position of lieutenant on the 44-gun frigate *United States* during the naval war with France. He then served in the Mediterranean Sea and during the Tripolitan War (1801-1805) commanded the schooner *Enterprise*. Among his many exploits was the boarding and burning of the captured and grounded frigate *Philadelphia* in Tripoli Harbor in 1804. Lord Nelson described this as "the most bold and daring act of the age." Decatur was promoted to commodore in 1810. In 1812, during the war with Great Britain, he commanded the *United States* in its victory over the 38-gun frigate *Macedonian*. In 1815 he commanded the 44-gun frigate *President* in its victory over the *Endymion*. The latter fell in with other ships of the British blockading squadron and forced the *President* to surrender. Later in the year he led a nine-ship squadron to the Mediterranean to put down the Barbary pirates. He captured the Algerian flagship *Mashuba* and quickly forced the bey of Algiers to accept peace on United States terms and to declare the American flag inviolable. He then forced peace on the bey of Tunis and the pasha of Tripoli, thus making the Mediterranean safe for U. S. ships. Decatur then became a naval commissioner in Washington, D.C. He was killed in a duel with James Barron near Bladensburg, Md.

DECAY, the natural reduction of the protoplasm of dead animals and plants to simple inorganic compounds. All dead animal and plant organisms will undergo decay unless it is prevented by artificial means. Decay is caused by the action of various bacteria on the once-living protoplasm of dead animals and plants. These bacteria, which come chiefly from the soil, break down into inorganic compounds the organic proteins, carbohydrates, and fats that constitute protoplasm.

The decomposition of proteins is the most complex chemical reaction that occurs during the decay of animals and plants. All proteins contain nitrogen. When the action of bacteria from the soil causes proteins to decompose, they first are changed into ammonia or ammonium compounds, then into nitrites, and finally into nitrates. Nitrates—principally sodium nitrate and potassium nitrate—are the most important inorganic compounds that result from the decay of animal and plant proteins. These nitrates become part of the soil. Later they may be absorbed by the roots of growing plants and made into living proteins. Carbon dioxide and water are other inorganic products of protein decay. The carbon dioxide is dissipated into the atmosphere, and the water usually evaporates. Sulfates and phosphates also result from the decay of many animal proteins and become part of the soil. The foul odor that usually accompanies the decay of animal flesh is generated during the decomposition of those proteins that contain sulfur and phosphorus. The decay of animal flesh is also termed putrefaction.

The organic carbohydrates and fats that also constitute animal and plant protoplasm decompose into the simple inorganic compounds carbon dioxide and water. Again, the carbon dioxide is dissipated into the atmosphere, and the water usually evaporates. When animal bones decompose, their constituent sodium, calcium, and phosphorus are returned to the soil in the form of salts.

Animal and plant decay is one example of the law of the conservation of matter. The chemicals contained in present-day animals and plants are the same as those contained in animals and plants that lived millions of years ago. Perhaps molecules of sodium chloride in our bodies are the same molecules that existed at one time in the bodies of dinosaurs or in giant ferns.

DECEMBRIST UPRISING, a revolt led by Russian army officers after the death of Czar Alexander I in December, 1825. Though the uprising failed, it inspired Russian liberals for years to come.

The rebel leaders were liberal noblemen, members of secret societies that advocated among other things abolishing serfdom and replacing the autocratic imperial government of Russia either with a republic or with a constitutional monarchy.

These noblemen took advantage of the doubt existing after Alexander's death about who was to be his successor to convince their soldiers to declare for Alexander's brother Constantine, demand a constitution, and rebel. Alexander's younger brother, Nicholas, the rightful successor, rallied loyal troops and put down the rebellion, which occurred in St. Petersburg (now Leningrad), the capital.

By order of the new czar, the despotic Nicholas I, the Decembrist leaders were executed or deported to Siberia and a severe police regime was imposed on the country. For later Russian generations, however, the Decembrists became the founders of the 19th-century revolutionary tradition.

DECIBEL, a unit for measurement of power or intensity, often applied to sound. The intensity of a sound is its energy per surface of the sound wave; loudness increases as intensity increases, but loudness also depends upon frequency.

If two sounds are compared, and the ratio of their intensities is written as I/I_0, then ten times the logarithm of this ratio is their difference expressed in decibels. That is,

decibels = $10 \log_{10} I/I_0$.

If both sounds have a frequency of 1,000 cycles per second, then this is also their loudness difference in decibels. If one sound has an intensity 100 times that of the other, the decibel difference is 20, since $\log_{10} 100 = 2$. Usually, a barely audible sound is said to be at zero decibel level. The unit of loudness is the phon.

Average intensities in decibels of several common sounds, ranging from countryside sounds to the almost painful din of a pneumatic rock drill, are shown on the scale below.

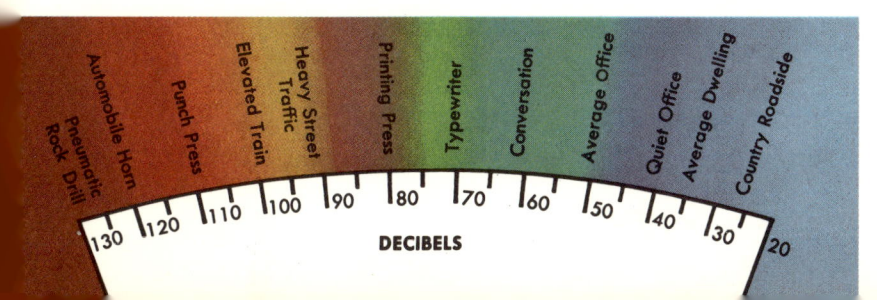

DECIMAL, a fraction expressed only in tenths, hundredths, thousandths, and smaller sizes each divisible by ten. In fact, the word *decimal* comes from a Latin word meaning "ten." These special sizes of fractions are useful because they can be written as part of the system we use to write whole numbers. In that system each position to the left of another stands for a unit ten times larger, the position on the right end being always for units of one. The number in each position tells only how many units of that particular size are to be counted. For example, 72 means two units of one and seven units of ten. Decimals simply extend this system to positions to the right of the "one" position. A period, called the decimal point, marks the beginning of this decimal part of the number. The decimal positions are related in exactly the same way as the whole number positions. Each is ten times smaller than the position on its left. Since all the positions after the decimal point are less than one, they are all fractions. The first decimal position, usually called a decimal "place," shows units of one-tenth. If the number 5 is in that decimal place, written as .5, it stands for $\frac{5}{10}$. The next decimal place shows units of one-hundredth. The decimal number .05 means $\frac{5}{100}$, and .55 means $\frac{5}{10}$ plus $\frac{5}{100}$. From fractions we know that this equals $\frac{55}{100}$. It is customary to read decimal numbers this second way, that is, in terms of the size of the last position. You would read 72.512 as "seventy-two and five hundred twelve thousandths." Written as a fraction it would appear $72 \frac{512}{1,000}$.

The great advantage of decimals is that we can add, subtract, multiply, and divide with them just as we do with whole numbers without having the complication of fractions. Also, we can compare decimal fractions at a glance. For example, it might not be obvious whether $\frac{3}{5}$ or $\frac{5}{8}$ is the larger fraction. In decimal form they are .600 and .625, and the difference is immediately plain.

To add or subtract decimal numbers, position them with the decimal points in a straight line up and down. The decimal place in the answer is in the same straight line.

To multiply decimal numbers, position them without regard for the decimal points and perform the multiplication. Count the number of decimal places in both of the numbers. This total is the number of decimal places in the answer.

To divide decimal numbers, count the number of decimal places in the divisor and move the decimal point in the dividend that number of decimal places to the right. The decimal point in the quotient is directly above this point. For a discussion of the decimal system, see NUMBER.

DECLARATION OF INDEPENDENCE is a document that states the reasons for the American colonies' denial of English sovereignty over them. The Declaration of Independence is not the official announcement of American independence. That was a resolution passed by the Continental Congress two days before it approved the Declaration of Independence on July 4, 1776. The real title of the Declaration of Independence is "The Unanimous Declaration of the thirteen united States of America."

More than a year passed between the beginning of the Revolutionary War and the approval of the Declaration of Independence. In the meantime, the colonies had attempted a reconciliation with England, but their offer, the Olive Branch Petition, had been rejected. The resolution for independence was presented by Richard Henry Lee, of Virginia, on June 7, 1776, and it was debated for several days. Congress decided to postpone a decision on the resolution until July and at the same time appointed the committee to prepare the document.

The declaration begins with a statement that it is only fair for the colonies to explain the reasons for their break with England. It states the purposes of government and claims that when a government goes against these purposes the people have a right to change or abolish it. This most famous part of the declaration reads:

"We hold these Truths to be self-evident, that all Men are created equal, that they are endowed by their Creator with certain unalienable Rights, that among these are Life, Liberty, and the Pursuit of Happiness—That to secure these Rights, Governments are instituted among Men, deriving their just

This picture of the signing of the Declaration of Independence was painted shortly after the Revolutionary War by the American artist John Trumbull. The signers of the declaration included Thomas Jefferson, Benjamin Franklin, John Adams, and Samuel Adams, who are depicted in the painting.

Powers from the Consent of the Governed, that whenever any Form of Government becomes destructive of these Ends, it is the Right of the People to alter or to abolish it, and to institute new Government, laying its Foundation on such Principles, and organizing its Powers in such Form, as to them shall seem most likely to effect their Safety and Happiness."

The declaration then states that the colonies have declared their independence only because the king had tried to establish an absolute despotism over America. To prove this statement the king's wrongs against America are listed. Mention is also made of the failure of all protests to the English king and people.

DECLINATION is one of the two measurements needed to give the direction from the earth of a star or other object in space. It measures the angular distance of the object north or south of the celestial equator. The celestial equator is the direction straight out from the earth's Equator. (See CELESTIAL SPHERE.) The distance is measured in plus degrees north of the celestial equator and in minus degrees south of it. For example, a star on the celestial equator would have a declination of 0 degrees. At the north celestial pole its declination would be plus 90 degrees.

Declination is similar to latitude measurement on the earth's surface. Its companion measurement, called right ascension, corresponds to longitude on the earth. See RIGHT ASCENSION.

DECORATION. See MEDAL AND DECORATION.

DEEP-SEA EXPLORING. Until the 1930's man's knowledge of the topography of the ocean floor derived from soundings. The development and improvement of breathing apparatus, such as the diving suit and the aqualung, enabled him to descend and observe marine plants and animals, but not until the development of closed vessels, such as the bathysphere and the bathyscaphe, was he able to reach great depths. The atomic submarine has

DEEP-SEA FISH

Milton Mild

A deep-sea diver must wear a protective suit and helmet and be supplied with air.

enabled man to stay under water longer and range more widely than ever before. See BATHYSCAPHE; BATHYSPHERE.

Sounding remained the principal method of exploring the ocean depths until the invention of the bathysphere. However, sounding with a line long remained a laborious and time-consuming task. Even with improved gear a deep-water sounding required several hours or sometimes an entire day. Development of sonic sounding instruments, which use sound waves bounced off the ocean floor, made possible continuous sounding of the bottom beneath a moving ship. Only a few ships, however, could obtain profiles of the ocean floor at depths greater than 12,000 feet.

The use of underwater breathing apparatus was first recorded by the Greek philosopher Aristotle. The diving suit of canvas and rubber, with metal helmet, was invented in 1830 by August Siebe. Because it can be used to a maximum depth of only about 500 feet, the diving suit has had limited use in deep-sea exploring. It is used mainly for underwater salvage and repairs. Aqualungs permit greater freedom of movement but do not permit descent into depths where pressures become great.

The greatest advances in deep-sea exploring have been achieved with closed vessels, such as the bathysphere and the bathyscaphe. William Beebe, an American scientist and author, and Otis Barton were the first men to reach great depths in the ocean. In 1934 they descended in the bathysphere to a depth of 3,028 feet, beyond the range of visible light. The bathyscaphe is a boat-shaped craft 50 feet long carrying a spherical crew chamber underneath it. Designed by Auguste Piccard, a noted Swiss scientist, the bathyscaphe carries gasoline for buoyancy and buckshot for ballast. On Jan. 23, 1960, Piccard's son Jacques and U.S. Navy Lieutenant Don Walsh descended in the bathyscaphe *Trieste* to the bottom of the Marianas Trench, a **depth of 35,800 feet. The area of this descent, 250 miles southwest of Guam in the Pacific Ocean, is the deepest known point in the world's oceans.**

Atomic submarines have opened up new possibilities in undersea exploration. Nuclear engines, unlike combustion engines, do not require oxygen; therefore atomic submarines can stay under the sea almost indefinitely, carrying only enough oxygen for the crew. When the atomic submarine USS *Nautilus* passed under the arctic icecap in August, 1958, it took continuous soundings of the floor of the Arctic Ocean, thus providing scientists and hydrographers with much new and important information. It also discovered a previously unknown deep-sea valley under the icecap. Between Feb. 16 and May 10, 1960, the atomic submarine USS *Triton* made the first known submerged voyage around the world, following as closely as possible the route taken by Magellan in 1519-1522. The trip produced a mass of scientific data about the ocean depths throughout the world. Soundings on the voyage revealed two uncharted 12,000-foot underwater peaks off Hawaii.

DEEP-SEA FISH. Zoologists know that some fish live in the ocean at a depth of 3,000 feet or more. Life of any kind at such a depth would seem almost impossible because of the darkness and pressure. Sunlight does not penetrate to a depth of 3,000 feet; there is never-ending black night at that depth. At lesser depths there is only a period of twilight each day. Below 600 feet the temperature both at the Equator and at the poles remains almost constant at 33° F., or just above the freezing point of water. The water pressure at a depth of 600 feet is 270 pounds per square inch. At 3,000 feet the pressure is 3 tons per square inch.

Within the bodies of these deep-sea fish there is pressure great enough to withstand the water pressure so that they are not crushed. When these fish are brought to the surface, their bodies burst outward

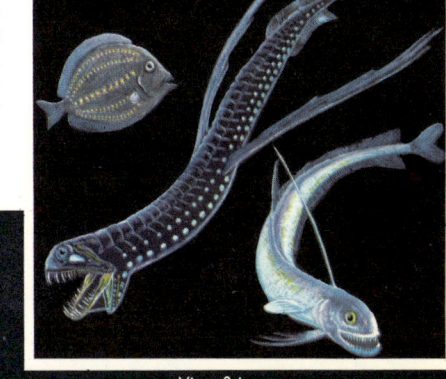

Most deep-sea fish are carnivorous. Some can ingest other fish larger than themselves.

Red Dory

Scorpion Fish

Ocellated Dory

Viperfish

Little Dory

Red Sea Bass

because the pressure within them is greater than normal air pressure. At depths where there is a little light, the eyes of these fish are very large so as to collect as much of the light as possible. At greater depths, where there is no light, some fish have no eyes. Many of these fish are illuminated so that they gleam brightly in the darkness. Their light comes from little bright patches along their sides and bellies. Some of the patches are arranged in beautiful designs. These strange fish were carefully studied by William Beebe in the course of many descents into deep water with his invention, the bathysphere.

DEER. The word *deer* is used to refer to any member of the deer family or, in a more restricted way, to refer only to those members of the deer family popularly called deer. The deer family is distributed throughout the world, except in Australia and central and southern Africa. It is distinguished from other families of mammals chiefly by a peculiar type of bony outgrowth on the head. This outgrowth is called antlers.

The largest member of the deer family is the moose, which is 6½ feet high at the shoulders. (See Moose.) Slightly smaller, but exceeded in size and strength among American deer only by the moose, is the American elk. It is unfortunate that the name elk became attached to this animal, since it is not closely related to the European elk; the name which was used by the Shawnee Indians, wapiti, is now in general use for it. (See Wapiti.) Another of the larger members of the deer family is the caribou or, as the domesticated caribou is commonly called, the reindeer.

None of these larger members of the deer family is the graceful animal deer are usually thought of as being. Among the more graceful deer are two North American species, the white-tailed, or Virginia, deer and the mule deer. The male Virginia deer is about 3 feet high at the shoulder and weighs up to 300 pounds or more. This deer moves with great spring and buoyancy of gait. It is found in the eastern United States and Mexico and has been much hunted, especially in colonial days, for its meat, known as venison.

The mule deer is found in western North America, from northern Mexico to Alaska. It runs with a peculiar, high-bounding gait, which, though it does not cover ground as fast as the rush of the Virginia deer when alarmed, is better adapted to the broken country over which the mule deer ranges.

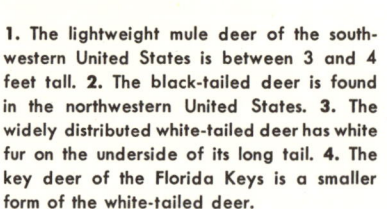

Male deer use their antlers to defend themselves. Female deer do not have antlers, except in rare cases which are found among the caribou or the reindeer. The antlers are shed each winter, and within a month or two new antlers begin to develop. The rapid growth of these antlers is one of the wonders of animal life.

Mating time is in the fall, when bucks fight savagely for their does. The antlers of two combatants occasionally become locked, and both bucks die of starvation. The enemies of the deer are legion, from man with his guns and hunting dogs to the great mountain lion of the West, which may kill deer once a week.

1. The lightweight mule deer of the southwestern United States is between 3 and 4 feet tall. 2. The black-tailed deer is found in the northwestern United States. 3. The widely distributed white-tailed deer has white fur on the underside of its long tail. 4. The key deer of the Florida Keys is a smaller form of the white-tailed deer.

DEFENSE, UNITED STATES DEPARTMENT OF, originally designated the National Military Establishment by the National Security Act of 1947. It was established as an executive department of the United States government by the National Security Act Amendments of 1949. The act established within the Department of Defense the Armed Forces Policy Council, the Joint Chiefs of Staff, the Joint Staff, and three military departments—the Department of the Army, the Department of the Navy, and the Department of the Air Force. It provided that there should be a secretary of defense (a member of the president's cabinet), a deputy secretary, and three assistant secretaries, one of whom should be the comptroller of the department. Later six additional assistant secretaries of defense and a general counsel were added to the newly created department.

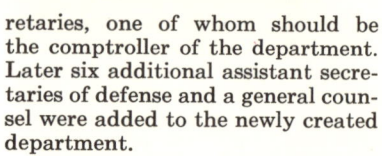

The department was created to provide for the security of the nation through the establishment of integrated policies for the departments, agencies, and functions relating to the national security. It is the duty of the department to coordinate and direct the Army, Navy, and Air Force, but not to merge them, under civilian control. The secretary of defense took the places that the secretary of war and the secretary of the Navy previously had in the cabinet.

DEFOE, DANIEL (about 1660-1731), English author and journalist, born at St. Giles, Cripplegate, London. He was educated at Morton's Academy. He engaged in Monmoth's Rebellion in 1685 but was allowed to escape. His career was a stormy one. When he wrote *The Shortest Way with the Dissenters* (1702), he was fined, pilloried three times, and imprisoned indefinitely. In prison he published his newspaper, *The Review*, in which he inaugurated the interview article. After his release he served the Whig and Tory ministries alternately and was imprisoned several times. He is best known for his fiction, including *Robinson Crusoe*, *Moll Flanders*, *Journal of the Plague Year*, and *Roxana*. He also wrote poetry, such as the satiric *True-Born Englishman*, pamphlets dealing with politics and economics, and history.